Brazil under Lula

Brazil under Lula

Economy, Politics, and Society under the Worker-President

Edited by
Joseph L. Love
and
Werner Baer

BRAZIL UNDER LULA

Copyright © Joseph L. Love and Werner Baer, 2009.

First published in 2009 by
PALGRAVE MACMILLAN®
in the United States—a division of St. Martin's Press LLC,
175 Fifth Avenue, New York, NY 10010.

Where this book is distributed in the UK, Europe and the rest of the world,
this is by Palgrave Macmillan, a division of Macmillan Publishers Limited,
registered in England, company number 785998, of Houndmills,
Basingstoke, Hampshire RG21 6XS.

Palgrave Macmillan is the global academic imprint of the above companies
and has companies and representatives throughout the world.

Palgrave® and Macmillan® are registered trademarks in the United States,
the United Kingdom, Europe and other countries.

ISBN-13: 970–0–230–60816–0
ISBN-10: 0–230–60816–7

Library of Congress Cataloging-in-Publication Data is available from the
Library of Congress.

A catalogue record of the book is available from the British Library.

Design by Newgen Imaging Systems (P) Ltd., Chennai, India.

First edition: January 2009

10 9 8 7 6 5 4 3 2 1

Printed in the United States of America.

This volume is dedicated to
Jorge Paulo Lemann
Whose long-term support of Brazilian Studies at the
University of Illinois made this book possible

CONTENTS

List of Illustrations   ix

List of Contributors   xiii

Introduction   1
Werner Baer and Joseph L. Love

Part One   The Problems the Lula Government Confronted in Politics and the Economy

One   Political Reform in Brazil: Recent Proposals, Diagnosis, and a Suggestion   9
José Antonio Cheibub

Two   The Macroeconomic Record of the Lula Administration, the Roots of Brazil's Inequality, and Attempts to Overcome Them   27
Edmund Amann and Werner Baer

Part Two   The Policy-Making Process

Three   Policy Making in the First Lula Government   47
Jorge Vianna Monteiro

Four   Brazil's Lack of Growth   67
Jocildo Bezerra and Tiago V. de V. Cavalcanti

Part Three   Specific Policy Issues

Five   Regulation during the Lula Government   93
Bernardo Mueller and André Rossi de Oliveira

Six   Exchange Rate Policy, Perceptions of Risk, and External Constraints under Lula   115
Donald V. Coes

Seven   Agricultural, Agrarian, and Environmental Policy Formation under Lula: The Role of Policy Networks   135
Charles C. Mueller

Eight   The Labor Policies of the Lula Government   151
          Michael M. Hall

Nine   Lula's Foreign Policy: Regional and Global Strategies 167
          Paulo Roberto de Almeida

**Part Four   The Impact of President Lula's
              Social Programs**

Ten   A Spatial Analysis of *Bolsa Família*: Is Allocation
          Targeting the Needy?   187
          Mônica A. Haddad

Eleven   A Report Card for Lula: Progress in Education   205
          Mary Arends-Kuenning

Twelve   Reforming Social Security under Lula: Continuities
          with Cardoso's Policies   221
          Maria Antonieta P. Leopoldi

Part Five   Regional Growth and Income Inequality

Thirteen Social Policies, Personal and Regional Income
          Inequality in Brazil: An I-O Analysis   243
          *Carlos R. Azzoni, Joaquim J.M. Guilhoto, Eduardo
          A. Haddad, Geoffrey J.D. Hewings, Marco Antônio Laes,
          and Guilherme R.C. Moreira*

Fourteen Regional Development Policies, 2003–2006   263
          Luiz Ricardo Cavalcante and Simone Uderman

Fifteen   Northeast Brazil under the Lula Government   283
          Alexandre Rands Barros and André Matos Magalhães

Part Six   The Long-run View

Sixteen   The Lula Government in Historical Perspective   305
          Joseph L. Love

Index   317

LIST OF ILLUSTRATIONS

Chart

13.1   Interregional flows considered in the model   252

Figures

3.1   Share of the executive in the law-making EC 32 regime   51
4.1   Panel (a): Logarithm of the real GDP per capita (chain series).
       Panel (b): Real GDP per capita relative to the U.S. level   69
4.2   Log of GDP (1990 US$) and GDP per capita in Brazil
       and in the world   70
4.3   Percentage deviations from GDP (1990 US$) in Brazil
       and in the world   71
4.4   Trended and de-trended growth rate of GDP (1990 US$)
       in Brazil and in the world   72
4.5   Panel (a): Kernel density of the average growth rate of
       real GDP from 2002 to 2005. Panel (b): Cumulative density
       of the average growth rate of GDP from 2002 to 2005   73
4.6   Growth rate of GDP (1990 US$) in Brazil: Data and
       predicted values   75
4.7   Realized and trended real interest rate and spread rate
       in Brazil   77
4.8   Realized and trended investment rate in Brazil   78
4.9   Government consumption over GDP   79
4.10   Brazil's tax burden as a share of GDP   80
4.11   Average years of schooling of the population 15 years
       and older   83
4.12   International comparison: Results from PISA 2000   83
5.1   Average length of vacancy in board of directors   98
5.2   Private investment in infrastructure by sector
       (US$ millions)   99
5.3   Private investment in infrastructure as percentage
       of GDP   100

5.4   Investments in Brazil as a percentage of worldwide private
      investments in infrastructure   101
5.5   Strategic choice of agency councilors   107
5.6   The judiciary as a safeguard   109
5.7   Strategic choice of agency structure and process   110
6.1   Real exchange rate index (August 1968–August 2007)   119
6.2   Current account and major components (US$ billions)   120
6.3   Emerging Markets Bond Index (EMBI) spread for Brazil
      (in basis points), 1995–2007   123
6.4   Reserves of foreign exchange—international liquidity
      (US$ billions), January 1990–April 2007   124
6.5   A subjective change in perceptions of risk   130
10.1 Research framework   192
10.2 *Bolsa Família* ratio relative to the sample average of
      Brazilian counties, 2006   193
10.3 Maps based on the allocated model for Brazilian
      counties, 2006   198
11.1 Net enrollment rates by age, Brazil 1981–2004   212
11.2 The proportion of first to eighth grade students delayed
      in school, 1992–2005   213
11.3 The proportion of high school students who are delayed
      in school   214
11.4 Mean Portuguese achievement test score, SAEB,
      1995–2005   215
11.5 Mean mathematics achievement test scores, SAEB,
      1995–2005   216
12.1 Open pension system—ranking of banks and insurers
      by revenue, 2006   224
13.1 Percent of Lula votes in relation to total votes   247
13.2 Moran scatterplot and global Moran's *I* statistic for
      Lula's performance in the first round of the 2006
      presidential elections   248
13.3 Moran significance map for Lula voting   249
14.1 Brazilian regions: GDP, population, and GDP per capita   269
14.2 BNDES disbursements (2003–2006) and GDP
      (2003–2004), Brazilian states   273
15.1 Per capita GDP in Brazilian states in 2003 (R$)   285
15.2 Share of Northeast per capita GDP of Brazilian
      per capita GDP   285
15.3 Share of population living under poverty line in
      Brazilian states, 2004   286
15.4 Performance of students of Northeastern urban schools as
      a proportion of performance of Brazilian students   287
15.5 Performance of students of Northeastern urban schools
      as a proportion of performance of Southeastern students   287

15.6   Performance of students in ENEM 2006   288
15.7   Share of Northeast GDP of Brazilian GDP   289
15.8   Brazil: Share of consumption of total GDP   290
15.9   Monthly standard deviation of sectorial shares in
        BNDES loans   291
15.10   Average default on checks—September to
        November, 2006   294
15.11   Share of Northeastern of total number of counties
        in each quintile of ranked fiscal and social
        responsibility index   295

Tables

1.1   Countries with district magnitude for legislative
        elections equal to or larger than 11   18
2.1   Gini coefficient: Brazil 1960–2005   30
2.2   Growth in GDP and real wages, 1976–2004   32
2.3   Consumer price inflation (IPCA index), 1980–2006   33
2.4   Growth of income by deciles of the distribution
        of incomes   33
2.5   Brazil: C4 concentration ratios   34
2.6   Poverty and indigence in Brazil: 1990–2004   36
2.7   Brazil: Years of education   40
3.1   Brazilian economy: Stability of constitutional rules,
        1988–2006   48
3.2   Quantity of Provisional Laws enacted by Lula government,
        2003–2006   49
3.3   MP 255 and scope of benefits (size of legislation in terms of
        number of articles in the law)   54
3.4   The making of Law 11,079   59
4.1   Growth rate of real GDP from 2002 to 2005:
        Selected countries and regions   73
4.2   Dependent variable: Brazil's growth rate of GDP. OLS and
        Prais-Winsten regressions   74
4.3   Counterfactual exercises based on table 4.2, column 3   76
5.1   Annual variation of GDP in real terms, per sector   102
5.2   Foreign investment in infrastructure as percentage of GDP 102
6.1a   Current account and major components, 1994–2006
        (US$ millions)   121
6.1b   Capital account, major components, and balance of
        payments, 1994–2006 (US$ millions)   121
6.2   Major economic indicators in the Cardoso and Lula
        governments (annual averages per term)   126
7.1   Phase of horizontal agricultural expansion (1500–1964):
        Developments and nature of policy networks   137

7.2   Phase of conservative modernization (1965–1990):
      Developments and nature of policy networks   137
7.3   Phase of gradual but radical reversal of the interventionist
      strategy (from the early 1990s to the present)   138
10.1 Summary statistics of all variables   194
10.2 Estimation results for the allocation model for
      Brazilian counties, 2006   197
10.3 Percentage of Brazilian counties under- and
      overpredicted based on the allocation model, 2006   199
11.1 The proportion of children delayed in school,
      by grade level, 1992–2005   213
12.1 Contributors to public and private pension
      systems: 2004 employed population   223
12.2 Assets of the 10 largest pension funds—January 2007   225
12.3 Private complementary pension plans (open
      and closed). Provision and assets 1994 to 2003
      (thousand R$)   233
13.1 Households eligible for benefits from *Bolsa Família*, 2000   246
13.2 Quantitative estimation results (dependent
      variable: Lula's vote as share of total)   251
13.3 Qualitative estimation results (dependent variable:
      Lula's vote as share of total)   251
13.4 Government transfers to families by region—
      Bolsa Família   254
13.5 Impacts on production by sector and region   255
13.6 Impacts on household income by region   257
13.7 Impacts on income inequality   258
13.8 Shares in production value and in income   259
14.1 Resources allocated by the federal government,
      2003–2006, current R$ millions   271
14.2 Tax expenditures, 1998–2006, current R$ millions   272
14.3 Regional share of BNDES disbursements, 2003–2006 (%)   273
14.4 Financial incentives (BNDES, FNO, FNE, and
      FCO), regions, 2003–2006 (%)   274
14.5 Direct investments by the federal government,
      2001–2006, current R$ millions   275
14.6 Family grant program, 2003–2006, current
      R$ millions   276
15.1 Investments predicted by the Programa de Aceleração
      do Crescimento (Program of Investment Acceleration—
      PAC) in R$ billions for the 2007–2010 period   297

LIST OF CONTRIBUTORS

Paulo Roberto de Almeida holds a doctorate in social sciences and is a Brazilian career diplomat. He is Professor of Legal Studies in the University Center of Brasília and teaches in the Graduate Program at Brazil's Diplomatic Academy. He has published widely on international relations, diplomatic history, and Brazil's foreign policy.

Edmund Amann is Senior Lecturer in Development Economics at the University of Manchester. His research interests concern the impact of trade and market liberalization on the economies of Latin America, especially that of Brazil. He is particularly interested in the ways economic liberalization has affected innovation in Latin American enterprises.

Mary Arends-Kuenning is Associate Professor of Agricultural and Consumer Economics at the University of Illinois. Her research focuses on economic and demographic issues in developing countries. She is especially concerned with child labor and children's schooling, and the impact of household structure on children's health and education.

Carlos R. Azzoni is the Dean of the School of Economics, Administration and Accounting of the University of São Paulo (USP). His specialty is Regional Economics, in which he is primarily concerned with regional inequality and its dynamics. He also studies personal income inequality and poverty.

Werner Baer is Lemann Professor of Economics at the University of Illinois. He has written extensively on Brazil's economy. The sixth edition of his book *The Brazilian Economy* was published in 2008.

Jocildo Bezerra is Professor of Economics at the Federal University of Pernambuco. He has been chair of the research group PIMES at that University, and a research fellow of the Centro Nacional de Pesquisa, the Brazilian national research foundation. He has also been president of Pernambuco's state development agency.

Luiz Ricardo Cavalcante holds a doctorate in administration at the Federal University of Bahia and is Professor at the University of Brasília (UnB). Cavalcante specializes in regional development, finance, and the economics of innovation.

Tiago V. de V. Cavalcanti has taught at the New University of Lisbon and the Federal University of Pernambuco. He is currently Lecturer in economics at the University of Cambridge. His research focuses on macroeconomics, economic development, and growth, and he has published in *Economic Theory*, the *Journal of Monetary Economics*, and the *Review of Economics and Statistics*.

José Antonio Cheibub is Associate Professor and Boeschenstein Scholar in Political Economy at the University of Illinois. He is the author of *Presidentialism, Parliamentarism and Democracy*, a coeditor of the *Democracy Sourcebook*, and a coauthor of *Democracy and Development*.

Donald V. Coes is Professor of Economics at the University of New Mexico. His research has focused on the economy of Brazil, where he was a Fulbright Professor in 1984 and a National Research Foundation (CNPq) Professor in 1995 in the Federal University system.

Joaquim J.M. Guilhoto is Professor of Economics at the University of São Paulo, and Adjunct Professor in the Regional Economics Applications Laboratory at the University of Illinois. He is concerned with structural analysis of the national and regional economies of Brazil.

Eduardo A. Haddad is Associate Professor of Economics at the University of São Paulo. He is the Director of Research of the Institute of Economic Research (FIPE), and is Adjunct Associate Professor in the Regional Economics Applications Laboratory at the University of Illinois. He is currently president of the Brazilian Regional Science Association.

Mônica A. Haddad is Assistant Professor at Iowa State University's Department of Community and Regional Planning, where she specializes in spatial analysis and geographic information systems. Haddad alternates her research focus between Brazil and the U.S. Midwest.

Michael M. Hall is Professor of History and Vice Director of the Center for the Study of International Migrations at the State University of Campinas (UNICAMP). His work has dealt primarily with the history of the Brazilian labor movement and immigration.

Geoffrey J.D. Hewings is Director of the Regional Economics Applications Laboratory as well as Professor of Geography & Regional Science, of Economics, and of Urban and Regional Planning at the University of Illinois. His research interests focus on the development and application of regional economic models. His geographic interests include the U.S. Midwest, and Brazil, Chile, Korea, Japan, and Indonesia.

Marco Antônio Laes is a graduate student in economics at the University of São Paulo. He is also a member of the research team at the Regional and Urban Economics Laboratory (NEREUS) at USP.

Maria Antonieta P. Leopoldi teaches political science and international relations at the Fluminense Federal University in Niteroi, Rio de Janeiro. She has published on industrial associations, corporatism, and economic policy making in Brazil. Her present work concerns the complexities of reforming the social security system.

Joseph L. Love is Professor of History Emeritus at the University of Illinois. His publications include *Rio Grande do Sul and Brazilian Regionalism*, *São Paulo in the Brazilian Federation*, and *Crafting the Third World: Theorizing Underdevelopment in Rumania and Brazil*.

André Matos Magalhães is Professor of Economics at the Federal University of Pernambuco. His research interests are applied econometrics and urban-and-regional economics, and he edits the *Revista Brasileira de Estudos Regionais e Urbanos* (Brazilian Review of Regional and Urban Studies).

Jorge Vianna Monteiro is Professor of Economics at the Pontifical Catholic University in Rio de Janeiro, where he specializes in the area of Public Choice. Among his recent books are *As Regras do Jogo* (The Rules of the Game), *Lições de Economia Constitucional Brasileira* (Lessons from Brazilian Constitutional Economics), and *Como Funciona o Governo: Escolhas Públicas na Democracia Representativa* (How the Government Works: Public Choices in Representative Democracy).

Guilherme R.C. Moreira is the Head of the Department of Economics at Fundação Padre Anchieta de Ensino in Jundiaí, Brazil. He is part of the team of researchers of the Institute of Economic Research (FIPE) in the Department of Economics of USP.

Bernardo Mueller has been teaching at the University of Brasília since 1995. His areas of interest are the New Institutional Economics, Positive Political Theory, and Regulation and Environmental Economics. Mueller is also Associate Editor of *Environment and Development Economics*.

Charles C. Mueller is Professor Emeritus and Senior Associate Researcher at the University of Brasília. For three years he was also Director and President of the Instituto Brasileiro de Geografia e Estatística, Brazil's national statistical office. His main areas of interest are agricultural economics, environmental economics, and development economics.

André Rossi de Oliveira is Associate Professor of Economics at the University of Brasília, and Deputy Director of UnB's Center for Studies in the Regulation of Markets. He is concerned with Regulation of Infrastructure, Game Theory, and Applied Microeconomics.

Alexandre Rands Barros is Professor of Economics at the Federal University of Pernambuco. He is the author of some 40 articles and the C.E.O. of Datamétrica, a consultancy, research, and telemarketing company.

Simone Uderman teaches at the State University of Bahia, where she received her Ph.D. in administration. Uderman has published in the field of regional economics, her special interest, and she is advisor to Bahia's State Development Agency.

Introduction

WERNER BAER AND JOSEPH L. LOVE

Luiz Inácio Lula da Silva, the former trade union leader and head of Brazil's Workers' Party, was elected president of Brazil in October 2002. At the time many Brazilian and foreign observers expected a dramatic shift to the left in the governance of the country. They shared the expectation that the Lula government would provide a radical alternative to the previous policy mix, and many domestic and foreign investors feared that irresponsibility in macroeconomic policies and the erosion of established property rights would become the order of the day. These early expectations were confounded by subsequent developments. Many of the early radical supporters were bitterly disappointed in the policies adopted by President Lula, while the domestic and foreign investment communities were not just pleasantly surprised by the actual policies adopted, but they gradually became strong *supporters* of the government.

Following President Lula's reelection in October 2006, the Brazil program of the Center for Latin American and Caribbean Studies of the University of Illinois organized a conference to examine the impact of the first mandate of the Lula government. The gathering was held on the campus of the University of Illinois at Urbana-Champaign on April 20–21, 2007. Brazilian and Brazilianist scholars presented papers evaluating the impact of the Lula administration from various disciplinary points of view. These papers are presented as chapters in this volume.[1] We also want to mention the following scholars who critiqued and improved the papers presented here: Marcos Holanda, Maria Eugenia Mata, Cláudio Paiva, Riordan Roett, Luciano Tosta, and John Welch.

Although papers by economists and regional scientists predominate in this collection, three of those—by C. Mueller, B. Mueller and Rossi, and Vianna Monteiro—deal with the political process itself. Furthermore, political scientists, historians, and a specialist in education have also contributed studies. Most of these papers emphasize continuities (in varying intensities) with the policies of Lula's predecessor, Fernando Henrique Cardoso (president, 1995–2002).

Thematically, income inequality is an issue that concerns virtually all the contributors. Brazil is one of the most economically unequal countries in the world, and President Lula himself has made income inequality the most salient issue in his second term. One major dimension of inequality is regional disparities in per capita income, and consequently, the last group of chapters in this volume concerns Brazil's poorest region, the nine-state bloc of the northeast.

The book opens with a chapter by José Antonio Cheibub, who shows how the institutional configuration of Brazilian politics led to corruption scandals, and he examines an array of reform proposals to remedy the situation. However, given that transformative electoral reforms are unlikely to be implemented because of entrenched interests favoring the present system, Cheibub offers suggestions for improving the status quo incrementally.

Edmund Amann and Werner Baer survey the forces that underlay the fact that economic inequality has persisted from colonial times to the present, and they ask whether President Lula's social policies have effectively broken with the past. The authors show that slavery and the monopoly of land tenure produced extreme inequality from the colonial era through Brazil's first century of independence, and they argue that new causes of inequality arose with the era of import-substitution industrialization (1930–1980). Subsequently the sources of inequality changed again, as differential access to education became the leading cause in our own time. The authors judge that the Lula government has effectively combated abject poverty, but that income distribution has changed little.

Jorge Vianna Monteiro shows how and why politicians in Congress have delegated powers to the federal bureaucracy. Private interest groups can deal more efficiently with bureaucrats, and these quiet negotiations allow special interests and Congress itself to escape public criticism. Thus democracy is partially neutralized by administrative mechanisms that get around cumbersome constitutional processes. In addition, Lula has frequently issued executive orders that forced Congress to accept faits accomplis, because members of Congress wanted to avoid shouldering the blame for unpopular government actions.

Jocildo Bezerra and Tiago V. de V. Cavalcanti provide an analysis of the reasons the Lula government could not produce higher levels of economic growth. Favorable conditions for economic growth prevailed at the international level during Lula's first term, but Brazil's growth was nonetheless disappointing. They conclude that despite important reforms, Brazil continues to suffer low levels of institutional development and human capital stock; an ineffective tax regime; and unsecured property rights.

Bernardo Mueller and André Rossi de Oliveira show how President Lula greatly reduced the power of regulatory agencies, and used the power of the presidency to maintain macroeconomic stability, perhaps even beyond that of any recent president. Nonetheless, there was continuity with the preceding Cardoso administration's efforts to reform the cumbersome regulatory system.

Donald V. Coes finds that the relatively robust state of the Brazilian economy owes in significant measure to the exchange rate policy of the preceding Cardoso government. Coes looks at the current exchange rate policy and the underlying internal constraints that still appear to be operative. The multiple goals of external balance, internal price stability, and the maintenance of access to international capital markets continued to impose important constraints on Brazil's longer-term growth prospects.

Charles Mueller points out that in the areas of agriculture and the environment, Lula took on huge policy challenges, but the government failed to coordinate its efforts. In agriculture, the government has been more effective in distributing land to peasants than in turning them into surplus producers. Leading "environment" issues included forest conservation and pollution, but policy in these areas overlapped the bailiwick of agriculture, because of the issue of genetically modified organisms. Such overlap caused conflict within the administration.

Michael M. Hall stresses the continuities of labor policy from the corporatist *Estado Novo* ("New State," 1937–1945) to the present. Authoritarian elements survived into the generally democratic constitutional regime of 1988, though thereafter the right to strike was specifically guaranteed. The increasingly important informal sector and employer demands for labor "flexibility" in employment weakened organized labor. Hall considers why the Lula government's efforts to reform the structure of labor unions and invalidate the labor code of the *Estado Novo* have stalled. Collective bargaining, as opposed to court arbitration, has yet to be implemented, and meanwhile deregulation of the labor market occurs on a piecemeal basis.

Paulo Roberto de Almeida surveys the Lula government's relations with major powers and power blocs, paying special attention to its ambiguous relations with the United States, arising from trade policy conflicts. He considers the differences between the Free Trade Area of the Americas (FTAA), sponsored by President Bush, and Mercosul, the South American regional trade agreement. Lula, more than his predecessors, has also asserted Brazil's claim on a permanent seat in the Security Council of the United Nations. The author also points out the implicit contradiction between Lula's professed ideals of national sovereignty and the regional integration that an effective Mercosul would entail.

Mônica A. Haddad examines the *Bolsa Família* (family subsidy) program from the perspectives of need and equity. She shows that, under Lula, counties characterized by higher need (i.e., those with a high Gini coefficient of inequality, high infant mortality rate, and high illiteracy rate) are receiving more funds than counties characterized by lower need. This happened in both the Northeast-North and the Center-South. Mary Arends-Kuenning, however, notes that the Lula government did not give priority to education. Access to schooling continued to improve, as it did under President Cardoso, but achievement levels remained stagnant, and Brazil is close to the bottom on international rankings when its students are measured on standardized tests. This alerts us to the fact that the quality of education is as important as the quantity (number of years of schooling). The challenge of raising educational performance continues into Lula's second term.

Maria Antonieta P. Leopoldi describes Brazil's changing and complex social security system, and notes the relative success in reining in the huge cost of pensions. Lula's efforts continued the reforms of the government of Fernando Henrique Cardoso, who introduced the taxation of private pensions. Lula succeeded where Cardoso failed in taxing government employees' pensions. He also put a ceiling on bureaucrats' salaries. Some pension and social security reforms—such as prohibiting "double-dipping" and limiting the scale of pensions—are still in process, and their fate is uncertain.

Carlos R. Azzoni and his five coauthors examine regional income inequality and the impact of the *Bolsa Família* on income distribution in the poverty-stricken northeast and the nation as a whole. They note a small but significant improvement in the Gini index of income inequality, but the authors emphasize that other programs need to be undertaken in the areas of social investment, especially in health and education. Otherwise, social transfers like the *Bolsa Família* will have little positive effect.

Luiz Ricardo Cavalcante and Simone Uderman demonstrate that fiscal and related financial incentives under the Lula government did not favor the northeast, but rather the northern and central-western states. They show that even when compensatory funds to backward regions are considered, the government still lacked an active regional development policy. On the other hand, Alexandre Rands Barros and André Matos Magalhães demonstrate that changes in the policy framework to benefit poorer regions had an impact on regional per capita GDP, and the northeastern states grew impressively in per capita income during Lula's first administration. New investments occurred in the shipbuilding and petrochemical industries, and small farmers gained greater access to technology and credit. These improvements led to a smashing electoral victory for Lula in 2006, when he received 77 percent of the vote in his native northeast.

Joseph L. Love concludes the volume by considering how the Lula administration might be viewed historically in terms of Daron Acemoglu's model of "the primacy of politics" to achieve greater economic equity in Brazil. The author looks at long-term social and political obstacles to decreasing the enormous inequality in income distribution in Brazil, the third most unequal country in the world, according to the World Bank. He considers some classical interpretations of Brazil's historical development, as well as recent monographs that help explain Brazil's long-standing failure to address the equity issue. He argues that Brazil now appears to have achieved the necessary maturity of civil society and the requisite level of political mobilization to significantly reduce economic inequality.

Note

1. The conference was mainly financed by a grant from the Hewlett Foundation. Other sponsors included the Lemann Chair, International Programs and Studies, the CIBER program of the College of Business, the Center for Latin American and Caribbean Studies, the Department of Political Science, and the College of Agricultural, Consumer and Environmental Sciences—all of the University of Illinois.

PART ONE

The Problems the Lula Government Confronted in Politics and the Economy

CHAPTER ONE

Political Reform in Brazil: Recent Proposals, Diagnosis, and a Suggestion*

JOSÉ ANTONIO CHEIBUB

Introduction

If we count the indirect, but competitive, election of 1985, Brazil has already experienced six presidential and six legislative elections since the end of the military dictatorship (1985, 1989, 1994, 1998, 2002, 2006; 1986, 1990, 1994, 1998, 2002, and 2006). Democracy has been in place for over 20 years now and, contrary to the image that is often projected by both the popular press and academics, both lamenting the fact that it has not brought about paradise-on-earth, it is operating reasonably well. Yet, political reform has been perennially on the agenda and seems to have gained a boost from the allegations of corruption in the middle of 2005 involving members of the executive and Congress. It is unclear if the proposed reforms are meant to prevent and, if implemented, whether they will be at all capable of preventing what is considered the high levels of corruption of the first Lula government. What is clear is that the 2005 corruption allegations provided a new impetus to those who seek to overhaul of the political system.

In this chapter I do three things. First, I characterize the current reform proposals and the diagnosis that led to them. Second, I argue that this diagnosis is theoretically and empirically problematic and, consequently, the proposals that follow from them suffer from similar limitations. Beyond that, I argue that these proposals, if implemented, are unlikely to achieve their intended goals. Third, I suggest one change in the current system that, I believe, will improve the performance of electoral institutions in Brazil. It should be noted that neither the executive (under Lula, but also all other presidents since the 1988 constitution was approved) nor any political party has a comprehensive proposal for political reforms. Reform proposals consist of specific bills introduced by members of Congress, and much of the discussion about political reform takes place through newspapers articles and essays written by academics and politicians. My views are based on a distillation of what I perceive to be the most important reform proposals.

Why Are Reforms Needed? The Standard
Diagnosis and Current Proposals

As in most countries, political reforms in Brazil have been forever on the agenda. They appeared more frequently in the discourse of political actors after the scandals revealed in winter 2005, involving legislators, members of the government, and the leadership of the governing *Partido dos Trabalhadores*.

We can discern a common thread running through most of the proposals under discussion because they are generally based on the same diagnosis of the current institutions and the problems they are thought to generate. Most proposals concern perceived weaknesses in the form of government; the electoral system for Congress (in particular the Chamber of Deputies) and the federal system of government.

Presidentialism

This regime is generally considered to be inherently problematic. The literature arguing this point is vast and there is no need to reproduce these arguments here.[1] Suffice it to say that presidentialism is thought to be too rigid and prone to conflict between the executive and the legislature. The main reason for this is that incentives under presidentialism are considered to be stacked against cooperation—between political parties and the government, among political parties themselves, and among individual legislators within parties. This implies that governments have a hard time putting together stable coalitions to support their policies in Congress, that parties prefer to stay in the opposition rather than support the government, and that even if they choose to support the government, such support is ineffective, given the chronic, inherent and structural inability of parties to discipline their members. Contrary to parliamentarism, where a vote of no-confidence and the possibility of early elections are believed to be sufficient to induce all sorts of cooperative behavior, no such mechanism exists in presidential democracies. Because the system does not possess, the built-in solution to eventual conflicts, governing under presidentialism is thought by its critics simply to be more difficult than under parliamentarism. With a multiparty system, presidential governance can be even harder (Mainwaring 1993). Multipartyism, however, prevails in most presidential systems, including Brazil. When many parties exist, the argument goes, the likelihood of minority governments increase, the need for coalition formation becomes stronger, but the disincentives for cooperation remain the same.

Legislative Elections

The existing electoral system for the Brazilian Chamber of Deputies almost guarantees a fragmented party system (and hence exacerbates the problems of presidentialism). Proportional representation (PR) is notoriously and uncontroversially associated with multiparty systems. The kind of proportional representation that exists in Brazil—with low barriers to entry and decentralized, state-based party structures—only reinforces this general tendency. The system currently in place, thus, for its critics, leads to a fragmented legislature and the pulverization of government support in Congress, thereby tending to paralyze presidential government.

If proportional representation in general is problematic because of its tendency to generate multiple political parties, the specific kind of PR used in Brazil to elect the lower house of Congress—open list as opposed to closed list—only makes things worse. For example, it charged with producing weak political parties (or, one should say, weaker than presidentialism would already make them): since voters are the ones who rank the names in electoral lists, parties are deprived of one of the most important instruments of influencing those who get into Congress—manipulating placement in the party lists. Moreover, the fact that it is the voter who ranks the candidates in the list implies that candidates compete against their fellow party members as well as against other parties.

Given these features of the electoral system, the argument goes, the best strategy for politicians is to cultivate a personal following rather than the party vote since what matters are individuals, not parties. This would not be necessarily problematic if it were not for the fact that electoral incentives readily translate into legislative behavior: the incentives to cultivate the personal vote lead to individualistic behavior inside Congress.[2] As a consequence, governing becomes a process of forming ad hoc coalitions, of buying individual legislators in a spot market where prices quickly become very high, with obvious political and economic costs for the country as a whole. Clientelism, then, becomes the norm: legislators have an incentive to secure particularistic bills for their constituencies. Given the need for legislative support, the government has an incentive to provide the resources for legislators' clientelistic projects. Legislative action, consequently, is centered on projects that are narrowly defined based on special interests, rather than those that are broad and national in scope.

The current electoral system is also supposed to generate low levels of accountability on the part of legislators, a situation that flows from the low level of intelligibility of the elections. Open list PR requires vote pooling across candidate lists, and vote pooling leads parties to maximize the number of candidates they present at election. Party lists in each state are large—each party can present one-and-a-half times as many candidates as there are seats in the district. Moreover, candidates, once elected, often switch parties, thus violating the relationship that was established at the time of election (Tavares 1998).[3]

Federalism

Finally, federalism only compounds these problems. Unlike the "good" federalisms observed in other countries—notably in the United States—the one in Brazil introduces a regional dimension into politics that prevails over the national dimension and, therefore, weakens national political parties (Stepan 2000). In this view, Brazilian federalism reinforces the system's tendency to generate narrowly defined legislation since governors operate as leaders of their states' representatives in the national legislature, thus preventing the approval of legislation that is general or national in character (Abrúcio 1998, Samuels 2003). It also distorts representation since malapportionment, exaggerated in the Senate, is high even in the lower chamber (Samuels and Snyder 2001). In sum, federalism introduces additional veto players in a system already saturated with them (Ames 2001).

Given these problems, what are the solutions?

The best way to avoid the problems of presidentialism, it seems, would be to get rid of it. The parliamentarism versus presidentialism debate in Brazil has been going on at least since the mid-1980s and it seems that it will never go away.[4] There seems to be a sense among proponents of political reform in Brazil that a parliamentary form of government is inherently superior to a presidential form of government. Interestingly, the parliamentary option in Brazil has always meant a mixed constitution, where the assembly-dependent government headed by a prime minister also faces a directly elected president. Whether such a misnomer originated in strategic considerations or in the belief that such systems are inherently superior to the "pure" formula is irrelevant here. What matters is that proponents of parliamentarism still roam the political landscape, in spite of the fact that the chances that it will ever be adopted are virtually nonexistent.[5]

The best way to fix the problems generated by the electoral system of Congress would be to make it less permissive, either by introducing short-term fixes to the current system (such as setting a higher minimum number of voters for each qualifying party) or by simply jettisoning the principle of proportional representation altogether. Proponents of a system based on single-member districts or of a mixed system such as the one that exists in Germany are numerous and are likely to increase.[6] As a matter of fact, there seems to be a large overlap between those who propose the introduction of some form of majoritarianism in the legislative electoral system and proponents of the parliamentary formula. This connection, of course, is not theoretical; but it is real nonetheless.

Regarding federalism, I do not know of anyone who proposes to abandon it. But much of the discussion about changing the electoral system and strengthening political parties are couched in the idea that parties and elections—and by extension, it seems, the behavior of legislators—need to be nationalized, set free from the influence of local and narrowly defined interests.

Ideally, then, one would want to get rid of presidentialism, of the proportional principle for legislative elections, and of federalism. Yet, no one believes that such changes are likely. Existing reform proposals, therefore, are second-best alternatives. Their goal is to minimize the problems of presidentialism and federalism, and to introduce changes in the electoral system that will make entry harder and will shift power from candidates/legislators to party leaders.

Bills have been introduced in Congress dealing with many aspects of the country's political and institutional organization. They include, in no particular order, the introduction of a vote of no-confidence on the president; the end of reelection for executive positions; the establishment of a popular referendum on ordinary legislation; the specification of conditions under which second rounds of elections seeking absolute majorities would not be required; provisions regulating electoral campaigns;[7] changes in the way party lists are composed and presented to voters; changes in the territorial basis of representation; changes in the form of government; and restrictions on the access to representative bodies and/or participation in them. Most of the projects, as noted by Soares and Rennó (2006: 13), were introduced by individual legislators without specific coordination and died before they reached the floor of either house of Congress. In this thicket of legislative proposals, the most important ones still alive include the adoption of closed lists in legislative elections (which would presumably strengthen the power of national over regional party leaders); public campaign financing (which would presumably establish a level playing field among candidates and remove incentives for corruption); and the establishment of electoral thresholds (which would reduce the number of political parties in Congress).[8] The few measures of relevance that have already passed include limits in the number of candidates presented by coalitions in proportional representation, revocation of the constraints in the type of coalitions that could be formed in these elections, and, the weakening of presidential powers through changes in the rules for "provisional laws." By limiting the number of times the president can reissue the same decree to one, this measure aimed at limiting the president's ability to undertake unilateral legislative action and, thereby, strengthening the role of Congress in the legislative process. Whether the measure succeeded in these goals has not yet been established.

The Inadequacy of Existing Reform Proposals

In this section I make three broad points: 1) that most of the reform proposals under discussion are based on what I consider to be a misdiagnosis of existing political institutions, in particular of the broad ones that define Brazil's overall constitutional framework; 2) that some of these reforms may not have the desired consequences; and 3) that supporters of current reform proposals fail to see some of the positive aspects of the institutions they are criticizing. Let me briefly develop each of these points.

There is a relatively large body of research showing that the premises on which these proposals are based are not supported by either theory or data. To begin with, it is not true that presidential democracies are chronically prone to deadlocks between the executive and the legislature. One estimate of the frequency of the institutional and political conditions under which deadlock emerges puts it at about one-third of all cases (country-years) of presidentialism (Cheibub 2002).

Moreover, it is a misconception to think that parliamentary democracies do not experience deadlock. Deadlock under parliamentarism is certainly not the same as deadlock under presidentialism; but it occurs. Under parliamentarism, deadlock occurs when, following elections, no clear majority emerges in the legislature, the government has weak legislative support, and faces a vote of no-confidence. Then a new government is formed, equally weak, a new vote of no-confidence is passed, no other combination of parties will form a government, new elections are held, and, again, no clear majority emerges, and so on. The fourth Republic in France and Italy prior to the collapse of the party system in 1992 are often cited as the best examples of deadlocked parliamentary democracies. Thus, given their different constitutional structures, the form the deadlock takes is necessarily different in parliamentary and presidential systems; but the outcome in one is not necessarily better than in the other. In both cases, there is no majority that will support government policies.

In addition, it is not true that political actors in presidential regimes have no incentives to form coalitions. The notion that political parties under presidentialism have an overwhelming incentive to play it alone, that they will not cooperate with each other and will not support the president even when they are part of the government, is simply false. My own research (Cheibub 2007 and Cheibub, Przeworski, and Saiegh 2004) shows that incentives for coalition formation are more or less the same under the two regimes; it also shows that presidential systems permits a type of legislative paralysis that does not occur under parliamentarism, but it only occurs under very specific institutional conditions. Furthermore, it happens only if one of the parties to the conflict prefers the status quo. The difference in coalition formation between parliamentary and presidential democracies, therefore, is merely quantitative, not qualitative.

Furthermore, presidential regimes are not incompatible with multiparty systems. Presidential democracies actually face higher risks of collapsing into an authoritarian regime when the number of parties is moderate (Cheibub 2002, 2007). Therefore, whatever the problems of governability inherent to multiparty presidential democracies are, the cause is not the inability of parties to form coalitions.

Finally, there are institutional features other than the form of government that may act to induce cooperation among political parties in Congress and of parties with the government. Governments with strong agendas and legislative powers can induce reliable legislative cooperation even if their parties do not hold a majority of seats in Congress. Analogous to the way prime ministers operate under parliamentarism, presidents under presidentialism can bargain from an advantageous position with legislative majorities in order to gain support for policies that are acceptable to both (Figueiredo and Limongi 2000a, 2000b, Huber 1996). The image of a spot-market for legislative support is simply not adequate for many presidential democracies, in particular the Brazilian one. Presidential democracies, as we know, vary considerably in terms of presidential powers to legislate directly and to set the legislative agenda (Shugart and Carey 1992). They range from cases such as the United States, where presidents are institutionally weak, to those of Brazil and Chile, where the president can issue decree-laws, has exclusive power to propose the budget, and may set the pace with which bills go through the legislature. (Figueiredo and Limongi 2000b, Siavelis 2000). Thus, the details of the way executive-legislative relations are structured in presidential democracies matter for the system's ability to neutralize whatever centrifugal forces may stem from the principle of separation of powers.

Regarding federalism, concern may also have been overstated. It is undeniable that governors play a central role in the political-legislative process, principally because electoral districts for national legislative contests are all contained inside state borders. This does not mean, however, that national legislators respond to state pressures rather than to partisan and national considerations. Recent research based on the analysis of roll-call votes taken in Chamber of Deputies shows that, although present, the local influence on the behavior of national legislators is not any stronger than the influence of the political party or the national government (Carey 2007, Cheibub, Figueiredo, and Limongi 2009, Desposato 2004). Consequently, one cannot say that federalism in Brazil introduces a bias toward the status quo that cannot be overcome by the national government.

In addition, the claim that the electoral system denies political parties the ability to control their candidates is based on an incomplete view of the instruments political parties can deploy. Although unable to rank candidates in their lists, parties can exclude individuals from them.[9] They also control the most effective instrument in Brazilian national electoral campaigns, namely, access to television and radio.

Finally, the irrelevance of political parties in structuring the vote in the broad electorate is more presumed than demonstrated. The evidence often invoked to support this claim—the relatively high proportion of preference votes as opposed to vote for the party, or the short political memory that is supposed to characterize the Brazilian voter—are at most ambiguous since it says very little about how voters actually decide. Given that in the current system a vote for a candidate is also a vote for his or her party, a high proportion of preference vote says nothing about the relative weight of individuals over the party. For it to do so, it would have to be true that voters who vote for a specific candidate would have voted for that candidate even if he or she were to change parties. This, however, we do not know to be true as there are no studies that address this issue. Available evidence, however, suggests that representatives who switch parties in the middle of the legislative term are *less* likely to be reelected (Schmitt 1999; Pereira and Rennó 2001, Samuels 2003), which implies that they are not able to carry with them the votes that got them into the Chamber. Moreover, not remembering whom one voted for in past elections may simply indicate that what matters for the voter is the party and not the candidate.[10] Finally, evidence from survey research indicates that parties do play a role in voters' electoral deliberations (Figueiredo 2005).

The second broad point I want to assert is that the proposed reforms may not bring about the desired outcomes or, if they do, they may have additional consequences that may well outweigh any positive effects. Thus, attempts to weaken the president may undermine the mechanism—the president's ability to shape the legislative agenda—that generated the higher-than-expected degree of legislative success of post-1988 Brazilian presidents. Closed lists for legislative elections will empower the party leadership at the expense of voters, something of dubious value. Moreover, closed lists will severe the direct link that now exists—at least potentially—between voters and legislators. If accountability is said to be low now, what will it be when voters cannot punish representatives directly? As recent research has shown (Kunicova and Rose-Ackerman 2005 and Persson, Tabellini, and Trebbi 2003; but see Chang 2005 for a contrary view), corruption is higher under closed list than under open list PR electoral systems; and the reasons are precisely the greater power of parties and lower accountability of legislators in the former systems. Moreover, public funding of political campaigns will do nothing to address the biggest problem of campaign financing in Brazil, namely under-the-table financing.

Finally, their haste to condemn the broad institutions—the form of government, the electoral system, the political organization of the country—supporters of the current reforms fail to see some of the positive aspects of these institutions. As emphasized by Shugart and Carey (1992), presidentialism gives voters two agents, elected on the basis of different constituencies, that allow the calibration of the two fundamental goals of democratic regimes—representation and governability—in a way that parliamentarism does not. The electoral system for the legislative chamber, in turn, is flexible enough to allow for a high degree of heterogeneity in the forms of representation. One study of the geographic distribution of the votes of successful candidates for legislative elections (Carvalho 2003) demonstrates that in 1994 and 1998 only about 17 percent of representatives adopted an electoral strategy of carving up a de facto geographic constituency. In Ames' (2001) terminology, these were the representatives who constructed successful "bailiwicks" by dominating elections in a cluster of geographically concentrated counties. The remaining 83 percent adopted different strategies that are less compatible with the clientelistic relationship implied by the existence of bailiwicks, such as sharing with others a relatively defined geographic area, dominating localities that were geographically separated, or obtaining relatively small shares of their vote in a geographically dispersed way. Thus, clientelism, at least as indicated by the existence of electoral bailiwicks, does not properly characterize the ties between representatives and voters induced by the current open list PR system. As a matter of fact, the current system is characterized by a *heterogeneity* in the strategies of representation pursued by successful candidates.

We might say that federalism is perhaps a small price to pay for keeping a country such as Brazil "in business." Those who identify federalism as one of the main sources of difficulties related to governance are possibly disregarding the importance of representation, in particular, regional representation, in accommodating interests that might otherwise seek nonpeaceful solutions to their demands. In order to consider both aspects—governability and representation—simultaneously, one has to perform a thought experiment and imagine what a country like Brazil would look like if it had a unitary constitution. Or imagine that the electoral system were one with closed list PR with national leaders in Brasília deciding who would constitute the party lists in each state. The problems of representation in such a framework might very well lead to worse problems of governability. Thus, a certain tolerance for sub-national concerns in the political process—both cause and consequence of the necessity of accommodating a diversity of interests through intense bargaining— may be the price to be paid for the continued unity of the country.

To conclude, because the constitution is hard to change (see Cheibub 2007: 152–153), most of the reform proposals will never be enacted. The insistence on changing what is hard to change, on altering the fundamental principles of the political system only serves to delegitimize that system. Moreover, such insistence obfuscates alternatives that maintain the broad constitutional framework, but try to improve it. I will address an important one in the next section.

Reducing Competitiveness and Preserving Representativeness of Legislative Elections

The high degree of representativeness is one of the positive attributes of the current Brazilian political system and this feature must be preserved. The system is highly representative not only because it imposes low barriers to entry but also, as noted above, because it is compatible with several strategies of representation. Yet, the system is based on excessively large electoral districts that in turn generate a tremendous degree of competitiveness in legislative elections. This, I argue, is an undesirable attribute of the current system and reforms should be designed to minimize it.

That districts in Brazil are comparatively large, both in relative and absolute terms, is not in question. According to Cox's (1997) study of 77 national legislative electoral systems in the mid-1990s, there were 27 cases with districts that returned more than 20 representatives. The vast majority had one or two such districts, and Slovakia had three. Only

Table 1.1 Countries with district magnitude for legislative elections equal to or larger than 11

Country	Year	Assembly size	Total districts	Median district magnitude	Electorate	Voters/District
Netherlands	2002	150	1	150.0	9,515,000	9,515,000
Brazil	**2002**	**513**	**27**	**11.0**	**115,254,000**	**4,268,667**
Israel	2003	120	1	120.0	3,200,000	3,200,000
Italy	2001	630	42	17.0	40,195,000	957,024
Namibia	2004	78	1	72.0	835,980	835,980
Slovakia	2002	150	4	44.0	2,913,000	728,250
Czech Republic	2002	200	8	23.5	4,789,000	598,625
Austria	2002	183	9	13.0	4,982,000	553,556
Bolivia	2002	130	9	13.0	2,994,000	332,667
Sweden	2002	349	28	11.0	5,385,000	192,321
Finland	2003	200	21	13.0	2,815,000	134,048
Slovenia	2002	90	8	11.0	1,050,000	131,250
Luxembourg	2004	60	4	15.0	199,846	49,962
Liechtenstein	2001	25	2	13.0	14,178	7,089

Source: Cox (1997)

Brazil and Italy had more than that: eight in Brazil and eleven in Italy. Still, according to Cox (1997), the median district magnitude in Brazil is 11, the same as in Slovenia and Sweden. There are 14 countries where the median district magnitude is 11 or larger. In most of these cases the absolute size of the electorate, as well as the average electorate in each district, is small compared to the ones in Brazil. As table 1.1 indicates, Brazil has the largest electorate of the countries that possess districts with large magnitudes—115,000,000. On average, districts in Brazil have about 4,200,000 voters, which is less than the total electorate of the Netherlands but more than the total electorate of Israel (both countries have only one national district). No other country with a large number of large magnitude districts has districts with more than 1 million voters. In Brazil, 22 of the 27 districts in the 2006 elections had more than one million voters; 12 had more than 3 million voters; 8 had more than 5 million voters; 3 had more than 10 million voters and 1 had over 28 million voters!

The combination of relatively large magnitudes with large electorates implies a high level of competitiveness in legislative elections. In 2002, there were 4,298 candidates for the 513 congressional seats in the country; on average, therefore, there were 8.4 candidates per seat. In only two states was the number of candidates per seat less than 6: in Bahia it was 3.4 and in Ceará it was 5.6. In six states the number of candidates per seat was over 10. In 2006 there were 4,946 candidates and competitiveness increased in virtually every district, with an average of 9.6 candidates per district (ranging from a low of 5.5 in Bahia to 15.4 in Rio de Janeiro).

Wanderley Guilherme dos Santos (2003) defends the level of competitiveness of the Brazilian system, using as an indicator the number of candidates per seat. Although I agree with him that the system has become more competitive and that competitiveness is something to be valued, I also believe that the number of candidates, and the degree of competition it implies, may be excessive. According to Fabiano Santos (1999), one of the consequences of large districts is the difficulty in identifying the constituency that supports the successful candidate. Yet, I find it unlikely that politicians do not know where their support comes from—given sophisticated polls and analysis of aggregate electoral results. The problem is that whatever constituency representatives choose to build, it is vulnerable to attacks by the numerous competitors they face.

High levels of competitiveness translate into high turnover rates in Congress: 62.8 percent of those who served in the Brazilian Chamber of Deputies in 1991 were not serving in 1987; 52.7 percent of those who served in 1995 were not serving in 1991; and about 41 percent of those who served in 1999 and 2003 were not serving in 1995 and 1999, respectively.[11] Of these, many chose not to run (Samuels [2003] estimates that this number is around 30 percent of the incumbents), in part because they anticipate not being able to win, in part because they pursued opportunities elsewhere. In any event, on average, half of the members of each legislature since 1991 were newcomers. Data on turnover are not widely available, in particular for other new democracies. The information available shows that incumbency return rates for Brazil's Chamber of Deputies are comparatively quite low. In a study of 25 industrialized democracies, Matland and Studlar (2004) found that the mean incumbency return rate over three to four elections was 67.7 percent, ranging from 53.1 percent in Canada (standard deviation = 21.25 percent) to 84.9 percent in the United States (standard deviation 6.14 percent). At 50.3 percent (standard deviation = 10.2 percent) for the four elections held between 1990 and 2002, Brazil is at the bottom of the list.

The high level of competitiveness of legislative elections, in turn, raises a number of issues that must be seriously considered. For one, at the current levels of competition, successful candidates—incumbent legislators—are not always rewarded for building strong ties with their voters. The risk involved in this kind of investment is extremely high as any such action is vulnerable to encroachment by the many competitors the incumbent faces. Thus, the problem with the current system for legislative elections is not that it provides incentives for politicians to cultivate the "personal vote," as it is frequently asserted; rather, the problem is that it does not provide enough guarantee that politicians who do so will be sufficiently rewarded.

Moreover, high legislative turnover causes difficulties for the institutionalization of the Congress. Short career paths are not conducive to the development of policy expertise, the establishment of permanent staffs, and, most importantly, the assertion of the assembly's institutional powers, in absolute terms as well as relative to the other branches of the government.

A high degree of competitiveness, and the lack of job security that it implies, also affects the recruitment of candidates for legislative elections and the very institutionalization of the national Congress. To the extent that congressional service requires specific attributes and qualifications, some of which are of relatively high market value, providing a degree of job security would be a way to lure into Congress those who might otherwise choose less risky careers. Moreover, to the extent that a strong institution depends on a degree of personnel continuity, short career paths are not conducive to the strengthening of Congress as an institution.

Another consideration is that high levels of competitiveness have an impact on legislative campaign financing, which was at the root of the scandals that came to light in 2005. When competition is very high, coordination among donors to support candidates and parties becomes harder, and significant resources are directed toward unsuccessful competitors. The overall cost of an election, therefore, is larger than it could have been had coordination over campaign financing been possible. At the same time, individuals and political parties are under extreme pressure to raise the money that will provide them with the edge they require. Incentives for corruption are, therefore, strong. Note that public campaign finance will do nothing to alleviate these pressures and reduce corruption; under-the-table funding will only become more prevalent if an absolute cap on political expenditures is instituted.

Thus, the reduction in the degree of competitiveness in legislative elections in Brazil can be an effective way of strengthening the ties between representatives and voters, for providing legislators with incentives to invest in their careers, for strengthening Congress, and for reducing corruption associated with campaign financing. Yet, this should not be achieved through a forced reduction in the number of parties, for example, by establishing legal thresholds or instituting a single-member district system. While these are common solutions to the issue of excessive electoral competitiveness and legislative fragmentation, these are measures that throw the baby out with the bath water. For measures such as these will cause the system to lose one of its best attributes, namely, that it allows for a variety of forms of representation in a way that systems based on single-member districts (SMD) or closed list PR do not; representation in these systems is exclusively individual or party-oriented, respectively.

A reduction in the level of competitiveness could be achieved by giving legislative incumbents an advantage over challengers, which they do not have right now. Incumbency advantage is anathema to most people, but the fact is that more secure legislators will significantly improve the system of representation in Brazil.

One way to achieve this goal—that is, to keep the level of representation relatively intact while providing a modicum of job security to legislators—is to keep the open list PR system but create electoral districts smaller than the existing ones. In so doing we can reduce the competitiveness of the system and keep intact both the heterogeneity of representation and the possibility of a direct link between voters and representatives afforded by the current system. The magnitude of these districts, I believe, should range from three to no more than six seats. In such a system, each state could still have its congressional delegation and "state" interests could be potentially protected if need be; but this delegation would be composed of groups of representatives elected in different—and legally protected—areas of the state. This system would also secure the same heterogeneity of representation that exists now—single-issue representation, personal representation, broad based representation—but those who are elected will have better information about who elected them. They will also be able to more credibly claim responsibility for benefits to their districts and, most importantly, they will be more protected from challenges. Moreover, and this is very important in view of the practices that came to light in July 2005, lower levels of competitiveness in smaller districts may affect the pressures on campaign spending, thus reducing the incentives for candidates to fund their campaigns however they can. Contributors will be better able to forecast the winners and losers; convergence and coordination among campaign contributors will be more easily achieved; and the need for blind spending and blind contribution will be weaker. This, of course, will not reduce the need to reform other aspects of campaign financing—most of these aspects can and should be dealt with by strengthening the agencies in charge of monitoring electoral spending and punishing illegal activities. But these measures suggested do reduce the incentive for corruption that is the direct product of the high degree of competitiveness in current electoral contests.

No discussion of electoral districts in Brazil can avoid the issue of their correspondence with state borders and, most importantly, the distortion of representation that the existence of floors and ceilings for state delegations entails. As mentioned above, a redrawing of electoral districts with the view of reducing their size does not require abandoning these two attributes of the current system; districts can be drawn so that no state border is crossed and provisions can be made to guarantee a certain number of representatives per state. However, neither of these aspects are defensible in principle and, therefore, there is no reason to preserve them.

In a system of equal-sized districts (in terms of population), most states will lose representatives in favor of São Paulo and marginally Minas Gerais. Assuming that the size of the Chamber of Deputies remains the same, under such a system, five states—São Paulo, Minas Gerais, Rio de Janeiro, Bahia, and Rio Grande do Sul—will together hold a majority, which some analysts see as undesirable. I fail, however, to see why this is a problem and why it should be taken as a reason to justify the distortion of representation that floors and caps entail. For instance, we should not expect that the common interests these five states share will always be stronger than the ones that divide them. Even though the five are among the most industrialized and urbanized, their economies and social structures are sufficiently diverse to prevent them from forming a united front against the rest of the country. The power of partisan and national interests, which are articulated in the current system by the combination of a strong president with a centralized congress (Figueiredo and Limongi 1999), will be equally felt under a system of representation that better implements the principle of one person-one vote. Finally, if fear of a collusion of states or excessive power of state-level concerns persisted, one easy if radical solution would be to simply dissociate electoral districts from state borders.

Conclusion

Redistricting, the end of malapportionment and disregard for state borders in electoral competition—these are proposals that, if ever considered, will entail intense conflict. Twenty-five states would lose influence if these measures were enacted. For instance, there is little chance that an adjustment of representation to correct malapportionment will ever be passed. It is not surprising that of the hundreds of legislative proposals introduced in the Congress to reform the political system, not one questioned the territorial basis of representation. Thus, barring a legislative revolution or some kind of judicial intervention (which, given the level of activism of the Brazilian courts is not a far-fetched possibility),[12] there is little chance that we will see any time soon a significant change in the organization of electoral districts in Brazil. Yet, were such changes to pass, the institutional apparatus for their implementation is already in place: the Tribunal Superior Eleitoral has impartially and efficiently administered recent elections and is equipped to oversee the drawing of sub-state electoral districts; and agencies such as the Instituto Brasileiro de Geografia e Estatística (the national statistical agency) can easily provide the necessary demographic information to design such districts.

Yet, my goal is simply to raise some points for discussion. I would like to move the political reform debate away from the overall institutional framework and the need to replace it toward considerations about improving the existing system.

There is nothing intrinsically conservative about this position, since there is no presumption that the status quo is optimal. The recognition that current political institutions do have positive aspects does not imply, contrary to Rennó's interpretation (2006: 260), a belief that no reforms are necessary. I do find, however, that the failure to realize that existing institutions can be improved at the margins is more harmful to the preservation of democracy than imperfect institutions themselves.

Notes

* I would like to thank Argelina Figueiredo and André Modenesi for comments on earlier versions of this paper.

1. Linz (1978, expanded in 1984) is, of course, the seminal work on the pitfalls of presidentialism.
2. See Carey and Shugart (1994) for a general discussion and Mainwaring (1991) and Ames and Nixon (1993) for a discussion specific to Brazil.

3. Note that this argument is in contradiction with the notion of individualism and clientelism that underlies the rest of the criticism of the electoral system. If the link between voters and legislators is personal, then parties do not matter and switching is of no consequence for that link; voters would follow their representative to whatever party he or she goes.

4. It was revived in the wake of the events of July 2005 by at least one journalist—Merval Pereira—and one academic—Octavio Amorim Neto (newspapers in July 2005). For a recent defense of parliamentarism by an influential politician, see Serra (2002).

5. Amorim Neto (2006) seems to be one of the few voices who explicitly advocate the "parliamentary" formula, but giving it the proper name. Proposals for a mixed system are boosted by the fact that many recent democracies have adopted this kind of constitution: whereas in 1946 there were three democracies in the world with mixed (or semipresidential) constitutions representing 9 percent of all democracies, in 2002 there were 25, which represented 22 percent of existing democratic systems (Cheibub and Chernykh 2008).

6. Mixed-member electoral systems are increasingly popular among political scientists and "institutional designers." See Shugart and Wattenberg (2001) for a collection of essays discussing the pros and cons, but mostly the pros, of such systems. Cintra (2005) provides an excellent historical discussion of the different electoral reform proposals in Brazil.

7. For example, concerning the execution of electoral polls, distribution of television and radio time across and within political parties, campaign financing and accounting, and political rallies.

8. Electoral thresholds constitute an interesting case. A perennial demand by those who see the fragmentation of the party system as a major source of institutional difficulties, thresholds were finally approved in 2002 to apply to the 2006 elections and later ones. The legislation stipulated a threshold of 5 percent of the total (valid, blank, and null) national vote and 2 percent of the total vote in at least nine states. Parties that failed to reach the threshold would still participate in the distribution of seats but, once in Congress, would not be able to participate in any leadership position (including committees) and would not benefit in equal terms from the distribution of public funds reserved for political parties (they would have to share 1 percent of these funds among themselves, while 99 percent would go to parties that reached the threshold). Only seven parties reached this threshold in the 2006 elections. At the same time that a process of consolidation of small parties started to take place, some of them lobbied intensely for the revocation of the threshold provision. In December 2006, in response to a popular initiative, the Supremo Tribunal Federal, the nation's highest court, judged the threshold provision unconstitutional. A new proposal for a similar threshold was introduced in Congress in 2007.

9. The infamous provision of candidato nato, according to which incumbents were guaranteed access to the party list, only existed in two democratic elections: 1990 and 1998. The legislation regulating the 1994 election did not grant incumbents automatic access to the party list. The provision was finally revoked in 2002, when the Supremo Tribunal Federal declared it unconstitutional. Note that even with it, parties were not powerless if they wanted to confront a disloyal incumbent. They could, for instance, sponsor a candidate competing with the incumbent.

10. Almeida (2006) laments the fact that a high proportion of Brazilian voters fail to remember the name of the individual who received their vote for federal representative. He does not wonder how many remember, or fail to remember, the party that received their vote.

11. Computed by the author from CEBRAP roll-call data.

12. As a matter of fact, the highest court in Brazil has not been shy to intervene in political matters. Most recently (September 2007), it has ruled on the issue of party switching, deciding that mandates belong to the parties. Representatives and elected executive officers who change parties in the middle of the electoral term will lose their seats.

References

Abrucio, Fernando Luiz. 1998. *Os Barões da Federação: Os Governadores e a Redemocratização Brasileira.* São Paulo: Hucitec.

Almeida, Alberto. 2006. "Amnésia Eleitoral: Em Quem que Você Votou para Deputado em 2002? E em 1998?" In Gláucio Ary Dillon Soares and Lucio R. Rennó, eds. *Reforma Política: Lições da História Recente.* Rio de Janeiro: FGV. pp. 34–46.

Ames, Barry. 2001. *The Deadlock of Democracy in Brazil*. Ann Arbor: Michigan University Press.

Ames, Barry, and David Nixon. 1993. "Understanding New Legislatures: Observations and Evidence from the Brazilian Congress." Presented at the Annual Meeting of the American Political Science Association, September 2–5.

Amorim Neto, Octávio. 2006. "A Reforma do Sistema de Governo: Rumo ao Parlamentarismo ou ao Semipresidencialismo?" In Gláucio Ary Dillon Soares and Lucio R. Rennó, eds. *Reforma Política: Lições da História Recente*. Rio de Janeiro: FGV.

Carey, John M. 2007. "Competing Principals, Political Institutions, and Party Unity in Legislative Voting. *American Journal of Political Science* 51(1):92–107.

Carey, John M., and Matthew Soberg Shugart. 1994. "Incentives to Cultivate a Personal Vote: A Rank Ordering of Electoral Formulas." *Electoral Studies* 14(4):417–439.

Carvalho, Nelson Rojas. 2003. *E No Início Eram as Bases: Geografia Política do Voto e do Comportamento Legislativo no Brasil*. Rio de Janeiro, Editora Revan.

Chang, Eric. 2005. "Electoral Incentives for Political Corruption under Open List Proportional Representation." *Journal of Politics* 67(3):716–730.

Cheibub, José Antonio. 2002. "Minority Governments, Deadlock Situations, and the Survival of Presidential Democracies." *Comparative Political Studies* 35(3):284–312.

———. 2007. *Presidentialism, Parliamentarism, and Democracy*. New York: Cambridge University Press.

Cheibub, José Antonio, Adam Przeworski, and Sebastian Saiegh. 2004. "Government Coalitions and Legislative Success under Parliamentarism and Presidentialism." *British Journal of Political Science* 34(October):565–87.

Cheibub, José Antonio, Argelina Figueiredo, and Fernando Limongi. 2009. "Political Parties and Governors as Determinants of Legislative Behavior in the Brazilian Chamber of Deputies, 1988–2006." *Latin American Politics and Society*, Spring.

Cheibub, José Antonio, and Svitlana Chernykh. 2008. "Constitutions and Democratic Performance in Semipresidential Democracies." *Japanese Journal of Political Science*. Forthcoming.

Cintra, Antonio Octávio. 2005. "Majoritário ou Proporcional? Em Busca do Equilíbrio de um Sistema Eleitoral." In *Reforma Política, Agora Vai?* Cadernos Adenauer, vol. 2. Rio de Janeiro: Fundação Konrad Adenauer.

Cox, Gary W. 1997. *Making Votes Count: Strategic Coordination in the World's Electoral Systems*. New York: Cambridge University Press.

Desposato, Scott W. 2004. "The Impact of Federalism on National Political Parties in Brazil." *Legislative Studies Quarterly* 29:259–285.

Figueiredo, Argelina, and Fernando Limongi. 1999. *Executivo e Legislativo na Nova Ordem Constitucional*. Rio de Janeiro: FGV/FAPESP.

———. 2000a. Presidential Power, Legislative Organization, and Party Behavior in the Legislature. *Comparative Politics* 32(2):151–170.

———. 2000b. "Constitutional Change, Legislative Performance and Institutional Consolidation." *Brazilian Review of Social Sciences, Special Issue* 1:73–94.

Figueiredo, Marcus. 2005. "O Eleitor, a Preferência e o Voto." *Insight Inteligência* 7(30):65–70.

Huber, John. 1996. *Rationalizing Parliament*. New York: Cambridge University Press.

Kunicova , Jana, and Susan Rose-Ackerman. 2005. "Electoral Rules and Constitutional Structures as Constraints on Corruption." *British Journal of Political Science* 35:573–606.

Linz, Juan J. 1978. *The Breakdown of Democratic Regimes: Crisis, Breakdown, and Reequilibration*. Baltimore: Johns Hopkins University Press.

———. 1984. "Presidential or Parliamentary Democracy: Does It Make a Difference?" In Juan J. Linz and Arturo Valenzuela, eds. *The Failure of Presidential Democracy: The Case of Latin America*. Baltimore: Johns Hopkins University Press. pp. 3–90.

Mainwaring, Scott. 1991. "Politicians, Parties and Electoral Systems: Brazil in Comparative Perspective." *Comparative Politics* 24:21–43.

———. 1993. "Presidentialism, Multipartism and Democracy: The Difficult Combination." *Comparative Political Studies* 26(2):198–228.

Matland, Richard E., and Donley T. Studlar. 2004. "Determinants of Legislative Turnover: A Cross-National Analysis." *British Journal of Political Science* 34:87–108.

Pereira, Carlos, and Lucio Rennó. 2001. "O Que É Que o Reeleito Tem? Dinâmicas Político-Institucionais Locais e Nacionais nas Eleições de 1998 para a Câmara dos Deputados." *Dados* 44(2):133–172.

Persson, Torsten, Guido Tabellini, and Francesco Trebbi. 2003. "Electoral Rules and Corruption." *Journal of the European Economic Association* 1(4):958–989.

Rennó, Lucio. 2006. "Críticas ao Presidencialismo de Coalizão no Brasil: Processos Institucionalmente Constritos ou Individualmente Dirigidos?" In Leonardo Avritzer and Fátima Anastasia, eds. *Reforma Política no Brasil*. Belo Horizonte: UFMG. pp. 259–271.

Samuels, David. 2003. *Ambition, Federalism and Legislative Politics in Brazil*. New York: Cambridge University Press.

Samuels, David, and Richard Snyder. 2001. "The Value of a Vote: Malapportionment in Comparative Perspective." *British Journal of Political Science* 31(3):651–671.

Santos, Fabiano. 1999. "Instituições Eleitorais e Desempenho do Presidencialismo no Brasil." *Dados* 42(1):111–138.

Santos, Wanderley Guilherme dos. 2003. "A Universalização da Democracia." In Maria Victoria Benevides, Paulo Vannuchi, and Fábio Kerche, eds. *Reforma Política e Cidadania*. São Paulo: Fundação Perseu Abramo. pp. 33–43.

Schmitt, Rogério Augusto. 1999. "Migração Partidária e Reeleição na Câmara dos Deputados". *Novos Estudos Cebrap* 54 (July):127–146.

Serra, José. 2002. *Ampliando o Possível*. Rio de Janeiro: Campus.

Shugart, Matthew S., and John M. Carey. 1992. *Presidents and Assemblies: Constitutional Design and Electoral Dynamics*. New York: Cambridge University Press.

Shugart, Matthew S., and Martin P. Wattenberg. Eds. 2001. *Mixed-Member Electoral Systems: The Best of Both Worlds?* Oxford: Oxford University Press.

Siavelis, Peter. 2000. *The President and Congress in Post-Authoritarian Chile: Institutional Constraints to Democratic Consolidation*. University Park: Pennsylvania State University Press.

Soares, Gláucio Ary Dillon, and Lucio Rennó. 2006. "Projetos de Reforma Política na Câmara dos Deputados." In Gláucio Ary Dillon Soares and Lucio R. Rennó, eds. *Reforma Política: Lições da História Recente*. Rio de Janeiro: FGV.

Stepan, Alfred. 2000. "Brazil's Decentralized Federalism: Bringing Government Closer to Citizens?" *Deadalus* 129(2) (Spring):145–170.

Tavares, José Antonio Giuisti. 1998. *Reforma Política e Retrocesso Democrático: Agenda para Reformas Pontuais no Sistema Eleitoral e Partidário Brasileiro*. Porto Alegre: Mercado Aberto.

CHAPTER TWO

The Macroeconomic Record of the Lula Administration, the Roots of Brazil's Inequality, and Attempts to Overcome Them

EDMUND AMANN AND WERNER BAER

The concentration of income and property has been a constant throughout Brazil's history, no matter what the nature of its economic regime. Have the efforts of the Lula government to tackle poverty through the *Bolsa Família* broken away from this constant characteristic? In this chapter we shall review the reasons for the persistence of inequality in Brazil,[1] and we shall try to establish if this constant has been broken by the first mandate of President Lula.

Property and Income Concentration in Colonial Times

The first great export boom in colonial Brazil, centered on sugar from the Northeast, was based on large rural estates that used slave labor. In his masterful essay on colonial Brazil, Caio Prado, Jr. offers a generalization that was backed by previous and subsequent studies when he states that "Seen as a whole, the colonization of the tropics appears as one vast commercial enterprise, more complex than the old trading stations...the foremost objective being the exploitation of the natural resources of a virgin land for the benefit of European commerce. This is the true meaning of tropical colonization, of which Brazil is one of the results, and this explains the fundamental elements, both economic and social, of the historical formation and evolution of the American tropics" (Prado, Jr. 1967: 20). And further on he states that "in all sectors, whether agricultural, mining, or extractive, organization was based on the large unit of production.... insofar as it brought together a relatively large number of workers under the orders and on the behalf of a single entrepreneur. It is this fact that

we should chiefly consider, since it is in this system of organizing labor
and property that lies the origin of the extreme concentration of wealth
that characterizes the colonial economy. The fact that thirty percent of
the population was made up of slaves, and that an unknown but surely
high percentage was made up of individuals who possessed no worldly
goods whatsoever and vegetated in obscure poverty with the lowest type
of material living standards, is both the immediate consequence and sure
symptom of this concentration of wealth which was the result of the
country's economic organization" (Prado, Jr. 1967: 140–141).

He came to the conclusion that "It was from the technique of production
and organization adopted by Brazilian agriculture that was derived the
entire structure of the country: the arrangement of classes and categories
of the population, and the particular status of each and that of the individuals who composed them. In other words, the whole complex of social
relations at their deepest and most essential level derived from this basis"
(Prado, Jr. 1967: 166).

Agricultural production dominated colonial Brazil. This was notable especially when the sugar export cycle prevailed and "Beneath the
dominance of agricultural production, there naturally lay the dominance
of land as by far the most important economic resource. Consequently,
land tenure... was from the outset a key factor governing the social,
political and economic history of the country. Under Portuguese rule, a
system of landholding was imposed that divided the producing regions
into a very few big estates... This excluded (along with the black population already excluded by slavery and the Indians....) the vast majority
of the free population from any access to the only asset that could have
given them a basis for economic stability and political power" (Maia
Gomes 1986: 9).

The Primary Goods Export Economy of the
Nineteenth and Early Twentieth Centuries

In his analysis of Brazil's economy in the 1870–1930 period, when
the major dynamic sectors were based on the export of coffee, cotton,
sugar, and a few other agricultural products, Warren Dean noted that
"Concentration of landownership in Brazil was traditionally extreme.
The Portuguese crown had believed that only landed aristocrats would
produce for overseas markets, and therefore its grants were enormous,
typically 40 square kilometers in extent. Under the Empire this tradition
was maintained because the central government was too weak to make
effective its law (1850) determining the sale of crown lands at auction.
Instead locally powerful elites simply usurped public lands, employing
fraud in land offices and evicting in the process smallholding squatters"
(Dean 1986: 701–702). And with the coming of a republican government in the last decade of the nineteenth century, the state "granted, in

effect, amnesty to the land grabbers, when it bestowed the remaining crown lands upon the states. The state governments then demonstrated the same incapacity to guard the public patrimony as had the Empire" (Dean 1986: 702).

The end of slavery did not improve matters. Dean noted that "Although many freedman fled to the cities, most accepted wage and sharecropping contracts on nearby or even the same estates. Pressure upon smallholdings because of population growth (Brazilian law divided inheritances equally among offspring), recurrent droughts in the interior of the north-east, and the continued political impotence of the lower class forced many free men to work on the plantations. In the north-east the effective costs of free labor to the planters were apparently lower than the former costs of maintaining slaves" (Dean 1986: 704).

Another historian gives a similar description of conditions that existed in the post-slavery agricultural sector, which were still dominant in Brazil in the first decades of the twentieth century. He found that "the *colono system* combined a capitalist system of production with a non-capitalist system of renting land. This particularly so in the case of the type of contractual agreement which was common practice on new coffee plantations, and which in fact was preferred by immigrants. The colonist and his family would plant the coffee and tend the plantation for a period of four to six years, as the coffee bushes usually began to yield a small crop in the fourth year. The *colonos* received practically no monetary payment, but were able to dedicate themselves to the production of food crops" (Fausto 1986: 780).

In the years 1871 to 1914 "opportunities for *colonos* to become smallholders or owners of medium-sized properties were limited. Access to land required influence, although the price of land was not high, and prospective buyers needed resources which were relatively inaccessible in order to make the land profitable" (Fausto 1986: 780).[2]

Income Distribution during the ISI Period

Import Substitution Industrialization (ISI) extended from the 1930s to the end of the 1970s.[3] It was characterized by a closing of the economy, the attraction of multinationals, the creation of many state-owned companies, and some social legislation (such as the introduction of minimum wages, worker's retirement funds, etc.). The ISI of the 1930s contributed toward diminishing the impact of the Great Depression, and to periods of high growth rates in the 1950s and 1970s and toward dramatic changes in the structure of the economy. The agricultural share of GDP declined from 27.6 percent in 1947 to 19.1 percent in 1966 while industry's share grew from 19.4 percent to 27.2 percent over the same period. By 1984, agriculture's share had fallen to just 9.3 percent while industry's share stood at 39 percent (Baer 2001).

Table 2.1   Gini coefficient:
Brazil 1960–2005

1960	0.57
1970	0.53
1976	0.62
1977	0.62
1978	0.60
1979	0.59
1980	—
1981	0.58
1982	0.59
1983	0.60
1984	0.60
1985	0.60
1986	0.59
1987	0.60
1988	0.62
1989	0.64
1990	0.61
1991	—
1992	0.58
1993	0.60
1994	—
1995	0.60
1996	0.60
1997	0.60
1998	0.60
1999	0.59
2000	—
2001	0.60
2002	0.59
2003	0.58
2004	0.57
2005	0.57

Source: IPEA Date/IBGE

It is notable that the dramatic changes in policy and economic structure—from a primary open export economy to a closed import substituting economy—did not change the concentration of income. To the contrary, for many years the income concentration of Brazil rose. This is noted in table 2.1.

There are a number of explanations for this: 1) The capital/labor ratios of the new industrial sectors were higher than those of the traditional sectors of the economy. As the former were the dynamic sectors of the economy, their contributions to GDP were distributed in favor of capital (even though the earnings of labor in the new sectors may have been higher than in the traditional sectors). This led to a substantial rise in the capital-labor ratio of the economy over time: between 1945 and 2000 this ratio rose by a factor of three (Feu 2001); 2) Within this highly protected economy, many new sectors were characterized by an oligopolistic structure, enabling them to charge very high prices for their product.[4] Most of the benefits from these high prices went to the owners of the firms rather than the workforce; 3) During the years of the military governments (1964–1985) labor unions were suppressed and/or tightly controlled and real wages were allowed to lag behind; and 4) When the census of 1970 revealed that during the high growth rates of the late 1960s the distribution of income worsened, the government contracted an economist, Carlos Langoni, to examine this phenomenon.[5] He came to the conclusion that the worsening of the distribution of income was due to the very growth success of the military governments. High growth rates resulted in accelerated demand for skilled labor. As the latter was scarce, its earnings increased much more than the rest of the labor force, which explains the concentrating trend in the distribution of income.

In all probability, all these explanations have some degree of validity in accounting for the observed distributional trends. What is important to note is that whereas the concentration of land ownership was the principal cause for the concentration of income in the colonial and subsequent primary export economy of the nineteenth and early twentieth centuries, the ownership structure of the industrial sector in the ISI economy was just as concentrated, if not more so. Relatively few manufacturing enterprises were held publicly by thousands of small investors. Instead, manufacturing was characterized by large state-owned or family-owned enterprises whose market share was somewhat higher than could be found in advanced industrial countries, for example the United States.[6]

Income Distribution during the *Lost Decade* of the 1980s and the Hyperinflations of the Early 1990s

As has been described in other places (Baer 2001, ch. 9), the 1980s was the time of the debt crisis, of periodic attempts to institute adjustment programs negotiated with the IMF and main private creditors, and of the spread of inflation, with a number of failed attempts at stabilization. The net result was many years of low growth and, from time to time a decline in real wages, especially in periods of hyperinflation as in 1987, 1990, and 1991 (tables 2.2 and 2.3).

The hyperinflations of the late 1980s and first years of the 1990s contributed to a further deterioration of the income distribution. As shown in table 2.4, during the hyperinflation of the second half of the 1980s the poorest tenth of the population saw the greatest deterioration in the share of income, while the substantial improvement of that group in the 1993–1995 period was due to the sudden stop in hyperinflation associated with the introduction of the Real Plan.

Table 2.2 Growth in GDP and real wages, 1976–2004

	GDP growth (%)	Growth in real wages (%)
1976	10.3	7.6
1977	4.9	5.1
1978	5.0	8.6
1979	6.8	4.4
1980	9.2	4.5
1981	−4.3	9.0
1982	0.8	11.5
1983	−2.9	−4.8
1984	5.4	3.2
1985	7.8	13.4
1986	7.5	14.2
1987	3.5	−7.2
1988	−0.1	8.5
1989	3.2	7.5
1990	−4.3	−12.0
1991	1.0	−4.3
1992	−0.5	15.9
1993	4.9	11.1
1994	5.9	9.5
1995	4.2	8.7
1996	2.7	5.5
1997	3.3	5.5
1998	0.1	4.6
1999	0.8	−1.6
2000	4.4	−2.7
2001	1.3	6.3
2002	1.9	5.5
2003	0.5	0.3
2004	4.9	7.1

Source: IBGE/IPEA Data

The Impact of Neoliberal Policies in the 1990s and Early Years of the Twenty-First Century

The constant pressures from the IMF, private creditors and the governments of creditor countries resulted in the adoption of neoliberal policies. These consisted of an opening of the economy by lowering tariff and nontariff protection, an opening of sectors to foreign investors that were previously closed, and the privatization of state enterprises. In 1994, the adoption of a stabilization plan, the *Plano Real*, finally succeeded in eliminating hyperinflation.[7]

Many of the neoliberal measures had a concentrating impact. The opening of the economy forced many sectors to improve their productivity in the face of foreign competition (Castelar Pinheiro

Table 2.3 Consumer price inflation (IPCA index), 1980–2006

1980	99.2
1981	95.6
1982	104.8
1983	164.0
1984	215.3
1985	242.2
1986	79.7
1987	363.4
1988	980.2
1989	1972.9
1990	1621.0
1991	472.7
1992	1119.1
1993	2477.1
1994	916.5
1995	22.4
1996	9.6
1997	5.2
1998	1.7
1999	8.9
2000	6.0
2001	7.7
2002	12.5
2003	9.3
2004	7.6
2005	5.7
2006	3.1

Source: IBGE

Table 2.4 Growth of income by deciles of the distribution of incomes

	1985–1986	*1986–1990*	*1990–1993*	*1993–1995*
First tenth (poorest)	95.9	−40.8	−12.7	99.9
Second tenth	44.2	−32.8	22.5	46.4
Third tenth	49.1	−37.7	35.1	−1.8
Fourth tenth	32.4	−35.3	12.1	31.7
Fifth tenth	44.7	−31.0	−2.1	37.2
Sixth tenth	42.6	−29.9	−1.1	27.3
Seventh tenth	41.2	−27.3	−7.4	33.6
Eighth tenth	38.6	−25.0	−9.0	34.0
Ninth tenth	33.7	−23.4	−9.0	33.9
Tenth tenth (richest)	39.4	−25.1	−3.3	24.6

Source: IBGE

Table 2.5 Brazil: C4 concentration ratios

	1993 (%)	2004 (%)
Transportation	73	73
Public utilities	46	69
Information technology	77	54
Telecoms	100★	72
Wholesale trade	56	80
Retail trade	54	66
Food, drink, tobacco	55	76
Auto parts	86	85
Textiles, clothing	45	62
Construction	47	67
Electronics	38	46
Pharmaceuticals and cosmetics	62	63
Construction materials	41★★	56
Machinery	51	56
Mining	59	79
Paper, cellulose	50	57
Plastics, rubber	61	68
Petrochemicals	80	91
Steel, metallurgy	58	72

Note: ★ Telecommunications were privatized in 1998; ★★ Data refer to 1994

Source: Amann and Baer. Forthcoming. *Quarterly Review of Economics and Finance* Calculated from data in *Exame*, August 1994 and July 2005

1999). This led many firms to incorporate the latest technology in their fields, which meant more reliance on capital intensive and labor saving technologies. The privatization process did not result in a widespread sale of shares to the general public, but rather in the auction of state firms to domestic and international oligopolistic groups, thus resulting not only in a concentration of property but also of market concentration as table 2.5 reveals.[8]

Additionally, many of the firms that were privatized shed an excess amount of labor.[9] The thousands who lost their jobs either found positions in traditional sectors, paying smaller wages and having smaller benefits, or joined the informal sector (Baer 2001: 289–294). Thus the net initial impact of privatization had a concentrating distributional impact.

The Economic Policies of the Lula Government

Although candidate Lula had a radical discourse in the 2002 election campaign, once in power he adopted a conservative set of policies that made him popular in the world's financial markets. This resulted in the continuation of the price stability inherited from the Cardoso administration. Central to the Lula government's orthodox macroeconomic strategy was the maintenance of stringent fiscal policy centered on the attainment of increasingly larger primary budget surpluses. For 2003, the latter was raised from 3.75 percent of GDP to 4.25 percent, while in October 2004 the surplus reached 4.7 percent of GDP (Amann and Baer 2006: 221). These surpluses were maintained for the remainder of the first mandate of the Lula administration.

The Central Bank's inflation-targeting policies that had been introduced under the Cardoso administration were retained and one of the principal instruments employed here was the setting of extremely high interest rates. The SELIC benchmark, the Central Bank's overnight lending rate, rose from an average of 17 percent in 2003 to 19 percent in 2005, decreasing only in the second half of 2006. While foreign direct investment continued to decline as the privatization program wound down, the high interest rates maintained in place large inflows of port-folio investment. This together with large trade surpluses (due mainly to high commodity prices for export staples such as iron ore and soya) lent support to the Real, which appreciated strongly against the U.S. dollar after 2002. The inflow of foreign exchange, facilitated by the favorable performance of the current account, allowed currency reserves to rise steadily from US$37.8 billion in 2002 to US$85.8 billion in 2006. This enabled the Lula government to pay off its entire debt to the IMF.

While high interest rates and fiscal austerity may have contributed toward the maintenance of low inflation and a healthy external balance, they nonetheless had a negative impact on growth. As table 2.2 indicates, only in 2004 did growth trend significantly upward (reaching 4.9 percent). In all other years, growth performance was anemic. Another disappoint-ing outcome was the low investment rate, which hovered around 19–20 percent of GDP. This was due to subdued foreign direct investment and to low investment by the government. As a result of this, much needed investment in infrastructure was foregone and the ground for accelerated growth rates in the future was not laid.

Poverty and Distribution under Lula[10]

Much attention has been drawn to the surprisingly orthodox economic policies of the first Lula administration. It might be supposed that such a policy stance would have done little to counter Brazil's ingrained tradi-tion of skewed income distribution. However, to the surprise of many, the Gini coefficient (the main measure of inequality) improved as it fell from 0.6 in 2002 to 0.58 in 2003 and 0.57 in 2005 (table 2.1). This has been attributed by many to the *Bolsa Família* program, created in 2003 by consolidating four other social security programs that had suffered major flaws in their administration.[11]

The *Bolsa Família* program gives out cash transfers ranging from R$15 to R$95 per month depending on the level of family income and the

Table 2.6 Poverty and indigence in Brazil: 1990–2004

Proportion (%)	1990	1992	1993	1995	1996	1997	1998	1999	2001	2002	2003	2004
Poor	44.19	44.00	44.09	33.23	34.13	34.09	33.43	34.95	35.03	33.99	35.59	33.21
Indigent	17.38	16.64	16.10	10.40	10.15	9.38	9.06	8.74	9.55	8.68	9.96	8.00

Source: Rocha (2006: 269). In Rocha's table "poverty" refers to that group of individuals existing below the poverty line in the PNAD survey while "indigent" refers to the subset of poor individuals subsisting on less than R$1 a day (PPP adjusted)

scale of previous benefits. Access to the benefits is conditional on parents' keeping their children in school and ensuring that they undergo regular medical checkups. The coverage of the *Bolsa Família* rose from 3.6 million families in 2003 to 11.1 million in 2006. This meant that by 2006, 44 million Brazilians were covered, roughly one quarter of the entire population.

There is evidence, especially in the historically disadvantaged Northeast that the *Bolsa Família* has been effective in alleviating extreme poverty. For example, in the state of Ceará where income from the program makes up 3.7 percent of the total, retail sales went up by 10 percent in 2006 while formal employment actually declined. For the Northeast as a whole, since the creation of the *Bolsa Família*, retail sales are up 54 percent compared with 26.4 percent in the economically more dynamic south.

Taking a longer view, one sees that the *Bolsa Família* may not have begun the declining trend of absolute poverty. In her exhaustive study on poverty in Brazil, Sonia Rocha found that there has been a steady decline in the proportion of the population that can be considered as poor or indigent from the beginning of the 1990s on. Table 2.6, which gives a summary of her findings, shows that the proportion of the population considered extremely poor—the indigent—declined from 44 percent in 1990 to 33.21 percent in 2004. However, the period in which the fall in the incidence of poverty is most concentrated lies between 1993 and 1995; in other words, the period straddling the introduction of the Real Plan. By contrast, the period 2002–2004, which saw the consolidation of initiatives comprising the *Bolsa Família*, saw only an extremely modest reduction.

Bolsa Família and Recent Trends in the Gini Coefficient

To what extent is the recent observed improvement in Brazil's income distribution attributable to the *Bolsa Família* and its predecessors? While there can be no doubt that there has been poverty alleviation for those on the lowest incomes, does that mean that the program has been responsible for a permanent improvement in the distribution of income?

The work of Paes de Barros et al. (2007) suggests that the introduction of the *Bolsa Família* has had a significant impact on the recent evolution of the distribution of income. However, it should be noted from table 2.1 that the improvement in the Gini has been rather modest: between 2002 and 2004 it fell by 0.02 percentage points. If one compares this to declines in the early 1990s, two points become apparent. In first place, the decrease in the Gini is small in relation to those previously experienced. Second, and more importantly, it is evident that declines in the Gini have been experienced in the past without the presence of an explicit antipoverty or income redistribution program. In other words, we need to be aware that factors other than the *Bolsa Família* and its constituent predecessors can drive downward movements in the Gini. In the early 1990s, the prime factor at work in this regard was the reduction (albeit temporary) in levels of hyperinflation (Thorp 1998). By the same token, it must be accepted that at least some of the credit for the recent reduction in the Gini may have to be attributed to lower inflationary pressures, and the rise of the minimum wage.[12]

The perception that the *Bolsa Família* can only have exerted a modest impact on the evolution of the Gini coefficient is underlined when one examines data on government spending. Our estimates from published government budgetary sources is that in 2006 the *Bolsa Família* amounted to 2.5 percent of government spending, or just 0.5 percent of GDP. If we compare this to government spending on debt servicing, which in 2006 amounted to 18 percent of total expenditures, one could almost argue that the overall pattern of government expenditure serves to worsen the distribution of income. Reading the figures in another way, it could be said that 2.5 percent of the budget goes to the poor whereas 18 percent go to the government's creditors that consist of financial institutions, wealthier individuals, and foreign entities. The argument that the *Bolsa Família* can only have had a limited impact on the distributional profile also finds support in a recent IPEA study, which highlighted the importance of other factors such as integration of local labor markets and more equality within different educational levels (Paes de Barros et al. 2006a).

Bolsa Família: A New Form of Clientelism?

The *Bolsa Família*, while undoubtedly one of the celebrated achievements of the Lula administration, has had, as we have pointed out, only a limited impact on historically ingrained patterns of income distribution. As will be argued below, income distribution remains highly skewed owing to deeply rooted structural drivers such as concentration in land ownership and, more recently, differential access to quality education. The sense that more distributional heat than light is emitted by the *Bolsa* program gives rise to the argument that its purpose may be less the tackling of inequality than the creation of clientelistic relationships that operate to the benefit of the Lula government.

Analysis of voting returns from the last presidential election shows that there may be some substance to this argument. In the poor North and Northeast, long the bastions of Center and Center-Right populist parties and politicians, Lula did particularly well. Perhaps not surprisingly, these regions, due to their higher than average poverty incidence, benefited especially from the *Bolsa*. It may follow, therefore, that the *Bolsa* has created a new client group beholden to the Lula administration and inclined to vote for it. If so, then the *Bolsa* represents the latest manifestation of an old tradition within Brazilian politics. It is long established Brazilian political practice that populist politicians in poorer areas seek electoral advantage by targeting groups of voters with "pork," whether in the form of infrastructure, temporarily enhanced public spending, or even cash handouts at polling time. For some opponents of President Lula, the *Bolsa* represents little more than clientelistic largesse, albeit on an unprecedented (and national) scale. Still, it cannot be denied that the *Bolsa*, unlike older, smaller-scale clientelistic schemes, has had real distributional impacts. The problem, though, is that such impacts need to be supplemented with redistributional structural reforms. It could be argued that in effectively pacifying the dispossessed, the *Bolsa* serves only to sap the political momentum to proceed with such reforms.

Continued Structural Underpinning of Income Concentration

It cannot be overemphasized that over the span of Brazilian history, income inequality has been underpinned by an accentuated concentration in asset ownership. Formerly, it was the concentration in land ownership that provided the major stimulus for income inequality. However, the role of inequality in patterns of land ownership has declined as a result of the diminishing share of agricultural output in overall GDP. Whereas agriculture accounted for 26 percent of GDP at the outbreak of World War II, by 2004 its share had fallen to 9 percent.

Still, it needs to be emphasized that despite efforts at land reform, land ownership remains highly concentrated. By 2000, farms of the size of 1,000 or more hectares that made up 1.6 percent of total farm units controlled no less than 43.8 percent of arable land (Abbey, Baer, and Filizzola 2006). Thus agriculture, although of declining relative importance to overall GDP, remains characterized by a high degree of ownership concentration. The same can also be said of the industrial sector that has expanded in its relative importance since the 1930s. Table 2.5 indicates that over the past decade, there has been a notable rise in industrial concentration across a range of sectors. Amann and Baer (2008) cite the importance of growing import competition and market liberalization as forces responsible for driving this trend. Thus, it is possible to argue that the potential boon to asset deconcentration of the declining role of agriculture has been at least partially offset by rising industrial concentration.

Alves Pinto (2006) finds evidence in a case study of Campinas (an important center for software and engineering and thus a center for nontraditional industry) of continuing and extremely high degrees of concentration in asset ownership. For 1996, Alves Pinto estimates a Gini for asset ownership of 0.92, while that for income stood at 0.58, the latter in line with national estimates. The implication of this is clear: given the scale of asset inequality, any administration faces a substantial challenge to remedy income inequality in the long run. Against this background it seems unlikely that the *Bolsa Família*, given its small scale proportionate to GDP, would be able to counterbalance the income effects of the enormous disparities in asset ownership.

Does the Ultimate Solution Lie with the Services Sector?

Brazil, like many emerging countries, appears to be moving in the direction of the OECD economies, where 70–75 percent of the economically active population is employed in the services sector. In 2004 the services sector accounted for 56 percent of Brazilian GDP, and 53 percent of the labor force. In an economy dominated by services, human capital rather than machinery or land, represents the most important asset. It would seem therefore that in order to substantially remedy the income distribution problem of Brazil, there needs to be an emphasis on addressing disparities in the distribution of human capital. This, of course, is likely to involve a heavy emphasis on the role of education and training.[13] Unfortunately, however, the distribution of human capital (at least as represented by access to *quality* education and educational attainment) has tended to be skewed. Some data might help to illustrate the scale of the problem here.

The average years spent in school in Brazil in 2000 was 6.4, compared to 10.1 years in Argentina, 10 years in Chile and 7.4 in Mexico, while in the United States, the United Kingdom, and Germany the average years were 12.25, 9.35, and 9.75 respectively. Besides Brazil's average lower years of schooling, it will be noted in table 2.7 that there also exists a substantial gap between the years of education of the lowest and the highest income quintile, indicating a substantial concentration in the distribution of human capital. Although this was reduced in the 1990s from 4.7 in 1990 to 3.0 in 2001, the gap was still substantial when compared to a country like Argentina, where it was only 1.8 in 2001.

In addition to concerns surrounding the issue of years of schooling, there are also questions about the quality of education to which the majority have access. According to a UNESCO survey, Brazil ranks 114th out of 125 countries for the quality of its educational system.

Table 2.7   Brazil: Years of education

	Quintiles					
	1	*2*	*3*	*4*	*5*	*Average*
1990	1.9	2.9	4.1	5.5	8.9	5.1
1995	2.3	3.4	4.5	6.1	9.7	5.6
2001	3.0	4.2	5.3	6.9	10.4	6.4

Source: World Bank (2004: 415)

India, whose GNI per capita[14] is significantly lower than that of Brazil (US$720 versus US$3460), ranked 25th in the survey while Gambia (GNI per capita US$290) ranked 55th. In other words, Brazil underperforms on educational quality compared with what its rank income per capita might warrant. Of the Brazilians making up the bottom two income quintiles of the distribution, only 5 percent have completed secondary school, compared with 73 percent of the richest decile. Equally troubling, another survey established that 75 percent of 15-year-olds found it impossible to complete only moderately difficult literacy tests. Regarding the quality of public education, the Ministry of Education found that in 2002 84.5 percent of the teaching in public institutions was "unsatisfactory to acceptable," compared with 37.6 percent in private institutions. The sense that public education (to which all have access) provides an inferior option to private education (to which access is based on income) is revealed in university admissions records. Data from the University of São Paulo in 2002 shows that over 67 percent of those who registered had gone to private secondary schools.

All of this suggests that there are systemic problems of equality and quality in the educational system, especially as regards its public sector component. While the Lula administration has pledged to improve the scope and quality of provision, progress so far has been limited and constrained by budgetary squeezes.[15] Whereas in 2003 (at the beginning of Lula's first mandate) R$4.3 billion of extra resources for education were proposed, by 2006 the extra budget allocation had been scaled down by a factor of four (Buarque 2006).

Conclusion

At the beginning of this chapter we pointed out that a constant in Brazil's economic history had been a highly skewed distribution of income. We have shown that the latter stemmed from an extremely concentrated pattern of asset ownership. In colonial times and during the primary export phase of Brazil's economic development, the skewed distribution of income was mostly explained by the concentrated pattern of landholding. With industrialization, the role of land was supplanted by industrial capital, ownership of which was, again confined to a small section of the population. It might be supposed that the growth in the relative importance of the services sector over the past 30 years could have acted to tackle ingrained patterns of skewed income distribution. This is because of the more fragmented structure of that sector compared with its agricultural and industrial counterparts. However, considering that human capital is the major input into the services sector, and that educational and training opportunities have been concentrated in the hands of the few, the growth in services has not, in fact, resulted in the significant evening out of the income distribution.

It could be argued that a concentration in asset ownership does not necessarily imply a concentration of income, since the state could act as a counterweight—taxing and redistributing the income flows emerging from the asset base. However, this is not happening, because both the tax system and the expenditure structure of the government continue to be regressive (Baer and Galvão 2008). Rather, such distributional improvements as there have been in recent years have stemmed from the positive income effects on the poor of reductions in inflation.

Our conclusion is that although the *Bolsa Família* program of President Lula has undoubtedly tackled successfully pockets of abject poverty, it has not succeeded yet in substantially improving Brazil's distribution of income.

Notes

1. A previous and somewhat different analysis of inequality in Brazil can be found in Luna and Klein (2006).
2. The situation was just as bad in Northeast Brazil. Fausto observes that "In the sugar plantation belt, the problem of wage labor was resolved by resorting to a practice which dated from the colonial period, and which involved the establishment of small landholders who were dependent on the large landed proprietor. Placed on small plots of land on which they cultivated subsistence crops, the workers were summoned for labor in the cane plantation whenever required. Labor was usually unremunerated or paid at a scandalously low rate…" (1986: 784). Graham found that in the middle of the nineteenth century in one *município* in Pernambuco, 15 percent of the mill owners account for 70 percent of all plantation land (1986: 749). It should be noted, however, that in the state of São Paulo in the 1930s there was a significant change in land tenure. See Holloway (1980)
3. See Amann (2000); Baer (2008); Bergsman (1970).
4. If one takes wages and social security as a percentage of value added in some of the dynamic sectors of the economy, one notes a clear downward trend. For instance, the share in metal-products declined from 35.4 percent in 1959 to 29.6 percent in 1975 and 19.3 percent in 1985; for machinery the share declined from 46.8 percent to 41.5 percent and 31.4 percent in the respective years; electrical equipment 38.7 percent, 28.1 percent, and 21.6 percent. Transport equipment, by contrast rose from 31.7 percent to 37.5 percent, declining to 21.4 percent. Chemicals fell from 23.8 percent to 11.7 percent and 11.4 percent. Textiles fell from 42.5 percent to 29.4 percent to 15.8 percent. (Baer 2001: 453)
5. Langoni (1973).
6. For Brazil, the average C8 ratio for manufacturing stood at 58 percent of sales in 1973, 59.1 percent in 1977, 49.7 percent in 1980, and 52.0 percent in 1983 (Baer 2001: 129). For the United States, the ratios tended to be somewhat lower. For the U.S. manufacturing sector, Pryor (2001: 309) finds C8 ratios of 52.6 percent in 1963, 52.1 percent in 1972, 50.1 percent in 1982, and 51.8 percent in 1992.

7. For more discussion, see Amann and Baer (2000) and (2002)
8. The C4 and C8 ratios respectively refer to the percentage of the market accounted for by the four and eight largest firms.
9. Many state enterprises had employed more workers than was needed for both political and social reasons (Baer, 2001)
10. Some parts of this section have benefited from the research of Gabriel P. Mathy (2006). See also Hall (2006).
11. The four programs in question were: 1) The *Bolsa Escola*, administered by the Ministry of Education, giving cash transfers to families with children in school; 2) The *Bolsa Alimentação*, which through the Ministry of Health gave money to poor families to purchase food; 3) The *Fome Zero* program performing similar food distribution functions but run by the Ministry of Agriculture; and 4) The *Auxílio Gás*, which subsidised gas prices for low income families and was administered by the Ministry of Mines and Energy.
12. For example, the minimum wage for São Paulo rose from R$287.75 in 2002 to R$376.75 in 2006. Paes de Barros, in a September 2006 article (Paes de Barros 2006b), summarizes the results of a simulation exercise that compares the impact of the minimum salary and the *Bolsa Família*. He found that the former is much less effective in combating poverty—especially extreme poverty—than the *Bolsa Família*. It should be noted, however, that this analysis is concerned with *absolute* standards of living of the extreme poor rather than the distribution of income.
13. A similar conclusion was reached by Giambiagi, Villela, Barros de Castro, and Hermann (2005) in which they argue, "The principal source of inequality in Brazilian income is the inequality between levels of education for groups of individuals. Various studies estimate that this influences the level of income inequality by a factor of 40%" (translation from Portuguese).
14. Gross National Income (GNI), unlike Gross Domestic Product (GDP), takes into account the impact of net property incomes (interest, profits, and dividends). It is thus a broader measure of national income.
15. Of course, the *Bolsa Família* is designed to increase participation in primary and secondary education. It remains unclear to what extent this has increased school attendance. To date, little has been done to increase resources for education and to improve the quality of education itself.

Bibliography

Abbey, Leonard, Werner Baer, and Mavio Filizzola. 2006. "Growth, Efficiency and Equity: The Impact of Agribusiness and Land Reform in Brazil." *Latin American Business Review* 7(2):93–115.

Alves Pinto, Nelson. 2006. "A Distribuição da Riqueza e o Multiplicador de Inventário", Unicamp, Campinas. Unpublished Paper.

Amann, Edmund. 2000. *Economic Liberalization and Industrial Performance in Brazil*. Oxford: Oxford University Press.

Amann, Edmund, and Werner Baer. 2000. "The Illusion of Stability: The Brazilian Economy under Cardoso." *World Development* 28(10):1805–1819.

———. 2002. "Neo-liberalism and its Consequences in Brazil." *Journal of Latin American Studies* 34(4):941–959.

———. 2006. "Economic Orthodoxy versus Social Development? The Dilemmas Facing Brazil's Labour Government." *Oxford Development Studies* 34(2):219–241.

Amann, Edmund, and Werner Baer. 2008. "Neo-Liberalism and Market Concentration in Brazil: The Emergence of a Contradiction?" *The Quarterly Review of Economics and Finance* 48(2):252–262.

Baer, Werner. 2001. *The Brazilian Economy: Growth and Development*. 5th Ed. Westport, CT: Praeger.

———. 2008. *The Brazilian Economy: Growth and Development*. 6th Ed. Boulder CO: Lynne Rienner.

Baer, Werner, and Antônio F. Galvão, Jr. 2008. "Tax Burden, Government Expenditures and Income Distribution in Brazil." *Quarterly Review of Economics and Finance* 48(2) (June):345–358.

Bergsman, Joel. 1970. *Brazil: Industrialization and Trade Policies.* Oxford: Oxford University Press.

Buarque, Christovam. 2006. "Lula's Education Program for Brazil: A Grim Comedy of Errors." *Brazzil Magazine* (January 30).

Castelar Pinheiro, Armando. 1999. "Privatização no Brasil: Por quê? Até onde? Até quando?" In Fabio Giambiagi and Maurício Mesquita Moreira, eds. *A Economia Brasileira nos Anos 90'.* Rio de Janeiro: BNDES.

Dean, Warren. 1986. "The Brazilian Economy, 1870–1930." In Leslie Bethell, ed. *The Cambridge History of Latin America.* Vol. 5. New York: Cambridge University Press. pp 685–722.

Fausto, Boris. 1986. "Brazil: The Social and Political Structure of the First Republic, 1889–1930." In Leslie Bethell, ed. *The Cambridge History of Latin America.* Vol. 5. New York: Cambridge University Press. pp. 498–509.

Feu, Aumara. 2001. "Evolution of the Capital/Product Ratio in Brazil and in OECD Countries." *Economy & Energy* 28(50):1–22.

Giambiagi, Fabio, André Villela, Vavínia Barros de Castro, and Jennifer Hermann. 2005.. *Economia Brasileira Contemporânea.* São Paulo: Editora Campus.

Graham, Richard. 1986. "From the Middle of the 19th Century to the Paraguayan War." In Leslie Bethell, ed. *The Cambridge History of Latin America.* Vol. 5. New York Cambridge University Press. pp. 311–321.

Hall, Anthony. 2006. "From *Fome Zero* to *Bolsa Familia*: Social Policies and Poverty Alleviation under Lula." *Journal of Latin American Studies* 38(4) (November):689–709.

Holloway, Thomas H. 1980. *Immigrants on the Land: Coffee and Society in São Paulo, 1886–1934.* Chapel Hill: The University of North Carolina Press.

Langoni, Carlos Geraldo. 1973. *Distribuição da Renda e Desenvolvimento Econômico do Brasil.* Rio de Janeiro: Editora Expressão e Cultura.

Luna, Francisco Vidal, and Herbert S. Klein. 2006. *Brazil since 1980.* New York: Cambridge University Press. ch. 8, "Inequality: Class, Residence and Race."

Maia Gomes, Gustavo. 1986. *The Roots of State Intervention in the Brazilian Economy.* Westport, CT: Praeger.

Mathy, Gabriel. 2006. "Bolsa Família: A Study of Poverty, Inequality and the State in Brazil." Unpublished Paper, Champaign: University of Illinois at Urbana-Champaign.

Paes de Barros, Ricardo, Samuel Franco Mirela de Carvalho, and Rosane Mendonça. 2006a. *Uma Análise das Principais Causas da Queda Recente na Desigualdade de Renda Brasileira*, IPEA Texto para Discussão No. 1203.

———. 2006b. "A efetividade do salário mínimo como um instrumento para reduzir a pobreza no Brasil." *Notâ Técnica: Boletim de Conjuntura* 74:91–97.

———. 2007. *A Importância da Queda Recente da Desigualdade na Redução da Pobreza.* IPEA Texto para Discussão No. 1256.

Prado, Jr., Caio. l967. *The Colonial Background of Modern Brazil.* Berkeley and Los Angeles: University of California Press.

Pryor, Frederic. 2001. "New Trends in US Industrial Concentration." *Review of Industrial Organisation* 18:301–326.

Rocha, Sonia. 2006. "Pobreza e indigência no Brasil: algumas evidências empíricas com base na PNAD 2004." *Nova Economia* 16(2):265–299.

Thorp, Rosemary. 1998. *Progress, Poverty and Exclusion: An Economic History of Latin America since Independence.* Baltimore: Inter-American Development Bank, Johns Hopkins University Press.

World Bank. 2004. *Inequality in Latin America and the Caribbean: Breaking with History?* World Bank: Washington.

PART TWO

The Policy-Making Process

CHAPTER THREE

Policy Making in the First Lula Government

JORGE VIANNA MONTEIRO

The General Framework of Unstable Rules

During the past two decades economic policy in Brazil has been the final product of a game of unstable rules when even constitutional rules—supposedly the most durable set of institutions in a representative democracy—have been changing with high frequency and variable range. Table 3.1 quantifies that low degree of institutional stability.

Qualifying the sheer number of changes in constitutional rules (column A), column B indicates the range over which those changes reverberate into other areas of the constitution.[1] An amendment is termed as having a large repercussion (or amplitude) when it affects, by addition or suppression, at least three articles of the constitutional text; in all other cases, the amendment is classed as having a small amplitude. Hence, the index computed in column B represents the proportion of broad amendments over the total quantity of amendments promulgated by Congress. By this measure, the proportion of large changes in constitutional rules along 1992–2006 is over one-third.[2]

It is also worth noting that so many and varied changes in that short period of time don't indicate a pattern that would amount to a new constitutional architecture. The improvements have been ad hoc, although in the long run they do reveal serious damage to the system of separation of powers (Monteiro 2000, 2004). Several instances of attempting to regulate the enactment mechanism for Provisional Laws (Medidas Provisórias—MPs), as well as the tugs of war between Congress and judiciary in 2005 and 2006,[3] exemplify this point of view.

The fact is that Brazilian political leaders do not seem to understand that the credibility of public choices demands respect for the constitution. The temptation to change constitutional rules so frequently is especially salient in election years, and also as a component of a solution to some political scandal.[4]

Table 3.1 Brazilian economy: Stability of constitutional rules, 1988–2006*

Period of time	Number of constitutional amendments (A)	Range of amendments (B)
1992	2	0
1993	2	0.5
1994**	6	0.16
1995	5	0.2
1996	6	0.16
1997	2	0.5
1998	3	1
1999	4	0.75
2000	7	0.28
2001	4	0.5
2002	4	0.25
2003	3	1
2004	3	0.33
2005	3	0.33
2006	5	0.2
Total*	59	0.37

Note: * There were no amendments in the 1988–1991 period; ** Revisional amendments; *** Includes revisional amendments. The Ato das Disposições Constitucionais Transitórias (Act of the Transitory Constitutional Rules)—included in the 1988 Constitution—set a period of five years, after which the new charter could be revised. Six "revisional amendments" were produced between October 7, 1993 and June 7, 1994.

Source: Data presented in this table is an update and given a new format to the index originally presented in J.V. Monteiro. 2006. "Regras do Jogo Instáveis & Dilema Contra-majoritário." *Estratégia Macroeconômica* 14(338):1–2

In July–September 2006, such requirements were presented simultaneously, and hence it causes no surprise that the stability of public choices was once again ignored as the following events show:

- For reasons purely internal to a single political party (the Partido da Social Democracia Brasileira—PSDB), its leaders announced that, if elected, their presidential candidate would not run for a second term, opening the possibility for other PSDB candidates to run in the 2010 presidential election.[5]
- On the other side, President Lula informally announced that he concurred with the idea of having a National Constitutional Assembly operating in 2007, with the single agenda item of achieving a "political reform."[6]
- Since the bill of budgetary directives of 2007[7] wasn't approved in time, political leaders suggested in mid-September 2006 that Congress should just ignore the directives in PLN 2-06 and concentrate its attention on the budget bill.[8]

Such proposals are not only a matter of constitutional change, but also reflect the low status constitutional rules themselves have in the preferences of political leaders. Why? Because these rules can be adjusted to the interests of political parties, and because the proposals are offered as ad hoc solutions to policy problems. However, to be effective, these rules should be treated as coherent and binding limitations.[9] By the same token, it is worth noting that little has been learned from the path of constitutional amendment No. 32 (September 11, 2001), which establishes a new regime for the legislative power of the president.[10]

The proposal of calling for a constitutional assembly in 2007 is still more intriguing because it supposes Congress is no longer the proper locus of the amendment agenda—which surely contradicts other classes of constitutional rules such as Article 60. If the presidential intent was to bypass the notorious bad behavior of most of the Brazilian legislators—as the political crisis begun in mid-2005 clearly reveals—the proposal could produce an even worse disfunction: namely, more intense damage to the credibility of the constitution, a result that would definitely undermine the very notion of the "reform" President Lula wanted to approve.[11]

Economic Policy by Provisional Laws (MPs): Some Basic Considerations

To a great extent the substantial and extensive power of the executive in public choices has its origin in the very decision process exercised by Congress, since it is the executive who implements the laws voted in Congress. As a consequence, resources and discretionary power incorporated in the legislative output of Congress inevitably sustain and even enlarge the power of the president (Macey 2006: 105).

However, since 1988 the president[12] and, by extension, the high-level officials in the executive (the bureaucrats) have the power to enact laws that require an ex post agreement by the Congress. Representatives and senators must react to faits accomplis generated by the executive.[13] In 2003–2006[14] that peculiar power to propose legislation amounted to around 40 percent of the laws generated autonomously by Congress, as shown in table 3.2.[15]

Table 3.2   Quantity of Provisional Laws enacted by Lula government, 2003–2006★

Status	2003	2004	2005	2006
Converted into law	55(30)	76(49)	35(18)	58(43)
Waiting to be voted	27(27)	10(10)	16(16)	19(19)
Revoked	1(1)	—	1(1)	19(19)
Rejected by Congress	—	4(4)	3(3)	2(2)
Loss of purpose	—	—	2(2)	—
Loss of efficacy★★	—	2(2)	3(2)	3(3)
Total★★★	58	65	42	67
MP/Laws★★★★	46.4%	36.5%	29.4%	51.5%

Note: ★ Numbers in brackets show the quantity of MPs issued in the year indicated at the top of the respective column; ★★According to the Constitution (Article 62, §3°.) and Resolution 1, 2002-CN, 5.8.02, if not converted into law in the constitutionally set period of time, an MP loses its validity; ★★★There is also an inventory of 53 other MPs which were issued under the old regime (before EC 32, 9.11.01), but still maintain their status as MPs; ★★★★The quantity of MPs issued monthly divided by the quantity of bills approved by Congress, less the bills that originated in MPs (the so-called conversion laws) and the MPs that Congress decided to revoke

Source: Raw data obtained from www.planalto.gov.br

As a matter of fact, this has been the core of the legal format of economic policy in Brazil. Provisional Laws are a sort of a protean legal mechanism, a placeholder for multiple forms of intrusion of government in the economy. Although there always have been formal rules disciplining its enactment, it also true that the top-level bureaucrats have managed to explore uncharted routes and produce a large volume of innovative MPs.

The use of MPs has been associated with the conventional thought that policy problems appear in windows of opportunity that may close very quickly, and so they demand prompt decision making (Kingdon 1995: Ch. 8). The mechanism is also linked to the usual advantages of centralizing decision making in the executive: the availability of information, control of operational decisions, and the capacity of managing external shocks.

Given the substantial legislative power held by bureaucrats, some fundamental questions about economic policy making in Brazil are those of J. Gardner (2005: 298):

- Why—and under which circumstances—could the Executive expand its powers to usurp prerogatives usually exercised by Congress and, in some situations, even by the judiciary?
- How—and by what means—can the executive seek to exercise authority formally allocated to Congress?
- How have deputies and senators reacted to that sort of intrusion?[16]
- What persuades the executive—moved by the goal of enlarging its legislative program—to retreat, when faced with resistance?
- Could the usurpation of such authority be forestalled, and if not, why not?[17]

Party politics tends to reconfigure the incentives by which legislators and the president play the public choice game. An example of this is the fact that one or more parties can transform the executive into a genuine counterweight to Congress (Levinson and Pildes 2006: 2321). Political interests of the president sometimes conflict with the supposedly proper role that he would play in a constitutional system; instead, such interests are linked to his party or its allies.

For the past 10 to 15 years, both Congress and the judiciary could have been more active in neutralizing the power-grabbing efforts of government agencies. In fact, the eroding of the separation of powers system is largely due to Congress's acceptance of the laws enacted by the president (especially in the field of economic policy) and to the consequent diminution of its own role to legislating on marginal themes.

That legislative expansionism of the executive has occurred because of its overall convenience to all parties involved in the game rather than because of the fear of an institutional stalemate of enormous proportions. The autonomy of the two legislative houses has assumed an ad hoc configuration, negotiated theme by theme, according the interests of the coalition in power.[18]

As mentioned above, the enactment of MPs sets a "counter-majoritarian dilemma" (Monteiro 2004: 41) and the reaction of legislators has been to seek to transfer decision-making power to Congress. Thus, instead of trying to enforce the separation of powers, Congress's usual behavior is to enlarge its own sphere of authority. Unfortunately, this strategy only contributes to further entangle the powers of the three branches of government, rather than to reestablish a viable form of separation.

Until mid-2001, the MP phenomenon developed through a trajectory in which the ratio MP/L*, that is, the monthly quantity of MPs measured in units of laws produced by Congress, was well above the proportion of 1:1 (Monteiro 2004: 232, Fig. 16). Figure 3.1 showing the trajectory under the new MP regime has revealed a much more restrained behavior.[19]

Since 2000 such a behavior of the production of MPs may also be viewed from the perspective of the relation of the executive with itself, that is, from the point of view of the internal division of powers exercised by bureaucrats (Katyal 2006). In such a reconfiguration of the separation of powers, the role played by the top economic managers is fundamental to holding the de facto initiative to enact an MP.

The Increasing of the Tax Burden: MP 232

At the end of 2004, MP 232 (December 30, 2004) contributed to one more wave of tax increases by altering tax rules of the Income Tax and CSLL (Social Contribution on Net Profit):

- The rates of the CSLL and of the Corporate Income Tax were increased by 25 percent (Article 11 of MP 232).
- The coverage of both taxes was furthermore expanded to the extent they have an impact on foreign exchange gains of firms with foreign capital participation in their assets (Article 9).

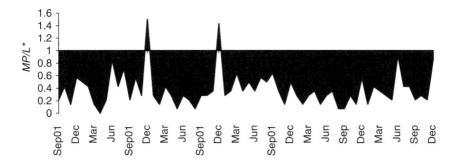

September 12, 2001 to December 31, 2006

Figure 3.1 Share of the executive in law-making EC 32 regime

Source: Raw data obtained from www.planalto.gov.br

The official justification for this expansion was that it roughly compensates for the loss in revenue (R$2.5 billion) brought about by simultaneous changes in parameters of the tax tables and of deductions in the personal income tax (articles 1 to 3).

The use of the MP mechanism provided government with various excuses:

- Several benefits were granted to state governments (to compensate for the loss of tax revenue from exports, for instance) and to private groups (exporters, auto industry).
- The tax increase brought by MP 232 was related to the preferential treatment granted by the government to those private groups in response to their lobbying efforts, media expenses, and campaign financing.
- The government resists cutting public expenditures and in implementing policy actions that would increase the productivity of those expenditures.

After local elections of 2004, it was no surprise that the administration issued an MP to ostensibly redistribute the tax burden, according the preferences and objectives of the fiscal bureaucracy.

The passage of MP 232 in Congress was quite confrontational, with legislators pointing to the tax increase that the MP brought about. However the MP 232 case is far more complex. There was no citizen-taxpayer-voter revolt against the tax increase. The turbulence was precisely because of the format the executive chose to promote the tax change. Furthermore tax policy is too complex to be clearly understood by most taxpayers. Even the monetary indexation introduced in the tax table of the personal income tax as presented in the text of MP 232 has an opaque net incidence on taxpayers.[20]

The president was cornered by Congress' reaction and he substantially revoked MP 232,[21] thus changing the transaction costs in order to pass the new tax. Also the intense interest group mobilization (the FIESP, Federation of Industry of the State of São Paulo; CNI, National Confederation of Industry; CNC, National Confederation of Commerce, among other groups) possibly established a new level of lobbying government, which will arise whenever public policies pose any substantial (positive or negative) impact to those groups.

Decision Impasses: MP 252

MP 252 (June 15, 2005) was a highly complex preferential provision that later lost its validity (October 14, 2005). With its 74 articles it was a prey to the lobbying of interest groups. As such, MP 252 had two important characteristics:

- Setting tax incentives for a variety of economic activities and sectors, it immediately became the target of new potential beneficiaries.

  To the original contemplated sectors—exports, information technology, private security, and real state construction—the coverage of that tax incentive was extended to small firms, air transportation, and even segments of the public sector such as local governments with budget imbalances.
- It increased transaction costs in Congress.

The list of activities and sectors demanding to be covered by the benefits of MP 252 enlarged the possibilities of logrolling, since each legislator noted the higher present value of the costs of obtaining a favorable decision for his electoral district. In other words, negotiation costs rise. At the same time, the external costs also rise: with the higher present value of the burden, each legislator knows that such costs will be transferred to his jurisdiction as a consequence of the fact that his jurisdiction will be left out of the tax incentive.

On the side of organized beneficiaries, the invalidation of MP 252 was linked to various losses to the private sector as vocalized in the media: several businesses imported equipment based on the exemptions created by MP 252, and many of the orders couldn't be canceled, since the shipments were already on their way to Brazil.[22] Canceling MP 252 also created obstacles to competitiveness of the Brazilian economy and to GDP growth, as argued by the National Confederation of Industry. The invalidation is an obstacle to cost cutting, even with the benefits concentrated on a small number of firms, says the CIESP (Center of the Industries of the State of São Paulo).[23]

Decisional Improvisations: MP 255

As it neared its expiration date, MP 255 (July 1, 2005) ended up being used as a host of a complex set of tax exemptions that distribute—under different intensities and following a variety of formats—benefits to activities such as information technology exports, capital goods acquisition by export firms, technology innovation, widening access to digital technology, naval construction, the pulp and paper industry, the petrochemical industry, cereal production, recycling, small and micro firms, civil construction, real estate, the manufacture of machinery and equipment, local governments' social security debts, alcohol, automobile parts, personal capital gains, private pension funds, long-term loans,[24] and ranching. Table 3.3 offers a quick glance at the dimensions of this thicket of preferential benefits brought about by MP 252.

Table 3.3 MP 255 and scope of benefits (size of legislation in terms of number of articles in the law)

MP 252	MP 255	PLV*a*25★	PLV 28★★	PLV 28★★★
(June 15, 2005)	*(July 1, 2005)*	*(October 25, 2005)*	*(October 26, 2005)*	*(October 27, 2005)*
74	3	139	140	134

Note: ★Alternative text, as suggested by the legislator acting as spokesman-reviewer of the MP 255, Senator Amir Lando; ★★Conversion Bill (Projeto de Lei de Conversão or PLVª) approved on the Senate floor (October 26, 2005); ★★★Final version approved by the House (October 27, 2005); ªA bill by which Congress can convert a Provisional Law into a permanent statute

Source: Raw data obtained from www.camara.gov.br, and www. Senado.gov.br

The 74 original articles in MP 252 were incorporated into the MP 255 to reach the status of a super text of 134 articles (and their ramifications) in the form of a bill growing out of a Provisional Law. It was finally approved in Congress a few days before the expiration of the PLV.[25]

Why Reforms were Postponed

Another sign of the low credibility of constitutional rules in policy making is given by the practice of ad hoc decisions as a way of bypassing the constitution. Two examples of this attitude are the initiatives to get social security and tax reforms underway. Both would be introduced outside Congress: at a meeting of the 27 state governors[26] and at the CNDES (the National Council of Economic and Social Development) created on January 1, 2003 (MP 103).[27]

As to the governors' association:

- At its face value that grouping is a copy of analogous experiments observed in a variety of other national economies. However, it is unequivocal that its purpose—and also of the CNDES—is to control the agenda of Congress.
- To some extent those ad hoc arrangements are an effective means of bypassing the constitutional separation of powers.

The decisions reached at these two deliberative stages would confront public opinion as well as legislators with faits accomplis eventually supported by the government majority in Congress.

In 2003, the dominant theme in Congress were discussions of two Proposed Constitutional Amendments (PEC 40–03, Social Security and PEC[28] 41-03, Tax Structure). Both proposals combine elements such as:

- Unifying criteria for the Social Security system in all segments of public choice and in the transition from the old to the new social security regime.

- Establishing separate criteria for tax policy and social security policy; compromises between those two policies; and bargains to adjust their impacts in the three government jurisdictions.
- In relation to the CPMF (Provisional Contribution on Financial Movement), a special tax on banking transactions: its renewal as a federal tax, the definition of its maximum tax rate; the sharing of its revenue with state and local governments;[29] and the amount of earmarking of its revenue.
- The choice of the initial and terminal dates for a variety of fiscal mechanisms, such as incentives to set up factories in the Zona Franca (Manaus Free Trade Area) and state-level fiscal incentives to attract new investments.
- Limits under which new sources of compulsory public revenues could be activated.
- The tax burden, especially in relation to tax ceilings, the amount of earmarking (CPMF, CIDE[30]), and the "reversion" policy—adjusting the rates downward after economic recovery sets in.

All these attributes are currency for legislative bargaining.

This exemplifies the shift of attention from the processes to the final results of the public choices. Taking into consideration some of the characteristics of the political intermediation in the case of PEC 40-03 and 41-03, discussed above, one can highlight:

- The proximity of two electoral years, 2004 and 2006, strongly influenced legislative decision making. Owing to their long duration, the versions of both PECs will certainly be amended again in postelection periods.
- The majority coalition tends to frame constitutional changes in terms of the timing to achieve its public policy priorities. That has been observed in the dominant "treasury perspective"[31] that usually frames stabilization policies discussions.
- All Congress constitutional decisions are not linked to any sort of formal justification by legislators or their corresponding rationale.

The path of PEC 41-03 is quite complex and illustrates why and how reforms can be postponed.

PEC 41-03 extends the validity of mechanisms that were originally introduced during an economic crisis: the CPMF, the additional rate of 10 percent in the personal income tax and the Desvinculação das Receitas da União (Separation of the Union's Receipts—DRU).

Under its MP format, policy decisions can be made to better fit the interests of state governors and eventually of some private groups. Furthermore, the approval of an MP (when converted into a formal law) can be sustained by a simple majority while a constitutional supermajority can block that decision. The supermajority has the attribute of raising the quality of legislation, especially in the case when the MP produces effects that diminish the commonweal.

It is also relevant to note:

- The attempts to split PEC 41-03 (see below), as originally approved by the House, into segments defined by the needs of the central, state, and local governments.
- The amendment that after its passage by Congress will be used as a benchmark for the questions left open, although those questions were originally central to the "tax reform."

With such a status, the amendment in question would be a political football, and would constitute a powerful currency for building future political alliances. In addition, it would have a substantial electoral value.

A Relevant Example: MP 135

The controversy over MP 135 is much more related to the fact that its enactment took everybody by surprise to the extent that PEC 41-03 was supposed to be a firm commitment as a tax reform proposal. MP 135 is notable because:

- The size of the text is unusually large. It consists of 69 articles that deal with the end of the cumulative incidence of the social security tax paid by employers (Contribuição Financeira Social—COFINS). However, the rules defined directly or indirectly a variety of other taxes, such as the IPI (Federal Tax on Industrialized Products), CPMF, the Civil Servants Savings Program (PIS-PASEP[32]), the income tax, and import duties.
- It triggers a procedure already used in the previous administration that allows the bureaucrats to get around the MP already in operation.

    When constitutional amendment 32 (September 11, 2001) passed Congress, a bundle of 59 former MPs were issued under the old MP regime.[33] These 59 MPs were not converted into law and therefore expired. Because of this peculiar configuration, the government can issue a new MP and rework the terms and validity of one or more of those MPs in that bundle. Hence the new rules of amendment 32 can be evaded.[34] (Monteiro 2004: 277–278).

On the other hand, one may notice that MP 135 is tied to a set of inducements:

- The government at last bowed to the demands of industrial interest groups, especially the export sector represented by Brazilian Association of Foreign Trade.

- The new COFINS is also a source of additional federal tax revenue: by then estimated to be 8 percent above the 2002 COFINS revenue.
- MP 135 also signals the government's preference for rules that can be altered accordingly to short-run needs of economic policy rather than through a more stable path of changes that would have followed from PEC 41–03.
- Last but not least, in presenting Congress with a set of faits accomplis, the executive abets the postponement of true tax reform.

One is led to conclude that Congress operates under substantial constraints set by the executive. The case in point is the combination of a PEC with some ordinary legislation that ends up informally reconfiguring the text of the PEC. The following sequential process illustrates the slicing strategy that can be legitimized by the enactment of an MP: Slicing strategy applied to PEC 41–03 → Lower coordination cost of constitutional change → Lower stability of the rules of the policy game → Higher discretionary power of bureaucrats → Greater flexibility in issuing Provisional Laws (MP 135).

Finally, it is worth noting that the issue explored here can be viewed as a classic question on the compatibility of democracy with the administrative state: That is, to what extent does legislation by the executive lessen the weight of Congress in public choices?

Tax Exemptions and Reinforcement of Discretionary Policy Instruments

In February 2003 the minister of Finance presented the new stage of policy commitments: He proposed maintaining the tax burden at 36.4 percent of the GDP (implying a transfer of private income to government of about R$477 billion). He also projected a primary surplus in the public accounts of 4.25 percent of the GDP, an increase of 13 percent over the level of the previous administration. Such announcements were mainly aimed at showing the good intentions of the new government regarding the stabilization effort. However, that was a risky bet in terms of the political capital it might build.

At a second level of the policy goals, the Lula Government did what everybody expected any new administration would try to do:

- The Central Bank raised (February 19, 2003) the short-run basic interest rate from 25.5 percent to 26.5 percent.
- It was announced that the CPMF would have its validity extended beyond 2003.

- As for the DRUs[35]—a discretionary tax allowing bureaucrats to allocate some 20 percent of federal revenues according to their preferences—their validity would also be renewed and its 20 percent coefficient could even be raised.

Delegations of power such as the DRUs are effective (Mashaw 1997: 141–147) in reducing the degree of responsibility among those in charge of policy implementation; by conditioning complex political bargains with interest groups; and in giving legislators the chance of selectively serving information to their voters, allowing them to legislate even without reaching consensus as to the details of public policies; and by hiding policy positions that are ideologically or programmatically inconsistent.

On the other hand one may look at the DRU from the president's perspective. National themes (such as the fight against poverty and unemployment) are less associated with the prestige of a congressman or a senator, and much more with the president. That is why ample delegations such as the DRU have a more direct relationship with the electoral preferences of the citizens in presidential elections. Accordingly, by enlarging the discretionary power to the executive in the implementation of public policies, the DRU acts as a mechanism of substantial weight in the political capital formation of the government.

To the extent that large parts of the central government's budget consists of constitutional entitlements, the DRU is also an attempt to create an environment in which public spending is determined by internal considerations of the bureaucracy. In such a world, public spending is on "automatic pilot."

In fact, there is a hidden tug of war between legislators and bureaucrats in terms of constitutional reforms and even in the renewal of the validity of a mechanism such as the DRU: the other side of that coin is the question of the discretionary power of bureaucrats in allocating a large share of public resources.

- As to the old theme of Central Bank autonomy, the Lula administration bypassed it with a vague promise to start the discussion of the issue in Congress in the second half of 2003.[36]
- Another recurrent policy theme is the partial or total removal of tax burden on selective economic activities. This policy results from intensive lobbying activity, such as that of FIESP to minimize the tax burden of large industrial firms.

A Unique and Virtuous Policy Case: The Law of
Public-Private Partnerships

The policy of supporting public-private partnerships (PPPs) (Monteiro 2006) offers some unique characteristics in the institutional environment

Table 3.4   The making of Law 11,079

Stage	Decision
November 19, 2003, President	Bill 2546: Presentation to the House of Representatives
February18, 2004, House	Voted at the Special Committee
March 17, 2004, House	Voted on the House Floor
May 4, 2004, Senate	Voted at the Infrastructure Committee
November 18, 2004, Senate	Voted at the Economic Committee
September 12, 2004, Senate	Voted at the Constitution and Justice Committee
December 22, 2004, Senate	Voted on the Senate Floor
December 22, 2004, House	Voted on the House Floor
December 30, 2004, President	Signing of the Law 11 079

Source: Basic information obtained from www.planalto.gov.br, www.camara.gov.br, and www.senado.gov.br

of the Brazilian economy in recent years. Instead of framing PPP policy on an MP format, the executive preferred to follow the more representative decision-making process of submitting a bill to Congress and engaging in a long and collaborative path toward the final text of Law 11 079 (December 30, 2004).

Table 3.4 shows this virtuous path of cooperation between the executive and Congress during 2004 for the enactment of the PPP law. (In fact, this is a rare example of formulation of a public policy following the typical decision format requiring two majoritarian decisions in Congress and the president's decision not to exercise his veto power.) This can be contrasted with the usual workings of the presidentialism by MPs. In that sense it is one of the greatest institutional contributions of the Lula administration to the operational enhancement of the Brazilian representative democracy. Despite the institutional disorder under which the economy operates (Monteiro 2004), it was possible to observe such a well-behaved interaction between Congress and the executive.[37]

After all, by realizing some PPP projects in their respective jurisdictions, they would be showing political agility and administrative proficiency. Furthermore, such virtues could always bring short-term gains to the PSDB candidacies in the 2004 local elections. Therefore, not only were several PPP state laws approved[38] before the federal PPP law was available, but also even some private-public partnerships got started on a limited basis.

The federal government had a similar interest. The synchrony of PPP with a sustainable GDP growth of at least 5 percent would be the achievement of "the growth spectacle," in the now famous phrase of the president. In that context, PPP gained political salience when it was associated with the complex negotiations concerning a fateful constitutional amendment permitting the reelection of the chairmen of both of the House and the Senate. Also, powerful lobbies were on the move—by using the media and acting directly on legislators—as exemplified by

FIESP and ABDIB (Brazilian Association of Infrastructure and Basic Industry).[39]

It would be difficult to identify a comparable source of gains to be allocated through the political process. The possibility of regaining momentum in investments under the partnership regime was quite tempting for private industry. In fact, this was the most wide open rent-seeking operation in the Brazilian economy, only comparable to the privatization policy in the 1990s.

The fact that the PPP policy was frozen for the rest of the first term of the Lula government, despite the approval of the PPP law (December 30, 2004), cannot be attributed only to electoral maneuvers on the side of the government: there wasn't sufficient time for the signing of partnerships contracts and putting private consortia into operation to gain significant visibility during 2005–2006. Even interest groups (such as machinery and equipment producers, private pension funds, and the financial market in general) understood that this was not a good occasion to obtain the maximum gains on the various economic policy fronts. Hence, there was also some degree of uncertainty as to the preferences of the future administration as far as the PPP was concerned, during the October–November 2006 electoral campaign.[40]

Conclusion

In the end we are led to ask: why all the potentially damaging events mentioned above were not reflected in the macroeconomic "success" of the Brazilian economy, as summarized by lower inflation rates, the persistent control of the public accounts, the extraordinary results of the trade balance, or even GDP growth (although at modest rates) in the 2003–2006 period?

That is a question that has not received a convincing answer. It also constitutes a sort of paradox to the extent that the fragility of the constitutional state, as shown above, is in some measure being neutralized by the operation of managerial-administrative mechanisms that block the negative consequences that an unstable—or even inoperative—set of constitutional rules can bring to economic performance as a whole.

Once we recognize the complex web of the delegation of authority in public choices, we see a large cession of decision making to the executive: legislators have chosen to transfer responsibilities on policy issues that involve diffused benefits and concentrated costs; not to do so would be politically unpopular (Komesar 1994).

This motive explains the tolerance of legislators not only of the unpopular fiscal measures associated with the stabilization policy, but also of the legal devices used in many policy decisions: provisional laws, presidential decrees, and administrative regulations. Even when we recognize that there are broader legislative concerns framing bureaucrats' actions in the ministries and regulatory agencies,[41] the details of such actions are poorly perceived by voters.

Hence the delegation of powers, functions, and resources is doubly convenient to politicians:

- They profit indirectly by serving the private interests of those who act, so as to minimize the costs that economic policy transfers to those groups. In order to do that, private groups manage to move opaquely within the executive, and can attenuate or even neutralize the costs that a policy may impose on them.
- More directly, legislators may get recognition from the positively affected segments of society. The blame for the costs—if they are at all recognized—can always be attributed to the executive by the minority; meanwhile, politicians of the majority can highlight the benefits and to try to take credit for them.

In an election year,[42] politicians of all parties know how to use those maneuvers available to them.

The question of electoral accountability for public policy is also very complex:

- To some extent, those policies were recognized as being the responsibility of the Workers' Party and, as such, the PT used its perceived successes in campaigning for the next election (2004 or 2006).
- However, some segments of public policy were allocated to other parties in the coalition controlling the executive. In 2006, this was the case of the Ministries of Transportation, Communications, and Agriculture.

Such a situation not only results in systematic cleavages on several policy issues (Bawn and Rosenbluth 2006: 251), but also makes it more difficult for voters to get a coherent perception of the net result of economic policy.

The PT, the majority party in the government, may claim to be responsible for those policy segments showing "good results," even if those segments are allocated to decision units that enjoy high autonomy in their operation and technical expertise. That is the case of the Central Bank and the success of the stabilization policy. On the other hand, there are ministries that operate without formal party ties, and they are relatively autonomous in setting policy in their special bailiwicks. The Ministry of Development, Industry, and Foreign Trade is the most notable example of this class. Finally, there are the "general interest" programs, such as *Bolsa Família, Fome Zero*, and the expansion of access to the university. These are policies showing a pattern of dispersed costs and benefits, and in consequence they also show a low lobbying activity, both for and against them.

Once again, the central point is: how does this sort of institutional accountability—or nonaccountability—translates into voters' preferences?

Notes

1. Two other variants of constitutional change are not represented in table 3.1: judicial interpretation of constitutional rules by the Federal Supreme Court (STF) and the implementation of those rules by bureaucrats in the Executive (Monteiro, 2004:95–99).
2. This amplitude index reflects the usual attributes of a broad amendment: it is a long subset of new rules, and hence it redefines several constitutional procedures.
3. See "Eleições 2006: Samba do Crioulo Doido nas Alianças," *O Globo*, March 4, 2006, *O País*, 3–4.
4. As shown along the political crises in 2005–2006.
5. "Criada pelo PSDB, Regra Gerou Crise Entre Tucanos," *Estado de São Paulo*, August 3, 2006, A4. To be on the safe side, those interested in the revision of rules (especially constitutional Articles 14 and 82) opted for an interparty agreement (PSDB, PFL, and PT) and then, approved in the Justice Committee (CCJ) of the Senate (August 2, 2006) an Amendment Proposal (PEC 41, May 29, 2003, with changes) eliminating the reelection rule for president, governors, and mayors, to be enforced from 2010 on. "Acordo Suprapartidário Leva CCJ do Senado a Aprovar Fim da Reeleição," *Estado de São Paulo*, August 3, 2006, A4.
6. "Lula Propõe Constituinte Exclusiva," *O Globo*, August 3, 2006, O País, 3. That constitutional power would furthermore apply without the approval of the National Congress. See also, "Constituinte Exclusiva," *Folha de São Paulo*, August 8, 2006, A3; "Enfim, um Debate," *Veja*, August 9, 2006, 54–55.
7. PLN 2, and the corresponding EM 59–06/MP, April 12, 2006. A PLN (Projeto de Lei apresentado ao Congresso) is a bill presented directly to Congress as a whole, such as the federal budget; "EM" or "Exposição de Motivos," is a formal statement by the president, justifying a bill he or she sends to Congress.
8. "Relatores Querem Votar o Orçamento e Relegar a LDO," *Valor Econômico*, September 19, 2006, A10.
9. One cannot pretend that by changing essential rules defining the power to govern, one will be able to preserve one pillar of the whole architecture of the Brazilian constitutional democracy: the separation of powers.
10. In the end this regime introduced new sources of disfunctions in the shared power to govern (Monteiro 2004).
11. Once again, consideration of the path of constitutional amendments helps to explain why the strategy behind the two above-mentioned proposals (a new electoral rule ending reelection and a "political reform") is inappropriate. Constitutional Amendment 32 (mentioned above) redefining the peculiar legislative power allocated to the executive, generated serious distortions in the definition of the power to govern.
12. Article 62 of the Constitution sets rules under which the MP mechanism works. There are two distinct MP regimes: 1) from May 10, 1988 to September 11, 2001; 2) the current regime set by EC 32, September 11, 2001.
13. This certainly reduces the possibility that congress will have control over the processes by which policy differences between executive and the legislature are reconciled.
14. For detailed evidence on the golden period of the use of MPs, from 1994 to mid-2001, where the MP mechanism played the role of the main anchor of the *Plano Real*, see J.V. Monteiro (1997, 2000).

15. In some circumstances, the use of the MP mechanism may be still more significant than the one suggested by quantitative evidence presented in table 3.2, where such a production reaches 51.5 percent of Congress' legislative output. On some occasions the use of MPs can be more substantial: between January 1, 2006 and August 14, 2006, and also between January 1, 2006 and November 24, 2006 (not shown in table 3.2), that proportion reached over four fifths of the Congress' legislative output. It is then unquestionable that in some situations the system of separation of powers is virtually nonexistent in making public choices.

16. Knowing the strategic potential of MPs, all political parties opt for the degrees of freedom the enactment of MPs confers to those who possess the authority to govern. Recall that only on September 11, 2001 did political leaders agree to approve a new set of rules for MPs.

17. On several occasions, the mere threat of enacting an MP has conditioned the decision process of Congress.

18. Only in 2001 (EC 32, September 11, 2001), possibly led by electoral uncertainty (Monteiro 2004: 142), did politicians of all factions opt for a new and more restrictive regime of the enactment of laws by the Executive. This is the same uncertainty one notices in the election year of 2006 leading legislators to once more announce their interest in restricting the MP regime.

19. I follow here the same notation as in J.V. Monteiro (2000, 2004). In this figure, L* represents the quantity of laws approved in the legislature except for those bills that renew or convert MPs; a convert bill has its origin in an MP and so it does not characterize an entirely autonomous decision taken by Congress. At the same time, L* is the average quantity of laws calculated for all the 64-month period shown in the figure. By the way, in the mid-1990s—hence, under the regime before Constitutional Amendment 32—the equivalent dark shaded area in figure 3.1 would be systematically depicted above the horizontal axis (Monteiro 2004: 232). Between January 1995 and August 2001, for instance, the same variable MP/L* shown in figure 3.1 reaches an average value of 5.3, or approximately a proportion of 5:1 between MPs and laws approved in congress. However, figure 3.1 can be interpreted in a contrary way to what is said above. Congressional tolerance of the legislative power of the executive could diminish Congress's own scope of authority.

20. The MP 232 episode certainly indicates we are approaching a line of resistance against attempts to increase revenues. However, the rapid growth of the bureaucracy has its own limits.

21. Articles 4 to 13, according to MP 243, March 21, 2005.

22. "Para Ressuscitar o 'Bem,'" *Jornal do Brasil*, October 16, 2005, Editorial, A4.

23. "Competitividade Perde sem a MP do Bem," *Gazeta Mercantil*, October 13, 2005, A1.

24. This item is of special relevance as an additional benefit for the heavy industry planning to operating consortia in the by then highly visible public private partnerships (PPP) initiative (Monteiro 2006). On that, see the section on "A Unique and Virtuous Policy Case" discussed further.

25. That is a didactic case of interdependence of the functioning of majoritary democracy and the distribution of the tax incidence among citizens and organized groups. As such, we may notice that the tax system can be as discriminatory as public expenditures, or even more so (Tuerck 1967).

26. As seen by the meetings held in Brasília on February 22–23, 2003.

27. This group has around 90 participants, 82 of them representing several interests of civil society.

28. In this chapter, PEC stands for Proposta de Emenda Constitucional or Proposed Constitutional Amendment.

29. This demand would reappear at the beginning of the second term of the Lula government and it was presented by state governors as a fundamental condition to lend their support to the PAC, Programa de Aceleração do Crescimento: 2007–2010 ("Governadores Querem R$15,5 bi de Lula em Troca de Apoio ao PAC," *O Estado de São Paulo*, January 30, 2007, A4).

30. Federal Contribution of Intervention in the Economic Order.

31. It has been common to introduce vigorous spending cuts, ignoring almost completely the rationality of who will take such a decision, from which segment of society the corresponding benefits will be denied, and, correspondingly, what reaction one anticipates after that denial.

32. Programas de Integração Social (PIS) e de Formação do Patrimônio do Servidor Público (PASEP).

33. Currently that array is down to 53 MPs.
34. In the case under review, MP 135 reconditions several articles of MP 2158–35, August 24, 2001.
35. The DRU is a delegation of taxing power from congress to the executive. The reason why legislators permit this goes as follows: (Aranson, Gellhorn, and Robinson 1982); 1) legislators know that any given piece of legislation will probably benefit a segment of society; at the same time, it will impose substantial costs to other segments. To get credit from the first segment while professing to be against those costs, legislators favor broad delegations (such as DRUs). Thus, they can get political support of the first group, while transferring the responsibilities for the negative impacts of the legislative delegation to the bureaucrats; 2) when all the groups are potentially harmed by the legislation so they would prefer the status quo—but they are not capable to opt for a given course of action—the legislators' delegation of power allows bureaucrats to allocate gains and losses among those competing segments of the public.
36. *Folha de São Paulo*, February 10, 2003, A10.
37. Although trivially relevant in any constitutional democracy, that is certainly a notable achievement in the Brazilian case; however it didn't get the deserved attention in the national economic and political debate.
38. State Law 14 868, December 16, 2003, in Minas Gerais, and State Law 11 688, May 19, 2004, in São Paulo. By mid-October 2004, two other states had already passed their PPP laws: Goiás and Santa Catarina.
39. Indirect evidence on that is collected in footnotes in J.V. Monteiro (2006).
40. Tax exemptions and new regulations (such as "sectoral directive plans") are the demands of the private lobbying at the beginning of 2007 ("Para o Setor Privado, Menos Incentivos," *O Estado de São Paulo*, December 1, 2007, B3). The investment fund as proposed by ABDIB would reach R$70 billion (the estimate is that investments in infrastructure in 2006 amounted to R$ 65.7 billion). In mid-January of 2007, the ABDIB sought to have such an investment fund included in the Programa de Aceleração do Crescimento, PAC: 2007–2010, as announced on January 22, 2007. It failed the processes of PAC were initially defined by eight Provisional Laws (MP 346 through 353), two bills enacted under the constitutional urgency clause (Article 64, §1°) and eight presidential decrees (Decree 6018 through 6025). Once again, this is a pattern that only reinforces the Executive's already substantial power of making proposals in the public choice process.
41. For example, the Central Bank, the Federal Revenue Service, and units such as ANATEL (telecommunications) and ANP (oil and gas).
42. Such as in 2006 and to some extent, in 2004.

References

Bawn, K., and F. Rosenbluth. 2006. "Short Versus Long Coalitions: Electoral Accountability and the Size of the Public Sector." *American Journal of Political Science* 50(2) (April):251–265.

Gardner, J. 2005. "Democracy without a Net? Separation of Powers and the Idea of Self-Sustaining Constitutional Constraints on Undemocratic Behavior." *St. John's Law Review* 79(2) (Spring):293–317.

Katyal, N. 2006. "Internal Separation of Powers: Checking Today's Most Dangerous Branch from Within." *Yale Law Journal* 115(9) (September):2314–2349.

Kingdon, J. 1995. *Agendas, Alternatives, and Public Policies.* 2nd. ed. New York: HarperCollins College Publishers.

Komesar, N. 1994. *Imperfect Alternatives: Choosing Institutions in Law, Economics and Public Policy.* Chicago: Chicago University Press.

Levinson, D. and R. Pildes. 2006. "Separation of Parties, Not Powers." *Harvard Law Review* 119(8) (June):2312–2386.

Macey, J. 2006. "Executive Branch Usurpation of Power: Corporations and Capital Markets." Paper Presented at the Yale Law Journal Symposium on the Most Dangerous Branch? March.

Mashaw, J. 1985. "Prodelegation: Why Administrators Should Make Political Decisions." *Journal of Law, Economics, and Organization* 1(1) (Spring):81–100. Reproduced in M. Stearns. 1997.

Public Choice and Public Law: Readings and Commentary. Cincinnati: Anderson Publishing. pp. 180–203.

Monteiro, J.V. 1997. *Economia & Política: Instituições de Estabilização Econômica no Brasil*. Rio de Janeiro: Editora FGV.

———. 2000. *As Regras do Jogo: O Plano Real, 1997–2000*. Rio de Janeiro: Editora FGV.

———. 2004. *Lições de Economia Constitucional Brasileira*. Rio de Janeiro: Editora FGV.

———. 2006. "Estado Oco & Parcerias Público-Privadas." *Revista de Economia & Relações Internacionais* 5(9) (July):56–73.

CHAPTER FOUR

Brazil's Lack of Growth

JOCILDO BEZERRA AND TIAGO V.
DE V. CAVALCANTI[*]

Introduction

It is high time for Brazil to seize its future. The world's fifth-most-populous nation needs a long-term vision for its economy, as well as a commitment at all levels of government to implement measures that could lead to a dramatic increase in productivity.[1]

Brazil's growth performance since the early 1980s has been lackluster. After several decades of high growth of per capita Gross Domestic Product (GDP), the Brazilian economy has gone through a long period of stagnation and slow growth. For instance, between 1950 and 1979 the average annual growth rate of Brazil's per capita GDP was 3.8 percent, while the same indicator grew at an average annual rate of 0.6 percent between 1980 and 2003.[2] At the latter rate, Brazil's per capita GDP would double in 116 years, and would only reach South Korea's current per capita GDP in about 150 years. The situation improved slightly between 2003 and 2006, when Brazil's per capita GDP grew at an average annual rate of 0.9 percent, but still much slower than most emerging market economies.[3]

This pattern of growth in the second half of the twentieth century is not only observed in Brazil. Most of Latin American countries experienced a period of high growth from 1960 to 1980 and an economic slowdown from 1980 to 2003. An exception is Chile, where per capita GDP grew at a higher rate in the last two decades of the twentieth century than in the period from 1960 to 1980.[4] Figure 4.4 shows that trended growth rate of GDP in Brazil started to decrease in mid-1970s, and this was also observed in the world economy. However, while the world economy started to grow at high rates again in the 1990s, growth in Brazil remained modest.

It is important to briefly describe the background to policies adopted by the Brazilian economy in the second half of the twentieth century. The period from 1950 to 1980 was characterized by the Import Substitution Industrialization (ISI) policies.[5] The government used protectionist instruments,[6] public subsidies, and some direct participation (state-owned enterprises)[7] to promote industrial growth.

From 1950 to 1980 the Brazilian economy grew at very high rates and diversified its industrial base. "But it was a base also characterized by capital scarcity and outdated and overused technology, requiring the support of either the state or foreign actors for sustained development."[8] In the 1970s Brazil continued to encourage a debt-led strategy that transferred the burden of high growth to future generations. This debt became unsustainable, especially when the debt crises of the 1980s hit the economy. The period from 1980 to the beginning of the 1990s was characterized by several heterodox attempts to control (hyper) inflation that resulted in a long period of low and volatile growth (see figure 4.4). Inflation was finally brought down in 1994. In the 1990s Brazil went through market-oriented economic reforms: It followed the world trend toward privatization and liberalization and opened the economy (i.e., the trade and the financial sector), exposing domestic producers to outside competition. Recently, Brazil implemented some microeconomic reforms, such as the one that changed the bankruptcy law. Despite a short cyclical recovery and some efficiency gains, the postreform period failed to fulfill the growth expectations.[9]

In this chapter we study the following questions: Why is growth low in Brazil? What are the policies that could improve economic performance? The investigation of these questions is important for at least three reasons: first, though Brazil is not a poor country, it has many poor people. Poverty has been decreasing in the last decade. However, data from Instituto de Pesquisa Econômica Aplicada (IPEA) show that still about 30 percent of the population lives below the poverty line. Therefore, faster growth might help the country to reduce poverty. Second, pushed by high growth rates of large developing economies (e.g., China and India), the world in the last years is growing at high rates again (see figure 4.4). This has boosted commodity prices (such as iron ore and soybeans) and exports in Brazil. In addition, international interest rates are at low levels and there is high liquidity in international financial markets. This is particularly important because it has shown (e.g., Klenow and Rodríguez-Clare [2005]) that a country's growth rate depends on other countries' growth. Given the current worldwide economic environment it seems even more critical to understand Brazil's recent economic performance.

What would be the effects of a worldwide economic slowdown on the Brazilian economy? Finally, as argued before, in the 1990s Brazil went through important market-oriented economic reforms, but the sluggish growth after the reform has given support to some analysts who think that the solution is to go back to old-style ISI and state-owned enterprises.

Therefore, it is important to make a careful diagnosis of the growth constraints of the Brazilian economy to shed some light on what policies are needed to promote steady growth and development.

Some International Comparisons

Long-run Comparisons

It is important to compare the growth experience of the Brazilian economy with some other successful emerging market economies that caught up with the industrial leaders in the second half of the twentieth century. In particular, we use two Asian countries and one Latin American economy. They are South Korea, Taiwan, and Chile. Figure 4.1 panel (a) shows the evolution of the logarithm of the real GDP per capita for Brazil and these three economies. Observe that South Korea and Taiwan had a similar pattern of sustained high growth in the period (figure 4.1 panel [a]) and as a result they caught up with the industrial leader (figure 4.1 panel [b]). For instance, in 1950, per capita income in South Korea was roughly 10 percent of the per capita income in the United States. Actual per capita

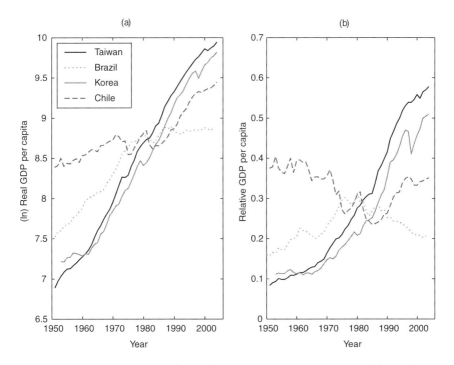

Figure 4.1 Panel (a): Logarithm of the real GDP per capita (chain series). Panel (b): Real GDP per capita relative to the U.S. level

Source: Heston, Summers, and Aten (2006)

income in South Korea is about 50 percent of what is observed in the United States. The Chilean economy had a growth experience that differed from what is observed in Brazil.[10] From 1950 to mid-1980s Chile's per capita income growth was modest, but from mid-1980s on, growth was steady and currently the per capita income is about 35 percent of what is observed in the United States. Despite the strong catch up from 1950 to 1980, we notice that Brazil's actual output per capita relative to the United States level is roughly the same as it was about 50 years ago: per capita income in Brazil is about 20 percent of that in the United States. It is not our goal to explain in details the difference in growth performance of these four economies,[11] but we seek to explain the actual growth constraints of the Brazilian economy.

We now compare the performance of the Brazilian and the world economy. Figure 4.2 shows the Brazilian and the world GDP (panel [a]) and per capita GDP (panel [b]) from 1950 to 2003. Observe that from 1950 to 1980, Brazil's GDP per capita caught up with the world economy, but since then the world has been growing at a faster rate than the Brazilian economy (see also figure 4.4). GDP and growth of GDP has also been more volatile in Brazil than in the world (see figure 4.3 and panel [b]) of figure 4.4). The standard deviation of the percentage deviations in world GDP is about 29 percent of that of Brazil's GDP. Interestingly, figure 4.3

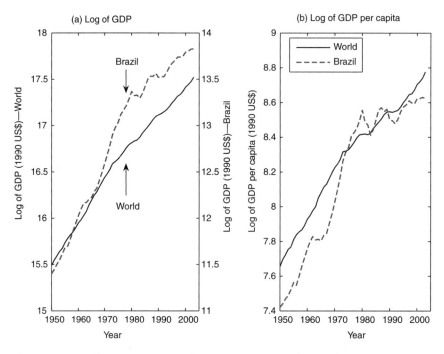

Figure 4.2   Log of GDP (1990 US$) and GDP per capita in Brazil and in the world

Source: Maddison (2006)

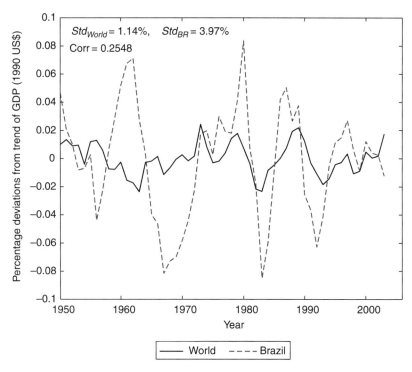

Figure 4.3   Percentage deviations from GDP (1990 US$) in Brazil and in the world

Source: Maddison (2006)

shows that from 1950 to 1970 GDP in Brazil and in the world correlated negatively, while the two series correlate positively from 1970 to 2003.[12] It is also worth noting in figure 4.3 that the control of inflation in mid-1990s is associated with a decrease in the amplitude of fluctuations in Brazil's GDP.

Short-run Comparisons

We now investigate the recent growth performance of the Brazilian economy. Figure 4.5 panel (a) shows the Kernel density estimate of the average growth rate of real GDP in about 170 economies from 2002 to 2005. In Figure 4.5 panel (b) we plot the cumulative distribution of growth rates in the world. According to the World Bank (2006), GDP in Brazil grew in this period at about 2.4 percent per year. As can be observed, this is below the mode observed among 170 countries in this period, which is roughly 5 percent. In fact, figure 4.5 panel (b) shows that from 2002 to 2005 only 30 percent of the countries in the world grew at lower rates than the Brazilian economy. This is critical, because we are including all industrialized countries, which in general are in their balanced growth

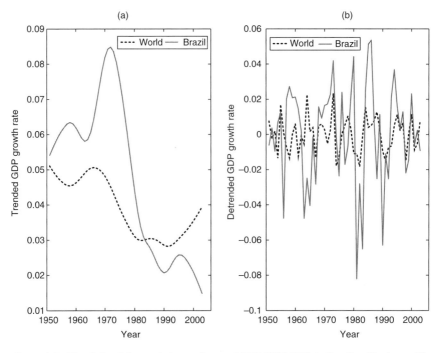

Figure 4.4 Trended and de-trended growth rate of GDP (1990 US$) in Brazil and in the world
Source: Maddison (2006)

path and do not grow at high rates, and countries in civil wars, such as Haiti and Zimbabwe, in which GDP shrank in the period.

Table 4.1 shows that the growth of real GDP in Brazil is different from the strong recent performance of the other three BRIC countries: Russia, India, and China. While from 2002 to 2005 average annual growth rate was 6.42 percent in the BRIC countries, Brazil had the lowest growth. The Brazilian growth rate of GDP is almost one-third of the average growth rate in BRIC countries and about one-fourth of the Chinese economy. In this period, the Brazilian economy has been growing at a rate lower than that observed in Latin America and just a bit higher than what is observed in OECD countries. However, population growth is much higher in Brazil than in industrialized countries. Therefore, in per capita terms growth has been lower in Brazil than in industrialized countries.

The Consequences of a Worldwide Growth Slowdown on Brazil's Growth

Recent research on growth and development has highlighted the role of international knowledge externalities on long-run growth[13] and on the interdependence of cross-country growth rates. One interesting issue is the effects of a worldwide growth slowdown on Brazil's growth performance. The recent years have been characterized by a time of record

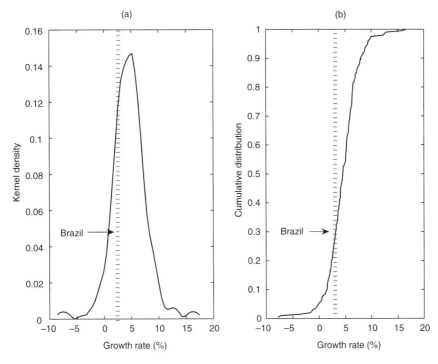

Figure 4.5 Panel (a): Kernel density of the average growth rate of real GDP from 2002 to 2005. Panel (b): Cumulative density of the average growth rate of GDP from 2002 to 2005

Source: World Bank (2006)

Table 4.1 Growth rate of real GDP from 2002 to 2005: Selected countries and regions

Country (region)	Growth rate of GDP (%)
BRIC	6.46
Brazil	2.42 (3.1)
Russia	6.41
India	7.24
China	9.77
Latin America	2.87
Chile	4.65
OECD Countries	2.31
United States	3.16

Note: Value in parentheses corresponds to the revised version of the growth rate of real GDP

Source: World Bank (2006)

high commodity prices, low interest rates, and robust global demand. The puzzle, as suggested by Velasco (2005), is: Why doesn't Brazil (and Latin America) grow more? What would be the consequences of a worldwide slowdown on the Brazilian economy?

Here we use Maddison (2006) data on the world and Brazilian growth rate of GDP from 1950 to 2003 to estimate how the average worldwide growth affects the Brazilian economy. Let y_t be the growth rate of real GDP in Brazil in a year and let x_t be the world growth rate of real GDP (minus the Brazilian component).We estimate the following equation:

$$y_t = \alpha + y_{t-1} + \beta x_t + \varepsilon_t \qquad (1)$$

We run two regressions: One without the lagged dependent variable ($\gamma = 0$) and another with the lagged dependent variable.[14] Table 4.2 contains the estimated coefficients. The first column uses ordinary least squares (OLS) procedure for the regression without the lagged dependent variable. Observe that the Durbin-Watson test indicates the presence of serial autocorrelation. In such cases, OLS procedures yield inefficient estimators. In the second column, we use Prais-Winsten iterations to correct for the presence of serial autocorrelation. However, observe in figure 4.6 panel (a) that such a model does not provide a good fit of the data. The third column of table 4.2 shows the OLS results with the presence of the lagged dependent variable. Note that the null hypothesis of no serial autocorrelation is not rejected, and the model has a good fit of the data (see figure 4.6 panel [b]). Observe also that in this regression all estimated coefficients (except the constant term) are statistically different from zero at a 95 percent confidence level.

We now use the estimated coefficients of table 4.2, column 3 to make some counterfactual exercises:

1. What would Brazil's growth of GDP be if there is a worldwide GDP growth slowdown of one percentage point? More specifically,
2. What would Brazil's growth of GDP during Lula's first term have been if the rhythm of worldwide GDP growth were similar to the one observed during the Cardoso administration?

Table 4.2 Dependent variable: Brazil's growth rate of GDP. OLS and Prais-Winsten regressions

	Specifications		
	OLS	*Prais-Winsten*	*OLS*
growthWorld	1.094** (2.66)	0.680* (1.81)	0.837** (2.36)
growthBR(-1)			0.444** −3.65
Constant	0.0049 (0.28)	0.02 (1.19)	−0.006 (−0.44)
Durbin-Watson test	1.165	2.134[a]	2.212
R-Squared	0.14	0.06	0.33
Number of observations	53	53	52

Note: t-Statistics are in parentheses. * ,** mean significant at 90 and 95 confidence level, respectively. [a] Durbin's h test
Source: Maddison (2006)

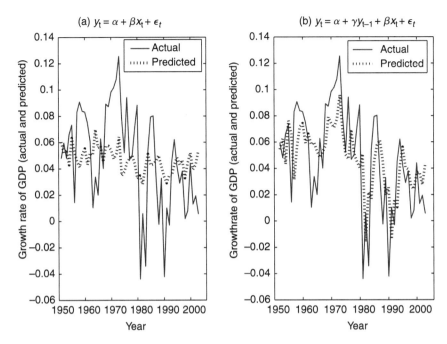

Figure 4.6 Growth rate of GDP (1990 US$) in Brazil: Data and predicted values
Source: Maddison (2006)

According to World Bank (2006), the world GDP grew in the last four years (2003–2006) at an annual rate of 4.1 percent. During Cardoso's first (1995–1998) and second (1999–2002) terms the worldwide GDP grew at 3.1 and 2.6 percent per year, respectively. During the whole Cardoso administration, worldwide GDP grew at 2.9 percent per year. This is about 1.2 percentage point lower than Lula's first term administration.

Table 4.3 contains the counterfactual exercises. It shows that Brazil's growth of GDP during Lula's first term would have been about 70 percent lower than its realized growth rate if worldwide growth of GDP were similar to what was observed during the Cardoso administration (counterfactual exercise [iii]). In particular, Cardoso's second term was a period characterized by a number of emerging market crises (e.g., Russia and Argentina crises) that negatively affected the Brazilian economy. If average world growth were similar to this turbulent period, Brazil's GDP growth during Lula's first term would have been roughly 60 percent of its realized growth rate (counterfactual exercise [ii]).

Observe that, whether we use the old series of Brazil's GDP or the new revised version, counterfactual GDP growth during Lula's first term would have been lower than the corresponding period during Cardoso's administration. Notice that a 2.28 percent growth of GDP would imply in Brazil a per capita GDP growth of 1.18 percent. At this pace, per capita

Table 4.3 Counterfactual exercises based on table 4.2, column 3

	Brazil's annual GDP growth rate (%)	
	Base year 1985	Base year 2000
Realized		
Cardoso's first term	2.57	
Cardoso's second term	2.1	
Cardoso's whole administration	2.34	
Lula's first term	2.7	3.35
Counterfactual		
(i) World-wide GDP growth similar to Cardoso's first term (1995–1998)	$0.72 \times 2.70 = 1.97$	$0.72 \times 3.35 = 2.51$
(ii) World-wide GDP growth similar to Cardoso's second term (1999–2002)	$0.60 \times 2.70 = 1.62$	$0.60 \times 3.35 = 2.01$
(iii) World-wide GDP growth similar to Cardoso's administration (1995–2002)	$0.68 \times 2.70 = 1.84$	$0.68 \times 3.35 = 2.28$

Source: World Bank (2006) and Instituto Brasileiro de Geografia e Estatística (IBGE)

income doubles in every 60 years. Now we turn to our understanding of Brazil's growth constraints.

Brazil's Growth Constraints

It is a much easier task to show that growth in Brazil has been disappointing in the last years than to identify Brazil's major growth constraints in order to define effective growth promoting policies. Larry Summers in his 2003 Godkin Lecture at Harvard University posited that:

> The rate at which countries grow is substantially determined by three things: their ability to integrate with the global economy through trade and investment; their capacity to maintain sustainable government finances and sound money; and their ability to put in place an institutional environment in which contracts can be enforced and property rights can be established. I would challenge anyone to identify a country that has done all three of these things and has not grown at a substantial rate.

According to Rodrik (2005) such recommendations are principles that countries should follow, but there is not a unique mapping from a determined set of policies that reach such economic principles. Policies and institutions are constrained by local formal and informal rules, and preferences. In addition, governments face political limitations, which makes relevant the definition of policies and reforms that have higher potential to promote sustained growth.

Unless the economy is facing an unstable macroeconomic crisis, it is not so trivial to identify which policy a country should undertake. It is clear that good macroeconomic policies, such as fiscal and monetary stability, make investors more confident and thereby help entrepreneurs to raise investment and productivity (see Bruno and Easterly [1998]). However, the experience of Brazil (and other Latin American countries), which made substantial progress in handling its macroeconomy in the 1990s, shows that macro stability is not enough to raise sustained productivity growth.

In a recent analysis of the Brazilian economy, Hausmann, Rodrik, and Velasco (2008) argue that "Brazil suffers from an inadequate business environment, high taxes, high prices for public services, low supply of infrastructure, insecure property rights and judicial enforcement, and inadequate education relative to some best-practice benchmark."[15] They hold that policy makers should make these problems priority areas for reform. "[A]ll these factors [tend to discourage] private investment by keeping private returns low." But they go on to say that "in spite of the sub-par atmosphere, private returns are very high and investment is constrained by the inability of the country to mobilize enough domestic and foreign savings to finance the existing investment demand at reasonable interest rates" (19).

Is that the case? Figure 4.7 shows that both Brazil's real interest rate (panel [a]) and the spread rate (panel [b]) have been decreasing in the last years in Brazil. Observe that in January 2003, the real interest rate in Brazil was about 19 percent and in January 2007, it decreased by half,

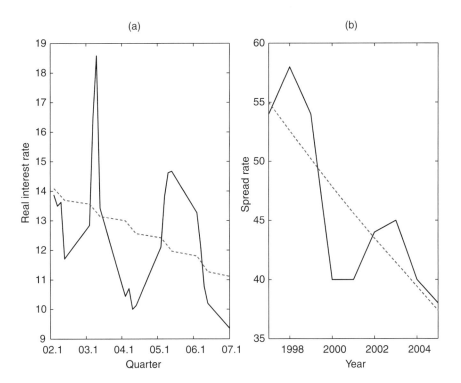

Figure 4.7   Realized and trended real interest rate and spread rate in Brazil

Source: International Financial Statistics

reaching 9 percent per year. A similar pattern is observed in the spread rate of the lending rate and the deposit rate.[16] However, despite the decrease in the real interest rate, spread rate, and country risk, investment in Brazil remained relatively stable in the last years around 20 percent (see figure 4.8).[17] Therefore, it does not seem that investment is constrained by the inability of the country to raise funds. We believe that Brazil now has a fair international credit record to mobilize foreign funds. We believe that investment is low in Brazil because part of it is not privately appropriated, due to high taxes, a swollen bureaucracy, and uncertainty.

Cavalcanti, Magalhães, and Tavares (2008) investigate the effect of improvements in institutions in Brazil's economic performance. They consider data from different institutions that indicate the regulatory costs of "doing private business," such as those related to bankruptcy law, start up costs, employment rigidity, and the expropriation of private investment. It can be observed that Brazil presents a lower level of institutional development than Chile, Taiwan, South Korea, and also Argentina. For instance, they show that the bankruptcy and collateral laws are much more effective in facilitating credit in Chile than in Brazil. As a result, the total private credit to output ratio is roughly two times higher in Chile than in Brazil. Brazil's low institutional development is also an important

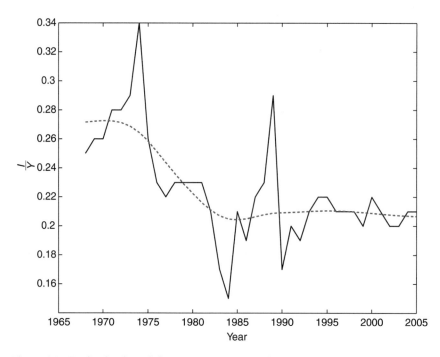

Figure 4.8 Realized and trended investment rate in Brazil

Source: International Financial Statistics

indicator that it can grow faster. The potential impacts of institutional reforms are quantitatively important.

It is important to highlight that the investment rates do not correlate strongly with growth rates. The investment rate is better in explaining differences in levels of growth than in growth rates (see Klenow and Rodríguez-Clare [2005]). Growth is more related to technical progress. Therefore, even if the investment rate does not increase, microeconomic reforms might still be able to increase Brazil's growth by increasing the intensity in the use of available factors of production and by increasing technical progress. Below we describe some of these reforms.

Government and Tax Reform

Although the investment rate has been at low and constant level over time in Brazil, government consumption as a share of GDP has had an opposite behavior. Figure 4.9 shows the behavior of government consumption over GDP in the last 40 years. Observe that it increased at a strong rate at the end of the 1980s.

Consequently the tax burden has also been increasing over time. Figure 4.10 shows that the increase of the tax burden is due mainly to the increase in revenue of "other taxes." They are mainly taxes on financial transactions (CPMF and IOF), and social security contributions, such

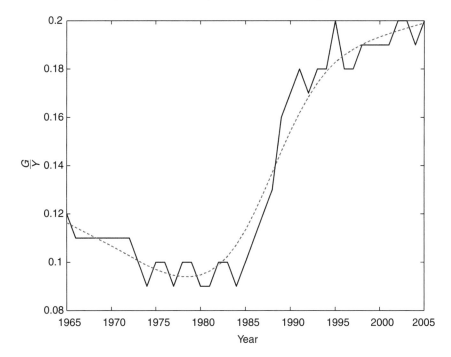

Figure 4.9 Government consumption over GDP

Source: International Financial Statistics

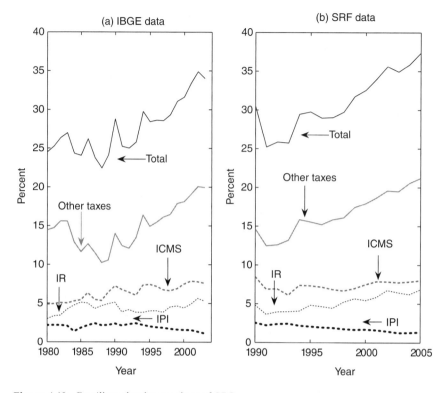

Figure 4.10 Brazil's tax burden as a share of GDP

Source: Instituto Brasileiro de Geografia e Estatística (IBGE) e Secretaria da Receita Federal

as PIS and COFINS. They were introduced to finance health care and federal government transfers.

Brazil's heavy tax burden is similar to that of some industrial countries.[18] High taxes and low enforcement generates informality. As a result, a large share of activities in Brazil is produced outside the realm of government regulation. Data from the World Bank show that the informal sector as a share of GDP is about 40 percent in Brazil, while in Chile it is roughly 20 percent. According to Capp, Estrodt, and Jones Jr. (2005), the informal sector in Brazil is one of the main barriers to increased productivity in the country (see also Elstrodt, Laboissière, and Pietracci [2007]). The reason is that companies gain cost advantages by operating in the informal sector. However, generally their productivity is lower than that of formal firms. Antunes and Cavalcanti (2007) provide a formal model that shows why informal entrepreneurs emphasize low-scale firms. They also provide simulation results that show that reforms that simplify bureaucratic procedures and decrease the tax burden might have a sizeable impact on productivity.

It is clear that, given Brazil's level of development, the country is an outlier in terms of government size, tax burden, and the size of the informal sector. A supply-side reform aimed at decreasing taxes and rationalize government spending is needed.[19] This is particularly important now, since both the ratio of total debt to GDP and interest rates are decreasing in the country. Therefore, a tax cut would make the government less tempted to increase current spending. A decrease in current government spending might also have positive effects on the provision of public infrastructure, of which Brazil is in need.

A related reform is the one of social security system. Brazil's social security system has undergone a series of reforms since the late 1990s. Despite all reforms, the social security deficit is still about 4 percent of GDP and is projected to increase over time (see Giambiagi and de Mello [2006]). Therefore, further reform is still needed to ensure the sustainability of this system over the long run.

Brazil's Recent Bankruptcy Reform

Brazil was in need of a reform in its bankruptcy system. The average time of insolvency proceedings is about twice of that in Chile (see World Bank [2005]), and total credit over GDP in Brazil is roughly half of what is observed in Chile (see World Bank [2006]). After roughly 10 years in the Congress[20] a new bankruptcy law was finally approved in December 2004. The old law gave first priority to workers, second to the tax authorities and third to creditors. The new legislation gives priority to creditors while limiting payments to workers. It also improved liquidation and reorganization procedures. It also provides the possibility of extrajudicial agreements (see Araujo and Funchal [2005]).

In a related article that investigates the impact of bankruptcy and judiciary reforms, Antunes, Cavalcanti, and Villamil (2008) show that the effects of such reforms on credit to output ratio and per capita output are sizeable for some Latin American economies. They show that financial market imperfections explain a significant part of the gap relative to the United States in per capita income for some Latin American countries (e.g., Brazil, Mexico, and Argentina) and transition economies (e.g., Russia and Poland). In particular, credit market imperfections account for roughly 64 percent of the difference in output per capita between the United States and Brazil.

Although Brazil's total credit over GDP is about 35 percent (a little lower with the new GDP methodology), it has been increasing in the last four years, and it has potential to increase further. However, it is not only the written law that is important. The judiciary is crucial to enforce the law. Therefore, it is essential to improve the efficiency of the judicial system to increase the effectiveness of the law. Studies have shown that the impact of such reforms on output per capita and total credit is sizeable.

Brazil's Labor Market Rigidity

One of the main supply-side factors that restrict the growth potentials of Brazil's economy is its labor market rigidity. According to data from "doing business" of the World Bank, the employment rigidity index (which combines the difficulties of hiring and firing in a given country) is higher in Brazil than the Latin American average.[21] The legislation protects workers in the formal sector of the economy. As a consequence, however, almost half of the labor force works in the informal sector[22] and such workers are predominantly guided by social objectives with adverse effects on economic efficiency.

Businessmen have pointed out that the current labor market legislation, which dates back from the 1950s and 1960s, is one of the main constraints for growth (e.g., CNI [2006]). The labor market rigidity increases the cost of operating in the formal sector, therefore decreasing productivity and firm size, as discussed previously. Such rigidity also has adverse effects on labor effort, since workers know that the costs of dismissing them are high. Workers also receive benefits in case of unjustified dismissals (e.g., through the Fundo de Garantia do Tempo de Serviço). In fact, if Brazil's goal is to raise the potential of economic growth it should make better use of its labor factor by deregulating it. See Cavalcanti, Magalhães, and Tavares (2008) for some quantitative estimates of labor market reforms on output and investment in Brazil.[23]

Human Capital Accumulation

There exists a large literature that shows that public education is favorable to growth because it increases the level of human capital and at the same time tends to produce a more equitable income distribution (e.g., Galor and Zeira [1993]). More egalitarian societies are also associated with fewer social conflicts and individuals have a lower tendency to report themselves happy when inequality is high (e.g., Alesina, DiTella, and MacCulloch [2004]). Then, why do some countries not adopt and implement a compulsory and efficient public educational system? Sokoloff and Engerman (2000) show how the "elite" of some countries protected their status quo by investing poorly in primary schooling and/or by erecting barriers to the right to vote and other privileges. It seems likely that education is related to social status, and therefore the elite might oppose the development of a strong public education system or any other reform that would threaten its political power.[24] This seems to be the case in Brazil.

Figure 4.11 shows the average years of schooling of the population aged 15 years and older for Brazil, Chile, Korea, and Taiwan. It is clear in this figure that compared to Chile, Korea, and Taiwan, Brazil's human capital accumulation was not government a priority from 1950 to 1980. Recall that this was a period of rapid industrialization and high growth rates. Since the 1990s, educational attainment has an upward trend in Brazil. However, the country still remains behind in education: The average number of years of schooling in Brazil is less than half of that observed in South Korea.

Brazil lags behind not only in the "quantity" of human capital, but according to the international evidence, the quality of education is also poor in the country (see figure 4.12). In the 2000 Program for International Student Assessment (PISA), which is the most comprehensive international

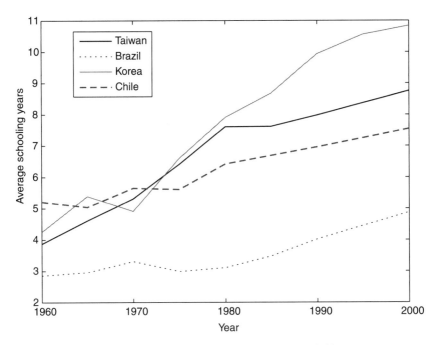

Figure 4.11 Average years of schooling of the population 15 years and older

Source: Barro and Lee (2000)

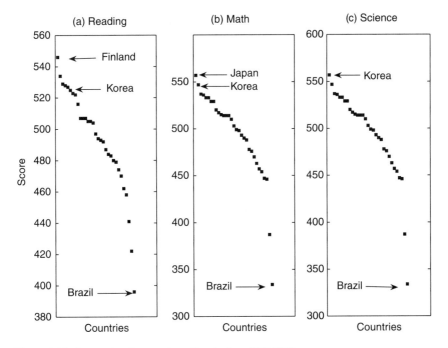

Figure 4.12 International comparison: Results from PISA 2000

Source: OECD (2000), data available at OECD website: www.oecd.org

assessment of educational outcomes to date, Brazil had the lowest score among 31 countries in all subjects: reading literacy, math literacy, and science literacy.

Using standard level accounting exercises, Pessôa (2006) shows that about two-third of the difference in income per capita between Brazil and Korea is explained by the educational gap of these two countries. Education explains about the same of the difference in output per capita between Brazil and Chile and Brazil and Taiwan. Although there were some recent improvements in human capital accumulation, Brazil surely needs to increase its effort to keep its population in school longer and to improve the quality of education. Again, the effects of such reforms on development might be sizeable.

Does Brazil Need an Industrial Policy?

One of the most intensive debates in development economics concerns the role of industrial policies to promote growth and development. By industrial policies we follow Pack and Saggi (2006) to define them as government "intervention or policy that alter the structure of production in favor of sectors that are expected to offer better prospects for economic growth." There are many arguments in favor of industrial policies, such as the creation and growth of infant industries, knowledge spillovers, and coordination failures without such policies.[25] It is not our role to discuss the details of each one here.[26] In economics we cannot use laboratory experiments to determine the impacts of different policies and institutions on economic development. We cannot, for instance, keep all "other" factors constant and adopt some industrial policy in one place and market-oriented policy in another to compare the growth results after some years.[27] Only in this way we would be able to evaluate the effectiveness of the two policies to promote growth and development.

Several developing countries have implemented industrial policies, such as subsidized loans, variable taxes, and differentiated tariffs to promote specific industrial sectors. However, countries and regions— Latin America and East Asia—had divergent development paths. The important question is: Was the difference in the path of development between East Asia and Latin America due to differences in the industrial policy? Or was it due to other policies?[28] It is important to highlight that economic fundamentals were sharply different in East Asia and Latin America. Besides their industrial policies, East Asian countries have a history of stable macroeconomic policies and fiscal discipline. They also invested heavily in education and in public infrastructure. In Brazil, macro stability occurred in mid-1990s, and the country remains behind in the provision of public infrastructure. Likewise, taxation is heavy, the bureaucracy is overly large, and the stock of human capital and the quality of education are both low. Therefore, it is hard to determine whether the industrialization policies in East Asian countries would have had long-run success in Brazil.[29]

Conclusion

The world in the last four years is growing at high rates and this has boosted commodity prices (such as iron ore and soya) and in Brazil's exports. In addition, international interest rates are at low levels and there is high liquidity in international financial markets. Despite this favorable situation, Brazil's growth during Lula's first term has been disappointing. Our counterfactual exercises suggest that if the world were growing at a rhythm similar to the one that prevailed during the Cardoso administration (first term, second term, or the eight-year period), then GDP growth during Lula's first term would have been lower than the period under Cardoso's administration.

Brazil went through important market-oriented economic reforms, but the postreform growth has been lackluster. This poor economic performance has raised the issue of whether Brazil should keep reforming its economy. In particular, our diagnosis shows that the country should remove the micro-level barriers that slowdown productivity growth. Brazil still presents a low level of human capital stock, a high level of expropriation of private investment, and unsecured property rights. However, Brazil's low level of institutional development is also an important indicative that it can grow faster. Studies have corroborated our view that the potential impacts of some institutional reforms on the country's development might be sizeable.

However, the impact of institutional change on development takes time (e.g., Fernandez and Rodrik [1991]). In fact, Méon, Sekkat, and Weill (2007) have shown that the full impacts of institutional reforms on productivity appear after approximately five to six years. Therefore, Lula's administration is benefiting from reforms taken in Cardoso's administration and might be constrained by the reforms not taken. In addition, there are always winners and losers from reforms. Consequently, those who fear losing their current benefits might erect barriers to institutional change.[30]

Reforms should be on the government agenda. Especially important are cutting taxes and government spending (e.g., through social security reform), and deregulating labor. Taxes should be cut in sectors with high tax evasion. This effort might combat informality and increase productivity at the same time. Another important reform would be to raise the efficiency of the judicial system in securing property rights and investment. Efforts to increase the stock of human capital and the quality of education are also crucial for Brazil's development. Given the lag between institutional change and its impact on development, Lula's administration might not benefit from these reforms. But the country surely will.

Notes

* The authors wish to acknowledge the financial support of the Conselho Nacional de Desenvolvimento Científico e Tecnológico (CNPq-Brazil). They also benefited enormously from conversations with Roberto A. Perrelli, who requested that he not be listed as a coauthor.

1. Elstrodt, Laboissière, and Pietracci, 2007:93.
2. Source: Maddison (2006) and Heston, Summers, and Aten (2006).
3. Based on World Bank (2006). It does not take into account the recent revision in the calculation of GDP in Brazil. With this revision GDP per capita annual growth between 2003 and 2006 increases by roughly 1 percentage point.
4. See Solimano and Soto (2006) and figure 1.
5. See Baer (2008) for a more detailed description of the Brazilian economy. The ISI period started in the 1930s in Getúlio Vargas' first presidential term. See Baer (2008) and Kohli (2004).
6. Some of these instruments were tariffs and nontariff barriers, such as the outright ban on the importation of similar goods (*lei do similar nacional*). Brazil's industrialization process also had a high participation of foreign capital.
7. Slow growth after reform is not unique to Brazil. For the New Zealand case, see, for instance, Evans, Grimes, Wilkinson, and Teece (1996).
8. Kohli, 2004:129.
9. Ferreira and Rossi (2003) provide evidence that trade liberalization strongly improved productivity. Their estimates suggest that the observed tariff reduction in the 1990s brought a 6 percent estimated increase in total factor productivity growth rate and a similar impact on labor productivity. Using Engel curves, de Carvalho-Filho and Chamon (2006) estimated that per capita household income in metropolitan areas from 1987 to 2002 increased by about 4.5 percent per year, which is much higher than the estimated GDP per capita growth rate.
10. According to Pritchett (2000), from 1960 to 1992 there were about 16 countries in the world that had growth rates in per capita GDP higher than 1.5 percent before a structural break (around the mid-1970s), but afterward growth fell to less than 1.5 percent, although it remained positive. Such behavior of per capita GDP is characterized by Pritchett (2000) as a plateau, and the classical example is Brazil.
11. See Kohli (2004) for a comparative study of the Brazilian and Korean industrialization process. For a study of South Korea and Taiwan see Rodrik (1995). Finally, De Gregorio and Lee (2003) provide a comparative study of Latin America and East Asia.
12. The correlation coefficient between the two series is -0.21 from 1950 to 1969 and 0.52 from 1970 to 2003.
13. See Eaton and Kortum (1999) and Klenow and Rodríguez-Clare (2005).
14. We added another lag but its coefficient was not statistically different from zero.
15. Hausmann, Rodrik, and Velasco (2008: 19). A similar diagnosis is found in Cavalcanti, Magalhães, and Tavares (2008).
16. Recently, country risk in Brazil reached its lowest historical level. Total debt over GDP has also been decreasing over time. Moreover, Brazil in the last four years has run a current account surplus that suggests that investment has not been constrained by the inability of the country to mobilize saving to finance investment.
17. The investment rate is about 22 percent in Chile, 30 percent in South Korea, 27 percent in Taiwan, and 20 percent in the United States.
18. According to the World Bank (2006) the tax burden in Chile is roughly 18 percent of GDP. In South Korea it is about 25 percent, a rate similar to that of the United States. Moreover, Baer and Galvão Jr. (forthcoming) give strong evidence that both the tax burden and government expenditures favor the higher income classes, which means that the country's fiscal system has a relatively low redistributional impact.

19. Given the high tax evasion in some sectors, a simple Laffer curve argument suggests that the government could cut taxes in such sectors without a necessary decrease in public revenues.
20. Although this reform was approved in Lula's first term, it also made important progress in Cardoso's second term. See the appendix of the working paper version of Araujo and Funchal (2005).
21. The cost of hiring in Brazil is about 26.8 percent of the worker's salary compared to 17 percent in Korea, and 3.4 percent in Chile. The cost of firing in the country is 165.3 percent in terms of a weekly wage. That number is 51.3 percent in Chile and 90 percent in Korea.
22. OECD (2006).
23. Evidence for New Zealand show that the unemployment rate decreased and productivity growth increased sharply after a labor market deregulation (Evans, Grimes, Wilkinson, and Teece [1996]).
24. Alexopoulos and Cavalcanti (2006) show that that one benefit for the elite is the specialization of skilled workers in high-paid jobs and the abundance of unskilled workers in the production of some cheap "home goods" in the market, such as painting and cleaning a house, babysitting, and/or cooking. They show that, depending on the level of inequality, the elite might oppose policies that improve the education system, even if there is no tax increases to finance such policies.
25. There are also criticisms of industrial policies. Some authors (e.g., Baldwin [1969]) claim that market failures that justify government interventions might be solved not by industrial policies (such as trade protection, differentiated taxes, or direct subsidies), but by correcting such market failures (e.g., policies to improve the functioning of the credit market).
26. See Pack and Saggi (2006) for details and references.
27. In the real world, however, there are various historical incidents that come close to the concept of a "natural experiment." Some examples are the divergent paths of North and South Korea, East and West Germany, and Hong Kong and mainland China.
28. One of the chief differences was that industrial policy in East Asia was export-oriented, while in Latin America it favored ISI policies.
29. See Canêdo-Pinheiro, Ferreira, Pessôa, and Schymura (2007) for an important discussion of industrial policies in Brazil.
30. See Parente and Prescott (2000).

References

Alesina, A., R. DiTella, and R. MacCulloch. 2004. "Inequality and Happiness: Are Europeans and Americans Different?" *Journal of Public Economics* 88:2009–2042.

Alexopoulos, J., and T.V. Cavalcanti. 2006. "Cheap Home Goods and Persistent Inequality." Working Paper, Universidade Federal de Pernambuco.

Antunes, A.R., and T. Cavalcanti. 2007. "Start Up Costs, Limited Enforcement, and the Hidden Economy." *European Economic Review* 51(1):203–224.

Antunes, A.R., T.V. Cavalcanti, and A.P. Villamil. 2008. "The Effect of Financial Repression & Enforcement on Entrepreneurship and Development." *Journal of Monetary Economics*. Forthcoming.

Araujo, A., and B. Funchal. 2005. "Past and Future of the Bankruptcy Law in Brazil and Latin America." *Economia* 6(1):146–216.

Baer, W. 2008. *The Brazilian Economy: Growth and Development*. Boulder, CO: Lynne Rienner Publishers.

Baer, W., and A.F. Galvão Jr. 2008. "Tax Burden, Government Expenditures and Income Distribution in Brazil." *Quarterly Review of Economics and Finance*. Forthcoming.

Baldwin, R.E. 1969. "The Case against Infant Industry Protection." *Journal of Political Economy* 77(3):295–305.

Barro, R.J., and J.-W. Lee. 2000. "International Data on Educational Attainment: Updates and Implications." CID Working Paper No. 42.

Bruno, M., and W. Easterly. 1998. "Inflation Crises and Long-Run Growth." *Journal of Monetary Economics.* 41(1):3–26.

Canêdo-Pinheiro, M., P.C. Ferreira, S.A. Pessôa, and L.G. Schymura. 2007. "Por Que o Brasil Não Precisa de Política Industrial." Working Paper, EPGE/FGV.

Capp, J., H.-P. Estrodt, and W.B. Jones Jr. 2005. "Reining in Brazil's Informal Economy." *The McKinsey Quarterly* 1:1–7.

Cavalcanti, T.V., A. Magalhães, and J. Tavares. 2008. "Institutions and Economic Development in Brazil." *Quarterly Review of Economics and Finance.* Forthcoming.

Confederação Nacional da Indústria (CNI). 2006. "Crescimento: A Visão da Indústria." Discussion Paper.

De Carvalho-Filho, I., and M. Chamon. 2006. "The Myth of Post-Reform Income Stagnation in Brazil." IMF Working Paper (WP/06/275).

De Gregorio, J., and J. Lee. 2003. "Growth and Adjustment in East Asia and Latin America." Central Bank of Chile Working Papers, 245.

Eaton, J., and S. Kortum. 1999. "International Technology Diffusion: Theory and Measurement." *International Economic Review* 40:537–570.

Elstrodt, H.-P., M.A. Laboissière, and B. Pietracci. 2007. "Five Priorities for Brazil's Economy." *The McKinsey Quarterly*, Special Edition: Shaping a New Agenda for Latin America.

Fernandez, R., and D. Rodrik. 1991. "Resistance to Reform: Status Quo Bias in the Presence of Individual-Specific Uncertainty." *American Economic Review* 81(5):1146–1155.

Ferreira, P.C., and J.L. Rossi. 2003. "New Evidence from Brazil on Trade Liberalization and Productivity Growth." *International Economic Review* 44(4):1383–1405.

Galor, O., and J. Zeira. 1993. "Income Distribution and Macroeconomics." *Review of Economic Studies* 60:35–52.

Giambiagi, F., and L. de Mello. 2006. "Social Security Reform in Brazil: Achievements and Remaining Challenges." OECD: Working Paper (ECO/WKP(2006) 62).

Hausmann, R., D. Rodrik, and A. Velasco. 2008. "Growth Diagnostics." In N. Serra and J. Stiglitz, eds. *The Washington Consensus Reconsidered: Towards a New Global Governance.* New York: Oxford University Press. Forthcoming.

Heston, A., R. Summers, and B. Aten. 2006. "Penn World Table Version 6.2." Center for International Comparisons of Production, Income and Prices at the University of Pennsylvania.

Klenow, P., and A. Rodríguez-Clare. 2005. "Externalities and Growth." In P. Aghion and S. Durlauf, eds. *Handbook of Economic Growth.* Vol. 1A. Amsterdam: North-Holland. pp. 817–861.

Kohli, A. 2004. *State-Directed Development: Political Power and Industrialization in the Global Periphery.* Cambridge, UK: Cambridge University Press.

Maddison, A. 2006. *The World Economy: Historical Statistics.* Paris: OECD Development Center.

Méon, P.G., K. Sekkat, and L. Weill. 2007. "Institutional Changes Now and Benefits Tomorrow: How Soon Is Possible?" Working Paper, Université Libre de Bruxelles.

OECD. 2006. OECD Economic Surveys-Brazil. OECD, Paris.

Pack, H., and K. Saggi. 2006. "Is There a Case for Industrial Policy? A Critical Survey." *The World Bank Research Observer* 21(2):267–297.

Parente, S.L., and E.C. Prescott. 2000. *Barriers to Riches.* Cambridge, MA: MIT Press.

Pessôa, S. 2006. "Prespectiva de Crescimento no Longo Prazo para o Brasil: Questões em Aberto." Ensaios Econômicos da EPGE, 609.

Pritchett, L. 2000. "Understanding Patterns of Economic Growth: Searching for Hills among Plateaus, Mountains, and Plains." *The World Bank Economic Review* 14(2):221–250.

Rodrik, D. 1995. "Getting Interventions Right: How South Korea and Taiwan Grew Rich?" *Economic Policy* 20:55–107.

———. 2005. "Growth Strategies." In P. Aghion, and S.N. Durlauf, eds. *Handbook of Economic Growth.* Vol. 1A. Elsevier: North-Holland. pp. 967–1014.

Sokoloff, K., and S. Engerman. 2000. "Institutions, Factor Endowments, and Paths of Development in the New World." *Journal of Economic Perspectives* 14(2):217–232.

Solimano, A., and R. Soto. 2006. "Economic Growth in Latin America in the Late Twentieth Century: Evidence and Interpretation." In A. Solimano, ed. *Vanishing Growth in Latin America: The Late Twentieth Century Experience.* Cheltenham, UK: Edward Elgar. pp. 11–45.

Summers, Lawrence. 2003. "Godkin Lectures." John F. Kennedy School of Government, Harvard University.

Velasco, A. 2005. "Why Doesn't Latin America Grow More, and What Can We Do About It?" Working Paper, Harvard Kennedy School of Government.

World Bank. 2005. *Doing Business in 2005: Removing Obstacles to Growth.* Washington DC: World Bank.

———. 2006. *World Development Indicators.* Washington DC: World Bank.

PART THREE

Specific Policy Issues

CHAPTER FIVE

Regulation during the Lula Government

BERNARDO MUELLER AND ANDRÉ ROSSI
DE OLIVEIRA

Introduction

More so than most other areas of economic activity, infrastructure sectors tend to exhibit large sunk investments, specific assets, economies of scale, and involve politically sensitive goods and service, often produced by foreign companies (Levy and Spiller 1996, Savedoff and Spiller 1999). These characteristics make the industries in these sectors particularly prone to governmental opportunism, so that investment will only materialize in an effective manner if investors can be convinced that there are reliable safeguards against governmental expropriation.

Mueller (2001a), written in the early days of regulation of infrastructure industries in Brazil, found an institutional environment that provided positive incentives for investment and growth in those sectors. Safeguards against opportunistic behavior by the government that were found in that study were 1) an independent judiciary that frequently ruled against the executive; 2) a credibility cost for the government that penalized undue interference by dissuading future investment, particularly in future privatization auctions (Mueller and Pereira 2002); 3) the coalitional nature of legislative-executive relations (Alston and Mueller 2006); 4) the governance built into the design of the regulatory agencies (Correa, Melo, Mueller, and Pereira 2006). This paper argued that these factors did provide significant safeguards to create an investment-friendly environment, but admitted they could possibly not be sufficient to resist a stronger shock, such as the election of a president with a hostile view toward the privatization process and the regulatory system that had been implemented (Mueller 2001a: 642). Two years later that hypothetical scenario actually became reality with the coming to power of the Lula government, which allows the opportunity to analyze how those safeguards fared once they were put to the test. That the shift in the presidency did in fact create a situation of uncertainty and tension, not only in the sphere of regulation and infrastructure, but in the economy more generally, was reflected by the sharp rise of the Brazil country risk and the exchange rate approximately five months before the election, when it started to become apparent that Lula would actually win.

The market's reaction reflected the fear that the policies that the new president would pursue, given the position expressed during more than 15 years as the main opposition voice in the country, would bring about abrupt and radical change both in terms of policy content, as well as form of governing. It is interesting, however, that immediately after the election, and even before effectively taking office, both the exchange rate and the country risk dropped precipitously, with the latter quickly reaching levels even lower than those that prevailed in the previous administration. This indicates that investors, for some reason, felt reassured that their fears were unfounded and that the new government would not in effect present as big a threat as had been expected. In part, this may have been due to the reassurance by the president-elect that there was no reason to fret, though any such declaration has little commitment value. More concrete was the quick announcement of the choice of Henrique Meirelles, a conservative banker with international experience and market-friendly credentials, as the head of the Central Bank. Important still, we argue, was the perception by investors that the complex set of safeguards mentioned above would both damp down the new government's motivation to act opportunistically as well as mitigate whatever inclination remained.

As it turns out, the new government did in fact take several actions, which will be detailed below, that were perceived by the market as an assault on regulatory autonomy and an undue change in the system that effectively reduced the role and power of the agencies. This situation, however, was not yet an equilibrium outcome, but rather the first impact of the Lula shock. A complete analysis must allow for the consequent reaction to these actions of the new government so as to see to what extent the institutional safeguards actually constrain opportunistic behavior. In this chapter we do just that by describing and analyzing first the content of regulatory policy in the Lula government (section titled Impact of Regulatory Changes in Infrastructure Sectors) and subsequently the process through which original policy goals got transformed as they met the constraints and restrictions imposed by political institutions (section titled Political Institutions, Policymaking Process and Regulation). It will be shown that in order to understand the policymaking process in the area of regulation, it is necessary to consider the broader policymaking process in the country, as many regulatory policy choices are motivated not by their direct impact on what gets regulated and how, but rather as a means to achieve other governmental objectives. In addition, we explore throughout this chapter the notion that despite the apparently sweeping changes in regulatory content and governance brought about by the Lula government, there prevailed strong elements of continuity.

Impact of Regulatory Changes in Infrastructure Sectors

Changes in the Regulatory Environment

In this section, we briefly describe the most relevant aspects of the reforms carried out by the two administrations of President Fernando Henrique Cardoso (1995–2002) in the telecommunications, electricity, and water and sewage sectors and discuss the main changes in their regulatory settings implemented by the Lula government during its first administration (2003–2006).[1]

Telecommunications

The reform of the Brazilian telecommunications sector started in 1995, when Congress brought to an end the state monopoly over telecommunications through Constitutional Amendment number 8. In 1997, the General Telecommunications Law was passed by Congress. It established the general principles governing the new structure of the telecommunications industry and created the sector's regulating agency, ANATEL, the National Telecommunications Agency. The following year, on the afternoon of July 29, 1998, the largest privatization Brazil has ever seen took place with the sale of the TELEBRÁS system through 12 separate auctions. As a result of the sale, three new local and regional long-distance companies and one national and international long-distance company were formed. Following the model of competition envisaged for the sector, which called for regional duopolies, the government issued authorizations for one entrant to compete with the incumbent (the old TELEBRÁS subsidiary, now a private company) in each one of the regions the country was divided into. The entrants, called "mirror" companies, were not subject to many of the obligations of the concessionaires, such as universal service and regulation by price cap.

There were no major changes in the regulatory rules for the telecommunications sector during the first Lula administration. This could be attributed to the fact that the backbone of the regulatory model instituted by the Cardoso government was written into law. The existence of a General Telecommunications Law configured a barrier to sweeping changes in the regulatory environment.

In fact, the existing model was in a sense sanctioned by the Lula government when in January 2006 the initial contracts signed by the wireline concessionaires (at the time of privatization) were replaced by new contracts, as required by law. The new contracts maintained the pricing system, based on a hybrid price cap scheme, with a few improvements, and did not bring about any major changes in the regulatory model.

Even though no major changes in the regulatory environment were registered during the first Lula administration, its impact on the telecommunications sector is not insignificant. Since the last president of ANATEL to be appointed by President Fernando Henrique Cardoso resigned in 2004, another incident we will discuss later, this regulatory agency has had three different presidents. Moreover, its board of directors (councilors) has been gradually neglected, with the government recurrently delaying the appointment of new directors.

Electricity

The approval, by the Brazilian National Congress, of Law 8.987, on February13, 1995, represented a fundamental legal landmark that became instrumental for the implementation of the new model of the Brazilian electricity sector. The model encompassed the creation of a regulatory agency, ANEEL, a system operator, ONS (National Electric System Operator), and a wholesale market, MAE (Wholesale Energy Market), where the sale and purchase of electric energy would take place. Competition in generation was considered feasible only with a substantial presence of the private sector in the distribution segment, and the privatization of distribution companies ensued. The first company privatized was ESCELSA, in 1995, a federal distribution company located in Espírito Santo, a state in the southeast region of Brazil. The privatization of generating companies, however, did not start until 1998.

The privatization process in the electricity sector was incomplete. Most of the big hydroelectric plants remained in the hands of generating companies whose main shareholder is the federal government. Some vertically integrated companies owned by state governments were not privatized either. Moreover, the predicted unbundling of generation, transmission, distribution, and commercialization activities was not entirely achieved. Some companies owned by the federal and the state governments kept their assets in those different lines of business.

Prompted in part by the shortcomings of the model and its implementation, like the dysfunctional wholesale market and the energy supply crisis of 2000, and in part by its own view of the role of the state in the electricity sector, upon taking office, President Lula determined that studies should be undertaken to revamp the electricity sector's regulatory framework. This process resulted in the publication of provisional measures[2] No 144 (December 10, 2003), which regulates the commercialization of electricity, and No 145 (December 10, 2003), which authorized the creation of the Energy Research Company (Empresa de Pesquisa Energética in Portuguese).

The main thrust of the new regulatory model established by the Lula administration is the requirement that purchases and sales of electricity be carried out through "least price" auctions. In addition, the electricity demanded and supplied by distribution companies is now traded through a pool, the idea being to reap economies of scale, to share the risks and benefits of energy contracts, and to equalize prices. Another feature of the new model is that electricity from new power plants (used to satisfy increasing demand) is now contracted separately from that of existing plants.

The Lula government replaced a model where there was supposed to be a bilateral market for electricity with a system with a central purchasing agency. Given the high level of sophistication of the Brazilian economy in general and of its electricity sector in particular, this move can be considered a step backward, but one must not forget that the model put in place by the Cardoso administration never delivered the goods it promised. In the light of the energy crisis of 2000–2001 and the high tariffs that ensued, the decision to switch to a model that tries to keep tariffs down is not unreasonable.

The new model has produced mixed results. The government is quick to point to the outcome of the two auctions that took place in 2006, where more than 70 percent of the energy contracted came from new power plants financed by private capital, as proof of its success. The critics, however, point out that the cost of such accomplishment was 35 percent higher tariffs, on average, than those of previous auctions, when energy from "old" power plants was sold, mainly by state-owned companies. Moreover, they recall that investment in capacity is still below that needed to keep pace with economic growth.

Water and Sewage

The institution of the National Sanitation Plan (Planasa) in 1971 is a milestone in the Brazilian water and sewage (W and S) sector. The plan laid out investment schedules for the sector, as well as tariff, credit, and other sector policies. It also promoted the creation of state water and sanitation companies (CESBs). Coverage of water provision in urban areas in Brazil augmented from 60 percent in 1970 to 86 percent in 1990 under Planasa, while coverage of sewage collection increased from 22 percent to 48 percent during the same period (Seroa da Motta 2004). The Planasa system was made obsolete by the Brazilian Constitution of 1988, conspicuously pro-decentralization, and was subsequently abandoned. After its collapse, no consistent set of policies for the water and sanitation sector was put in place to fill the void.

In an attempt to restructure the sector, in 2001 the Cardoso government submitted a bill to Congress, known as PL 4.147, which gave sanitation companies administrative and financial autonomy, established pricing principles and concession criteria. Moreover, it established the state as the authority with the power to grant concessions in metropolitan areas, instead of the counties. The bill ran into the opposition of many stakeholders. The counties were against it mainly because of its provision that states were to have the power to grant concessions in metropolitan areas. There was also resistance to the project coming from segments reluctant to accept its directives regarding privatization, universal service, and other issues.

One of the major concerns of the government of President Luiz Inácio Lula da Silva was to restructure and restore investments in the sanitation sector. A draft bill was submitted to Congress proposing that the concession power should be assigned to counties when the service was of local interest and that pricing as well as concession procedures should be regulated by autonomous authorities.

The bill was eventually approved by Congress and was signed into law on January 5, 2007. It establishes criteria for counties and states to access federal financing and determines the constitution of councils with the participation of the civil society. The bill does not clearly define powers of concession, a matter that apparently will have to be decided by the country's highest court.

It stands to reason that the new bill will change the face of the Brazilian water and sanitation sector, which still reflects the guidelines set by Planasa in 1971. But the lack of significant initiatives in W and S during the first Lula administration has only increased the need for massive investments in water and sewage systems to bring access and affordability indicators close to satisfactory levels.

Constraints on Regulatory Agencies

The central government has imposed two types of constraints on regulatory agencies during the first Lula administration: governance and budget constraints. Governance constraints are the result of delays in appointing higher-up officials, whereas budget constraints come from the practice of holding back agencies' budget entitlements. We will discuss budget constraints in the section dealing with political institutions, policymaking process, and regulation.

The governance constraint has tightened considerably since the beginning of the Lula government in 2003, as figure 5.1 illustrates.

In 2003, a seat in the board of directors of a regulatory agency was vacant an average of 29 days, a number already much higher than the

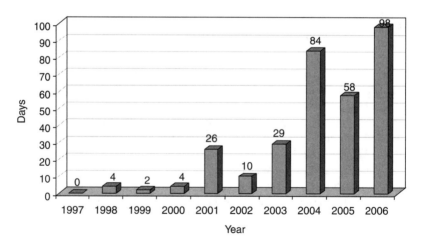

Figure 5.1   Average length of vacancy in board of directors

Note: Calculated as the average number of days a seat was vacant in any of the infrastructure regulatory agencies

Source: Brazilian Association of Infrastructure and Base Industries (Abdib)

average of the period 1997–2002. It skyrocketed to 84 in 2004, and after a recess in 2004 reached the peak of 98 days in 2006. The situation is worse in the transportation agencies. At ANTAQ, the average number of days a seat is vacant is 81 per year, whereas at ANTT it reaches 71 per year.

This situation lowers considerably the quality of the work done by the agencies, as each director becomes overwhelmed and the board, when it has enough members to convene, frequently postpones decisions and/or doesn't give each matter due consideration.

Effect on Investments and Growth by Sector

In this section, we evaluate if the changes in the regulatory environment put into effect by the Lula government have produced any sizeable side effects on investment levels and output growth in infrastructure sectors. We start with a look at private investment (see figure 5.2).

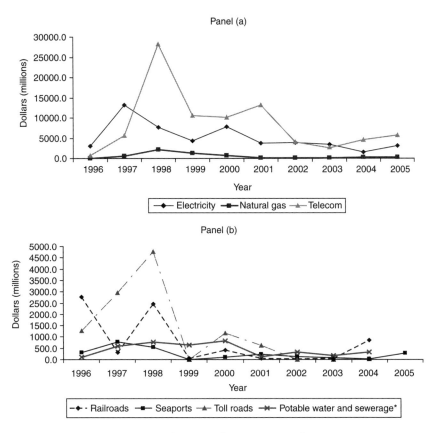

Figure 5.2   Private investment in infrastructure by sector (US$ millions)

Note: *Potable water and sewerage is a separate series provided by PPI and does not necessarily equal the sum of Potable Water and Sewerage series

Source: Private Participation in Infrastructure (PPI) Project Database, World Bank

Notice that, for all sub-sectors, investment levels (in US$) during the first Lula government (2003–2005) are well below their highs of the late 1990s. The same pattern emerges in aggregate investment in infrastructure, not displayed here. There is a boom in investment in the late 1990s and much smaller investment levels from 2003 to 2005.

However, one should not rush to the conclusion that the regulatory policies put in place by the Lula administration have resulted in a considerable drop in private investment in infrastructure sectors. The late 1990s were the period when most of the privatizations of the Fernando Henrique Cardoso era took place. The first Lula administration, true to its long-established stance against the sale of publicly owned companies to the private sector, did not any carry out any significant privatizations.

In the figure 5.3, we present the evolution of aggregate private investment in infrastructure as a percentage of GDP during the last three years of the Cardoso administration and the first three years of the Lula administration. This provides a better comparison of the two periods than do dollar figures. There is a clear decline in private investment in the 2003–2005 period when compared to the 2000–2002 period, but the beginning of the decline seems to have been in 2002, still during the Cardoso administration. At any rate, the average investment rate during the last three years of the Cardoso administration was 2.91 percent, compared to only 1.26 percent during the first three years of the Lula administration.

There is no question that during the first three years of the Lula government (2003–2005) the participation of private investment in Brazilian infrastructure sectors as a share of worldwide private investment in infrastructure was considerably below what it had been in the previous

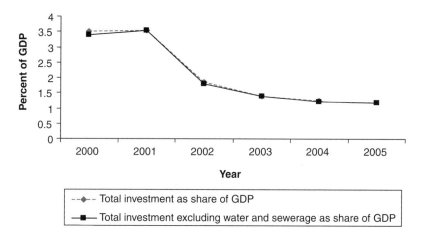

Figure 5.3   Private investment in infrastructure as percentage of GDP

Source: Private Participation in Infrastructure (PPI) Project Database, World Bank; Banco Central do Brasil—DEPEC

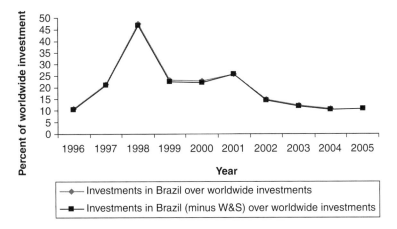

Figure 5.4   Investments in Brazil as a percentage of worldwide private investments in infrastructure

Source: Private Participation in Infrastructure (PPI) Project Database, World Bank

years (see figure 5.4). But again, this phenomenon seems to have started in 2002, the last year of the Cardoso administration.

The analysis carried out so far seems to indicate that, by many different measures, private investment in Brazilian infrastructure sectors during the first three years of the Lula administration was well below its average of the past 10 years. There is also evidence, however, that this declining trend started shortly before Lula came to power. It is not possible to determine the causes based on the data we have.

Another qualification to the results presented above is that we did not investigate whether there was a relative increase in public investment in infrastructure sectors during the first Lula administration. Even though that is an important issue—for increased public investment might have compensated for the decline in private investment—we do not address it here for two reasons. First, changes in regulatory policies have a direct impact on private investment and not necessarily on public investment. The government can dole out treasury money or require publicly owned companies to invest, even when the regulatory environment deteriorates, from the private sector's perspective. Second, the public sector in Brazil has been under pressure for quite some time to generate fiscal surpluses, which has limited its ability to invest, and this scenario is not likely to change much in the near future.

Let's now investigate how some of the infrastructure sectors in Brazil have performed in terms of output growth. Table 5.1 provides some interesting numbers.

Notice that there is a sharp decline in economic activity in the communications[3] sector in 2003, and it has not recovered since (up to 2006). In the public utilities sector,[4] output growth was not as high in the period 2003–2006 as it was in the mid-1990s, but it seems to be in

Table 5.1 Annual variation of GDP in real terms, per sector

	Communications (%)	Public utilities (%)	Transportation (%)
1994	13.87	4.19	4.06
1995	22.92	7.63	6.63
1996	10.85	6.00	2.58
1997	5.02	5.90	3.93
1998	8.31	5.19	−3.64
1999	12.12	1.36	−1.57
2000	15.60	4.23	3.07
2001	10.49	−5.63	1.69
2002	9.81	3.04	3.40
2003	1.81	2.68	1.44
2004	−1.36	4.61	4.93
2005	0.15	3.65	3.19
2006	−0.86	3.32	2.15

Source: Ipeadata

Table 5.2 Foreign investment in infrastructure as percentage of GDP

	2001	2002	2003	2004	2005
Electricity, gas and hot water	0.28	0.33	0.13	0.20	0.20
Post and telecommunications	0.81	0.91	0.55	0.49	0.24
Water and sewerage	0.01	0.02	0.01	0.00	0.00
Transportation	0.01	0.01	0.02	0.03	0.01

Source: Ipeadata

line with last decade's average. As for the transportation sector, average growth in the first Lula administration doesn't seem to have diverged from the previous average. Table 5.1 helps us visualize the evolution of these indicators.

A final measure of performance of infrastructure sectors we look at is foreign investment. Table 5.2 brings numbers on foreign investment in infrastructure sectors as a percentage of GDP from 2001 to 2005.

Starting in 2003, there is a noticeable decline in foreign investment in all infrastructure sectors except transportation. Once again, telecommunications took the hardest hit. When compared to 2002, foreign investment in telecommunications in 2005 dropped approximately 74 percent. The picture drawn by the data given in table 5.2 is one of shortage of foreign investment in infrastructure during the first Lula administration.

The abundance of evidence we provide above does not entail the conclusion that the regulatory policy put into practice by the first Lula administration has had a detrimental effect on investment in and growth of infrastructure sectors in Brazil. Nevertheless, it certainly is a strong indication that that policy, perhaps by design, has neither been able to attract the much-needed private (domestic or foreign) investment, nor to foster growth in infrastructure sectors.

Political Institutions, Policymaking Process, and Regulation

Introduction

In this section we analyze how political institutions and safeguards reacted to the attempts by the Lula government to change both regulatory policy and regulatory governance. The first step in order to do so is to make the point that the new government did in fact seek to change many aspects of regulatory policy, often through means that required changing the rules of the game. The second step is to pursue those cases beyond their initial impact to see how they played out in the end, once the institutional safeguards were allowed to react. Finally we broaden the scope of analysis to show how the government's regulatory policy choices are nested within the more general policymaking process. This provides insights into the more basic determinants of the government's motivations regarding regulatory policy.

Governmental Attempts to Change Regulatory Policy

Three related events in the telecommunication sector will be detailed to show the new government's approach to the regulatory system already in its first years in office. The purpose is to show that the government's attitude did in fact represent a desire to effect a sharp change in the role and power of regulatory agencies. The first case involves the government's attempt to lessen the increase in telephone rates that ANATEL authorized in June of 2003, in accordance with the concession contracts and the General Telecommunications Law (1996), which stipulated the use of the IGP-DI, calculated by the Fundação Getúlio Vargas, as the price index in the price-caps mechanism.[5] The average increase for fixed line telephones was 28.75 percent. The government took issue with the size of the increase, aware of the impact of public service tariffs on inflation, a sensitive issue for an incoming president seeking to dispel distrust over his capacity to manage the economy. Fluctuations in the exchange rate in the previous months had caused the IGP-DI index used in the concession contracts to be significantly higher than the IPCA[6] index calculated by the government's census bureau and used for most other purposes; 30.5 percent versus 17 percent. This divergence created a perception that the telephone companies were making windfall profits at the expense of consumers and prompted pressure for a tariff reduction through a change of index. This cause was taken up by the Ministry of Communications, which first tried to negotiate tariff reductions with the companies and then to pressure ANATEL. However, all of the councilors had been appointed by the previous president and the agency maintained the rate increase as stipulated in the concession contracts. In response, the minister publicly called out for civil society to fight against the rate increases by taking the case to the courts in what constituted an odd way to air disagreement among governmental entities. Over 30 cases were filed in state and federal courts across the country, including cases brought by consumer protection agencies and public civil suits by the public prosecutors in the *Ministério Público*.[7] The first of these cases to have an impact had been filed by the *Ministério Público* in the Federal Court in Fortaleza, with the judge deciding that ANATEL and the telephone companies should immediately change rates to reflect the government-calculated index, IPCA, rather than the nonofficial index, IGP-DI, subject to a daily fine of R$50,000 in case of disobedience. Several other cases in different courts followed suit with similar decisions. Given the national scope of the issue, the Superior Justice Tribunal ruled, two months later, that the various cases be unified into a single case that was assigned to a federal court in the Federal District. In January of 2004, the telephone companies that were the defendants in the case opened a suit in the Superior Justice Tribunal requesting the suspension of the decision that imposed the IPCA. At this point it was starting to become clear that due to the appreciation of the Real, the IPCA would tend to be higher than the IGP-DI. The court struck down the previous decisions imposing the IPCA and sustained ANATEL's decision to use the IGP-DI as stipulated in the concession contracts. The companies, however, were not allowed to recoup the difference for the period in which tariffs had been depressed.

The second case of government interference took place in January 2004 shortly after the court had ruled in favor of the telephone companies by sustaining ANATEL's tariff calculations. The president of ANATEL, Luis Schymura, originally appointed in the Cardoso presidency, was forced out of office and a new councilor, with strong ties to the telecommunication worker's union, and consequently the Worker's Party (PT), put in his place. The court eventually decided that the law did not allow the president, who appoints the councilors subject to Senate approval, to remove them as well. This aspect of the agencies' governance was specifically designed to provide autonomy against governmental opportunism, a feature common in regulatory agencies throughout the world. It was this lack of direct control that had led President Lula, in the height of the price index imbroglio, to state that the regulatory agencies had outsourced (*terceirizado*) the government. Arguably, the most the president could do was to remove Schymura from the presidency of the five-men council, but not to remove him from the council. However, although no formal mechanism exited to fire Schymura, the government had several means of pressuring him to quit by making his permanence in office unbearable. This event denounced an attempt by the government to play a more direct role in the decision-making process formally held by the agencies and raised serious concerns in the market regarding the agencies supposed independence.

The third related event involves the attempt by the Lula government to change the entire set of rules underlying the regulatory system. Already in March of 2003, just three months into his mandate, the president established a work group charged with drafting a proposal to "perfect the institutional model of regulatory agencies," (Brasil, Presidência da República, Casa Civil 2003). This led to the presentation of two law proposals in early 2004, which were put up for public consultation. Whereas the proposals did retain the overall model of regulatory agencies, there were several details that raised much concern. The first proposal focused on the extent of the agencies' jurisdiction and the second on issues of organization, governance, and social control.[8] Perhaps the most controversial proposed change was the transfer from the agencies to the ministries of the concession power, that is, the granting of the right to exploit public services. Ideally this should be a technical decision taken through objective criteria such as an auction. Although the proposal does establish constraints for how the concessions are to be granted, it is reasonable to presume that there are more incentives for political motivations when the power rests with a ministry than when it does with an agency. The proposals are emphatic that the locus of planning and decisions on concessions belong to the executive and its ministries.[9]

A second controversial change in the proposals was the creation of a management contract (*contrato de gestão*) that would establish goals for the agencies and punishment for when those goals are not met. The alleged intention of this device is to "make the agencies' polices compatible with the government's programs," which in principle can be a legitimate concern. The fear, however, is that the contract can be used as an instrument to impose the government's will on to the agency as the punishments may conceivably involve things such as firing councilors and budget reductions.

At this point we can step back and summarize the three cases described above to visualize what the perception might have been in early 2004 for investors, consumers, and other stakeholders in regulated sectors. After little more than a year in office the government: 1) forcibly ousted the president of ANATEL using informal and nonofficial methods; 2) tried to overrule the agency's upholding of the concession contracts and publicly prompted the public to challenge the agency's decisions; and 3) proposed a new law for regulatory agencies that contained the potential of severely reducing their autonomy and capacity to resist pressure from the executive. In other regulated sectors, similar if not so dramatic events also took place. It is easy to see that the events in the new government's early mandate could be construed as an alarming direct assault on the extant regulatory framework. Clearly, they reveal much about the government's intent and motivation. However, the mere fact that these events took place are not the entire story and do not warrant the conclusion that the regulatory framework had been subverted and that regulatory risk would have risen and stifled confidence and investment in those sectors. To tell the whole story, it is necessary to analyze second and third round effect, that is, how institutional constraints reacted to the government's offensive and how the government reacted to those constraints.

Institutional Constraints and Safeguards

The question that needs to be asked is not whether the government attempted to change regulatory policy and whether the changes and the means in which they were pursued were legitimate or not, but whether those actions impacted investor and consumer confidence in the system sufficiently to reduce social welfare. It is clear that the government's actions had the potential of increasing uncertainty and regulatory risk; however, it is not a sufficient condition. If a strong set of institutional constraints on governmental opportunism were firmly in place, then investors and other stakeholders would feel less at risk and would be less inclined to let those events change their economic decisions. Of course, in an equilibrium situation the government would perceive those constraints and would not even indulge in the opportunistic behavior in the first place. But given the nature of the historical moment we are dealing with, it is reasonable to assume that this was a period of change and learning in which the institutional constraints were being tested. None of the players had sufficient information to predict what outcomes would emerge from the tension between the government's actions and the institutional constraints, as these had never before clashed with such force. The purpose of this subsection is thus to analyze the development of the cases described above in their second and third round effects. In order to put this analysis in perspective, we will explore a simple spatial model that can be used to understand the issues involved in each of the three cases. This model will first be used to address the issue of choice of councilors for the regulatory agencies by the government. It will then be used to address the issue of governmental interference with regulatory policy, such as in the case of the choice of price-caps index. Finally, the model will be used to address the issue of the interference in the design of agency governance.

Figure 5.5 portrays the strategic choice that a president has to make when deciding who to appoint as a councilor in a regulatory agency.[10] The horizontal line represents the position of each of the players along a single policy dimension that can be thought of as left versus right, pro-consumer versus pro-industry, and so on. Point P shows the preferred point of the president, which is determined by both ideology and political incentives. He/she must choose a councilor for a regulatory agency according to where that councilor's preference lies on the dimension. The downward sloping lines that emanate from P show the president's utility, which declines the further the preference of the chosen councilor is from his/her own. Point T is the technical choice point. If the president were to choose a councilor with that profile, the market would consider it a purely technical, that is, nonpolitical, choice, and the president would face no credibility cost from that choice. Credibility costs are any costs that arise from market fears regarding uncertainty, regulatory risk, and government opportunism. They can manifest themselves as lower levels or quality of investment, higher required risk premiums, lower receipts in

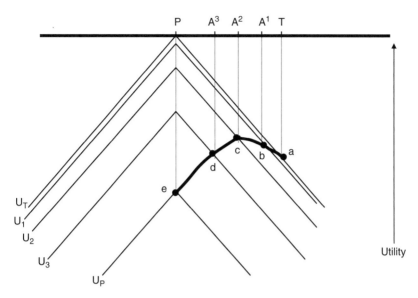

Figure 5.5   Strategic choice of agency councilors
Source: Authors' illustration

future privatizations, higher perceived country risk rankings, and the like. These costs are captured in the figure through a downward shift in the president's utility curve. If instead of choosing a "technical" councilor the president were to choose one with a profile at point $A1$, then the original utility curve (which is associated with point T) would drop to the second set of utility curves. The move from T to $A1$ has two effects on the president's utility. First, there is a marginal benefit from having a councilor slightly more in tune with his/her own preferences. Additionally there is a drop in utility associated with the credibility cost. Because $A1$ is relatively close to T, that cost is still small, so that, as drawn in figure 5.5, the net marginal effect is positive (b is higher vertically than a). The president will thus want to consider the effect of a further move from $A1$ to $A2$, which again entails marginal benefits and marginal costs of the same nature. As long as the net marginal benefit is positive, the president will continue to move his/her potential choice closer to his/her own preference. The optimal point is $A2$ as any subsequent move to the left yields a lower utility. More generally, the final outcome will depend crucially on the size and nature of the credibility cost.

What this model highlights is the trade-off between control and credibility cost. This is precisely the central issue of this chapter. The new Lula government has distinct preferences for the regulatory sector and acted forcefully on those preferences as soon as it came to power. This suggest that at that point in time, the government perceived low credibility costs. If one analyzes the government's subsequent behavior in relation to councilor choice, however, there is little evidence that the choice of pursuing greater control of regulatory policy at the expense of credibility actually became the norm. The government faced much criticism for the events regarding the forced exit of the ANATEL president in early 2004 and subsequently reverted to a relationship with agency councils well within the legitimate rules of the game. For ANATEL two councilors very close to the telecommunications worker's union (FITEL) were appointed during Lula's first term, which in the graph would be a choice close to *P* and thus associated with higher credibility costs. In the second term, however, the government actually chose not to immediately appoint new names to the seats that became vacant, which was many times interpreted as a strategy to weaken the power of the agencies.[11] This seems unlikely, as a better way to weaken the agencies would be to place loyal people in those seats so as to gain greater control of the agencies. More likely, we argue, the president in his second term opted for a more hands-off approach toward the agency, now fully recognizing the credibility cost, and also recognizing an additional benefit and an additional cost that had not been fully appreciated with regard to the choice of regulatory agency councilors. The cost is that the appointment of people based on their preferences compatibility but ignoring their technical capability and the compatibility of their preferences with the proper functioning of the sector may lead to losses through inefficient regulation.[12] The previously unrecognized benefit is the use of the agency positions as patronage with which to purchase support within Congress. Alston and Mueller (2006) argue that the exchange of "pork" for policy between the executive and Congress in Brazil is a key feature of the policymaking process in Brazil, with gains to both sides from participation. The consideration of a name for a vacant ANATEL seat in early 2007, closely associated to the fixed-line companies and to the PMDB party, thus on quite the opposite side of the spectrum from the two union-based councilors, is one of the first indications of the use of agency seats in the regular trade of government jobs for support. This took place as President Lula was reforming his cabinet for the second term to assure a strong and stable majority to pursue the reform agenda. Our conclusion from all this is that the forceful intervention in the agencies through the councilor appointment process that was observed in the first term soon gave way to a more considered attitude. This stance was more in line with the existence of credibility costs and other consequences that were perhaps not fully appreciated by the government earlier.

The attempt by the government to change the index in the price-cap contracts for telephone concessions can also be analyzed through a spatial model that highlights the strategic choice of action by the government. Figure 5.6 shows a single dimension that in this case represents the final price of telephone services after the price revision by ANATEL in 2003. The preferences of the players show that the firms prefer a monopoly price, the Supreme Court (*SC*) prefers the concessions contracts be upheld and the price be set at x_0, and the executive (*Ex*) prefers a lower price.

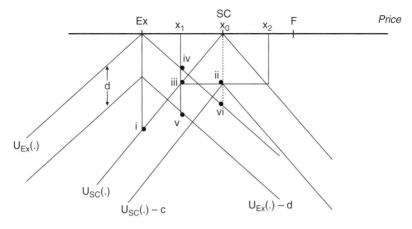

Figure 5.6   The judiciary as a safeguard

Source: Authors' illustration

The status quo is x_0 as until that point, the concession contracts had been respected. Once again utility is measured downward up, with the highest level at the price line. If the executive were to impose the use of the IPCA instead of the IGP-DI, his utility would have risen from the level in *iv* to his preferred point at *Ex*. But given the existence of an independent judiciary, this would not be an equilibrium, as the Supreme Court would simply strike down the change in index and reinstitute the rules from the concession contracts. The Supreme Court would want to do this, as it would raise its utility from *i* back to its preferred point at *SC*.

A more realistic analysis would want to consider that both actions by the executive as well as those by the Supreme Court are not costless. The SC would face political confrontation costs for overturning action initiated by the executive and probably very popular with the population. The executive would face credibility costs from overturning the concession contracts and changing the rules of the game. Once we consider these costs, very different equilibria become possible. Consider first the introduction of costs faced by the Supreme Court. The executive could now act strategically and set the new price not as far out as *Ex*, but at point x_1 where the Supreme Court would be indifferent between letting things stand and receiving utility at the level of *iii*, or reversing the executive's action and bringing the price back to x_0. This would entail the cost represented by the fall in the SC's utility curve, which leads to point *ii* and a utility equal to that at *iii*. The presence of costs of action for the Supreme Court allows the executive a greater scope of control over the sector. This can change once we introduce the credibility costs for the government, represented by a drop in its utility curve once it interferes. As drawn in figure 5.6 this would represent a fall from point *iv* to point *v* from having the price at x_1. As this is lower than the executive's utility from simply not interfering (utility at *vi*), the equilibrium would be no interference and letting x_0 prevail.

Clearly, different levels of both types of costs in the previous discussion would lead to different outcomes. The point here is to focus on the strategic interaction between the executive and the judiciary as a safeguard against opportunistic behavior within the rules established by the current regulatory institutions. The executive demonstrated a clear predisposition for breaking the concession contracts and changing the index used for yearly price revision but in the ended opted for not taking direct action. All this is consistent with the equilibrium described above, and the fact that the judicial system did in the end uphold the concession contracts. The executive did this even when lower courts had ruled in favor of a change in the index, and despite the pressure from the executive, much of Congress, and the public at large, which disliked the higher tariff charges. Thus, whereas this whole affair initially seemed to be a disquieting warning that would frighten off investors, the final resolution was quite the opposite. It offers evidence that there are powerful safeguards to uphold contracts and enforce the rules even in the face of stiff opposition.

Finally, we use figure 5.7 to analyze the Lula government's attempt to change the rules of the regulatory sector introducing a greater level of control over the agencies. As in figure 5.6, the single dimension represents a given policy issue, and P and A represent the preferred positions of the president and the agency, respectively.[13] Suppose that the agency is initially pursuing policy at A. The president can pull the policy closer to P by changing the rules of the regulatory system, formally or informally. This is represented by the function D. In order to achieve his preferred policy at P, the level of interference will have to be large, D^P in figure 5.7. However, associated with this interference is a credibility cost ($\Omega(D)$) that

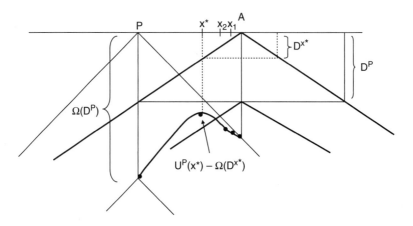

Figure 5.7 Strategic choice of agency structure and process

Source: Authors' illustration

is a positive function of D. This interference increases the cost to the agency of altering the policy so that the executive can tailor the initial policy to a point where the agency will not want to change it. In the case of D^P the president can set the initial policy at P and the agency will be indifferent between leaving it there and reverting to A, given the drop in its utility curve. Note however that, as drawn in figure 5.7 the executive would end up worse off from such a large intervention, as the size of $\Omega(D)$ would outweigh the gain from moving policy from A to P. The locus of net utilities associated with policy at different points between A and P shows that for that configuration of costs the equilibrium would be at point $x^\star$, associated with the level of intervention $D^{x\star}$.

When we use this model to analyze the Lula government's attempts to pass a new law for regulatory agencies, the first impression is that, if the model is correct, the size of the credibility cost ($\Omega(D)$) must have been small given that the chosen level of intervention was considerably large.[14] However, once we look at subsequent events and consider that the initial proposal was but the first step in the decision of how much intervention to effectively pursue, a different conclusion emerges. The initial stringent proposal was largely an attempt to gauge the reaction of economic groups and society in general to what the government wanted to do. The proposal was discussed in various forums including Congress. Subsequent versions of the proposal were watered down in many of the more controversial points. Eventually, the proposal got sidelined and remains to this day buried in Congress, possibly never to see the light again. Its ostracism was initially due to the problems the government faced in Congress with a cash-for-votes scandal called the *Mensalão* (big monthly payoff); however, the large outcry against what was seen as illegitimate meddling by the government in the regulatory sector was the key determinant of the government's reversal. This reaction provided the government more information on the size of $\Omega(D)$, leading in the end to a considerably lower D. Currently an amendment to the Constitution is finding its way through Congress that clarifies the role and powers of regulatory agencies (PEC 81/03, authored by Senator Tasso Jereisatti). It has been approved with near unanimity in the Senate (though still requiring a second vote before becoming law) and is broadly seen by the markets and pundits as removing the uncertainties that prevailed and creating a better environment for investors and for the agencies themselves.

That the government has altered the scope and magnitude of its intended regulatory policy in each of the three cases analyzed above, bringing it more in line with the original rules and concession contracts, is evidence of the existence of safeguards and institutions that do, to some extent, constrain opportunistic behavior of even a player as powerful as the Brazilian president. We are not saying that there is no need for investors and other stakeholders to worry when it comes to regulation, as even cases as those described above, where the opportunistic behavior was eventually checked, can lead to uncertainty and losses. We argue that the level of institutional development in Brazil is much higher than that which is generally presumed, and that rather than infer insecurity at the first sign of opportunistic behavior, it is important to consider full development of events to allow the second and third order reactions to unfold.

Conclusion

This chapter has described regulatory policy in Brazil during the first Lula government. This analysis covered both the content of regulatory policy and regulatory governance and policymaking process. In both cases it was found that the new administration brought about great change. In regard to content, there were changes in the basic model (e.g., electricity), important new legislation (e.g., water and sewage), and a significant fall in investment and shifts in its composition. In the area of regulatory governance and policymaking, the government worked hard to change the role and power of the agencies. But we also stressed throughout the chapter the continuity that prevailed within this change. In the first place it would not have been a complete surprise if the Lula government had decided to eliminate the regulatory system outright and even renationalize some parts of the services. The fact that the changes that were pursued did not reach the fundamental core of the regulatory system is already an element of continuity. Second, as noted, many of the changes in the content of regulation and its impact on investment were started before the Lula government was elected and to a great extent reflect changing economic circumstances and the natural learning curve, which is relatively steep, given that regulation in Brazil is barely 10 years old. The fact that many of the observed changes would in some measure have taken place regardless of who was in office is additional evidence of our claim of elements of the continuity.

Finally, we argued that, despite the Lula government's desire to change the rules of the regulatory system in order to reduce the power of the agencies, the final effect of those actions was not as drastic as is generally supposed. Despite the predominant power of the president in the policymaking process, there is a set of institutional safeguards that promptly sprung into action and mitigated the extent of the change, reinforcing continuity in the evolution of regulation during the Lula administration.

Notes

1. There were not many relevant changes in the regulatory environment of other infrastructure sectors such as transportation, oil, and gas during the first Lula administration.
2. A provisional measure is a bill sent to Congress by the Executive that takes effect immediately but becomes void if Congress doesn't approve it in due time.
3. The communications sector includes telephone, postal, and telegraphic services.
4. The activity "Public Utility Industrial Services" includes the services of water and sanitation and production and distribution of electricity supplied by public or private companies. It also

includes the electricity output of companies in other activities when it is possible to treat their electricity generating facilities independently. When that is not possible, their electricity generation is labeled "secondary generation in industrial activities" and is not accounted for under Public Utility Industrial Services.

5. The description of this event is based on Morais (2007). The IGP-DI (General Price Index—Internal Availability) is a general price index that is used in many contracts and as a general measure of inflation. It is calculated by the Fundação Getúlio Vargas, which is a private organization, and thus has credibility because it is not being manipulated by the government.

6. The IPCA (Consumer Price Index) is the official governmental price index calculated by the census bureau (Instituto Brasileiro de Geografia e Estatistica—IBGE).

7. Prosecutors in Brazil not only prosecute crime, but also act as watchdogs of the behavior of other political actors. Brazilian political institutions give the prosecutors the independence, legal instruments, and resources that have made them central figures in making and implementing policy.

8. For a detailed analysis of the proposals and their effects on the telecommunication sector, see Mattos and Mueller (2006).

9. Note, however, that this is not the same as stating that the actual concession process should be implemented by those entities, given the political motivations of elected officials.

10. This model is from Mueller and Pereira (2002). Although the choice being modeled is of a single regulator, rather than one regulator in a five-member council, as in most Brazilian regulatory agencies, the basic issues are the same.

11. For example, a popular blog (http://blog.estadao.com.br/blog/josemarcio/?m=20070320 accessed on November 4, 2007) linked to the *Estado de S. Paulo* stated on March 27, 2007: "The Lula government's actions to reduce the reach and power of the agencies are well known: Budget cuts, undue delays in appointing new directors, choice of union members and others who defend the control of the agencies by the Executive."

12. There is anecdotal evidence that by 2006 the Executive had regretted the appointment of the two union-linked councilors in ANATEL, due to their technical inability to create and implement efficient regulatory policy. The subsequent appointment of Ronaldo Sardenberg (March 2007) as the new president of ANATEL is seen as a recognition of the importance of placing competent people in these positions. Sardenberg is an ex-minister from the FHC era perceived as a strong and highly competent name despite his not being from the telecommunication sector.

13. In this case the regulators have already been chosen and are taken as given.

14. See Mattos and Mueller (2006) for an analysis along these lines.

References

Alston, L.J., M. Melo, B. Mueller, and C. Pereira. 2005. "Political Institutions, Policymaking Processes and Policy Outcomes in Brazil." Inter-American Development Bank.

Alston, L.J. and B. Mueller. 2006. "Pork for Policy: Executive and Legislative Exchange in Brazil," *The Journal of Law Economics and Organization* 22(1) (Spring):87–114.

Brasil. Presidência da República. Casa Civil. 2003. "Análise e Avaliação do Papel das Agências Reguladoras no Atual Arranjo Institucional Brasileiro: Relatório do Grupo Interministerial." Brasília, December.

Correa, P., M.A. Melo, B. Mueller, and C. Pereira. 2006. *Regulatory Governance in Infrastructure Industries: Assessment and Measurement of Brazilian Regulators.* Washington: The World Bank, Trends and Policy Options Series, No. 3.

Figueiredo, A., and F. Limongi. 2000. "Presidential Power, Legislative Organization, and Party Behavior in Brazil." *Comparative Politics* 32(2):151–170.

Gallup, J.L., J.D. Sachs, and A.D. Mellinger. 1998. "Geography and Economic Development." In *Annual World Bank Conference on Development Economics.* (April), Washington, DC: The World Bank.

Levy, B., and P.T. Spiller. 1996. *The Institutional Foundations of Regulatory Commitment: A Comparative Analysis of Telecommunications Regulation.* Cambridge, UK: Cambridge University Press.

Mattos, C.C.A., and B. Mueller. 2006. "Regulando o Regulador: A Proposta do Governo e a ANATEL." *Revista de Economia Contemporânea* 10(3):517–546.

Morais, L.E. 2007. "Risco Regulatório no Setor de Telecomunicações no Brasil," Dissertação de Mestrado (Master's Dissertation), Departamento de Economia, Universidade de Brasília.

Mueller, B. 2001a. "Institutions for Commitment in the Brazilian Regulatory System." *The Quarterly Review of Economics and Finance* 41:621–643.

———. 2001b. "Regulação, Informação e Política: Uma Resenha da Teoria Política Positiva da Regulação." *Revista Brasileira de Economia de Empresas* 1(1):9–29.

Mueller, B., and C. Pereira. 2002. "Credibility and the Design of Regulatory Agencies in Brazil." *Brazilian Journal of Political Economy* 22 n.3 (87) (July):65–88.

Pereira, C., and B. Mueller. 2003. "Partidos Fracos na Arena Eleitoral e Partidos Fortes na Arena Legislativa no Brasil: Conexão Eleitoral no Brasil." *Dados* 45:265–302.

———. 2004. "A Theory of Executive Preponderance: The Committee System in the Brazilian Congress." *Journal of Legislative Studies* 10(1) (Spring):9–49.

Pereira Filho, O.A. 2006. "Avaliação da Autonomia Orçamentária da Agência Nacional de Telecomunicações—ANATEL." Working paper, Department. of Economics, Universidade de Brasília.

Savedoff, W.D., and P.T. Spiller. 1999. *Spilled Water* Washington DC: Inter-American Development Bank.

Seroa da Motta, R. 2004. "Questões Regulatórias do Setor de Saneamento no Brasil." Working Paper No. 29, SEAE/Ministerio da Fazenda, January.

CHAPTER SIX

Exchange Rate Policy, Perceptions of Risk, and External Constraints under Lula

DONALD V. COES*

Introduction

Brazil stands out among the world's major economies as one whose growth has frequently been conditional on its access to foreign savings. This was dramatically clear several times in the past four decades, beginning with the exclusion of international financial markets to most Latin American borrowers following Mexico's moratorium in the early 1980s. The problem returned in the closing years of the twentieth century, when international capital markets once again showed the fragility of Brazil's access to external lending. Successive crises in the wake of Asian and Russian payments crises forced the government of Fernando Henrique Cardoso to end its use of exchange rate policy in support of domestic price stabilization. The new exchange rate policy has continued in the Lula government, in part because of its recognition that other options may be worse or simply unavailable.

The grudging acceptance of macroeconomic and external payments constraints by a government whose core supporters had little interest in them in the past is in itself an important chapter in Brazil's political evolution after the fall of the post-1964 military dictatorship. The other side of this story is the reaction of international credit markets that were uncertain about how successive groups of Brazilian economic policymakers would respond to the different constraints upon them. Much of the story of Brazil's recent and successful—possibly even overly successful—return to world capital markets may be viewed as the consequence of change in the perceptions of these risks between early 2002, when it became increasingly clear that Lula would be elected to the presidency, and his inauguration for a second term at the beginning of 2006.

In this chapter, the section titled The Long and Winding Road to a Flexible Exchange Rate Policy reviews the gradual evolution of Brazilian exchange rate policy over several decades, focusing on the developments that led up to the fundamental change in early 1999. The next section, The Rise of Brazil's Contemporary Exchange Rate Policy, examines some of the causes and effects of this change early in the second Cardoso administration, and the resulting exchange rate policy that his successor inherited and maintained. The chapter concludes with the section Brazil's Exchange Rate Policy: Some Conclusions and Prospects, offering some conclusions that may be drawn for Brazil's exchange rate experiences over the past decade.

The Long and Winding Road to a Flexible Exchange Rate Policy

Brazil's contemporary exchange rate regime is only the most recent chapter in a long history of arrangements dictated in part by external markets and in part by the rise and fall of Brazilian inflation. The roots of current exchange rate policies can be found in the early stages of the military dictatorship and its stabilization programs. These arrangements were modified both by military regimes, whose success in tapping international capital markets—beginning in the late 1960s—hid a number of problems until they exploded in the 1980s and by the civilian governments that followed. These governments struggled with the external payments problems that accompanied internal macroeconomic disequilibria. Exchange rate policy became a key piece of the internal price stabilization with the Real Plan of 1994, which in turn set the stage for the crises of the late 1990s.

Exchange Rate Policies in Pre–Plano Real Brazil

Early postwar exchange policies in Brazil look quaint in a world of exchange rate flexibility, internationally mobile capital, and within Brazil itself, an almost complete absence of "money illusion" after decades of inflation. Between 1945 and 1968 Brazil maintained fixed nominal exchange rates with the U.S. dollar interrupted at times with sharp nominal devaluations following payments crises. The devaluations were sometimes delayed though the use of multiple rates and a variety of controls on both capital and current account transactions. With price levels increasing more rapidly in Brazil than in its major international economic partners, however, fixed nominal rates inevitably led to major adjustments, usually visible to market participants well before they occurred.

In 1968 the military government adopted a "crawling peg" system of frequent but small adjustments in the dollar/cruzeiro nominal exchange rate. This policy change effectively extended the second-best policy of inflation indexation that was already being developed and implanted in domestic financial markets to the exchange market. Adjustments were generally in line with the difference between cruzeiro and U.S. dollar inflation, but not so regular in either frequency or size as to permit profitable speculation. There appears to be little question that the policy reduced substantially the real exchange rate uncertainty that had resulted from the combination of fixed nominal exchange rates and the high Brazilian inflation that began in the early 1960s. The greater stability in relative prices of tradable goods and the elimination of profitable bets against an overvalued domestic currency were both fruits of the new exchange rate policy.

In retrospect, the crawling peg policy replaced several decades of unsuccessful nominal exchange rate fixing with a decade of real exchange rate fixing. Real exchange rate fixing may have been superior to fixing nominal rates, but the need for greater real exchange rate flexibility became apparent with the successive oil price shocks of the 1970s. The current account deficit required adjustment through a real depreciation, and not simply financing through capital inflows and growing external indebtedness. Real exchange rate rigidity ended partially in late 1979, with a modest depreciation that was soon undone by rising domestic prices. It was more decisively ended in February 1983, with a larger depreciation whose real effects were more long lasting, but which reintroduced significant real exchange rate uncertainty.

Had these external policies been supported with domestic macroeconomic policies consistent with the maintenance of the price competitiveness, the departures from the post-1968 crawling peg policy might have been successful. Instead, Brazil embarked on a decade of failed stabilization plans, beginning with the *Plano Cruzado* of 1986 during the Sarney government, followed by the spectacular collapse of the *Planos Collor I* and *II* and a number of less ambitious but equally unsuccessful stabilization programs. All were failures in part because they did not address the underlying fiscal imbalance and the implied "unpleasant arithmetic" of increasing debt, either domestic or external, with its resulting servicing requirements. As private agents became more wary and sophisticated about price stabilizations that were not likely to be sustainable over the long run, the chances for success became ever more limited.

Exchange Rate Policy in the Plano Real *and the First Cardoso Term*

In contrast to its predecessors, the *Plano Real*, developed in late 1993 and the first half of 1994 by a group of economists working under finance minister and former federal senator Fernando Henrique Cardoso, and implemented in July 1994 during the Itamar Franco presidency, was a resounding success and a watershed in Brazilian macroeconomic history. Most analysts have understandably focused on the fiscal foundations of the plan and the de-indexation of the economy, and the credibility that these domestic policy measures generated among private agents. Some of its success, however, came from a more sophisticated use of exchange rate policy than had been the case in the earlier plans.

The bottom line for an evaluation of any exchange rate policy over the long run is how it attains and maintains competitiveness in international markets in a way consistent with domestic price stability. A summary measure of these trends is provided by the real exchange rate. A number of such measures exist, all of them related. For a large economy like Brazil's, with some activities only tenuously if at all linked to world markets and others closely linked, it is helpful to view the real exchange rate as the ratio of tradable to nontradable prices, P_T/P_{NT}. If this ratio increases, there is an incentive for producers to shift resources into the production of tradable goods—both exportable and import-competing goods—at the expense of nontradable production. Consumers would shift their buying in the opposite direction, toward those nontradable goods and services that were now relatively cheaper. Both shifts would work to increase the country's competitiveness and to improve its current account balance.

The general price level is a weighted average of these two groups of prices, or $P = P_T^{\alpha} P_{NT}^{(1-\alpha)}$. Although it is an oversimplification to view the prices of tradables P_T as completely set in international markets and those of nontradables P_{NT} as completely determined in domestic markets, this separation of prices into two groups highlights the role of the nominal exchange rate in domestic price setting. If the local currency price of tradables is simply the tradable price level P^* in foreign markets converted by the price of a unit of foreign exchange, or $P_T = eP^*$, then the response of the general domestic price level P to the exchange rate will depend on α, the weight of tradables in the price level. The two price definitions used here, moreover, then imply that the ratio of tradable prices to those of nontradables, or what is sometimes called the "internal terms of trade," is

$$P_T/P_{NT} = [eP^*/P]^{[1/(1-\alpha)]} \tag{1}$$

An increase in the relative importance of tradable goods in the general price level therefore implies a rise in their price relative to the numeraire nontradable price level P_{NT}. Figure 6.1 uses this definition of the real exchange rate to show the evolution of Brazilian exchange policy over nearly 40 years, from the inception of the crawling peg in August 1968 to August 2007. The decade of real exchange rate stability that followed the institution of the crawling peg is apparent, as is the breakdown in real exchange rate stability in the 1980s. The series of failed stabilization plans between the 1986 *Plano Cruzado* and the *Plano Real*, the first successful one, is also clear in the path of the real exchange rate.

In comparison with the Brazilian economy of the 1950s or even the early 1980s, Brazil in 1994 was an economy more closely linked to international markets. In terms of the equation above, this increase in openness implies a greater α.[1] The relatively greater importance of external prices permitted the nominal exchange rate to play a stronger role in price stabilization than it could have in earlier decades. The Real replaced a currency with a long history of inflation. It was strengthened by rules that converted

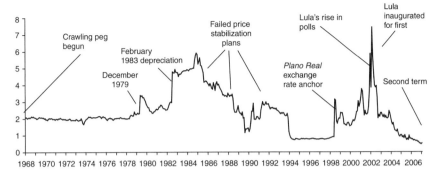

Figure 6.1   Real exchange rate index (August 1968–August 2007)

Source: Author's calculations from Br$/U.S. dollar exchange rate, US PPI, and Brazilian INPC

Primary Sources: Nominal exchange rate: Banco Central do Brasil, US PPI: US Department of Labor, Producer Price Index (All), INPC: Fundação Getúlio Vargas/*Conjuntura Economica*. An increase in the index (base August 1994) indicates a rise in real price competitiveness (a real depreciation)

old currency prices into Real prices without rewarding those who had received the most recent price adjustments, making the reduction of inflationary expectations more credible than it had been in earlier plans. Such a strategy, however, placed critical weight on the exchange rate as an anchor for the new price environment. As may be seen from equation (1), it now had greater leverage in influencing domestic prices than had been the case when Brazil was a more closed economy.

With successful price stabilization, the erosion of international price competitiveness that had accompanied most of earlier stabilization plans could be avoided. As is clear from the definition P_T, real appreciation can be obtained either by maintaining the nominal exchange rate e at a low level, or permitting the domestic price level P to rise. One of the important features of the *Plano Real* that distinguished it from its predecessors was that real appreciation of the Real in support of the stabilization plan during the first Cardoso administration relied on keeping the nominal exchange rate e low, rather than letting the domestic price level P rise. Since the general price level was a more politically visible target for macroeconomic policy than was the nominal exchange rate, this was a politically more viable strategy in the short or intermediate run. As a number of commentators have noted, the apparent ability of the government to bring down high inflation was an important electoral asset that paid large dividends in the next few years.[2]

Brazil's apparent success in reducing inflation in this way, however, depended critically on the willingness of external lenders to finance the capital inflows that are the counterpart of a real appreciation. With the fall in inflation and euphoria of a stable price level in the immediate post-1994 period, this was not initially a problem. Indeed, international capital markets were impressed—as they should have been—with both the speed and the sophistication of the new government's apparent ability to avoid the potentially hyperinflationary explosion that had loomed a few years earlier. Inflation as measured by the consumer price index fell from 2477 percent in 1993 to 22 percent in 1995, the first full year under the new currency, and to less than 2 percent in 1998.[3] In the first few years after 1994, the fall in inflation was regarded by international lenders as a mark of the macroeconomic management competence of the new government.

Such success in bringing down inflation, even though it was unprecedented in Brazil, was still not enough to avoid the real appreciation that had resulted from the one-to-one peg of the new Real with the dollar at the outset of the plan in July 1994. Brazil was to spend more than four years with the new currency's enjoying widespread popularity at home, while it imposed a growing cost on the country's price competitiveness in external markets. The stability of the real exchange rate in the first few years after the implementation of the *Plano Real* is clear in figure 6.1.

The fall in Brazil's price competitiveness was soon manifested in the current account, whose major components are shown in figure 6.2.[4] As a long-time recipient of capital inflows, the servicing costs of this debt had been financed in most years of the preceding decades by a surplus in the merchandise trade balance. The macroeconomic crises and slowing of growth in the late 1980s and early 1990s had further increased this surplus, which averaged about US$13 billion annually in the 1986–1993 period.

Within a few months of the inception of the *Plano Real*, however, this trend was reversed. Brazil had a trade deficit of more than half billion dollars in the fourth quarter of 1994, and over the next four years, the trade deficits grew to more than US$6 billion annually. Annual data for the major components of Brazil's current account and for the balance of payments is given for the post–*Plano Real* period in tables 6.1a and 6.1b respectively. These data show that much of the deterioration of Brazil's

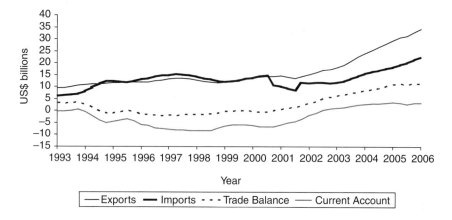

Figure 6.2   Current account and major components (US$ billions)

Source: Banco Central do Brasil, *Boletim*, Seção Balanço de Pagamentos. Series are four-quarter moving averages

Table 6.1a   Current account and major components, 1994–2006 (US$ millions)

	Trade balance	Services (excluding factor payments)	Net factor payments	Unilateral transfers	Current account balance
1994	10466	−5657	−9035	2414	−1811
1995	−3466	−7483	−11058	3622	−18384
1996	−5599	−8681	−11668	2446	−23502
1997	−6753	−10646	−14876	1823	−30452
1998	−6575	−10111	−18189	1458	−33416
1999	−1199	−6977	−18848	1689	−25335
2000	−698	−7162	−17886	1521	−24225
2001	2650	−7759	−19743	1638	−23215
2002	13121	−4957	−18191	2390	−7637
2003	24794	−4931	−18552	2867	4177
2004	33641	−4678	−20520	3236	11679
2005	44703	−8309	−25967	3558	13985
2006	46074	−9408	−27444	4306	13528

Source: Aggregated from Banco Central do Brasil, Boletim

Table 6.1b   Capital account, major components, and balance of payments, 1994–2006 (US$ millions)

	Direct investment	Portfolio investment	Loans, other capital flows	Capital account balance	Errors and omissions	Net balance of payments
1994	1460	50642	−43410	8692	334	7215
1995	3309	9217	16569	29095	2207	12919
1996	11261	21619	1088	33968	−1800	8666
1997	17877	12616	−4693	25800	−3255	−7907
1998	26002	18125	−14425	29702	−4256	−7970
1999	26888	3802	−13370	17319	194	−7822
2000	30498	6955	−18127	19326	2637	−2262
2001	24715	77	2260	27052	−531	3307
2002	14108	−5119	−985	8004	−66	302
2003	9894	5308	−10091	5111	−793	8496
2004	8339	−4750	−11112	−7523	−1912	2244
2005	12550	4885	−26898	−9464	−201	4319
2006	−8469	8622	17124	17277	−236	30569

Note: Net balance of payments is equal to the change in holdings of the monetary authorities

Source: Aggregated from Banco Central do Brasil, Boletim

current account between 1994 and 1999 was due to the sharp falls in the merchandise trade balance and in the net nonfactor payments service balance. These two components of the current account can be identified as the net balance for trade in goods and services, which we would expect to be more sensitive to the real exchange rate than other balance of payments items. Together, they moved from a surplus of about US$5 billion in 1994 to a deficit of more than US$7 billion in 1998. Whether or not one could ever take seriously the "elasticity pessimism" debate about the response of the trade flows in earlier times in Brazil, there should be no such argument today. Current account trends in the post-Real Plan period appear to provide strong support for the view that Brazil's current account today is strongly influenced by the real exchange rate.

The Rise of Brazil's Contemporary Exchange Rate Policy

Brazilian exchange rate policy as Lula's second term unfolds is more an inheritance from the second Cardoso government than it is a policy of Lula's government. Events in the second Cardoso term forced the abandonment of the exchange rate anchor early in the term. This was the major change, and the political transition from Cardoso to Lula four years later was more significant for what did not change in exchange rate policy and the macroeconomic influences behind it, than for what did change.

External Pressures and the End of the Exchange Rate Anchor

There is an interesting precedent for the attraction of Brazilian economic policymakers to the exchange rate anchor (*âncora cambial*) in the early *Plano Real* period. In the early phases of the *Plano Cruzado* in 1986, price controls were defended as a way of manipulating inflationary expectations to rid the economy of "inertial inflation." Had it ever really been that easy, subsequent stabilization plans like the *Plano Real* might never have been necessary. As the Sarney government became increasingly charmed by its success in temporarily interrupting the inflationary spiral with a price freeze, it ignored the nonviability of such a policy over the longer run. Critics of the *Plano Cruzado* noted that this short-run economic strategy was akin to administering anesthesia and then neglecting to do the surgery. Several subsequent stabilization efforts before the *Plano Real* repeated this tempting but fundamentally flawed strategy.

Rather like domestic price controls, the use of an exchange rate anchor makes it politically tempting for a government to rely on it too long, while neglecting to make the more fundamental adjustments that are required. To most of the electorate, an overvalued exchange rate is a "strong currency." Despite the economic sophistication both of policymakers in the first Cardoso administration and of Brazil's financial market operators, the political momentum of a successful stabilization with an exchange rate anchor as one of its centerpieces may have been unstoppable in the first few years. It is easier in retrospect than it was at the time to argue that Brazil should have put aside the exchange rate anchor far sooner. In addition, a number of economists at the time argued for this approach, most notably Gustavo Franco, president of the Banco Central for much of the period of the anchor.[5]

It was sudden external currency crises and not a leisurely internal policy debate that forced the abandonment of the exchange rate anchor. In July 1997 the Thai baht was floated, following several speculative attacks in preceding months. Shortly afterward, financial deterioration of Kia Motors in Korea sparked a wider decline in stock markets there, and depreciation of the won. Short-term financial capital outflows from both countries increased sharply, accompanied by similar financial downturns in Malaysia, Hong Kong, and Singapore. Similar events occurred in Russia in 1998. A downturn in the prices of petroleum and other exports, as well as financial market concerns about short-term state bonds led to a precipitous fall in foreign exchange reserves in the summer of 1998. Despite an IMF support package, the ruble depreciated sharply, and was finally allowed to float in September.

In earlier decades the potential for "contagion" between events in these markets and the Brazilian exchange market would have been much more limited. By the late 1990s, however, the parallels between Brazil's payments position and those of Russia and the Asian crisis countries were too strong to be ignored—especially by lenders actively involved with all of these economies. Like them, Brazil had engaged in extensive management of its exchange rate, in effect offering an opportunity for potentially profitable speculative attacks. By the time of the Asian and Russian crises, many market participants regarded the Real as overvalued.[6]

A variety of evidence supports the hypothesis that the Asian and Russian currency crises played a role in the deterioration of Brazil's external payments after 1997. Figure 6.3 shows the spread between yields on Brazilian government dollar-denominated bonds and comparable yields for U.S. securities, popularly known as the *risco Brasil*. As is clear from this series shown by month for the 1995–2007 period, both the Asian and the Russian crises appear to have had a noticeable effect on the spread, even though domestic political trends later had much larger effects. More formal tests of the "contagion hypothesis" include work by Goldfajn (2000), who considered a number of channels of transmission of the external shocks. His results suggest that Brazil was regarded

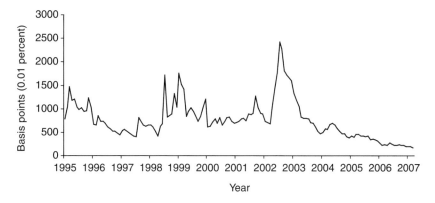

Figure 6.3 Emerging Markets Bond Index (EMBI) spread for Brazil (in basis points), 1995–2007

Source: JP Morgan Emerging Markets Research, EBMI+ Brazil, accessed at www.cbonds.info on March 28, 2007

by a number of foreign private lenders, especially those in the offshore markets, as similar enough to Russia to result in significant capital flight.[7]

The administered but flexible exchange rate, or "dirty float," that Brazil used between July 1994 and early 1999 differed markedly from a "pure" or completely market-determined one in that it required a high level of foreign exchange reserves. In the early years of the *Plano Real*, this requirement was not a serious constraint or threat to the credibility of the administered rate. All this changed with the changed perceptions of Brazil's payments position following the Asian and Russian currency crises. Figure 6.4 shows the monthly foreign exchange reserve position of the monetary authorities. Here the effects of both the Asian crises and of Russia can be seen. The fall of more than US$8 billion in September 1997 following the Asian crises was unprecedented in Brazil; September 1998's drop was over US$21 billion, the largest reserve loss in Brazil's history.

The response to this exchange crisis, which occupied the remainder of 1998, resulted in a profound change in January 1999, when all attempts to maintain the exchange anchor were abandoned. The use of inflation targets, based on a "fiscal anchor," rather than the exchange anchor had been advocated for some time by a number of economists, including the new president of the Banco Central, Armínio Fraga. With the deterioration of Brazil's reserve position in September, this was not only a preferable path, but probably the only viable one.

The ability of the Brazilian economy to handle this sharp policy change without a return of pre-Real Plan inflation has been the subject of much discussion. Although the downward trend in the inflation rate was interrupted by the 1999 policy change, this effect was far smaller than had been feared, with consumer price inflation rising from about 2 percent in 1998 to about 9 percent in 1999—hardly an explosion into high inflation. Among the reasons for this surprisingly small effect was the success

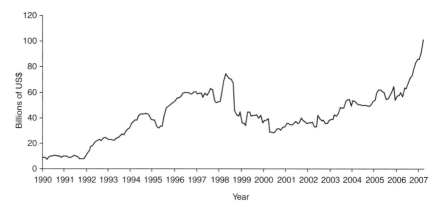

Figure 6.4 Reserves of foreign exchange—international liquidity (US$ billions), January 1990–April 2007

Source: Banco Central do Brasil, foreign exchange reserves—international liquidity, at www.ipeadata.gov.br accessed on March 28, 2007

of the *Plano Real* in de-indexation of the Brazilian economy. In earlier times, the pass-through effects of an exchange rate depreciation on the general price level would have been amplified significantly by indexation, as occurred quickly in 1979 and 1983. Another factor was a degree of softness in aggregate demand, with industrial production in early 1999 below levels of preceding years, due in part to the real appreciation in the 1994–1999 period. An adjustment in the *salário mínimo* of only 5 percent in 1999, when expectations for inflation of about 20 percent were common, further dampened the inflationary impact of the policy change. Most important, however, was probably the fact that the new fiscal anchor was credible, with a long-delayed increase in the primary budget surplus from about 0 in 1998 to over 3 percent in 1999. Underlying this change was the new Law of Fiscal Responsibility, widely discussed in the press and certainly responsible for part of the perception that the fiscal disequilibrium was at last being seriously addressed and not just talked about.

There were also advantages to being a latecomer to the currency crises of the 1990s. The earlier crises in the Asian countries and in Russia had been a learning experience for both monetary authorities and financial market participants. Despite the initial euphoria that had accompanied the *Plano Real*'s success in 1994, the worsening payments situation had been apparent for some time before the 1999 jettisoning of the exchange rate anchor. As is clear from figure 6.3, markets had increased sharply their assessment of the *risco Brasil*, so that when the adjustment finally came, it had been anticipated by many in the financial markets.[8] Foreseen crises may not really be crises.

The Exchange Rate Policy Inheritance of the Lula Government

Despite the market turmoil of 1998, the reelection of Cardoso to a second term as president marked an important milestone in Brazil's return to a democratic political culture after the 1964 interruption. Cardoso again faced Lula, his 1994 opponent, with the *Plano Real*'s success still helping him, despite the deepening external payments problems. The margin of his victory over Lula, the runner-up, in early October was slightly narrower than it had been in the first election (53 to 32 percent of the vote in 1998, versus 54 to 27 in 1994), but both were decisive enough to avoid a run-off election.[9]

The second Cardoso term was initiated with the mid-January 1999 decision to abandon the exchange rate anchor. Although this decision did successfully address some of the financial markets' concerns with Brazil's worsening external payments situation in the first term, domestic macroeconomic indicators in the second term help explain the decline in popular support for the Cardoso government and the rising strength of the Lula and the PT.

Table 6.2 shows the averages for the three government terms— Cardoso I, which ended two weeks before the abandonment of the

Table 6.2 Major economic indicators in the Cardoso and Lula governments (annual averages per term)

	Cardoso first term (1995–1998)	Cardoso second term (1999–2002)	Lula first term (2003–2006)
GDP growth rate (%)	2.6	2.1	2.7
Private consumption growth rate (%)	3.7	0.9	2.4
Public sector consumption growth rate (%)	1.8	1.5	1.0
Gross fixed capital formation growth rate (%)	4.4	1.5	3.4
Export growth rate (%)	3.4	9.7	12.9
Import growth rate (%)	13.4	−3.7	10.0
Inflation (IPCA percent change over year) (%)	9.7	8.8	6.4
Current account (US$ billions)	−26.4	−20.1	10.8
Real exchange rate (August 1994 = 1.00, with a higher value corresponding to a real depreciation)	0.60	2.68	1.92
Gini coefficient (PNAD)	0.580	0.565	0.544
Monthly income of lowest 50 percent of income earners in September 2004 reais (PNAD)*	234.0	232.0	234.7

Note: * The 1993 monthly income (in 2004 R$) for the lowest 50 percent of income earners in the PNAD sample was R$175

Sources: GDP growth rates: Author's calculations from Instituto Brasileiro de Geographia e Estatística (IBGE), Serviço de Contas Nacionais; IPCA: Fundaçao Getúlio Vargas; Current account: Banco Central do Brasil, *Boletim*; Real exchange rate: Author's calculations, shown in figure 6.1; Gini coefficient and monthly real income: IBGE, Diretoria de Pesquisas, Coordenação de Trabalho e Rendimento, Pesquisa Nacional de Amostra de Domicílios. Average for second Cardoso government omits 2000

exchange rate anchor, Cardoso II, and Lula, for which most of the data is given through 2006. The major exception is for data on income distribution and earnings in the National Household Sample Survey (PNAD), for which data are only available through 2004.

Overall GDP growth rates were comparable over all three sub-periods, and were mediocre by Brazil's performance in earlier decades. This similarity, however, masks some important changes in the growth rates of the components of GDP that followed the big change in exchange rate policy. Before the exchange rate anchor was abandoned, exports grew a little faster than total GDP, despite the increasing overvaluation. Their ability to grow even this fast in a period of extreme real appreciation suggests that non-price-related changes in the Brazilian export sector were operative after the *Plano Real*, as they also appear to have been in 2006 and 2007. This trend may help explain the rapid growth in exports under the new exchange rate policy, both in Cardoso's second term, and even more so in Lula's first term.[10]

The slowing of growth after the 1999 exchange rate policy change fell primarily on private consumption and on investment. The former change had major political implications, while the latter decrease was one of the causes of slower growth of the Brazilian capital stock in both the later Cardoso term and Lula's first term. The fiscal austerity imposed by the switch to a fiscally based anchor after January 1999, and its continuation under the Lula government is apparent in the slowing of public sector's contribution to GDP, which in recent years has grown at less than half the rate of total GDP.

Table 6.2 also provides some important clues to the electoral shift that put Lula and the *Partido dos Trabalhadores* in power in the 2002 elections. Price stabilization after the 1994 *Plano Real* had increased the standard of living of poorer Brazilians significantly, with real monthly earnings of the lower half of the income earners in the PNAD sample rising from R$175 to R$234 (in September 2004 prices). After the exchange rate policy change and the move toward much greater fiscal austerity, real wages appear to have stagnated, despite a slight improvement of the relative income distribution that has continued under the Lula government. Although the success of the *Plano Real* in eliminating the inflation of preceding decades was maintained in the second Cardoso term, this accomplishment had lost some of the luster it had in the first years of the plan.

Slowing growth and the stagnant real wages endured by a large part of the electorate after 1998 provide much of the explanation for the much better showing of Lula and the PT in the 2002 elections. The possibility that Lula might be elected had become apparent as early as 2001, when preliminary polls gave him the largest support than any candidate.[11] Over the following months, the government party's candidate, José Serra, rose in the polls. Meanwhile minor candidates abandoned their candidacies, while Lula's own share of voter intentions increased to about 40 percent.

The reaction of the exchange market to Lula's increasing chances was clear by May, when the real/dollar rate began a steep climb that took it to over 3.4 reais in July and nearly 4 in September, on the eve of elections. The effect of these sharp changes in the nominal rate on the real exchange rate was to produce the largest real depreciation in Brazil's history of flexible exchange rates, far outstripping the effect of the abandonment of the exchange rate anchor in January 1999.

Given the rapidity with which this trend subsequently unwound, it is understandable to interpret this market response as an overreaction. Statements by Lula himself in earlier campaigns and in interviews as late as 2002, however, provided some basis for these concerns. He harshly criticized the generation of large primary budget surpluses, and suggested that interest payments might be subordinated to wage payments.[12] Some PT figures close to him reinforced the market worries that the external payments and fiscal policies of the Cardoso government would be cast aside by a victorious PT. Federal Deputy Aloísio Mercadante, cited as a possible finance minister in a Lula government, voiced support for a plebiscite on foreign debt payments. Guido Mantega, one of his advisors and later minister of planning, characterized primary budget surpluses of 3 percent as "suicidal."

Although such statements, including those from the candidate himself, may have been accurate reflections of the "historical PT's" views about debt, interest payments, and public spending priorities, it was obvious as the PT edged closer to power in the later years of the Cardoso government that they were a political liability. Argentine payments difficulties in 2001 and 2002 showed how quickly a similar middle-income economy like Brazil's could be thrown into crisis if access to credit markets were to end. The general retraction of world capital markets in the wake of the September 11, 2001, attacks was another concern. Finally, extensive pre-election polling of Brazilian voters showed significant reservations about the "radical" PT portrayed both in the press and by some of the party's own earlier statements.

These factors, allied with the recognition that the many years of opposition to the government might be succeeded by actually having to govern, produced a profound change in the PT's position by 2002. Lula's June 22 "*Carta ao Povo Brasileiro* [Letter to the Brazilian People]" is a remarkable statement of how far the PT had moved away from its own past.[13] True, in its criticism of the Cardoso government, it did sound many traditional PT concerns—among them Brazilian income distribution, lack of "social justice," and agrarian reform. But far more significant from the point of view of financial markets were the criticisms that might well have come from market participants themselves, and the clear recognition that those markets needed some reassurances from the leading presidential candidate. Exchange rate policy during the 1994–1999 period was blamed for slow growth and market uncertainty. The lack of fiscal adjustment and the delay in tax reform were noted. And perhaps most striking were unambiguous promises that the primary fiscal surplus would be maintained as long as necessary, that inflation would not return, and that contracts would be honored.

Promises made by a candidate, however, are not as credible as they may become after an election and inauguration. Market behavior even after Lula's June statement suggests that it was not taken as seriously at the time as it was later. The sharp rise in the Real cost of a dollar continued, as did the increase in the Brazilian risk premium in international capital markets (see figures 6.1 and 6.3), peaking respectively in September and July. Some of the reduction in market panic may be due to changes within the PT leadership, in which the mayor of Riberão Preto and former federal deputy, Antônio Palocci, associated with more centrist parts of the party, emerged as the most influential economic policymaker and Lula's choice as finance minister. Another important signal to the markets was the choice of businessman and *Partido Liberal* leader José Alencar as Lula's vice-presidential running mate.

In the October 27 run-off between Lula and Serra, Lula won 61.3 percent of the vote (compared to 46.4 percent for Lula on the first round), against Serra's 38.7 percent. By November the *risco Brasil* had declined to about 1600 basis points, and in January, with Lula's inauguration, was about 1300. In the months following the election, several decisions of the incoming government added to the reassurances. Henrique Meirelles, formerly a Bank of Boston executive, was named as the new Banco Central president, with much of the senior staff carried over from the Cardoso administration. Support for that government's inflation targeting was reaffirmed, with targets of 8.5 and 5.5 percent set for 2003 and 2004 respectively. Perhaps most important, an increase in the primary fiscal surplus to 4.5 percent of GDP was set—a significant rejection of the PT's historical position on this issue.

Brazil's Exchange Rate Policy: Some Conclusions and Prospects

There are several lessons that emerge from the exchange rate experience of the Lula government's first term. First, as had been shown by the events that preceded the abandonment of the exchange anchor at the beginning of the second Cardoso term, Brazil's real exchange rate in the longer run is an endogenous variable, not set by the government.[14] Although an administered exchange rate may work for shorter periods, it is courting disaster to push exchange-rate setting to the degree that was done in the first years after the *Plano Real*. This was apparently a lesson that had been learned by the incoming economic team in 2003, even though it took financial markets a while to believe that the new team understood it.

Because the real exchange rate is an endogenous variable, the increasing openness of Brazil's capital markets in the 1990s made an administered exchange rate a potential source of risk, rather than a tool for reducing it. In contrast to the Brazil of earlier decades, when the exchange rate was viewed primarily as the relative price that reflected current account equilibrium—or the lack of it—the exchange rate in post-inflationary Brazil is one of the central prices in Brazilian capital markets. Lula and the PT's response in 2002 to market worries about his likely presidency showed that the constraints that a financially open economy faces are much more widely understood than they once had been. So too are the connections between the financing needs of the public sector, and the underlying fiscal position that drives these needs. Within the Lula government, there appears to be little support—or even interest—in the kinds of proposals for unilateral external debt restructuring that once were common when the PT was an opposition party.

A second and related conclusion that may be drawn from Brazilian exchange rate experience over the past decade is the importance of market expectations about events that may in fact never come to pass. Samuelson's quip that the U.S. stock market had successfully predicted nine of the past five recessions has its Brazilian counterpart in the rapid depreciation of the Real and the steep rise in the Brazil bond spread during the 2002 election period. The mechanism behind this kind of episode may be viewed as an expression of a change in the subjective probabilities held by market participants.

Figure 6.5 represents this kind of change in expectations in a highly stylized way. For simplicity, it is assumed that there are two outcomes, or

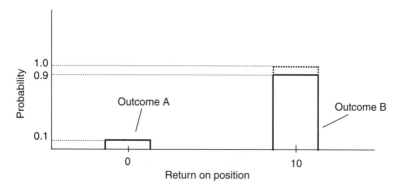

Figure 6.5   A subjective change in perceptions of risk

Note: Outcome A: Unilateral external debt moratorium, return of inflation, and fiscal disequilibrium
         Outcome B: Maintenance of debt service, attainment of fiscal and price targets
         ....: Addition to probability of Outcome B when Outcome A eliminated

Source: Author's illustration

states of nature, A and B. Under A, a moratorium on debt service would be declared, fiscal and inflation targets would be ignored, and inflation returns. Under B, events like these, which would yield a return in the neighborhood of zero, do not occur, so that the yield on the position is in the neighborhood of 10. In this simple example, it is assumed that even when there is a chance of A, the subjective probability that market participants assign to it is only 0.1, while they assume that there is a 90 percent chance that B will be the outcome.

If market participants become convinced that A will not happen, the mass of the distribution around zero is transferred to the neighborhood of 10. There are several important consequences of such a change in expectations, or in the subjective probability distributions. The mean return rises from 9 to 10, a modest increase. If agents in the markets cared only about mean returns, this might not appear to matter much. If agents are risk averse, however, the elimination of the low return outcome may have greater consequences. The variance of the distribution has been significantly reduced, adding to the attractiveness of situations in which A does not occur.

The international financial markets to which Brazil had access were deep by the 1990s and had developed a number of ways to permit risk sharing. Nevertheless, the assumption that private lenders to both public and private Brazilian borrowers were risk averse is hardly a controversial one. This implies that agents seek to maximize the expected utility of uncertain returns, and that they would be willing to buy fairly priced insurance against unfavorable outcomes.[15] Thus changes in subjective probabilities like those represented in figure 6.5 would have a stronger effect than would be the case if they simply preferred higher mean returns. The practical implication of this kind of behavior is that when small subjective probabilities of adverse outcomes first appear, they may have large and nonlinear effects on the behavior of those agents who now hold them. Such reactions might not just result from personal preferences that embody risk aversion. If major lenders were corporate entities, subject to minimum return requirements, bank runs by worried depositors, or other extreme sanctions, then the results might be similar.[16] We do not know just how traditional PT rhetoric was viewed by lenders in 2002 in terms of subjective probabilities, but the sharp rise in the *risco Brasil* and a depreciating exchange rate are both consistent with such an interpretation.

A third conclusion that one can draw from the Brazilian exchange rate experience of the past decade is that changes in the real exchange rate have strong and relatively prompt effects on the current account. The use of the exchange rate as a tool for domestic price stabilization in the first Cardoso term produced a sharp fall in the trade balance. In a reverse fashion, the real depreciation of the Real in 1999 resulted in a reversal of the export trend, making this sector one of the fastest growing ones in both the second Cardoso government and in Lula's first term. Since current account surpluses are necessary to generate the income to service the external debt, the real exchange rate also serves as a signal to creditors.

Both of these roles of the real exchange rate raise some important questions in the context of recent real appreciation of the Real. If the past decade's experience is a guide, Brazil's export growth may be constrained by the recent loss in price competitiveness. In real terms, the Real in 2007 has appreciated beyond the levels of the 1994–1999 period, as may be seen in figure 6.1. This has yet to be reflected in current account trends, but Brazil's trade surplus in 2006 was only slightly about US$1.5 billion higher than that of 2005, after consecutive increases of more than US$10 billion in each of the preceding four years. If the real appreciation induced by current capital flows continues, experience suggests that export growth will be much slower.

A return to some of the other conditions that produced the 1999 crisis still appears unlikely. But that period showed how quickly international capital markets can change their perceptions of an economy's external payments prospects. If Brazil's record current account surpluses appear to be ending, capital markets will take note rather quickly. Although the Lula government appears to have learned the lessons that Brazil's recent exchange rate history teaches, a reversal of recent current account trends and an accompanying downturn in capital flows would put their learning to the test.

Finally, we might conclude that some of Brazil's current success in attracting international capital flows rests on foundations beyond the control of the Lula government. The combined efforts of the preceding Cardoso government in ending high inflation, and that of the current government in sustaining the policies that eliminated it, have been recognized by international markets. This is the good news, since in the short and intermediate run, it eliminates an external constraint that has frequently conditioned Brazilian economic growth, as foreign capital markets allocate a larger share of the world's savings to Brazil.

In the longer run, however, such a portfolio shift carries with it some risks. The sharp increase in capital flows to Brazil in 2006 and 2007 represents in part a long overdue response by external financial markets to the elimination of high inflation in one of the world's important economies. If a major part of the capital inflow is in fact a portfolio shift induced by the end of high inflation, then flows of this magnitude are not eternal. Even if international capital markets were to permanently maintain a larger share of the world's stock of financial assets in Brazil, the flow that is currently increasing this stock eventually does its job. As the level of assets that external markets wish to hold in Brazil approaches its desired level, capital flows would grow more slowly. Such a maturing of the current boom may still be some time away, but if there is any lesson in Brazil's past external payments history, it is that external economic constraints can change quickly. It is apparent that the Lula government has learned this lesson, but it still must be careful that a soft landing does not become a hard one.

Notes

*I would like to thank Ed Amann, Cláudio Paiva, Heiko Wacker, and John Welch for helpful comments.

1. The real exchange rate shown in figure 6.1 is based on the simplified hypothesis that the degree of openness, averaged 0.5 over the whole period, beginning at 0.3 in 1968.
2. Goldfajn (2000), and Amann and Baer (2003).
3. Source: Fundação Getúlio Vargas, Conjuntura Econômica (IPCA index).
4. The current account data in figure 6.2 uses four-period averages of Banco Central quarterly data to eliminate the strong seasonal trends that have characterized the underlying series.
5. Franco (1995). Early critics of the use of the exchange rate for internal stabilization objectives included Dornbusch, Goldfajn, and Valdés (1995).
6. Franco (2005) has suggested that the Banco Central's almost continuous accumulation of reserves due to capital inflows calls this view into question.
7. It is sometimes argued that the channel operated through the restriction of private lending to Brazil by banks needing to restore their balance sheets after the Asian and Russian crises. Goldfajn finds less evidence for this, noting that a number of other Latin American borrowers were not as severely treated as was Brazil by lenders under such pressure.
8. Gruben and Welch (2001) attribute some of the speed with which Brazil emerged from the 1998–1999 currency crisis to the fact that most banks had positioned themselves for the longer-run economic consequences of the exchange rate anchor.
9. A run-off is not required if a single candidate receives 50 percent plus one vote of those cast. Run-offs were required in the following two presidential elections.
10. Estimates of equilibrium real exchange rates for Brazil by Paiva (2006) suggest that some of the recent real appreciation may result from higher productivity in tradable sectors and from significant growth in production capacity.
11. In mid-December, 2001, *DataFolha* surveys already indicated about 33 percent support for Lula. See Carreirão (2004) for an analysis of the 2002 presidential election process and polls. For an analysis of the principal candidates' positions on issues that affected the exchange market, see Williamson (2002).
12. For a summary of a number of these statements by Lula and other PT leaders, see Giambiagi (2004).

13. Luiz Inácio Lula da Silva (2002).
14. This point is emphasized by de Barros, Barbosa, and Giambiagi (2004).
15. Formally, this assumes that utility of profits π is concave, so that $U_1(\pi) > 0$ and $U_2(\pi) < 0$.
16. Garcia (2004) emphasizes the high degree of risk aversion by international banks in explaining the reversals of capital flows during Brazilian currency crises.

References

Amann, Edmund, and Werner Baer. 2003. "Anchors Away: The Costs and Benefits of Brazil's Devaluation." *World Development* (June):1033–1046. Working Paper at www.business.uiuc/ Working_Papers/papers/02–0122.pdf accessed on April 4, 2007.

Carreirão, Yan. 2004. "A Eleição Presidencial de 2002: Uma Análise Preliminar do Processo e dos Resultados Eleitorais." *Revista de Sociologia e Política* 22(junho). At www.scielo.br/pdf/rsocp/ n22 accessed on April 10, 2007.

de Barros, Octavio, Fernando H. Barbosa, and Fabio Giambiagi. 2004. "O regime cambial e o ajuste externo." In Fabio Giambiagi, J.G. Reis, and A. Urani, eds., *Reformas no Brasil: Balanço e Agenda*, Rio de Janeiro: Nova Fronteira. pp. 127–151.

Dornbusch, Rudiger, Ilan Goldfajn, and Rodrigo Valdés. 1995. "Currency Crises and Collapses." *Brookings Papers on Economic Activity* (2):219–270.

Franco, Gustavo H.B. 1995. *O Plano Real e Outros Ensaios*, Rio de Janeiro: Francisco Alves Editora.

———. 2005. "Auge e Declínio do Inflacionismo no Brasil." In Fabio Giambiagi, André Villela, Lavínia Barros de Castro, and Jennifer Hermann, eds. *Economia Brasileira Contemporânea (1945–2004)*. Rio de Janeiro: Elsevier Editora Ltda. pp. 258–283.

Garcia, Márcio G.P. 2004. "Brazil in the 21st Century: How to Escape the High Interest Rate Trap?" Working Paper No. 162, Center for Research on Economic Development and Policy Reform, Stanford University. At www.scid.stanford.edu/ pdf/credpr162 accessed on April 4, 2007.

Giambiagi, Fabio. 2004. "Rompendo com a Ruptura: O Governo Lula (2003–2004)." In Fabio Giambiagi, André Villela, Lavínia Barros de Castro, and Jennifer Hermann, eds. *Economia Brasileira Contemporânea (1945–2004)*. Rio de Janeiro: Elsevier Editora Ltda. pp. 196–217.

Goldfajn, Ilan, 2000. "The Swings in Capital Flows and the Brazilian Crisis." PUC Texto para Discussão 422, Pontifícia Universidade Católica do Rio de Janeiro.

Gruben, William C., and John H. Welch. 2001. "Banking and Currency Crisis Recovery." *Economic and Financial Review* (Fourth Quarter):12–23; Federal Reserve Bank of Dallas at www.dallasfed. org/research/efr/2001/efr0104.html accessed on March 23, 2007.

Lula da Silva, Luiz Inácio. 2002. "Carta ao Povo Brasileiro." Published on June 22 at www.iisg.nl/ collections/carta_ao_povo_brasileiro/pdf accessed on April 4, 2007.

Paiva, Claudio. 2006. "External Adjustment and Equilibrium Exchange Rate in Brazil." IMF Working Papers (WP/06/221) at www.imf.org/ external/pubs/ft/wp accessed on March 31, 2007.

Williamson, John. 2002. "Is Brazil Next?" Policy Brief 02–07, Institute for International Economics, Washington at www.iie.com/publications/pb/pb02 accessed on March 23, 2007.

CHAPTER SEVEN

Agricultural, Agrarian, and Environmental Policy Formation under Lula: The Role of Policy Networks

CHARLES C. MUELLER

Introduction

Our evaluation of agricultural, agrarian, and environmental policy formation in Lula's first term combines the rationality dimension, empha-sized by economists, with a fundamental social dimension of power, resulting from the action of influential agents interested in specific policy decisions. Policies are regarded as stemming from the interaction between the regime—the administration in power—and influential agents with interests in policy issues, organized in sectoral policy networks. The regime is considered as having two main objectives: the attainment of a view of "good society"; and maintaining or increasing its hold on power. Influential agents, in turn, have conceptions of good society—that may or may not coincide with the regime's—which are reflected in their policy demands (C. Mueller 1982).

Both the regime and sectors have resources—not only economic, but also political and social; in our conceptual background we under-line the latter. The regime uses its resources in pursuit of its two main objectives, and for this it values resources of influential sectors. Policymaking involves, therefore, the exchange of economic, political, and social resources between the regime and influential sectors. The moving factor in this exchange is essentially a search for gains, both by the regime and by sectors; through the policy exchange sectors attempt to increase their welfare, and the regime seeks advances in its pursuit of a good society while maintaining or increasing its hold on power.

It is helpful, moreover, to regard policymaking as a dialectical process (Marsh and Smith 2000). Certain agents initiate a policy proposal (the thesis), but influential sectors with differing views on the proposal bring in suggestions to "improve" it (the antithesis), usually leading to a new proposal (a synthesis)—with elements of the "thesis" and of the "antithesis"—with a better chance of being approved. And in the process, certain organizations assume a crucial role: the *policy networks* (Marsh 1998).

A policy network is not a mere sectoral grouping of public agencies. These agencies exist and may have central positions in the network, but private agents—components of sectors—also participate; they usually have well-defined views regarding policy proposal and policy needs, and power to influence policy decisions.

There are different categories of policy networks. Some are fluid, and tend to change as a result of shifts in the political environment. Others, however, are crystallized and experience only minor and infrequent changes: they are *tight policy networks*. A characteristic of tight policy networks is that they tend to strictly control their policy areas in almost all circumstances.

The Recent Truncated Dialectical Policy Process

In Lula's first term, there were several instances of policy proposals that failed to complete the dialectic cycle: cases of *truncated dialectical policymaking*. Some blame this on managerial deficiencies but a factor in stalling policy proposals has been the operation of tight policy networks. We review below two policy areas in which this has prevailed: those of the environmental and of agrarian policies. A problem with these networks is that they have stalled policy decisions in their fields, helping to give to the Lula administration the impression of an inherent lack of ability to effectively decide. But we also examine the agricultural policy area in which a strong policy network receded to the background, giving way to the constitution of several sub-sectoral policy networks. Our review focuses initially on rural—agricultural and agrarian—policymaking; and then appraises of the environmental policy in Lula's first term.

Agricultural Policy Formation in Lula's First Term

It is useful at this point to outline the main phases of agricultural development in Brazil, and the evolution and nature of the policy networks in each. In a broad overview, we identify three main phases (Mueller and Mueller 2006):

- From the early colonial period to the late 1960s: a period of horizontal agricultural expansion.
- From 1965 to 1990: a period of induced conservative modernization.
- From the early 1990s onward: a stage of radical reversal of the interventionist strategy.

As indicated in table 7.1, a major factor in the expansion of agriculture in the first period was the incorporation of new land at the agricultural frontier. The productivity of agriculture remained low and stagnant but road construction allowed production to expand into new areas in Brazil's center-south. It is important to stress that in this period there was nothing resembling a concerted agricultural strategy; accordingly, there was no overall agricultural policy network. But there were a few commodity policy networks, the most influential of which was that of coffee.

At the end of the period however, the agricultural frontier was reaching the Cerrado, a region that, given the technologies then existing, was basically unfit for commercial agriculture. This, together with the recognition by the military regime, then in its early stage, of the crucial role of an adequate performance of agriculture in its economic strategy, led to the conservative modernization approach of the second phase.

As shown in table 7.2 there was, in the late 1960s, a critical move to a strong interventionist stance, with ample use of subsidies and incentives,

Table 7.1   Phase of horizontal agricultural expansion (1500–1964): Developments and nature of policy networks

Developments	Nature of policy networks
Increases in agricultural production through the incorporation of land in the agricultural frontier.	Absence of a national strategy of agricultural development.
Persistence of low productivity, primitive agriculture.	The Ministry of Agriculture, created only in the early 1930s, remained largely inoperative.
Until the late 1960s Brazil had a considerable stock of relatively fertile land that could be accessed, requiring only the expansion of the transportation infrastructure.	There was no overall agricultural policy network; there were, however, influential commodity policy networks: first for coffee and later for sugar, and for cotton.

Source: Author's illustration

Table 7.2   Phase of conservative modernization (1965–1990): Developments and nature of policy networks

Developments	Nature of policy networks
Period of officially induced conservative modernization led by the perception of the strategic role of an adequate performance of agriculture and of the inadequacies of the model of horizontal expansion.	Decline of influence of the traditional commodity networks (coffee, sugar). Emergence and strengthening of an overall agricultural policy network.
Main instruments of the modernization strategy: • Subsidized financing. • Development of a research network in agriculture (the EMBRAPA system). • Promotion of agribusiness complexes. • Highly interventionist stance; on the one hand there were subsidies and incentives, on the other there were frequent interventions in markets.	Main goals of its private agents: • Rent seeking; making the most of the subsidies and incentives of this period. • Protection of agriculture from the unfavorable effects of a hectic macroeconomic policy milieu.

Source: Author's illustration

and with frequent interventions in markets for products and inputs, in credit, foreign exchange, exports, and imports. The strategy was conservative, since it did nothing to change the highly concentrated pattern of land ownership.

This period saw the loss of influence of commodity networks (coffee, sugar) and the emergence of an overall agricultural network that became quite active. Its efforts were mostly directed toward rent seeking for its private agents and the search for protection from the unfavorable effects of macroeconomic policies.

Regarding the public agencies of the agricultural policy network, the interventionist stance of this period required the modernization of the Ministry of Agriculture, and the establishment or reform of other policy organizations. Among the most important are the EMBRAPA system of agricultural research, and the minimum price agency. Moreover, as the main dispenser of agricultural credit, the Banco do Brasil assumed an important position in the network's architecture. There were similar reforms in the main agricultural states.

These changes, however, did not enable the Ministry of Agriculture to become more influential in overall agricultural policy. The ultimate control over agricultural credit and the minimum price policy remained entrenched in the "economic" area of government—for example, the Ministry of Finance—limiting the reach of the agricultural policy network (C. Mueller 1988). In fact, prominent private agents of the policy network would often bypass the Ministry in attempts at influencing the economic ministries and agencies directly.

As indicated in table 7.3, in the third phase a growing resource scarcity and the inability of the public sector to cope with a complex and rapidly

Table 7.3 Phase of gradual but radical reversal of the interventionist strategy (from the early 1990s to the present)

Developments	Nature of policy networks
From the early 1990s onward there was a gradual reversal of the interventionist strategy.	Declining role of an overall agricultural policy network; it still exists, but with less influence in the policy process.
A hands-off approach was implemented; the resources for subsidies and support policies dwindled, and market interventions decreased.	Emergence of several sub-sectoral policy networks, with varying influence, each focusing the peculiarities of its own area of concern.
This notwithstanding, there was a considerable expansion of agricultural production and increase in productivity.	Very recently, however, there has been a revival of the agricultural policy network (see below).
Important factors in the process: the contributions of new agricultural technology; and the expansion, diversification, and the intricacy of Brazilian agribusiness.	

Source: Author's illustration

expanding modern agriculture, combined with the liberalizing trends of the 1990s, led to a gradual but profound change in agricultural policy-making. But the resulting hands-off stance was far from detrimental to Brazilian agriculture. In this phase, still in progress, agriculture—as the central component of thriving agribusiness complexes—experienced quite impressive increases in production, productivity, and became a major contributor to the country's balance of trade. The declines in subsidies and incentives were more than compensated by the removal of the distorting interventions of the previous period.

The third phase saw actions to curtail the number and/or size of the public organizations of the agricultural policy network, and to streamline the operation of the remainder. The role of EMBRAPA continues to be perceived as fundamental, but this institution constantly struggles to assure minimally adequate funding.

Regarding the private agents of the agricultural policy networks, the growth and the diversification of Brazilian agriculture brought about a dramatic increase in the number and scope of agribusiness organizations. Involved in a given agribusiness complex is a composite of economic organizations of which those linked to agricultural production as such are only a part. There are also agents that provide inputs and services to agriculture, and are involved in processing of agricultural commodities and in different phases of commercialization. Virtually all segments of agribusiness have specific associations, and most of them have composed particular agribusiness networks. As such, they engage in lobbying. Together with the official agricultural institutions mentioned above, and with less formal but important organizations such as the Rural Group of Congressmen (the *Bancada Ruralista*) and the Democratic Rural Union, they compose a broad agricultural policy network. The web operates parallel to many sub-sectoral agribusiness policy networks, each focusing on aspects of its area of concern. This was the situation faced by Lula in the outset of his first term, when it seemed that Brazilian agriculture had freed itself from government intervention.

Agricultural Policy in Lula's First Term

The new president did little to change the essence of the agricultural policy architecture he inherited. As he was forming his first cabinet, it was already clear that he could not embark in a radical agrarian policy, involving the confiscation of land from commercial producers, since this would destabilize one of the few sectors of the economy that was then growing; moreover, it was contributing decisively to ease the foreign exchange restriction.

Examining the political events of Lula's first term, one cannot fail to recognize his preference for placing emblematic figures in high levels of the administration. An instance is the choice of Roberto Rodrigues, a highly regarded leader of the Brazilian agribusiness association, for the Ministry of Agriculture. This was a surprising move; the campaign rhetoric created the expectation of an agrarian strategy hostile to commercial agriculture, which completely failed to materialize (C. Mueller 2004). But Lula also did not disregard an important segment of his constituency—the landless movements. Therefore he placed in the Land Reform Ministry Miguel Rossetto, an active member of PT and one committed to sharply increase the settlement of the landless peasants (more on this below).

In his term in office—ending late in 2006—Rodrigues attempted to improve the operation of the Ministry, but in doing this he had to struggle continuously to overcome the lack of resources, an arduous task given the priorities set by the "economic" area of government in the Palocci era. He also did his best to organize agribusiness policy networks; to this end he created a series of Sectoral Chambers (*Câmaras Setoriais*) operating under the sponsorship of the Ministry, one for each major agribusiness segment.

But Rodrigues also endeavored to revive the overall agricultural policy network, somewhat dormant since the late 1990s; the 1999–2004 agricultural boom had generated a certain complacency on the part of the Brazilian farmers. However, the effects of severe droughts in 2005 and 2006 coupled with an increasingly appreciated domestic currency and declines in agricultural commodity prices engendered a major debt crisis that threatened not only farmers, but also input producers, processors of agricultural commodities, and financial organizations (Rezende and Kreter 2006). It soon became obvious that the situation could not be effectively dealt with through sectoral policy networks. As a result, there were efforts to revitalize the agricultural policy network.

At the head of the agricultural policy network, Rodrigues actively pressured for means to help alleviate the crisis, but a number of policy packages were approved only in the first half of 2006. They dealt with the more immediate effects of the crisis, creating conditions for a substantial recovery of production in the 2006/2007 period. Negotiations were arduous; it took the downfall of Palocci and the direct involvement of Lula to obtain approval of the relief packages. But in a state of near exhaustion, Rodrigues left the Ministry.

The process of negotiation contributed to the resurgence of the overall agricultural policy network. A question remains however: what is the future of negotiation? Will booming commodity markets lead to a reversal to the semi-dormant state it had reached before the crisis? And what will be the role of negotiation for the substantial agricultural debt that remains?

Agrarian Policy in Lula's First Term

The other component of the rural policy scene has to do with the agrarian issue rooted in Brazil's highly skewed pattern of land ownership, and fueled by the pressure exerted by landless organizations and by the availability of underutilized agricultural land. For several decades the issue has produced heated debates, but until recently it generated very little agrarian reform. In the 1990s, however, significant changes began. Contributing to this was the foundation in 1988 of a pressure group of landless farmers, the *Movimento dos Sem Terra* (MST), a result of the growing pressure exerted by the waves of displaced farm workers and the dismal results of the Amazon frontier settlements of the military government (Alston et al. 1999). From the outset MST directed its claims to fertile lands closer to markets. Its main approach has been to promote the invasion of private "unproductive" farms and to employ violence to attract attention to the country's highly skewed distribution of landholdings. In response, the government was forced to intervene, expropriating land for agrarian reform.

The second half of the 1990s saw a marked increase in land reform initiatives. The main factor in this was the growing pressure of the squatter groups, but also contributing was the sharp declines in land prices stemming from the *Plano Real*, which resulted in substantial increases in the supply of land for sale to the government.[1] Between 1995 and 2005, more than 42 million hectares of land was redistributed to some 800,000 families (over 3 million people) at a cost of over 17 billion reais, roughly US$7.7 billion at the August 2006 exchange rate (Mueller and Mueller, 2006). This was certainly a remarkable achievement.

The Agrarian Policy Network

The creation of a specific ministry to administer agrarian policies is fairly recent; in the past some of its functions were executed by organizations of the Ministry of Agriculture. A Land Reform Ministry was created by the first administration after the end of the military regime, and it remained in operation until the present under different names; it is now called the Ministry of Agrarian Development (MAD). A result of this arrangement was that the agrarian issues were removed from the purview of the Ministry of Agriculture.

The agrarian ministry remained largely ineffective until 1994, when land reform initiatives began gaining momentum. As this happened, the ministry became increasingly captured by the landless movements in the formation of a tight policy network.

At present the agrarian policy network is basically composed, on the one hand, of the Ministry of Agrarian Development and of INCRA (the ministry's executive arm) and of parallel organizations at the state level; and, on the other hand, by landless organizations and allies such as the (Catholic) Land Pastoral Commission, and by NGOs acting in the agrarian field. In the second half of the 1990s the network had acquired enough power to critically influence land distribution initiatives. During the administration of Fernando Henrique Cardoso and particularly that of Lula, the network "tightened" the close relationship established between the landless groups, and the MAD and INCRA.

Agrarian Policy under Lula

We saw that Lula tried to compensate for his agricultural strategy by placing Miguel Rossetto in the Ministry of Agrarian Development, a figure closely linked to the landless movements. However, this did not appease the MST and its allies. To express their displeasure, during Lula's first term, they staged frequent waves of demonstrations, road blocks, and invasions of farms, federal offices, and banks. The government reacted by trying to appease the landless movements with promises of increases of land distribution programs and of more resources for credit for settlers and agrarian development cooperatives (C. Mueller 2004).

But the acquisition of land for redistribution became increasingly difficult. This is a recent dilemma of the land reform policy. Nowadays, unlike previous decades, few of the farms targeted for invasion by the landless were really unproductive. A significant share of the stock of idle farms had been taken up by the settlement programs of the 1990s and early 2000s, and the 2000–2004 agricultural boom induced a more intensive use of land in much of the remaining area. Thus, the recent episodes of invasion were mostly staged on farms that could not be easily expropriated for settlement projects (C. Mueller 2004). From the beginning of this decade, the government has been forced to purchase land at market prices, with only part of the payment in long-term bonds. As payments in cash became substantial, settlement programs soon felt a budget crunch.

This notwithstanding, as indicated, the redistribution of land has been considerable. However, progress in transforming the land reform settlers into self-sustained, productive farmers was less significant (C. Mueller 2004). With a few exceptions, the settlers have continuously depended on handouts by the government; now the landless organizations exert substantial effort to guarantee such resources for their members and their cooperatives.

It is important to stress that this is a tight policy network, one that at times seems tame and subdued—this was the case during the 2006 electoral period—but on other occasions comes out quite forcefully with invasions, blockages, and even destruction of plantations, laboratories, and buildings perpetrated by agents of the network. Of course, the MAD and satellites do not condone most of these actions, but they rarely take effective steps to curb excesses. Moreover, they have adopted a more positive stance, actively engaging in initiatives to strengthen the agrarian policy. As a result, there has been a striking increase in the budget allocated to agrarian policies to the detriment of resources for initiatives of interest of the agricultural policy network.

Agricultural and Agrarian Policies: Aren't There Tradeoffs?

We have claimed that a study of policymaking that ignores the fundamental dimension of power is likely to originate misleading results; the above discussion brought out the importance of considering this dimension. But given the usual division of labor between economists and political scientists, one may argue that economists should continue to concentrate on the dimension of rationality, leaving to political scientists the dimension of power. A further look into agricultural and agrarian policies illustrates how this procedure can result in misleading analyses and inadequate prescriptions.

In their comprehensive study of these two branches of rural policies, Chaddad et al. (2006) have identified a sharp reduction, since 1985, of the federal combined real expenditure in the two policy areas. In addition, the study found a declining trend in the proportion of the rural federal resources destined to traditional agricultural policies and a corresponding increase in the proportion of such resources devoted to agrarian policies; and this trend was stepped up in Lula's first term.[2] Arguing that currently the social returns of expenditure in traditional agricultural policies—in areas such as agricultural research and extension, food security, animal and vegetable health—is much higher than the returns to the handouts of agrarian programs, the study proposes the fusion of the two rural ministries (Ministry of Agriculture and the Ministry of Agrarian Development) and the pooling of the resources devoted to each, establishing as a criterion of resource allocation the marginal social return of each specific policy. Asset or income transfer expenditures should be maintained based on equity considerations, but they should be moderate and should not involve never-ending grants.

This is a typical instance of a recommendation founded on rationality considerations; but it is clearly unfeasible. The tight agrarian policy network would fiercely oppose such a recommendation, and an administration attempting to implement it would fail, and would probably pay a high political price in the process. A recommendation such as this, based solely on social returns of policy expenditures, would almost certainly produce unintended and undesirable results.

Environmental Policymaking in Lula's First Term.

The emergence of an environmental policy network in Brazil is fairly recent. Most of the more significant legislation regarding environmental policy dates from the 1980s, with emphasis on the environmental provisions of the 1988 constitution. There is also a strict Forest Code and a harsh law on environmental crimes. Moreover, numerous laws and decrees were passed—in all levels of government—with a direct bearing on environmental policy.[3] Along with this legislation a policy structure was formed, culminating in the 1980s with the creation of a Ministry of the Environment (MMA) and of its executive arm, the Brazilian Institute of the Environment and of Renewable Natural Resources (IBAMA).

Moreover, numerous environmental NGOs also sprung up. In the early 1990s, Brazil already had a large number of environmental NGOs, many "amateurish and ineffective, but a few highly professional" (Baer 2001: 412); and some with constructive behaviors, but others with fundamentalist outlooks and aggressive conducts. And the expansion of environmental NGOs persisted in the 1990s.

Some of these NGOs were able to exert influence on environmental policy, becoming a factor in "tightening" the environmental policy network. More recently, the influence of public actors outside the executive branches of government dealing with environmental policy increased noticeably. Among those that deserve mention are public prosecutors operating in the area of environment protection (B. Mueller 2006). Their actions often contribute to the achievement of the objectives of the environmental policy network.

The tightening of the environmental policy network began almost with the inception of the environmental policy. In fact, the policy network was already tight before Lula's inauguration in 2003, but under him it received a considerable thrust. One of the emblematic figures Lula placed in high position at the outset of his first term was Senator Marina Silva, chosen to lead the MMA. The reputation of Marina Silva was established by her association with Chico Mendes—the leader murdered in a struggle for a less destructive use of the Amazon forest—and it was enhanced by her outstanding career in the Senate.

Marina Silva has firmly pressed to increase the power of the environmental policy network. In fact, she aims at much more. She claims that since almost all public policies have environmental consequences, some of which can be substantial, environmental sustainability considerations should be taken into account in development planning, in investment in infrastructure, and even in the regulation of the actions of private agents. Moreover, this should reach the highest level and not only that of individual projects.[4] She has actively pursued this goal, but as should be expected, with scant results. Nevertheless, leaving aside lamentations and denunciations, she has devoted her energies—with substantial success—to the improvement of the operation of the MMA and IBAMA, and to strengthening the environmental policy network.

The environmental policy network became able, on various occasions, to stop or considerably delay the implementation of decisions and the execution of projects it regarded as unsustainable. In fact, the obstructionist tactics went on to a point that they began to concern Lula himself. We shall review two instances of the action of this tight environmental policy network in obstructing policy decisions considered unsustainable.

The Environmental Policy Network and the Licensing of Genetically Modified Organisms(GMOs)

Research in biotechnology and the use of products of biotechnology, are the object of a specific law (the Biosecurity Law), and the National

Commission of Biosecurity (CTNBio) is the institution that regulates this area. The Law and the Commission in its present configuration have achieved notoriety in the context of the introduction in Brazil of the cultivation of soybeans from genetically modified seeds.

The genetically modified soy seeds developed by Monsanto were engineered to resist a herbicide produced by this company. With one important exception, farmers of the main soybean producing countries have wholeheartedly adopted the "transgenic soybeans" technology since it substantially reduces production costs. The exception was Brazil, thanks to the action of the environmental policy network. Due to the impact it had in tightening the policy network, we outline the progression of transgenic soybeans in Brazil.

Before 1998, the cultivation and trade of genetically modified soybeans in Brazil were modest; it was first authorized in that year by a resolution of what we term, the old CTNBio—a commission of scientists to which the new technology was submitted, and who judged it environmentally safe. The old CTNBio, instituted by a 1995 law, provided technical support to the federal government on decisions related to the research and use of GMO technologies.[5] It was assumed that the endorsement by the old CTNBio would be enough to allow the cultivation of transgenic soybeans. However, according to the environmental legislation, for such an authorization to be granted, it has to be cleared by a formal Study of Environmental Impact. Since Monsanto had not carried out such a study, a judicial embargo suspended the authorization.

There has been a fierce opposition by the environmental policy network to the transgenic soybean technology. Fearing its environmental impacts, loathing the multinational Monsanto, and disregarding the experience of other countries, the network went out of its way to block the formal introduction of genetically modified soybeans. In spite of its efforts, however, the genetically modified soybean technology spread rapidly; this took place initially in the southern state of Rio Grande do Sul, but gradually the transgenic soybeans moved into most of the other producing states.

This created an awkward situation; when the judicial ban was decreed, many thousands of farmers were already cultivating transgenic soybeans, and it would be impossible to enforce the ban without huge economic losses and political turmoil. As a result, in 2001 the government issued a Medida Provisória—which the Congress later ratified—allowing, exceptionally, for a limited period, the cultivation and commercialization of transgenic soybeans in Brazil's south (Medida Provisória 113, later Law 10,688). But since in the succeeding years the cultivation of transgenic soybeans increased, similar schemes were implemented. Thus in 2003 and 2004—during Lula's first term—the Medidas Provisórias 131 and 223—later ratified by Congress—were enacted. This way, in spite of legal impediments (Monsanto never conducted the Study of Environmental Impact), transgenic soybeans became a fact of life in Brazil.

How did this affect the environmental policy network? Regardless of its failure in banning the genetically modified soybeans, the network gained strength. It did this in the process of reform of the Biosecurity Law and of the National Commission of Biosecurity. A new Biosecurity Law enacted in 2005 recreated CTNBio with a different structure; instead of a commission composed only of scientists, it became a larger body, including representatives of environmental NGOs, consumer groups, and similar organizations.[6] Moreover, the Biosecurity Law mandated a two-third majority of the 54 members of CTNBio for the approval of any authorization for the research, and for the use in production of the outcomes of research in biotechnology.

The new CNTBio was created with a majority of scientists in the field, but in practice, vocal "representatives of society" were able to dominate the deliberations, leading the commission to a virtual standstill. This was achieved by making nearly impossible the attainment of a two-thirds majority of the members in considering a request the policy network did not endorse. Under the banner of "a Brazil free of GMOs," representatives of civil society, almost all connected to the environmental policy network, transformed the meetings of the CTNBio into rallies in which politico-ideological arguments and slogans prevailed over rational, scientific arguments. This tactic discouraged the involvement of the technically motivated members of the commission,[7] and CNTBio became unable to make decisions. A large number of requests for research and application of biotechnology are waiting for rulings, which are constantly postponed.

But recently the lower house of Congress reacted to the stalemate by approving a bill changing the criterion for decisions by CNTBio, from the two-thirds rule to that of a simple majority (*Boletim ANBIO*, January 3, 2007). The environmental policy network lost the struggle to stop the bill, during which it had to fight the agricultural policy network. However, a final outcome is still pending; the bill still has to be approved by the Senate, and signed by Lula. The environmental policy network will surely try to prevent this.

The Environmental Policy Network and the Issue of Permits for Large Projects

The Brazilian Constitution mandates that the implementation of infrastructure projects—be it by the government or by private agents—must be preceded by a formal authorization, issued—depending of the magnitude and the geographical scope of the project—by environmental organizations at the federal, state, or county level. A Study of Environmental Impact must be submitted, and it has to be subjected to public hearings.

This is no doubt an adequate way of tackling projects with potentially large environmental impacts. Brazil offers important instances of projects executed without this safeguard that engendered extensive negative environmental externalities. The problem, however, is that the fundamentalist members of the environmental policy network oppose in principle the execution of large projects, and endeavor to block their execution. This is often done by obstructing the approval of Studies of Environmental Impact and delaying or preventing the execution of infrastructure projects.

This practice has been conspicuous in the case of hydroelectric projects, but was used in road construction projects, and in oil exploration.[8] Such tactics are affecting, for instance, the execution of the two proposed hydroelectric plants at the Madeira River, in the Amazon, with the capacity of over three thousand megawatts each. A successful completion of these plants is considered fundamental to reduce the threat of blackouts at the end of the present decade, similar to those that decelerated economic growth in 2001 (*O Estado de S. Paulo*, July 23, 2006, A3). However, because the projects are located in the Amazon and have potential impacts over large geographical areas, their licensing is being obstructed by the environmental policy network.

An observation is in order here: the impression from articles in the press is that environmentalists have entirely dominated the licensing process, systematically opposing progress. This view can be overstated. According to José Goldemberg, a respected scientist who, until recently, was the secretary of Environment of the state of São Paulo (see Goldemberg 2006), two types of extremists have interfered in the area of environmental licensing: those who place growth and progress above all considerations—for them, environmental licensing should be drastically simplified; and the environmental fundamentalists, who demand extreme rigor in licensing, regardless of the importance of a project. Goldemberg acknowledges that initially the first group dominated project appraisal, and Studies of Environmental Impacts were perfunctorily executed. But this has changed; licensing became much more rigorous, more technically complex, but there weren't appreciable improvements in the technical capability of the public sector to deal with licensing. Moreover, the statutes regulating the process are confusing and misleading.

But it is true that the environmental fundamentalists take advantage of these weaknesses to block projects and initiatives they decided to contest. In line with the truncated dialectical policy model that prevailed in Lula's first administration, initially obstruction was allowed to persist almost without interference. But at the outset of his second term, Lula announced accelerating the country's growth as a major goal, and a central component of the proposed strategy for this was the expansion of investment in infrastructure, with emphasis in the area of hydroelectricity. Thus, protracted environmental licensing became identified as an obstacle to growth.

The president himself expressed apprehension in this regard, and on December 17, 2006, he held a special meeting with high-ranking governmental officials concerned with development and environment protection to tackle the problem (*O Estado de S. Paulo*, December 18, 2006, B1). The main decision that emerged was that a bill would be sent to Congress to streamline the legal statutes on the matter considered too vague.[9] It is interesting to note that, following this meeting, high-level officials of the Ministry of the Environment went out of their way to downplay its importance. Before the meeting Marina Silva had already expressed her opposition to fundamental reforms in the environmental legislation.[10] In a January 7, 2007, interview to the *Estado de S. Paulo*, she argued that problems of environmental licensing are essentially the result of the inadequate preparation of investment projects and of governmental organizations ill equipped to deal with licensing. For her, the environmental establishment is merely doing its job; and following suit, the secretary general of the MMA publicly expressed a similar view.[11]

This was the situation at the time of this writing. It is worth observing how the government will go about in removing obstacles interposed by licensing for the proposed infrastructure investments. Will the full dialectic cycle of policymaking run its course, or will it remain truncated by endless dissension? The situation is especially striking regarding the large hydroelectricity projects considered essential to minimize the risk of an energy crisis.[12] This is a particularly delicate issue for Lula; in 2001 an energy crisis caused by insufficient rain in the region of major hydroelectric reservoirs curtailed growth. Lula and the PT reacted by sharply censuring the Cardoso administration for its incompetence in energy management. This reproach was reiterated during the 2002 and 2006 presidential campaigns. An energy crisis on the eve of the next presidential campaign could be disastrous for the Lula coalition. Therefore, one can expect a major effort to avert such a crisis. But will it happen? And will the effort produce satisfactory results?[13]

Conclusion

Our overview of agricultural, agrarian, and environmental policy formation was undertaken against the backdrop of the truncated dialectical policy process that evolved during Lula's first term, highlighting the makeup of the policy networks in these areas. The study is just a preliminary step in the investigation of policy formation in the three fields. Further research is needed to identify in more detail the operation of the respective policy networks and to establish the degree of acceptance or of resistance of each to different types of policy proposals. Such scrutiny would clarify the roles played by tight policy networks and by sheer incompetence in the truncated dialectical policy process that seems likely to continue during the remainder of Lula's second term.

Notes

1. Holders of idle land for protection against inflation endeavored to sell their holdings, given the expectations of further decreases in land prices.
2. Between 1985 and 1989 traditional agricultural policies received 94 percent, and agrarian policies, 6 percent of the federal resources for agriculture; in the Lula 2003–2005 period,

traditional policies received 55 percent, and agrarian policies 45 percent of the total rural resources. Chaddad, Jank, Nakahodo (2006, Table 2).
3. A Legislative summary regarding the environment can be found in Annex I of MMA, 2000. See also Scalzilli et al. (2005).
4. An instance of her outlook is in the interview she gave to the *O Estado de S. Paulo* (see issue of January 7, 2007). Her views are much more forcefully voiced when she addresses sympathetic audiences.
5. A complete survey of the legal instruments regarding transgenic soybeans in Brazil up to the end of 2005 is in Scalzilli, Scalzilli, and Dia 2005. This portion of the paper makes extensive use of the material contained in their article.
6. The rationale for this change in the composition of the CTNBio was that decisions regarding biotechnology should not be taken only by scientists but, given their potential impacts, also by representatives of society at large.
7. The articles by Leila Oda (2006), and by Jank and Lima (2006) provide an overview of the situation from the standpoint of the scientific minded members of the commission.
8. See, for instance, *O Estado de S. Paulo*, November 19, 2006, for a survey of blocked projects and initiatives leaked to the press by the government; licensing problems in the area of oil extraction are mentioned in Cardoso (2006: 27).
9. As reported in *O Estado de São Paulo*, November 18, 2006, p. B1.
10. *O Estado de São Paulo*, December 9, 2006, B10.
11. In a press release of the Ministry of the Environment (Mattos, 2006) the Secretary General states: "The debate on environmental licensing…is marred by irrationality. Licensing has been used as a smokescreen to hide other problems, such as the lack of planning of the areas of government dealing with infrastructure, the lack of resources for investment and insufficient managerial skill of certain sectors."
12. The risk of an energy blackout is considered substantial. The *O Estado de São Paulo* (January 28, 2007) printed excerpts of a technical report by the Secretariat of Economic Studies of the Finance Ministry stressing the likelihood of such a blackout by 2010 if there is to be a resumption of growth. Annual growth rates higher than 4 percent for the 2007–2010 period, together with long delays is the completion of hydroelectric projects and with problems in the supply of natural gas for thermal plants would substantially increase the likelihood of a blackout.
13. Since the seminar for which this paper was written, the network was defeated on the licensing issue. Pressured by the government on the licensing and on other issues, in May 2008 Marina Silva resigned her post at the Environment Ministry and was replaced by Carlos Minc, a more "pragmatic" environmentalist. Needless to say, both hydroelectric projects were granted environmental licenses.

References

Alston, Lee J., Garry D. Libecap, and Bernardo Mueller. 1999, *Titles, Conflict, and Land Use—the Development of Property Rights on the Brazilian Amazon Frontier*. Ann Arbor: The University of Michigan Press.
Baer, Werner. 2001. *The Brazilian Economy—Growth and Development*. 5th Ed. Westport, CT: Praeger.
Boletim ANBIO, January 3, 2007. Bulletin released by the Associação Nacional de Biosegurança titled Bio Notícias Semanal at www.anbio.org.br.
Cardoso, Beatriz, 2006. "A energia dos investimentos." *Conjuntura Econômica* 60(10) (October):20–27.
Chaddad, Fabio, Marcos S. Jank, and Sydney Nakahodo. 2006. "Repensando as políticas agrícola e agrária do Brasil." São Paulo, *Digesto Econômico* (November/December): 6–45.
Goldemberg, José. 2006. "Ambientalistas ameaçam o desenvolvimento?" *O Estado de S. Paulo*, December 19, A2.
Jank, Marcus Sawaya, and Rodrigo C.A. Lima. 2006. "Carl Sagan e a vela na escuridão." *O Estado de S. Paulo*, December 20, p.A2.
MMA. 2000. Ministério do Meio Ambiente, IBAMA, Gestão dos Recursos Naturais—Subsídios à Elaboração da Agenda 21 Brasileira. Brasília, Edições IBAMA.

Marsh, David, 1998. *Comparing Policy Networks*. Buckingham: Open University Press.

Marsh, David, and Martin Smith. 2000. "Understanding Policy Networks: Towards a Dialectical Approach." *Political Studies* 48:4–21.

Mueller, Bernardo. 2006. "Who Enforces Enforcement? Can Public Prosecutors in Brazil Break the Endless Regress?" Paper Presented at the 3rd World Congress of Environmental and Resource Economists, Kyoto, Japan, July 3–7.

Mueller, Charles. 1982. "Formulação de políticas agrícolas." *Revista de Economia Política* 2/1(5) (January/March):89–122.

———. 1988. "Conflitos intragovernamentais e a formação de preços agrícolas no Brasil." *Pesquisa e Planejamento Econômico* 18(3) (December):685–708.

———. 2004. "Brazil: Agriculture and the Agrarian Problem and the Lula Government." Paper Presented at the 2004 Meeting of the Latin American Studies Association, Las Vegas, Nevada, October 7–9.

Mueller, Charles, and Bernardo Mueller. 2006. "The Evolution of Agriculture and Land Reform in Brazil: 1950–2006." Paper Prepared for the Conference in Honor of Werner Baer, University of Illinois, Urbana/Champaign, December 1–2.

Oda, Leila. 2006. "CTNBio parada." *O Estado de S. Paulo*, November 4, p. A2.

Rezende, Gervásio Castro de, and Ana Cecília Kreter. 2006. "Política Agrícola, dez., 2006." *Boletim de Conjuntura*, Rio de Janeiro, IPEA (75) (December):63–75.

Scalzilli, João Carlos Lopes, João Pedro Scalzilli, and Lucas M. Dia. 2005. "Soja transgênica no Brasil: anotações sobre a legislação de plantio, comercialização e direitos de propriedade intelectual." *Última Instância—Revista Jurídica* at http://ultimainstancia.uol.com.br/editorial/ler_noticia.php?id.Noticia=19475 accessed on January 22, 2007.

CHAPTER EIGHT

The Labor Policies of the Lula Government

MICHAEL M. HALL

One of the mysteries of Brazilian politics has been the survival of the Vargas-era system of labor relations into the twenty-first century.[1] It has practically no open defenders, though there are some who see positive aspects to one or another of its features. Yet, the system has survived virtually intact through dictatorships and democracy, governments of Left and Right, two "democratic transitions," and enormous economic and social changes over more than 60 years.

The system is a form of state corporatism implanted in stages between 1931 and 1943, and clearly fascist in inspiration.[2] While it is not particularly surprising that Brazil adopted corporatist measures in the 1930s, most such arrangements elsewhere did not long survive the fall of the dictatorships that implanted them. It must be said, however, that the lawyers who carried out the initial planning in Vargas's new Labor Ministry in the early 1930s had long associations with the Left and seem to have been influenced by interwar debates among European socialists over the use of corporatist solutions as a means of restricting what they regarded as the chaos of the capitalist market and the wasteful effects of the class struggle. Moreover, as Zeev Sternhell and others have shown, important elements of fascist doctrine originated with the political Left.

In any case, the Vargas regime codified the Brazilian system in 1943 in the highly detailed Consolidation of the Labor Laws (CLT), still in effect. Armando Boito Jr. argues that the essential elements of the system are: 1) state recognition as a condition for the existence of unions; 2) the principle of *unicidade*,[3] the single union system, which permits only one union per category in a given territorial unit; and 3) the union tax (or "contribution"), by which all workers in a category, union members or not, have the equivalent of one day's wage per year deducted and paid to the union system.[4] It seems to me that there has also been a fourth element, now disregarded in practice in some cases, which is the effective exclusion of unions from the workplace. Various repressive elements historically associated with the system have disappeared, largely as a result of the 1988 Constitution. There is now a broad right to strike, for example, and the Labor Ministry can no longer take over unions and replace their officers. In addition, formerly prohibited *centrais*,[5] nationwide associations of unions, have existed since the 1980s, though with limitations on their powers, as will be seen below.

Demands for changes in the labor laws have a long history in Brazil, as unions tied to the state and under the sway of *pelegos* (complacent leaders subservient to the state and unresponsive to rank-and-file demands) represented very imperfectly the interests of their members. Although there are some earlier precedents, the "new unionism" that emerged in the 1970s forcefully rejected the essential features of the system and called for their abolition. In the struggle against the military dictatorship, workers' demands for union autonomy and democracy occupied a significant place.[6] In 1985, the first civilian government, that of José Sarney, proposed a law to legalize strikes and change the corporatist union structure, although his labor minister, Almir Pazzianotto, made clear that the measures would be subject to negotiation. In fact, they drew so much hostile fire from both employers and unions that they were withdrawn and a more elaborate bill introduced only in 1987. This would have ended the Labor Ministry's powers of union recognition and intervention, gradually eliminated the union tax, created a form of plural unionism, and permitted the existence of *centrais*. The government only presented its proposal as the Congress began debate on the 1988 Constitution and apparently had little expectation that the measures would be approved, intending instead simply to signal its responsiveness to public pressures.[7]

In the 1980s, a combative union movement, under conditions of very high inflation and relatively low unemployment, won some dramatic victories and helped to consolidate and extend the democratic process after 20 years of military dictatorship. The Constitution ratified in 1988 included a considerable range of social rights and served to strengthen the position of the labor movement although many found it somewhat contradictory in promising full freedom to unions while keeping the principle of *unicidade*, which retains the state as regulator of the union structure.

The election of Fernando Collor in 1989, however, represented a drastic change. The new president embarked on a program of neoliberal reforms, including a measure to abolish the union tax immediately. The Congress amended the original bill so as to eliminate the tax gradually over a period of five years. Collor then refused to negotiate and vetoed the measure, thus leaving the union tax in force.[8] The government introduced other proposals concerning union organization and collective bargaining, but a hostile congressional committee modified them drastically, and they never came to a vote. (The measures were finally withdrawn a decade later by Fernando Henrique Cardoso, who had other plans.) Following Collor's impeachment, his successor, Itamar Franco, and particularly the latter's labor minister, Walter Barelli, attempted to establish an institutional dialogue with the labor movement through such mechanisms as the Sectorial Chambers later abolished by the Cardoso government.[9]

Unions faced a much more hostile environment in the 1990s than they had in the previous decade.[10] Workers proved harder to mobilize under the conditions of low inflation prevailing after 1994 while recession and, in particular, high rates of unemployment created an atmosphere of fear and insecurity that left the labor movement very much on the defensive. Moreover, Brazilian industry modernized considerably during the 1990s, introducing new technologies and new management techniques on a considerable scale. The effects of restructuring and government economic policies included the marked growth not only of the unemployed, but also of those "precariously employed," who were unorganized, without social benefits and enjoyed little legal protection. About half the labor force was thought to be in the informal sector by the end of the 1990s. According to one study, of the 290,000 workers in the ABC industrial suburbs of São Paulo who lost jobs in the metalworking sector between 1989 and 1997, only half returned to the formal labor market, often in low paid and rarely unionized service sector jobs. Unemployment in metropolitan areas reached 14 percent in 1999. Some of the workers heavily affected by restructuring to reduce labor costs, such as those in banking and the automobile industry, had been among the most combative and organized in the struggles of the 1980s.

Not only did the labor movement have to deal with a weakened and increasingly heterogeneous labor force, but employers took the ideological offensive through courses and training programs that aimed at creating new mentalities among workers by dissolving class identifications and distancing them from the unions. Employers sought to identify their employees with the firm, emphasizing common interests, loyalty, work quality, skill, productivity, and what was often termed the new rationality of productive relations in a period of globalization.

A broader ideological operation served to change the basis of political debate in the society as a whole. Invoking the mantras of neoliberalism triumphant elsewhere, employers and their spokesmen succeeded in creating a new discourse in Brazil, whose key terms became "agility," "modernity," and "flexibility." The existing labor legislation was depicted as "rigid," "authoritarian," and above all, "old." Metaphors involving straitjackets and plaster casts abounded. Flexibility, generally a euphemism for taking away workers' rights, was said to be the way to create new jobs, while the political objective became the removal of the state from labor relations, which were to be left, insofar as possible, to the free play of market forces.

The labor movement also suffered from internal divisions, when the *Central Única dos Trabalhadores* (CUT), whose origins lay in the "new unionism" of the 1970s and 1980s, faced the emergence of the *Força Sindical* (FS), aligned with neoliberalism.[11] The FS, which grew out of unions historically tied to the state structure, promised a "unionism of results" and received much encouragement from conservative forces of various types. While sometimes combative in economic questions, the FS generally sought to cooperate with management in labor disputes and criticized the often-confrontational style of the CUT.

Moreover, the number of unions grew to immense proportions as one of the perverse consequences of the 1988 Constitution, which eliminated the need for new unions to secure prior recognition from the Labor Ministry. Approval became perfunctory, workers could define new categories, and the number of unions is thought to have reached the extraordinary figure of 20,000. While the frequently cited Union of Astrologers may actually be apocryphal, there apparently is a Union of Ministers of Evangelical Churches and Similar Workers. Since the new unions can receive substantial sums from the automatic union tax, the so-called pulverization of existing unions and the creation of new ones proceeded apace. Not all the new entities were fraudulent, and some reached previously unorganized categories of workers, but the general result hardly seems to have made unions any more legitimate or more representative of Brazilian workers. As one observer noted, all that is needed currently to form a new union is "a little creativity and a good lawyer."[12]

Fernando Henrique Cardoso, who occupied the presidency from 1995 to 2003, never attempted a comprehensive reform of Brazilian labor relations, but introduced a number of significant changes, particularly in the field of individual employment relationships.[13] Various figures in his government proposed dramatic changes in labor relations at one time or another, including the abolition of the Labor Court system and an amendment to eliminate the section on labor rights from the 1988 Constitution.[14]

Cardoso's initial priority, however, was to ensure the success of his economic stabilization policy, and this led to often difficult relations with the more combative parts of the labor movement. Shortly after taking office, the new government faced a strike by several categories of public employees over the nonfulfillment of promises made by the previous government, along with some other issues. The government considered the strike a threat to its economic policy and reacted harshly, securing a decision by the Supreme Labor Tribunal (TST) that the strike by the most important category, petroleum refinery workers, was illegal. Petrobrás, the state company that held a monopoly on refining, started firing strikers. The army occupied key refineries, and the TST began to charge the union heavy fines, as well as blocking the union's bank accounts. The government thus broke the strike, certainly with the intention of intimidating other parts of the union movement from attempting similar actions. The government's admirers likened the defeat of the refinery workers to Thatcher's victory over the British coal miners a decade earlier.[15]

The Cardoso administration implemented an important initiative that had been proposed at the end of Itamar Franco's government, Participation in Profits and Results by workers (Participação nos Lucros ou Resultados—PLR). This system became a means for firms to pay workers without having to raise formal wages. Since payments via the PLR are exempt from the requirement of paying "social charges"[16] and have the effect of creating a variable form of pay, the program proved popular with employers. How benefits are calculated depends entirely on negotiation between firms and their workers. Unions participate in some cases, but elected commissions of workers' representatives can also conduct the negotiations, thus excluding unions. There have been complaints about access to information concerning the firms' operations, but the program has spread widely and, in many cases, negotiations over PLR payments have become more significant than those over wages. It is also important to note that bargaining necessarily concentrates on individual firms, the level at which unions have historically been weakest in Brazil. Presumably, one intention of the PLR was that workers would concern themselves with the firm's competitiveness and thus take a more sympathetic stance toward such matters as cost cutting and the introduction of new methods of production.

The Cardoso government also introduced several measures designed to increase flexibility in labor contracts. One law authorized contracts for specific periods of time with lower benefits and lower social charges, which also served to reduce the costs of firing workers. Other laws authorized part-time contracts and permitted layoffs (the temporary suspension of contracts) for up to five months, during which time workers would receive a payment for retraining courses. Perhaps the most interesting measure was the Bank of Hours, originally a program instituted in 1995 by the metalworkers in São Bernardo to try to avoid dismissals.[17] Although it created some disruption in workers' lives, the scheme certainly made work time more flexible. It also drastically reduced overtime pay.[18]

Cardoso introduced his most ambitious reform only at the end of his second term, when his popularity and bargaining power had fallen considerably. The history of this incident reveals quite a lot about the difficulties of labor law reform in Brazil. The essential idea of the proposal sent to the Congress in 2001 was that "what is negotiated should prevail over what is legislated," meaning that guarantees in the CLT would henceforth be subject to bargaining between workers and employers. Since the Constitution mentions various labor rights in rather generic terms, their details depend on the CLT. Thus, the guaranteed 30 days of annual vacation can be divided, according to the CLT, into no more than two parts. The government argued that workers and employers should be able to negotiate three 10-day vacation periods. Most of the other examples cited by supporters of the proposal seem equally unexceptional.

The weekly day of rest could fall on any day if the parties so agreed, for example. Payment of the 13th monthly wage[19] could be divided into several parts rather than being paid in December. There was always, however, considerable doubt about the extension and possible effects of opening up rights guaranteed in the CLT to collective bargaining. Critics pointed out that many unions are small, unaccustomed to bargaining, and might not be able to defend workers effectively. Others considered the general principle of "negotiated agreements prevailing over laws" as potentially quite dangerous.

The CUT mobilized demonstrators against the proposal, while the FS defended it vehemently, echoing the government's argument that the changes would create more jobs.[20] Public opinion is hard to interpret, since only a minority of the people polled were familiar with the proposals. In São Paulo, among those who said they knew something about the bill, 47 percent favored it and 46 percent opposed, though class differences were marked and, among those who considered themselves well informed, the proposal lost by a 2 to 1 margin.[21] The government lobbied the Congress hard for the bill and the press reported that "those who vote against the President cannot count on good will in the authorization of resources for budgetary amendments designed to please their electoral bases."[22] Dornelles, the minister of labor, spent his weekend telephoning deputies and also "asked for help from big businessmen in order that they contact politicians with whom they have ties."[23]

Nevertheless, the government's supporters showed considerable apprehension about the vote. Nelson Marchezan, deputy leader of the PSDB, said that "the government has no way of coming out well in this affair, even if it wins the vote, because it lost the battle of communication to the parties of the Left and the unions." Yeda Crusius, then a PSDB deputy, commented that "the harm to us has already happened and is irremediable." A PFL deputy, Felix Mendonça said that the "the business unions dealt with the question badly, defending the proposal in a very ostensive and intransigent way, giving the impression that the big winners would be the bosses"[24] Aécio Neves, president of the Chamber of Deputies, asked the president to withdraw "constitutional urgency" from the bill, which would have effectively killed it, but Cardoso refused.[25]

On the day of the vote, the electronic voting panel in the Chamber of Deputies "unexpectedly and inexplicably" broke down.[26] Government supporters left the hall so there would be no quorum for a vote. Despite this fiasco, and following intense pressure, including the personal involvement of the president, the deputies finally passed the measure the following week by a margin of 264 to 213, though the deputies from São Paulo voted against it by a margin of 43 to 26. The situation in the Senate seemed more difficult, and early in 2002 the government withdrew constitutional urgency from the bill, ostensibly in order to pass the extension of the CPMF, a special tax on banking transactions. Apparently, the political costs of tampering with the labor laws in an election year simply struck many politicians as too risky. In any case, the measure never came to a vote in the Senate, and the president's often-expressed intention to "put an end to the Vargas era" suffered another defeat.

Cardoso provided a curious explanation for his intense efforts on behalf of changes in the CLT. "In private conversations, FHC gives vent to his feelings that he can no longer bear to hear businessmen charge that he changed nothing in the relations between labor and capital during these seven years in office." According to the report, "FHC now considers that he has something to say in his meetings with businessmen." Maliciously enough, the journalists then cited unnamed government deputies who opposed the project and suspected that Dornelles and Cardoso supported it so strongly because they were thinking about the upcoming elections, seeking to "please some economic sectors, potential contributors to election campaigns."[27]

In the presidential campaign of 2002, Lula promised a broad reform of the labor laws, which was to be prepared democratically through extensive deliberations organized by a tripartite National Labor Forum (FNT).[28] Such a procedure contrasted sharply with that of previous governments, whose proposals and decrees had often been drafted rather surreptitiously by sympathetic specialists. Upon taking office in 2003, the new government hoped to secure a sufficiently broad consensus among workers and business interests to give labor law reforms a good chance of approval by the Congress.

The process turned out to take considerably longer that the government originally expected. The newly established Forum organized extensive debates in the various states during the second half of 2003. The government quickly concluded that it would separate the question of reforms in union structure from that of changes in the CLT and individual workers' rights. The two matters had quite different histories: the call for union reform came from the new unionism of the late 1970s, while CLT revisions formed part of the neoliberal agenda of the 1990s. Employers and their allies wanted the Congress to consider the two questions simultaneously, and it is not difficult to image what might have happened. Never far below the surface were possible bargains of the sort: "we'll allow some union presence in the plant if you'll agree to let the thirteenth wage, extra pay for night work, overtime, and so on, be freely negotiated."

The government's clear intention was first to strengthen the unions through legal reforms, and only after the Congress had approved these would they proceed to debate proposed changes in the CLT. Since so many principles of labor law are enshrined in the 1988 Constitution, even the first stage had to include a constitutional amendment as well as a second separate bill specifying union reforms dealt with in ordinary law. The actual drafting of these first two measures took quite some time, since Brazil is a civil law country, whose traditions call for highly detailed legal specifications designed to cover all eventualities and thus to reduce the discretionary powers of judges to a minimum.[29]

In March, 2005, the government sent the proposed constitutional amendment, PEC[30] 369/05, to the Congress, where it would require a difficult three-fifths majority. The ordinary law proposal was drafted but would formally go to the Congress only after the approval of the PEC. These measures represented in most cases the consensus reached by the FNT, though when the representatives of workers and employers failed to come to an agreement, the government included its own choices. Among the principal areas of disagreement were the question of unions in the workplace and the number of union officials who would receive job guarantees against reprisals by employers. The definition and punishment of "anti-union conduct," particularly strike breaking, also provoked insurmountable disagreements.

In fact, the consensus arrived at by the FNL was rather shaky, as can be seen in Carlos Henrique Horn's analysis of the debates in the various State Labor Conferences. Only some of the participants supported, in one form or another, the central theses of the proposed reforms, while a large number actually preferred to retain major aspects of the existing system, such as *unicidade* and the union tax.[31] In retrospect, this should not be too surprising, given that the government decided to base the FNT on the *centrais*, most of which depend in one way or another on precisely those two features of the Vargas system.

The government never explicitly confronted the "discourse of flexibility," triumphant as it was, after all, in most of the world. Nor did it intend to compromise the international competitiveness of Brazilian industry, but rather to seek some acceptable balance between flexibility and rights. Nevertheless, the proposals included quite enough innovation to infuriate business interests and the Right generally. The main principle is clear: the government wanted to ensure the existence of representative and democratic unions, strong enough to face employers successfully in future collective bargaining. In order to secure this objective, they were willing to give up ground in a number of areas.

Perhaps the two key proposals are the strengthening of the *centrais* and the assurance of a union presence in the workplace. While the *centrais* would have to meet some criteria of representativity, they would be recognized as legal bargaining agents, a right they did not have at the time. The government's expectation seems to have been that the bargaining power of *centrais* would permit stronger and more uniform workers' demands, a considerable innovation in Brazil. They would also have considerable powers in certain areas over their affiliated unions.

Brazilian workers have long called for effective representation in the workplace, which the 1988 Constitution authorizes in general terms for firms with more than 200 employees. However, such representation currently operates only where strong unions have managed to impose their presence. The government proposal includes a number of safeguards to protect the elected representatives and to assure an important role for the unions in the operation of the system. The expectation is that workplace representation will permit the resolution of many day-to-day disputes at the plant level, as well as adding a new and dynamic component to union activity and to collective bargaining. However, the decision to exclude from these obligatory arrangements those workplaces with fewer than 30 employees would presumably leave the possible representation of a very large number of workers to the vagaries of future collective bargaining.

The proposals also take on the historic essentials of the corporatist system. The union tax is to be abolished over a period of three years, and unions' revenues will henceforth depend on the services they provide. While dues can be charged only to members, the unions will receive a collective bargaining fee from all workers covered by the resulting contract. An assembly open to all will set the level of the fee. Since most strong unions no longer depend heavily on the union tax and a few even return it to their members, the effects of abolition will presumably be felt most strongly by the so-called rubber stamp unions, probably closing them down.

The measures eliminate *unicidade* and open the possibility of there being more than one union among a category of workers in a given area. However, in order to secure some kind of consensus, the government accepted a number of qualifications. Existing unions may secure exclusive representation by meeting certain criteria, such as enrolling 20 percent of the workers, and complying with requirements for internal democracy that a new National Labor Relations Council (Conselho Nacional de Relações de Trabalho—CNRT) will specify at a future date. In addition, the government accepted the mechanism of "derived representation" by which a *central* or federation can transfer "representativeness" from one union possessing it to another that would otherwise fail to meet the necessary standard. The result of these reforms might well be a hybrid system with a considerable potential for conflicts among unions.

The basis for union organization would change and, rather than representing often fragmented occupational categories, as at present, unions will be set up by economic sector or by divisions of economic activity. The CNRT will define these. The government's objective here is to reduce "pulverization" and eliminate some current problems with collective bargaining in firms where a number of unions are present. The preponderant economic activity of a firm will determine the union category to which its employees may belong. The result should be larger unions and a much smaller total number of them.

Among the more controversial proposals are changes involving the Labor Justice (Justiça de Trabalho—JT) system. These courts, for example, will no longer be able to declare strikes illegal, a power much abused in the past, but would have some limited and specific powers to order strikers back to work under certain circumstances in what are deemed to be essential services. An earlier judicial reform sought to restrict the power of the labor courts in judging collective accords to those cases in which both sides agree to the JT's jurisdiction. In any case, the JT's presence in collective disputes has declined drastically in recent years.[32] Collective bargaining is to become the main means for resolving labor conflicts, and the proposals include a number of articles seeking to facilitate these procedures, which can be conducted at various levels. In any case, the negotiated will not prevail over the legislated, and those who drafted the proposals seem quite aware of the very unequal negotiating capacity of unions, especially under the threat of high unemployment. The provisions for public and private arbitration provoked hostile reactions from many observers, since recent experience with these mechanisms has been mixed at best.[33] A legal device by which unions can represent workers with similar individual claims before the labor courts (*substito processual*) predictably infuriated business groups (although it was later authorized by the Supreme Court in 2006). The government also included in its proposals a controversial topic on anti-union conduct, specifying practices that would become illegal, most of which deal with persecutions of union members and the abusive use of strike breakers.[34]

The government introduced the first part of the reforms, the Proposed Constitutional Amendment (PEC), in the Congress a few weeks before the scandals broke that were to occupy Brazilian politics for the rest of 2005 and most of the following year. Faced with run-away congressional committees investigating such matters as garbage collection contracts in Ribeirão Preto during the 1990s and the finance minister's sex life, the question of labor relations reform fell off the government's agenda. Even without such distractions, approval of the proposals would never have been easy. In part, this is only one more consequence of a perverse electoral system that elects presidents by large margins but leaves them without majorities in the Congress.

However, in this case, there were a number of specific problems. Much of the Left came to oppose the reforms, and even within the CUT support was far from unanimous.[35] The other *centrais* (six participated in the FNT), despite having initially agreed to most of the forum's conclusions, also eventually came out against the proposals, in part because many of the *centrais* would probably have had difficulty in meeting criteria for representativeness.[36] While workers in the most advanced sectors have called for the end of the corporatist structure since the 1970s and no longer depend very much on the protections of the CLT, many of them came to feel that in an era of neoliberal advance and unfavorable economic conditions, changes in the labor laws could be hazardous even for them.

In any case, Lula and his government, distracted by the scandals and attacks, made no real effort to pressure the Congress on behalf of labor relations reform. The CUT remained sufficiently divided and ambivalent not to undertake mobilizations in defense of the proposals. Left to itself, the Congress was not going to take the initiative and, in any event, the lobbies of *pelegos* and others threatened by the reforms remained very strong.[37]

Luiz Marinho, while labor minister in early 2007, said that he still had hopes for the reforms, but few shared his optimism. When Lula, as part of efforts to secure a reliable majority in the Congress, gave the Labor Ministry to Carlos Lupi, head of the Partido Democrático Trabalhista,[38] the latter declared—in the midst of considerable populist kitsch—that his party was the heir of Getúlio Vargas and he had no intention of ever changing the CLT "unless workers want to."[39]

Apparently, the government's intention is to present piecemeal some of the measures it considers most important, such as a bill granting full legal and union recognition to the *centrais*. The opposition concentrated its fire on the provision of the bill that would allocate a portion of the compulsory union tax to *centrais* meeting certain criteria of representativeness. This reform passed the Chamber of Deputies in October 2007, but the opposition added an amendment that would summarily eliminate the compulsory union tax.[40] However, the Senate eventually dropped the amendment when it passed the bill at the end of 2007.

In fact, the Brazilian labor relations system has proved more flexible than its critics charge and, in any case, with half the workforce outside the formal economy, the labor market has already been considerably deregulated—often, of course, under much degraded conditions. Noncompliance by employers and limited state enforcement of the labor laws also provide substantial de facto flexibility.[41] Even the CLT has shown considerable adaptability in practice.[42] A number of the proposed reforms, such as union representation in the workplace and the elimination of the union tax, simply recognize practices that are already present in some places, even without formal legal sanction.

Nevertheless, there is something more than a little tragic in the failure of the Congress to pass the labor reforms proposed by Lula's government. This is so in part because reforms undertaken by a subsequent government are likely to be far more restrictive of workers' rights than those proposed in 2005. Lula's government, in seeking to strengthen the labor movement through changes in collective labor law, clearly ran counter to powerful trends in Latin America and elsewhere.[43] The stakes could be high, not just because of possible future institutional handicaps for the union movement, but also on account of potential limitations on workers' rights and on the possibilities for social justice in Brazil. After all, labor law exists precisely because employers and employees are not equal in the market place, and the law has proved to be a way of imposing some limits on economic power. The workers who played such an important role in ending the military dictatorship and in the subsequent democratization of Brazilian life—some of whose most notable results being the presidential elections of 2002 and 2006—deserved better.

Notes

1. Thanks to Hélio da Costa, friend and former student, for suggestions and assistance on this paper.
2. The system is often wrongly said to copy Mussolini's *Carta del Lavoro*. The union measures, however, echo an earlier fascist law, "On the Juridical Disciplining of Collective Labor Relations," of 1926. For interpretations in English, see Hall (2000), and French (2004), who downplays the fascist origin of the labor laws.
3. *Unicidade* is usually translated as "exclusive representation." However, the 2005 reform proposals to be examined below use "representação exclusiva" in a more specific sense and, to avoid confusion, it is probably clearer to retain the Portuguese neologism *unicidade*.
4. Boito Jr. (1991).
5. The translation would be national "Federation" or "Confederation," but since "Federação" and "Confederação" are used in Brazil to designate, respectively, state and nationwide associations by category, the best solution may be to leave *central* and its plural, *centrais*, in Portuguese.
6. See Sader (1988) and Barros (1999).
7. See Diniz (2005: 344–345).
8 Diniz, ibid. Gomes and D'Araújo (1993: 341–347), provide an informative discussion of the implications of the tax, the ambivalence of much of the labor movement about it, and the debate provoked by Collor's attempt to abolish the union tax/contribution. The authors wrote the article in 1992 and concluded: "it is clear that the abolition of the Union Contribution is a question of time."
9. On this interesting experiment, see Arbix (1996) and Zauli (1997).
10. There are a number of excellent studies dealing with labor policies during the 1990s, which are the basis for the following paragraphs. In addition to the article by Simone Diniz, cited above, see Martins and Rodrigues (2000); Krein and Oliveira (1999); Pochmann (1998); Costa (2005); Pessanha and Morel (1999); Rodrigues (2005); and, for a catastrophic view, Alves (2002).
11. For some background, see Cardoso and Comin (1997); Rodrigues (1997); Giannotti (2002).
12. Horn (2005: 54).
13. For an extensive and critical review of the labor policies of the Cardoso government, see Krein (2003). Krein analyzes several measures not dealt with here, such as Brazil's denunciation of ILO Convention 158 on standards and procedures for the dismissal of workers.
14. The latter, advocated by Francisco Dornelles, sometime labor minister, was actually sent to the Congress in 1998, but later withdrawn. Aloysio Nunes Ferreira, general secretary of the presidency, defended the abolition of the Labor Courts.
15. Rizek (1998) describes the successful manipulation of public opinion against the strikers.
16. Employers' contributions to the retirement funds and other benefits for registered workers.
17. Blass (1998).
18. The legislative history and precise details of these measures are quite complex, in part because the government introduced them as Provisional Measures (MPs), a kind of presidential decree eventually subject to congressional decision. At the time, an MP could be reintroduced dozens of times, as several of these were, with important changes in detail as the government responded to pressures from various sources. The clearest presentation I found is the article by Simone Diniz, cited in note 7.
19. A benefit paid to all officially registered workers at the end of the calendar year.
20. It later turned out that the Labor Ministry, though a foundation it funded, had given R$2.7 million to the FS before the vote for programs in the "health area." *Folha de S. Paulo*, December 6, 2001.
21. *Folha de S. Paulo*, December 2, 2001.
22. *Estado de S. Paulo*, November 29, 2001.

23. *Folha de S. Paulo*, November 27, 2001.
24. The three quotes are from *Estado de S. Paulo*, November 28, 2001. The government's allies were equally unhappy. Geddel Vieira Lima, leader of the PMDB in the Chamber, complained, "I don't see the need for bringing this to a vote and submitting the allies to this kind of attrition in a pre-electoral year." *Folha de S. Paulo*, November 27, 2001.
25. Ibid. "Constitutional urgency" can be requested by the president and requires the Congress to vote on a bill within a short period. It also prevents other bills from being voted.
26. *Folha de S. Paulo*, November 29, 2001.
27. Cruz and Alencar, *Folha de S. Paulo*, November 29, 2001.
28. *Coligação Lula Presidente 2002*, p.23, as cited in Horn (2005: 44).
29. These and other documents are available at www.fnt.mte.gov.br
30. Proposta de Emenda Constitucional—proposed constitutional amendment.
31. Horn (2005).
32. DIEESE (2006).
33. *Folha de S. Paulo*, May 19, 2002; *Folha de S. Paulo*, May 27, 2002; *Estado de S. Paulo*, May 20, 2007.
34. For details and some of the possible implications, see Kaufmann (2005).
35. On the opposition by the PCdoB and its union allies, for example, see Borges (2004).
36. In 2007, three of them merged to form a new central in order to satisfy such requirements in the government's proposal, discussed below, for legalizing *centrais*.
37. See, for example, *Estado de S. Paulo*, February 27, 2005. Zylberstajn (2005) is helpful on the entrenched interests, from both labor and management, opposed to the reforms.
38. A party founded by the populist Leonel Brizola in 1979 and once strong in Rio de Janeiro State.
39. *Folha de S. Paulo*, March 29, 2007.
40. For some idea of the heat generated, see the editorial in the *Folha de S. Paulo*, October 24, 2007, expressing indignation at the provisions for financing the *centrais* and at the CUT's opposition to the amendment eliminating the union tax. The president of the CUT replied in a letter to the newspaper (October 26, 2007), arguing that the central continued to favor abolishing the check off, but not without rules for the transition or provisions concerning a negotiating fee, approved in assemblies, for unions meeting criteria of representativeness.
41. Cardoso and Lage (2005). The power of the inspectors gave rise to a major controversy in 2007, when the opposition amended a tax bill so as to deprive labor inspectors of the authority to intervene directly in cases where firms used subterfuges to avoid paying social charges for what were effectively regular workers. The amendment required that such cases be submitted to the Labor Courts, which would then take years to reach a decision. Lula vetoed the amendment and submitted legislation seeking to eliminate possible abuses in the area. See Singer (2007).
42. Such is the argument of Cardoso (1999) and other writings.
43. See especially Cook (2007), chs. 2 and 3. She also emphasizes how difficult labor law reform has proved to be in most countries under democratic conditions.

References

Alves, Giovanni. 2002. "Trabalho e sindicalismo no Brasil: um balanço crítico da 'década neoliberal' (1990–2000)." *Revista de Sociologia e Política* 19:71–94.

Arbix, Glauco. 1996. *Uma aposta no futuro: os primeiros anos da câmara setorial da indústria automobilística*. São Paulo: Scritta.

Barros, Maurício Rands. 1999. *Labour Relations and the New Unionism in Contemporary Brazil*. Basingstoke: Macmillan.

Blass, Leila. 1998. "Jornada de trabalho: uma regulamentação em múltipla escolha." *Revista Brasileira de Ciências Sociais* 13(36):67–78.

Boito, Jr., Armando. 1991. *O sindicalismo do estado no Brasil*. São Paulo: Hucitec.

Borges, Altamiro, ed. 2004. *A reforma sindical e trabalhista no governo Lula*. São Paulo: Anita Garibaldi.

Cardoso, Adalberto. 1999. *Sindicatos, trabalhadores e a coqueluche neoliberal: a era Vargas acabou?* Rio de Janeiro: Editora Fundação Getúlio Vargas.

Cardoso, Adalberto M., and Álvaro A. Comin. 1997. "Centrais sindicais e atitudes democráticas." *Lua Nova* 40/41 (1997):167–192.

Cardoso, Adalberto M., and Telma Lage. 2005. "A inspeção do trabalho no Brasil." *Dados* 48(3):451–489.

Cook, Maria Lorena. 2007. *The Politics of Labor Reform in Latin America*. University Park: Pennsylvania State University Press.

Costa, Márcia da Silva. 2005. "O sistema de relações de trabalho no Brasil: alguns traços históricos e sua precarização atual." *Revista Brasileira de Ciências Sociais* 20(59):111–131.

Cruz, Valdo, and Kennedy Alencar. 2001. "Promessa a empresário faz FHC ordenar voto." *Folha de S. Paulo*, November 29.

Diniz, Simone. 2005. "Interações entre os Poderes Executivo e Legislativo no processo decisório: avaliando sucesso e fracasso presidencial." *Dados* 48(2):333–367.

DIEESE. 2006. "Taxa de judicialização das negociações coletivas do trabalho no Brasil 1993–2005." *Estudos e Pesquisas* 21 (June).

Estado de S. Paulo. 2001. "Governo busca vitória apertada para mudar CLT." November 28.

———. 2001. "Após confusões, votação da CLT é adiada de novo." November 29.

———. 2005. "Lobby dos velhos sindicalistas se mobiliza para barrar reforma." February 27.

———. 2007. "Tribunais anulam 42% das arbitragens que examinam." May 20.

Folha de S. Paulo. 2001. "Câmara vota hoje projeto de mudança na CLT." November 27.

———. 2001. "Painel quebra, governo foge, CLT emperra." November 29.

———. 2001. "Paulistanos se dividem sobre 'nova CLT.'" December 2.

———. 2001. "Força é acusada de apoiar nova CLT em troca de verbas." December 6.

———. 2002. "Acordo de conciliação lesa trabalhadores." May 19.

———. 2002. "Justiça privada é cilada para trabalhadores." May 27.

———. 2007. "Lula confirma Lupi apesar de pressão da CUT." March 29.

———. 2007. "Trama fracassada." October 24.

Fórum Nacional do Trabalho. www.fnt.mte.gov.br accessed on February 20, 2007.

French, John. 2004. *Drowning in Laws: Labor Law and Brazilian Political Culture*. Chapel Hill: University of North Carolina Press.

Giannotti, Vito. 2002. *Força Sindical: A central neoliberal de Medeiros a Paulinho*. Rio de Janeiro: Mauad.

Gomes, Ângela Castro, and Maria Celina D'Araújo.1993. "A extinção do imposto sindical: demandas e contradições." *Dados* 36(2):317–351.

Hall, Michael M. 2000. "Labor and the Law in Brazil." In Marcel van der Linden and Richard Price, ed. *The Rise and Development of Collective Labour Law*. Bern: Peter Lang. pp. 79–95.

Horn, Carlos Henrique. 2005. "Limites do consenso na reforma da organização sindical." *Revista de Direito do Trabalho* 119:42–56.

Kaufmann, Marcus de Oliveira. 2005. "A anti-sindicalidade e o anteprojeto de lei de relações sindicais." *Revista de Direito do Trabalho* 119:210–255.

Krein, José Dari, and Marco Antonio de Oliveira. 1999. "Mudanças institucionais e relações de trabalho: as iniciativas do governo FHC no período 1995–1998." *Anais do VI Encontro Nacional de Estudos do Trabalho*, 2 Vols. São Paulo: Associação Brasileira de Estudos do Trabalho, 1999. pp. I:639–671.

Krein, José Dari. 2003. "Balanço da reforma trabalhista do governo FHC." In Marcelo Weishaupt Proni and Wilnês Henrique, eds. *Trabalho, mercado e sociedade: o Brasil nos anos 90*. São Paulo: Editora da Unesp. pp. 279–322.

Martins, Heloisa de Souza, and Iram Jâcome Rodrigues. 2000. "O sindicalismo brasileiro na segunda metade dos anos 90." *Tempo Social* 11(2):155–182.

Pessanha, Elina da Fonte, and Regina Lúcia Morel. 1999. "Mudanças recentes no modelo de relações de trabalho no Brasil e Novo Sindicalismo." In Iram Jâcome Rodrigues, ed. *O novo sindicalismo vinte anos depois*. Petrópolis: Vozes. pp. 95–112.

Pochmann, Márcio. 1998. "Adeus à CLT? O 'eterno' sistema corporativo de relações de trabalho no Brasil." *Novos Estudos Cebrap* 50:149–166.

Rizek, Cibele. 1998. "A greve dos petroleiros." *Praga* 6:97–105.

Rodrigues, Iram Jâcome. 1997. *Sindicalismo e política: a trajetória da CUT.* São Paulo: Scritta.

———. 2005. "Peculiaridades da ação sindical dos metalúrgicos do ABC." *Revista de Direito do Trabalho* 119:117–131.

Sader, Eder. 1988. *Quando novos personagens entraram em cena: experiências, falas e lutas dos trabalhadores da Grande São Paulo.* Rio de Janeiro: Paz e Terra.

Singer, Paul. 2007. "A Emenda 3 e os direitos do trabalhador." *Teoria & Debate* 20(71):14–16.

Zauli, Eduardo. 1997. *As condições sociais da emergência e decadência da câmara setorial da indústria automotiva no Brasil.* São Paulo: Annablume.

Zylberstajn, Hélio. 2005. "A reforma sindical de Lula." *Revista de Direito do Trabalho* 119:94–116.

CHAPTER NINE

Lula's Foreign Policy: Regional and Global Strategies

Paulo Roberto de Almeida

Introduction

This chapter presents the chief diplomatic initiatives of the Lula government since 2003, against an analytical background of the potentials—and limitations—of Brazil as a regional and global actor. Brazil is an important player at both levels, obviously possessing greater powers of "intervention" in South America. But Brazil also shows some degree of leadership in a few multilateral issues (such as trade negotiations), and is also acquiring growing leverage in special topics of global impact (such as renewable energy sources). Lately, the country has been seen as an important player in the evolution of the world economy, as one of the so-called BRIC countries, together with Russia, India, and China.[1]

Brazil and the World Order: Changes and Continuities in Foreign Policy

In the same way (but perhaps not with the same rhythm or intensity) as the world has undergone profound political-economic transformations since the end of the Cold War, with a new order based on global markets and the progressive emergence of new players, Brazil has also been going through marked changes in its regional role and as a new global player. These changes in Brazil's relative position within the region and the world have taken place as a consequence both of objective processes in the regional and global domains, which affect the South American giant in diverse ways, and of decisions taken by the government of Luiz Inácio Lula da Silva, better known as Lula, who ended his first mandate (2003–2006) and began, in January of 2007, a second presidential term (until 2010).

The structural and systemic changes that have marked Brazil since the early 1990s require a brief examination. First, there was a huge effort toward an opening up of the economy, begun under President Fernando Collor (1990–1992), followed by the *Plano Real*, a successful macroeconomic stabilization plan, taken up by the minister of Economy Fernando Henrique Cardoso (FHC), under the administration of Itamar Franco (1992–1994). The *Plano Real* was then consolidated during the two presidential terms of FHC (1995–1998 and 1999–2002), despite successive financial crises that affected Brazil, leading to the negotiation of stand-by agreements with the IMF (1998, 2001, 2002).[2] The FHC years brought a complex process of regulatory and institutional changes that exerted their most significant impacts on the Brazilian domestic macroeconomic reality, but also with some relevant elements in the realm of foreign policy, most of them in the regional integration schemes, with Mercosur and the negotiations under the U.S. proposal to create a Free Trade Area of the Americas (FTAA).

The stabilization process allowed for a new international projection of Brazil, thanks to the good relationship achieved by FHC vis-à-vis some world leaders (especially in the G-7). Regardless of the relative weight of Brazil in the regional and global power schemes of the 1990s, it is worth noting that due to its own economic mass, its diplomatic projection, its ability to regularly attract direct foreign investment, and to other factors, Brazil already held a certain degree of influence in the region, prior to the intense process of structural changes in the world economy during the last two decades.

Market operators feared that Lula's election could represent sweeping changes in economic policy, thus opening the way for a significant deterioration of the "Brazil risk" during the 2002 campaign, with a marked increase in interest rates, inflation and exchange rate parity, and the decline in the value of the Brazilian foreign debt bonds negotiated in the financial markets. In fact, Lula promised that he would not only preserve IMF agreements, but also maintain the core of the mechanisms put in place by the *Plano Real*: fiscal responsibility (that is, budgetary surplus in order to pay public debt), the inflation target regime, and the floating exchange rate. He also announced significant changes in foreign policy, starting by the regional integration process.

Brazilian leaders have always been aware of Brazil's outstanding position in the region—South America in the first place—but they have also aspired, at certain stages, to achieve for Brazil a position of greater importance at the world level. This is why, for example, starting with the Versailles peace conference (1919) and the creation of the League of Nations, Brazilian diplomats stated their aim to see Brazil promoted as a member of its directive body, an objective ultimately frustrated by the choice of Germany to enter it, which provoked Brazil's withdrawal from the League (1926). Along these same lines, at the end of World War II, Brazil hoped to assume one of the permanent seats in the new UN Security

Council, an equally frustrated goal, due just as much to the opposition of some of the heavyweight players (the UK and the USSR, for example), as to Brazil's lack of military or financial capacity.

This aspiration to a prominent status in the so-called *inner circle* of the world's political oligarchy is recurrent among Brazilian military and political leaders. Coinciding with a phase of rapid economic growth (1969–1979), during the military regime (1964–1985), those leaders hoped to consolidate Brazil's position as a new economic, and eventually also atomic, power, in order to enable the country to join the leading group at the head of global economy and politics. This objective was frustrated repeatedly by the recurring economic crises endured by Brazil in the last three decades of the twentieth century: oil crises in 1973 and 1979, external debt in 1982 and beyond, uncontrolled inflationary process in the following years, culminating with the financial crises of the late 1990s. The country was increasingly seen as a candidate lacking the real conditions for leadership, thus confirming the judgment of the Austrian writer Stefan Zweig in 1941, that Brazil was the eternal "country of the future."

Despite the setbacks in the process of economic growth, the financial difficulties, and the inflationary process of the 1980s, José Sarney, the president during the redemocratization period (1985–1990), announced in 1989 that Brazil was ready to assume a permanent seat on the Security Council if and when the issue of UN Charter's reform was once again included in the agenda. At that moment, aware of the difficulties that could arise in the region (especially with Argentina), Sarney did not present Brazil as a "regional candidate," highlighting only the fact that it could accept the seat even without the veto power. Much more important than this claim, however, was the decision by Sarney to decisively engage Brazil in the process of regional integration that began with sectoral deals and bilateral protocols with Argentina. In 1986, Brazil and Argentina started a bilateral program of integration and economic cooperation, followed by an integration treaty in 1988, having in sight a full common market in 10 years' time.

After a decision taken in July 1990 by both countries—under President Fernando Collor de Mello (1990–1992) and Carlos Saul Menem (1989–2000)—to shorten the time frame and anticipate the common market to 1995, the negotiations were enlarged under the request of other neighbors, and the treaty creating the Southern Common Market, or Mercosur, was signed in Asunción in 1991, joining Paraguay and Uruguay to the two big South American countries. Yet, the methodology to achieve a common market was greatly modified: instead of a gradual and sectoral approach for the dismantling of reciprocal trade barriers, a process of free trade was begun, with a view to complete a full customs union by December 31, 1994.

Collor de Mello took decisive steps toward redirecting Brazil's foreign policy toward nonproliferation, the abandonment of a military nuclear program, the reduction of trade protectionism and of the slightly "third-worldist" stance of professional diplomacy, bringing Brazil a little closer to the economic philosophy of the OECD countries. President Collor (impeached for reasons of corruption less than two years into his term) is said to have declared that he preferred to see Brazil take the "last place in the developed countries group" than as "the first of the developing countries." This meant a significant change by the traditional standards of professional diplomats, who had always fought to maintain Brazil's status as a "developing country" (with all of its implications in terms of the General Agreement on Tariffs and Trade [GATT], the Generalized System of Preferences [GSP], and other preferential trade schemes).

During the presidency of Itamar Franco, Brazilian diplomacy also began to operate a small but relevant conceptual change toward the abandonment of the old adherence to the "Latin America" geographical dimension in exchange for new emphasis on the "South America" concept. This was put forward by repeated attempts to enter into association or trade liberalization agreements between Mercosur and all of its South American neighbors. Also, reacting to the U.S.-backed FTAA, Brazil responded by proposing a SAFTA, or a South American Free Trade Area (which aroused little enthusiasm in the region at that time, 1994).

Fernando Henrique Cardoso's two consecutive terms are relevant in view of the notable economic reforms, with important constitutional amendments that opened the Brazilian economy to globalization. His presidential diplomacy aimed to secure a larger Brazilian presence on the international scene, in large part thanks to the ease with which FHC moved in international circles. The president also confirmed Brazil's total denuclearization upon adhering to the Nuclear Non-Proliferation Treaty (NPT), the 1968 nonproliferation treaty, for three decades considered by diplomats and military officials as iniquitous and discriminatory. With the exclusive support of professional diplomats—and the indifference or light opposition of entrepreneurs—he took on the difficult issues raised by the remaining asymmetries within Mercosur, which hindered the consolidation of its customs union. His second term was plagued by problems created by huge and growing deficits in foreign transactions, seriously aggravated by the Asian, Russian, and Argentinean crises and partially relieved through three successive financial deals with the IMF (1998, 2001, 2002) and the developed countries. Also relevant in the diplomatic agenda of the late 1990s and thereafter was the U.S.-sponsored FTAA, neither welcomed by industrial sectors, nor by diplomats or other government officials.

FHC never got to attend any of the G-7 meetings. In fact, as other leaders in some important emerging democracies, he was never invited to any of the closed G-7/8 meetings—at this stage involving post-Soviet Russia—but maintained very close contact with various social-democrat leaders of the group, such as Bill Clinton and Tony Blair. This approximation translated into a sort of informal partnership between FHC and the American president, who had true personal empathy for FHC and was inclined to see Brazil take on a role of greater importance in regional conflicts, such as that in Colombia and its fight against the narco-guerillas of the FARC. This kind of involvement was seen with some reluctance on the part of FHC, who was aware of the limitations on Brazil's ability of foreign projection in terms of display of power. FHC also did not insist on Brazilian candidacy to a permanent seat on the Security Council, mindful of the objections that would be brought up, as a matter of principle, by neighboring Argentina, whose relations with Brazil in the Mercosur he had always considered to be so strategic in nature that they could not be endangered by some exhibition of Brazilian willingness to play alone in the tableau of great powers game.[3]

The most significant changes in Brazil's foreign economic and political position and in some lines of its external policies happened during President Lula's first term (2003–2006). His diplomacy, backed by his Partido dos Trabalhadores (PT—Workers' Party) brought new emphases and preferential alliances. Among these was a marked change in the discourse of foreign relations, with some corrections in style and also of priorities in the beginning of his second term (2007). Although a large part of the diplomatic agenda has shown more elements of continuity than of rupture with prior policies, some innovative elements should be highlighted as identifiers of the new emphases and priorities. Besides a strong emphasis on political multilateralism traditional to Brazilian diplomacy (but now with an evident "anti-hegemonic" leaning, i.e., against American unilateralism), the focus fell sharply onto South-South diplomacy, as well as in a great effort to see Mercosur reinforced and broadened as the basis for political integration and of consolidation of a unified economic space in South America. Together with the very intense lobbying for a permanent seat on the Security Council and the election of some privileged partners as "strategic allies"—namely South Africa, India, and China, with the eventual inclusion of Russia, on some topics—the reappearance of a Third World stance and the reaffirmed integrationist vocation in South America clearly make up the main axes of Lula's new diplomacy.[4]

Although the rhetoric about Brazilian leadership in South America abated substantially throughout the first mandate, the intention was clear at the start and was affirmed even if in an indirect manner. President Lula talked about a "diplomacy of generosity," based on the size and industrial might of Brazil on the continent, recommending that domestic importers buy more from neighboring countries, even at relatively disadvantageous prices, as a way of balancing the flux of commerce and contributing to common prosperity in the region. However, promises made to neighbor countries for direct financing by the National Bank of Social and Economic Development (BNDES) did not materialize, and only the engineering projects of Brazilian companies working in these countries were approved. Diplomatic activism in South America, preferably with an expanded Mercosur, and the setting up of a coordinated policy as the background for diverse initiatives undertaken in the region, may paradoxically have resulted in adverse reactions to an expansion of

Brazil's influence. Even in Mercosur, the worries about Brazil's "excessive weight" may have influenced the decision of the smaller countries to support the "political admission" of Venezuela into the integration scheme of the Southern Cone.

In a broader sense, what the diplomatic authorities and Brazilian leaders had to propose, to regional partners and other developing countries outside the region, was a "Southern coalition" to "change the power relationships in the world." Other proposals, included in the diplomatic speeches by president and the foreign minister, concerned the capacity of Southern countries to open the way for a "new world trade geography" based much more on South-South exchanges than on the supposed "dependence" on "unequal" trade with the North. Countries that Brazil courted could have realized that what was in fact at stake was that Brazil gave priority, on the one hand, to its objective of a permanent seat on the Security Council, and on the other, to its desire to imprint the mark of Brazilian economic interests on South America, that is to say, two national objectives presented as being the expression of a new multilateral order supposedly taking everyone's interests into consideration. On both sides, the results were fairly modest, despite the large diplomatic (and financial) investments that were made in South America, Africa, and elsewhere. Special attention was given to Lusophone countries in Africa—Angola, Mozambique, Guinea Bissau, Cape Verde, and São Tomé e Príncipe—to which programs of technical cooperation, professional training, and scholarships were directed.

To explain the gap between the objectives and the achievements realized, some observers argued that the problem was not the operation of Brazil's diplomatic service, but the flawed idea at the very heart of Brazil's new diplomacy. This new foreign policy draws from various political elements from the party diplomacy of the Workers' Party (formulated while it was still an opposition party), such as "solidarity among developing countries," and "national liberation movements," the reform of economic institutions (presumably dominated by the great powers), the "essential identity of the South" (of course, against "hegemonic countries") and so on. Partner countries designated as the selected target of Brazilian priorities do not necessarily share those assumptions. Those presumptions have, as a matter of fact, much more to do with the political idea within the dominant party in the governmental coalition—that is, the PT—than with the traditional ideas and diplomatic concepts of the Foreign Ministry, known as Itamaraty.

Summing up, the changes that effectively took place were much less significant or important than the suggested agenda of "sovereign integration" into the world economy, with the consequent redefinition of the international political and economic order. This is probably due to the fact that Brazil's weight in the relevant flow of goods, services, technology, and capital, as well as in the provision of technical assistance and cooperation on a world scale is relatively modest in relation to its more vocal and quite visible role in some of the main world forums. Based on the modest harvest of results achieved so far, the practical implementation of regional diplomacy and the South-South orientation (reaffirmed, nevertheless, at the start of the second term) seems to be moving toward greater pragmatism than was the case during the first term.

Main Priorities in Brazil's New Foreign Policy

The new priorities of Brazilian foreign policy were explicitly stated on several occasions, starting with President Lula's inaugural address in January of 2003. They were reaffirmed in Lula's trips abroad, also through an intense schedule of diplomatic contacts kept through regional and multilateral meetings, as well as through the reaffirmation of these same priorities during the second inauguration. Indeed, on January 1, 2007, Lula stated that Brazil had changed for the better "in monetary stability; fiscal consistency; the quality of its debt; the access to new markets and technologies; and in diminished foreign vulnerability." As the president noted, Brazil's foreign economic situation had improved considerably.

Lula reaffirmed "[Brazil's] clear choice of multilateralism," the "excellent political, economic, and trade relations [maintained] with the great world powers," but he also confirmed that the "ties with the Southern world" were a priority, especially with Africa, which he described as "one of the cradles of Brazilian civilization." Lula also remarked that "surrounding South-America" was the "center" of his foreign policy, adding that Brazil "associates its political, economic, and social destiny with the continent, Mercosur, and the South-American Community of Nations" (later renamed Unasur, the Union of South American Nations, at a meeting in Venezuela, in April of 2007).

These are Brazil's foreign policy priorities. They are based on a world vision that corresponds to traditional priorities of the establishment, that is, professional diplomats—the foreign minister is still a career diplomat—as much as with the views of the political left, the Workers' Party in particular. In fact, it is in foreign policy that the Lula government's emphases are most similar to original orientation of the Workers' Party. These policies are faithfully followed in many trends of the new external policy—in particular in the South-South diplomacy and in the strategic alliances with some of the large, nonhegemonic, players.

These priorities have been advanced by a variety of means, some of them traditional (that is, through Itamaraty's diplomacy reputed for the excellence of its diplomatic staff), or by an active presidential diplomacy. Yet, this diplomacy is not called "presidential," in an effort to distinguish it from the diplomatic style of President FHC. There is also a brand-new kind of external action that could be described as party diplomacy made up of privileged links and alliances between the progressive and leftist movements that were formerly in the opposition, that is, Latin American

Marxist parties (grouped together in the Forum of Sao Paulo[5]), as well as the so-called social movements, whose political agenda and focus are obviously much closer to those of the World Social Forum than to the World Economic Forum of Davos.

These new objectives represent a combination of factors linked to national and sectoral policies, for example, the emphasis upon a progressive or social agenda (in order to compensate for the uneasy acceptance of a conservative economic policy). They also are linked to some very old traditions of Brazilian diplomacy, like the so-called independent foreign policy, put in place by the progressive governments that preceded the military regime that took power in 1964. This latest agenda may be seen as an affirmation of autonomy (with regard to the United States, obviously) in the fields of politics and the international economy or in matters of security. It also gives emphasis to national economic development and on "policy spaces" for sectoral measures aimed at developmental programs. Besides, Lula has reaffirmed the priority of South American regional integration, through the enlargement of Mercosur.

Given these objectives, Brazil has thrown itself into several diplomatic initiatives that have engaged not only professional diplomats, but also the president himself, who has become a major proponent of the new Brazilian activism. This activism has been in motion since the very first day of the new administration, when, taking advantage of the presence of the foreign ministers of India and South Africa in Brasilia at Lula's inauguration, Brazil proposed the creation of a G-3, consisting of India, Brazil, and South Africa, which has held two summits to date. The same activism was present at the inception of the G-20, created at the ministerial meeting of the WTO in Cancun (September 2003), and it is seen as an essential instrument for achieving a "change in world power relationships" and establishing a "new international geography of trade." The government also seeks to transform the BRIC concept into a truly diplomatic endeavor, by proposing regular meetings of the four foreign ministers and, if possible, the heads of their respective governments. In fact, all kinds of diplomatic activities are being developed, with the aim of reinforcing Brazil's capacity to influence politics at the regional and global levels. Those areas that have a direct interface with civil society—such as those involved with the environment, peasant groups or the fight against AIDS—are increasingly part of an activist and "progressive diplomacy."[6]

The players or political agents that participate in the formulation and implementation of current Brazilian foreign policy are many and are found at different levels. Sometimes, they move through apparently uncoordinated actions or have different kinds of discourses, which could give the impression that the decision-making process is fragmented. Foreign policy therefore stems from the convergence of distinct vectors, in contrast to the relative organizational and conceptual unity found in previous administrations. Traditionally, diplomacy was the monopoly of Itamaraty, which also "offered" presidential advisors and international advisors for other public agencies. In Lula's government, beyond the a priori positions taken by the Workers' Party on international policy, Professor Marco Aurélio Garcia, the PT's former secretary for International Relations, has chaired the presidential foreign advisory staff.[7] Trade unions and social movements have also rallied around their favorite topics, be it in support or in opposition to certain issues on the international agenda: most important have been the FTAA hemispherical trade negotiations, South American integration and the so-called South-South diplomacy.

The various foreign policy actors are, however, taking a political-diplomatic route different from the old patterns of Itamaraty. Also, some of the new strategic alliances can, in principle, influence or even determine Brazil's position in multilateral forums of special interest: this could be the case, for example, in human rights issues (in relation to China or Cuba, among others), or in environmental or ecological matters, with the unheard of involvement of pressure groups—against GMOs or agribusiness, for instance—that have sympathizers in the government. This issue is especially relevant in the case of the peasant or landless movements that are openly against agribusiness and liberalized trade in farm products, weakening Brazil's negotiating position, while it attempts to merge irreconcilable demands in the same agenda.

Foreign policy is increasingly important in Brazil's domestic politics. The mass media, academia (generally in line with the Left), and businessmen and union leaders in industrial and agricultural sectors have mobilized around the central issues of the Lula government's foreign policy. For the first time, Brazilian diplomacy seems to have lost the unanimity that it long enjoyed in mainstream society, due, in large part, to the PT's original ideology.[8]

Brazil's Foreign Policy Strategies and Their Main Focus of Interest

Lula's administration put in motion all kinds of tools and all forms of foreign policy—multilateralism, bilateral relations, and informal mechanisms of cooperation—in order to promote its new diplomatic priorities. The multilateral forums are naturally in a good position to handle global issues, especially trade policy, the environment, technical and financial cooperation for development, human rights, and disarmament. In the area of regional integration, there is a combination of bilateral tools, most of all with Argentina, and of multilateral coordination efforts toward creating favorable conditions for the advance of physical integration in South America: infrastructure, energy, transports, and communications in general.

One of the main priorities of Lula's diplomacy is the quest for a permanent seat in the United Nations Security Council, an objective on behalf of which a variety of strategies and instruments are used by diplomats and the president himself. This topic has been inserted in all bilateral agendas and appears in practically all talks and bilateral statements agreed upon between Brazil's president and other leaders during state visits or even communiqués arising from working meetings. In order to obtain support for this cause, financial compensations or the canceling of old bilateral debts were offered in some cases—this was the case for various African and Latin American countries—as well as promised increases in bilateral technical cooperation for the least-developed countries. This objective was probably the underlying element in the Brazilian decision to lead the UN stabilization mission in Haiti, with the mobilization of important resources at the military, diplomatic, humanitarian, technical, and financial levels. It has furthermore provided the opportunity for a high-level debate and coordination efforts with other declared Security Council candidates. From these talks the G-4 arose, uniting Brazil with Germany, India, and Japan. The group aims to establish a common position for the enlargement of the Security Council, to include them and a representative from Africa. Brazil received support from at least two of the current permanent members, France and the United Kingdom, plus the ambiguous support of a third, Russia. But it faces the much more ambiguous "non-opposition" from the United States (in fact, the latter supports Japan and "one other country," which is probably India). Brazil also sought the support of China.

Despite open opposition in the region from Argentina, and the lack of enthusiasm of the United States for an "exaggerated" expansion, Brazil considers its efforts worthwhile. Brazil's diplomatic and military establishment sees winning a permanent chair in the Security Council, even without veto power, as a desirable symbol of the country's status as a major world player. Although the issue is being debated in terms of regional representation, Brazil does not consider its candidacy as necessarily emanating from any mandate arising from its geographic region. Rather, it sees a Security Council seat as an acknowledgment of the country's important global role in achieving peace and development.

Although the costs and compensations of obtaining a Security Council seat have been little debated outside the elite, there is an established consensus that there is support at every layer of society for this objective. The same consensus does not exist regarding another aspiration, accession to the OECD. Adherence to the Paris-based organization is seen as an unsought graduation into the rich countries club, a shift that could create obstacles to the coordination of positions with neighbors and developing countries as a whole.

Despite its firm engagement in nuclear nonproliferation, its adherence to the entire range of instruments of control of weapons of mass destruction of all types, as well as to the regimes to control sensitive equipment and dual use materials, Brazil does not consider acceptable schemes that perpetuate the currently existing discriminatory systems, as shown by the NPT. Conventional disarmament is not emphasized as such, by diplomats or the military establishment, but Brazil is one of the countries with the lowest per capita spending on the military, in the region and in the world; this fact has worked as an element of reassurance and political stabilization in the region. Brazil aspires to play the same role on a wider scale.

The focus of Brazil's political, economic, and diplomatic strategy is obviously centered on South America, an idea that has been emphasized by Brazilian diplomacy since the beginning of the 1990s, as a replacement for the politically vague and geographically diffuse notion of Latin America. After the United States advanced its idea of a FTAA for the entire hemisphere, Brazilian diplomats tried to regain the initiative, and proposed a SAFTA (see above), conceived as a network of trade deals between Mercosur and the South American countries. It did not succeed at the time, but reappeared later, first in the form of President Cardoso's idea for a South American Initiative for Regional Integration to be focused on infrastructure projects, and appeared afterward under Lula's more ambitious proposition for a South American Community of Nations, for which Brazil offered to supply the secretariat (declined by the neighbors). Lately, the same idea gained the support of more activist countries in the region and is now transformed in a political organization known as South American Nations Union (Unasur), with a formal secretariat established in Quito. The proper functioning of those political arrangements is however complicated by the political instability of many countries of the region by their inconsistent or erratic diplomatic actions. At the economic and financial level, the United States can outbid Brazil in market access, financing, trade in services, and investments—areas in which Brazil has notoriously less competitive resources and capabilities.

Disagreements among countries in the region regarding a common list of priorities, their respective, and not always coincident, national interests, and their historical mistrust vis-à-vis Brazil's specific weight—together with Brazilian protectionism—have made it very difficult for Brazil to exercise what many observers consider to be a natural leadership in the region. Besides, the continent is still not well integrated physically—geographical obstacles are very considerable in some areas—and great economic and social disparities, the so-called asymmetries, combine to limit the integration drive sought by Brazil. The very notion of a regional leadership was never an aspiration of traditional Brazilian diplomacy, because "old" diplomats were aware of the problems and suspicions that such a declaration would cause in the region. Lula's display nevertheless flirted with demands of the smaller countries, which were probably eager to get Brazil's technical, financial, and economic cooperation. The same requests—and the apparent acceptance of a Brazilian prominence—were made by African Lusophone countries with which Brazil's current government engaged in very ambitious cooperative programs, only limited by the scarcity of financial resources.

Indeed, despite the impressive magnitude of its GDP and the advancement of its industry and agriculture, Brazil has insufficient means to provide assistance and technical cooperation at the same levels as DAC-OECD countries. In South America, the country has voluntarily advanced infrastructure and economic capacity in the smaller countries. Brazil agreed to put up 70 percent of the financing for a compensatory mechanism within Mercosur called Focem, a fund for the "correction of asymmetries." Even adopting for itself much more cautious and orthodox economic policy principles than those in force in many other countries in South America (with the exception of Chile), Brazil participates in discussions and negotiations with an aim of creating financing schemes for regional development using public resources. Meanwhile, in October 2007, Venezuela's President Hugo Chavez proposed a Banco del Sur (Southern Bank), with norms and rules perhaps looser than those followed in the IADB (Inter-American Development Bank) or the CAF (Andean Financial Development Corporation).

Some disagreements arose between Brazil and some countries in the region, mostly oil and gas exporters, concerning energy cooperation and the relative weight of fossil fuels and the renewable energies. Brazil is a major producer and exporter of ethanol made from sugarcane. It has already proposed technological cooperation schemes with the United States to stimulate its use internationally, something that has not stopped the latter country from protecting its own corn-based ethanol by imposing high duties on the Brazilian product. Brazil, as it continues to seek a possible understanding for a full physical integration of the continent, has pursued a cautious strategy in the energy integration sector. This is much more complicated than was initially predicted, since it includes the net supplier countries of oil and gas, most notably Venezuela and Bolivia, but also Peru and Ecuador, and the net consumer countries of Brazil, Argentina, and Chile, whose interests are not necessarily conflicting or contradictory, but do not exactly coincide on all points. Bolivia has difficulties in fulfilling its treaties and gas exploration accords signed with Brazil in the 1990s, and in 2006 unilaterally modified them. (In fact, Bolivia expropriated some Petrobras assets in that country.) In addition, the Venezuelan proposal for an enormous gas pipeline to Brazil and Argentina must be carefully analyzed, as it implies enormous costs, environmental barriers, and as yet unspecified tariffs.

Lula's second term diplomacy in South America is being carried out under much more cautious and realistic assumptions and procedures than during its first term. Indeed, the enthusiasm for the cause of integration and the political initiatives adopted in a relatively impetuous manner in the initial phase soon came up against the distinct political realities in each sub-regional case. Lula's most ambitious project was to ensure the expansion of Mercosur as the basis for regional leadership, both for its own sake and as a kind of continental resistance against the U.S.-sponsored FTAA. But his government was unable to overcome the difficulties that had paralyzed the trade group in the exchange crisis of 1999: competition among members countries, a defensive posture against foreign competition, and the nonintegrated and nearly noncomplementary national industrial structures. All these factors continue to impede the operation of the customs union via a common external tariff.

The FTAA negotiating process was blocked at the presidential summit meeting of Mar del Plata (November 2005), at the instigation of Lula, Kirchner, and Chávez, only to come back in the form of a series of bilateral trade agreements drawn up by the United States for like-minded countries (including some partners in Mercosur, such as Peru). In 2006, Mercosur was expanded to include Venezuela, but its adhesion was an essentially political decision, still leaving unresolved whether the deadlines for its full incorporation into the customs union.

On the bilateral level, for example, Brazil had to accommodate Argentinean complaints, accepting various unilateral restrictions to free trade before agreeing to consolidate the new regime of trade exceptions in a protocol of safeguards, euphemistically called the Competitive Adaptation Mechanism. In the South American integration plan, the "burden of leadership" was never taken on, since the South American Community of Nations remained a project that was still being put into place when Brazil was rebuffed in its intension to acquire the secretariat; during its inception, for example, in a regional meeting held in Peru (December 2004), none of the three other Mercosur presidents showed up for the ceremony. The new Community has taken the name Unasur, proposed by Hugo Chávez, with a secretariat in Quito. But it is far from obvious that the new entity can overcome the differences in vision and objectives among the region's leaders.

Interactions between Brazil's New Diplomacy and the International Order

Brazil occupies a singular position, not necessarily unique, but specific in its own way within the contemporary system of international relations. Together with Russia, India, and China, who are emerging or are already categorized as large powers, Brazil is presumably destined to play a future role of prominence in the changing scenarios of global governance, but probably as a raw economy rather than as a strategic-military power. As the first worldwide producer of a long list of raw materials that are mostly agricultural, Brazil is blessed with immense reserves of biodiversity and natural resources.

For a long time, in its first three or four centuries as a nation, Brazil, quite efficiently, offered to the world basically dessert products: sugar, coffee, cocoa, and a few others. Currently a wide range of other raw goods—grains, meat, orange juice, minerals—complements this line of raw materials, besides manufactured goods of low technological intensity (textiles, shoes, some appliances). Today, Brazil continues to be a competitive commodities supplier—and it will certainly remain so, with more value-added primary products—but is also on the front line of state-of-the-art technology, like the civil aircraft of Embraer. In the future, and for the first time in its economic history, Brazil will become a major supplier of renewable energy products, from sugarcane ethanol to biofuels in general, not only because of its raw products, but also because of its technological and scientific achievements.

For the first time in world economic history, Brazil also will have the chance to put its imprint on something really valuable at the world level, that is, the energy matrix emerging from the gradual depletion of petroleum: this prospect is still distant, but it offers the opportunity to define a new strategic industry that has truly geopolitical dimensions. Properly managed, the Brazilian know-how and technology of sugarcane plantation, its transformation into ethanol, and the associated farms and plants for many kinds of biofuels can in the near future be transferred to lagging developing countries like those in Africa—starting by Lusophone Angola and Mozambique, which have plenty of arable lands.

Historically Brazil has been penalized for its lack of abundant sources of energy—coal and petroleum in the first and second industrial revolution—which, together with the population's low educational level, has hampered its entry into the modern industrial economy. Today, fully industrialized but still dragging the heavy baggage of a lagging educational system and low standards of technology (despite a notable rise in academic and scientific output), Brazil is preparing to take on a more prominent role in globalization. The low economic growth rates of the last two decades followed a sustained and impressive rise in GDP during the first 80 years of the twentieth century. Sluggish growth could persist long into the future, taking into account Brazil's high fiscal burden compared to the rest of the emerging countries: public expenditures make up around 38 percent of the GDP, similar to OECD's average, compared with an average of 28 percent for emerging countries and an even lower rate for the most dynamic among these (17 percent and 18 percent for China and Chile, for instance).

Indeed, an analysis of the BRIC countries by two Goldman Sachs economists confirmed that Brazil is the least dynamic country relative to this group, only managing to surpass France and Germany after 2030.[9] But, even maintaining just the average, fairly modest rate of 3.5 percent GDP annual growth, up to 2050, this would be enough to place Brazil into a new G-6 of the world economy predicted in this study. Of all BRICs, Brazil is the country with the best market structures, the fruit of capitalism that has developed in a relatively orthodox manner throughout the twentieth century (in comparison to the diverse socialist experiments in the other three).

Despite overall dysfunctions generated by an intrusive government and by the heavy tax burden, in large part responsible for the high costs of transactions and the high rate of informality in the economy in general, the fact is that modern Brazil has a relatively developed and functional state and corporate institutions, allowing for its smooth entrance into the circuits of a globalized economy. If the country is able to put forward a new social pact that could reduce the weight of overtaxation and excessive regulation, Brazil could break into the virtuous circle of sustainable growth (although at more modest rates than those of a few other emerging countries), while still preserving macroeconomic stability. Brazil will retain, for one or two generations more, a significantly skewed pattern of its income distribution, with a higher Gini coefficient than the world average. Yet the trend seems to be gradually downward, because of macroeconomic stability, investment in education, and government transfers.

The overall orientation of the Brazilian elite is to seek out alliances of a pragmatic rather than ideological character, and to develop the country's potential according to a combination of political elements, including diplomatic and economic factors. Obviously, a favorable evolution toward the desired sovereign integration into the world economy and the assumption by Brazil of a larger economic and political presence in the world depend on the country's successfully carrying out domestic reforms to allow for faster economic growth. Brazil also has to consolidate the process of structural transformations necessary to place it among the fully developed nations. Although much of this complex process depends on objective conditions—most of all on capital accumulation and technological capabilities—policy measures and elite attitudes are also crucial.

This path to full development cannot be guaranteed. In a pessimistic scenario, reflected in a study by the National Intelligence Council, an entity affiliated with the CIA, which saw in *Project 2020* perspectives for Brazil and Latin America, there was an attempt to visualize trends for Brazilian and regional evolution. According to this study Brazil will likely have failed to deliver on its promised leadership in South America, due as much to the skepticism of its neighbors as to its frequently overwhelming emphasis on its own interests. It will, nevertheless, continue to be the dominant voice on the continent and a key market for its Mercosur partners. Brazil will still not have won a permanent seat on the Security Council, but it will continue to consider itself a global player. Although Brazil's economic improvements are not likely to be spectacular, the size of its economy, along with its lively democracy, will continue to have a stabilizing effect on the entire region. Trade arrangements with Europe, the USA, and large developing economies, mainly China and India, will help to keep its exports growing steadily enough to offset its overall lack of economic dynamism. Even after twenty years, efforts to pass vital reforms to Brazilian institutions will still be underway. Though the situation is bound to improve somewhat, the so-called 'Brazil cost', itself a governance issue, will continue to thwart efforts to modernize the economy thoroughly. Brazil's complex and burdensome taxation system, fiscal wars between its states, and the limits of its internal transportation infrastructure, will persist. Taking advantage of Asia's hunger and improved ties with Europe, Brazil will endeavor to offset its structural limitations through its robust agribusiness sector. Brazil's sizeable debt and vulnerability to inflation will also remain matters of concern.[10]

Conclusion

Summing up, Brazil will continue to advance, but apparently not at a rhythm that will put it at the head of the world economy in the near future, provided, of course, that no big economic or social problem disturbs the relatively optimistic prospective scenario laid out in the Goldman Sachs study. In any case, its presence in this hypothetical G-6 brings economic implications, but nothing is said about the consequences for Brazil on the strategic or military levels, areas not at all covered by the study. It is predictable that Brazil will continue to show features similar to those currently seen in the actual implementation of its very cautious and at the same time participative diplomacy: a leading position in trade forums, a strong presence in the regional context, a relatively small importance in the financial and technological areas, and the continuity of its active engagement in multilateral bodies. The Southern alliances, especially those in the South American region, will continue to have a great emphasis in its foreign policy, at the same time that the dialogue with the leading powers will continue to intensify, not to exclude its eventual entrance into the OECD and in an expanded G-8.

The preferred scenario for diplomatic action will continue to be in South America and possibly in some African countries—especially the big Lusophone ones, Angola and Mozambique—but the quality of diplomatic interaction with developing partners will also presumably be improved. The United States and the great European countries that have a strong corporate and cultural presence in Brazil, like Germany, will continue to have an outstanding role in this complex web of economic, financial, and technologic relationships. In 2007, the European Union and Brazil decided to open a high-level dialogue about a strategic partnership, which should have implications for Mercosur. Such a scheme might allow Brazil to offset the weighty presence of the United States in South America.

In conclusion, it may be said that the emergence of Brazil as a major regional and global player depends much more on continuity of its internal economic reforms and policies than its ability to project itself abroad, a process that seems guaranteed.

Notes

1. Wilson and Purushothaman (2003).
2. For a global view of the reform era in Brazil, see: Giambiagi, Reis, and Urani (2004); Font and Spanakos (2004); Purcell and Roett (1997).

3. On FHC's presidential diplomacy and the main international relations issues of his term, see Almeida (2004: 203–228); the argument about UNSC and Argentinean reaction about it was carried in an interview with FHC himself.
4. There is not yet a detailed or complete study of Lula's diplomacy. For a brief analysis of foreign policy during Lula's first term, see Almeida (2007: 3–10); available at http://www.usp.br/cartainternacional/modx/assets/docs/CartaInter_2007–01.pdf accessed in January 2008.
5. This is a conference of left-wing parties and social movements in Latin America. It was organized by the PT, and the first meeting was held in Sao Paulo in 1990. Since that time, it has met in other Latin American cities, but the organization retains the name Forum of Sao Paulo.
6. See Almeida (2004: 162–184).
7. On the PT's foreign policy positions, see Almeida (2003: 87–102); available at http://www.scielo.br/scielo.php?script=sci_arttext&pid=S0104–44782003000100008&lng=en&nrm=iso&tlng=pt accessed in January 2008. French version: "La politique internationale du Parti des Travailleurs, de la fondation du parti à la diplomatie du gouvernement Lula." In Denis Rolland and Joëlle Chassin, eds. *Pour Comprendre le Brésil de Lula*, Paris: L'Harmattan, 2004. pp. 221–238.
8. See Almeida (2006: 95–116).
9. See Wilson and Purushothaman (2003); available at http://www2.goldmansachs.com/insight/research/reports/99.pdf accessed in January 2008.
10. See "Latin America in 2020: Two Steps Forward, One and a Half Back," in National Intelligence Council, part of the project *Mapping the Global Future: 2020 Project*, Washington: Government Printing Office, 2004; available at http://www.dni.gov/nic/NIC_2020_project.html accessed in January 2008 cited in Almeida (2004: 157–190, cf. p. 189).

Bibliographic References

Almeida, Paulo Roberto de. 2003. "A política internacional do Partido dos Trabalhadores: da fundação do partido à diplomacia do governo Lula." *Sociologia e Política* (20) (June): 87–102.

———. 2004. "Planejamento no Brasil: memória histórica." *Parcerias Estratégicas* (18) (August): 157–190.

———. 2004."A relação do Brasil com os EUA: de FHC-Clinton a Lula-Bush." In Reis Giambiagi and Urani, eds. *Reformas no Brasil: Balanço e Agenda*. pp. 203–228.

———. 2004. "Uma política externa engajada: a diplomacia do governo Lula." *Revista Brasileira de Política Internacional* 47(1): 162–184.

———. 2006. "Uma nova 'arquitetura' diplomática?: interpretações divergentes sobre a política externa do Governo Lula (2003–2006)." *Revista Brasileira de Política Internacional* 49(1):95–116.

———. 2007. "A diplomacia do governo Lula em seu primeiro mandato (2003–2006): um balanço e algumas perspectivas." *Carta Internacional*, São Paulo: Nupri-USP, 2(1) (January–March):3–10.

Font, Mauricio A., and Anthony Peter Spanakos, Ed. 2004. *Reforming Brazil*. Lanham, MD: Lexington Books.

Giambiagi, Fabio, José Guilherme Reis, and André Urani, Eds. 2004. *Reformas no Brasil: Balanço e Agenda*. Rio de Janeiro: Nova Fronteira.

Wilson, Dominic, and Roopa Purushothaman. 2003. *Dreaming with BRICs: The Path to 2050*. New York: Goldman Sachs at http://www2.goldmansachs.com/insight/research/reports/99.pdf accessed in January 2008.

PART FOUR

The Impact of President Lula's Social Programs

CHAPTER TEN

A Spatial Analysis of Bolsa Família: Is Allocation Targeting the Needy?*

MÔNICA A. HADDAD

Introduction

Social inequality is a continuing problem in Brazil, but as president, Luiz Inácio Lula da Silva has focused more attention on the issue than his predecessors. When he took office in January 2003, Lula created the new Ministry of Social Development and Fight against Hunger (*Ministério do Desenvolvimento Social e Combate à Fome*) to manage the country's investments aimed at reducing poverty, combating hunger, increasing school attendance, and improving the number of people—especially children—who receive basic health care. One such program, *Bolsa Família* (Family Fund), is based on a direct transfer of funds to low-income families that agree to keep their children in school and provide them with basic health care. Its main purpose is to provide "households the incentives to invest in human capital and thereby reduce poverty [and minimize social inequalities] in the long-run" (de Janvry et al. 2005: 1).

Based on the Ministry of Social Development and Fight against Hunger's database, *Bolsa Família* (*BF*) benefited 3.6 million families in its first year (2003) at a cost of R\$3.4 billion; in 2005 the program helped 8.7 million families at a cost of R\$5.7 billion. Furthermore, in 2005, more than 21 percent of the federal budget was allocated to social welfare programs like *BF*, while in 1987, only 3 percent of the federal budget was. There is no denying this is a significant change. While this program has been the topic for important studies (Brière and Lindert 2005, Hall 2006, Lavinas 2006, Soares et al. 2006, and Oliveira et al. 2007), only one study assesses *BF* from a spatial perspective (Haddad 2008); it examines whether this program is contributing to greater social equality within the country.

As Lula began his second term in January 2007, he promised to continue to allocate a substantial part of the federal budget to social programs. The federal government set aside approximately R$8.6 billion for *Bolsa Família* in 2007. Therefore, it is crucial to assure that these resources are directed to areas where there is greatest need and they can do the most good. Focusing on *BF* in 2006, the most recent full year for which data are available, this chapter addresses the following research question: Are the investments allocated in counties that need them the most? If investments are not allocated and distributed where the majority of needy families live, Lula's compensatory policies may be reinforcing the traditional patterns of poverty and social injustice.

Why should we address this issue? A previous study (Haddad and Nedović-Budić 2006) examining the relationship between public intervention and the reduction of social and economic intra-urban inequalities in São Paulo City showed that in 2002 (pre-Lula), social programs, public services, and utilities were allocated in areas with lower needs, that is, in areas with higher levels of human development. It is possible that this was an anomalous situation that did not reflect conditions elsewhere in the nation, but other studies about Brazil lead us to doubt that. It is not unusual to see "wealthy people influencing government officials to attract public investments and services to the [areas] they live in, at the expense of low-income [areas]" (Werna 2000: 4). Allocation practices also are related to the "processes of political representation, [and] the rationale for action of the bureaucratic segments responsible for the provision of services" (Torres and Oliveira 2001: 16). Low-income households typically do not have enough education or power to participate effectively, if at all, in political processes. Finally, Coady, Grosh, and Hoddinott (2002), when reviewing targeted programs in developing countries, found that more than a quarter of the programs were characterized by "regressive benefit incidence." In other words, "in approximately 25 percent of cases targeting was regressive so that a random allocation of resources would have provided a greater share of benefits to the poor" (Coady, Grosh, and Hoddinott 2004: 84). Based on these previous studies, if new allocations are about to be made, it is important to assure that the distribution of resources is consistent with the spatial distribution of the disadvantaged.

To better examine *Bolsa Família* allocation, we introduce a spatial dimension in our analyses. In this way we overcome the limitations of analyses that neglect to consider the dependency of each county[1] on its geographic location. Hence, to answer the research question posed above, we rely on Exploratory Spatial Data Analysis (ESDA) and Confirmatory Spatial Data Analysis (CSDA) methods. By using ESDA methods we are able to test for spatial autocorrelation, which occurs when value similarity and locational similarity coincide (Anselin 2001). By using CSDA methods we are able to specify spatially explicit regression models, that is, models that incorporate spatial autocorrelation in their specification.

Our intention is to spatially analyze this contemporary social program and devise responses to policy makers. With our spatial analyses, policy makers will be able to better comprehend the allocation of funding for Lula's main social program with maps that are easy to understand. This examination may guide policy makers toward a new system of allocation, if needed, or the continuation of the same system. The chapter proceeds as follows. The section Thinking Socially focuses on social development, social policies, and a description of the *Bolsa Família* program. In the Methodology section we explain the methodology, focusing on the data, the spatial weight matrices, spatial autocorrelation test, and model specifications. The next section, Modeling Results, focuses on the modeling results, including some maps as an alternative to understand the results. The last section concludes, suggesting some recommendations for policy makers.

Thinking Socially

Traditional economic development theory holds that economic growth generates income gains for the poor and promotes welfare benefits to them, such as access to school and health care. The overall outcome of this process is an improvement in the social development status of the population. Nevertheless, as Ghai (2000) states, "It is commonly observed that levels of economic development tend to be roughly correlated with levels of social development in countries throughout the world. This observable cross-country correlation, however, does not necessarily indicate a direct causal relationship between economic and social development in any particular case" (1). Numerous studies indicate that growth alone is not sufficient to overcome social problems (Haddad et al. 2002, Morley and Coady 2003; Hall and Midgley 2004, Arbache 2006, Haddad and Nedović-Budić 2006). Therefore, attention to social development should be part of the public policy agenda, and President Lula is on the right track when deciding to allocate public resources to social programs such as *Bolsa Família*.

Complementary to that, Hall and Midgley (2004) propose that "the best hope of raising standards of living and eradicating poverty lies in an approach that combines a commitment to economic development with the introduction of social policies that specifically and directly address the poverty problem" (45). As Lula entered his second term as president, not only did he continue his social policies, but he also delivered an economic development package called Programa de Aceleração do Crescimento (Program for Accelerating Growth—PAC). Its objective is to reach a sustained annual GDP growth rate of 5 percent by stimulating private investment, and securing higher rates of public investment in economic infrastructure.

Mkandawire (2004) also advocates social policies as key instruments that work in combination with economic policy to ensure equitable and socially sustainable economic development. He defines social policy as "collective intervention in the economy to influence the access to and the incidence of adequate and secure livelihoods and income" (1). *Bolsa Família* ensures children's access to school and health care and provides income to their families, offering a good example of how a social program can be implemented in the real world. Social policy may target different objectives such as rural development and urban environment improvement (Hall and Midgley 2004). *BF* lies in the categories of poverty reduction and social inequality minimization.

Conditional cash transfer programs—a specific type of social policy—appeared in Brazil prior to Lula's first term as president. The idea behind *Bolsa Família* is not a new approach for Brazilians. As Morley and Coady (2003) point out, conditional transfer-for-education (CTE) programs have been in place in many different countries since the mid-1990s. Examples are *Progressa* in Mexico, Food for Education in Bangladesh, *Red de Protección Social* in Nicaragua, and *Bolsa Escola* (School Fund) in Brazil. *Bolsa Escola* started as a county program whose rules and financing were decided locally. In 2001, *Bolsa Escola* was implemented at the national level (under Cardoso's administration).

In October of 2003, *Bolsa Família* was created, and the existing cash transfer programs—including *Bolsa Escola*—were slowly merged with the new *BF*.[2] The same system initiated by *Bolsa Escola* is now being used by *BF* beneficiaries. The system lowers the cost—transportation and time—of "making transfer payments to both the donor and the recipient.... The mother of each beneficiary family is given an electronic card and an account at *Caixa Econômica Federal*. Monthly payments are directly credited to this account from the national treasury, and the mother can make electronic withdrawals at any of the local outlets of the bank or in thousands of other authorized commercial outlets" (Morley and Coady 2003: 33). *BF* monetary values for the beneficiaries vary according to poverty level and number of children, pregnant women, and nursing mothers per family.[3]

Each county is responsible for the implementation of *BF* in its territory. Eligible families apply by contacting the responsible party in the county where they live, and presenting personal documents (social security number or voter's card). These families apply only once to the *Cadastro Único dos Programas Sociais do Governo Federal*, which is a federal government tool to collect data to identify all the existing poor families in Brazil. This single application allows families to be officially eligible for all federal social programs available, including *BF*.

Concerning the selection criteria, the Ministry of Social Development and Fight against Hunger organized a database—based on data from the 2000 IBGE Census and the 2004 Brazilian National Household Survey[4]—that contains the estimated number of poor families living in each county. By cross-referencing information from *Cadastro Único* and this database, the ministry allocates public funds in the counties. As Barth (2006) alerts, with this distribution system, "the federal government continues to have great influence on the lower government units. It is...an indicator that decentralization of social policies is still at an early stage [in Brazil]" (261).

The price Brazil is paying for its social agenda is expensive. According to Arbache (2006), one way to fund Lula's social agenda is through tax increases, but "the tax burden plus the nominal deficit amounted to about 38.5 percent of the GDP. In view of the fiscal constraints and the firm decision of the government to keep inflation at low levels, funding an ambitious pro-poor program [*Bolsa Família*] was the highest challenge of the government" (341). Clearly, the economic infrastructure—needed for economic development—suffered in this trade-off. To illustrate, in 2005, the federal government spent 3 percent of its budget on economic infrastructure and 21 percent on the cash transfer programs.

Bolsa Escola—predecessor to *Bolsa Família*—has been the subject of several studies (Bourguignon, Ferreira, and Leite 2003, Barrientos and DeJong 2004 and 2006, Cardoso and Souza 2004, de Janvry et al. 2005). To illustrate, Cardoso and Souza (2004) find a positive and significant impact of *Bolsa Escola* on school attendance. In the same direction, Bourguignon, Ferreira, and Leite (2003) simulated the effect of *Bolsa Escola* and found that it had a big impact on school enrollments, but less on poverty levels, since families lose the income of children who leave the labor force to attend school. As they state, "results suggest that 60 percent of poor 10- to 15-year-olds not in school enroll in response to the program" (229). Contrary to this, Barrientos and Dejong (2006), when examining different social programs—including *Bolsa Escola*—concluded that cash transfer programs targeting children in poor households are an effective way of reducing poverty.

Schwartzman (2005) examined education-oriented programs using the 2003 Brazilian National Household Survey—applying descriptive statistics—and concluded that these programs are "reasonably well focused in lower-income families, in spite of a bias against poor in urban areas, some regional distortions and the fact that, in 2003, of the 8.3 million children in families receiving the benefit, 1.5 million, or 17 percent, were in the upper 50 percent income bracket" (21). However, he states that the programs "are mostly out of focus as an education policy instrument, since most of the stipends are given to families that would keep their children in schools in any case" (21).

Several scholars propose different ways to assess *Bolsa Família*. Marques et al. (2004) examined the July 2004 *BF* beneficiaries for some Brazilian counties, comparing their regional location, population size, rating on the U.N. Human Development Index, urban or rural status, and leading economic activities. By using descriptive statistics, they found that the majority of the beneficiaries are located in the northeast region, in contrast with a lower number of beneficiaries in the south region. On the other hand, Neri (2005) observes that the proportion of people living below the poverty line fell significantly from 2003 to 2004, reaching the lowest figure since 1992; he credits this result to economic growth and *BF*.

In summary, based on this literature review, we can state that President Lula seems justified in investing significant public resources in a social program, since economic development may do no good for the poor per se. The proposition that *Bolsa Família* is an effective vehicle for social investment still requires assessment, because the program will not only continue during Lula's second mandate, but will be expanded.

Methodology

As stated previously, *Bolsa Família* lies in the social policy categories of poverty reduction and social inequality minimization. The question—are the investments allocated in counties that need them the most?—is related to poverty reduction. In this section, we explain the methodological approach to address this research question.

Research Framework

The central element of the research framework (figure 10.1) is *Bolsa Família* allocation that is either targeting the disadvantaged, or not. This practice is influenced by policy makers, who can decide on where to allocate *BF* funds based on county socioeconomic variables, such the Gini coefficient, illiteracy rate, and infant mortality rate. A feedback loop is constructed to allow for adjustments in public policies, if policy makers are willing to make changes in *BF* allocation.

Data

This study focuses on the large majority of Brazilian counties.[5] Data for the 2006 *Bolsa Família* beneficiaries come from the Ministry of Social

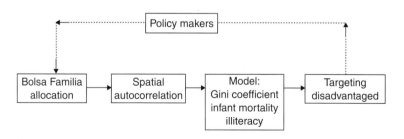

Figure 10.1 Research framework

Source: Author's illustration

Development. It is very important to highlight that this dataset is *stricto sensu BF*, not including the beneficiaries from the existing cash transfer programs (pre-Lula) that were merged with *BF*. We create a ratio in which we can express the percentage of the target population that benefited from the program in 2006. For the denominator—based on "interests, profits, dividends, and others"—we use families with per capita income of R$120 or lower (for counties located in the northeast region), R$130 or lower (for counties located in the north region), and R$140 or lower (for counties located in the southeast, center-south, and south regions) as a proxy to the program target population (Source: IBGE Census 2000).[6] Therefore, the ratio—which is the dependent variable of our model—is calculated as 2006 beneficiary families, divided by families with the per capita incomes described above.

Figure 10.2 shows the *Bolsa Família* ratio relative to the sample average of Brazilian counties, for the year 2006. Counties with low *BF* ratio (less

Figure 10.2   *Bolsa Família* ratio relative to the sample average of Brazilian counties, 2006
Source: Calculated by the author

Table 10.1 Summary statistics of all variables

Variables	Mean	Standard deviation	Minimum	Maximum
Gini coefficient (2000)	0.561	0.059	0.360	0.820
Bolsa Família ratio (2006)	0.584	0.208	0.045	1.209
Infant mortality rate (2000)	0.045	0.030	0.006	0.135
Illiteracy rate (2000) .	0.267	0.152	0.020	0.703

Source: *Atlas de Desenvolvimento Humano, Fundação João Pinheiro*, and *Ministério do Desenvolvimento Social e Combate à Fome*

than 90 percent of the sample average) are located in the center and south of the country. Counties with a high ratio (more than 110 percent of the sample average) are located in the north and northeast of Brazil. These facts suggest substantial intercounty variability in the spatial distribution of *BF* in Brazil.

We use as independent variables the Gini coefficient, infant mortality rate, and illiteracy rate, all for the year 2000 (Source: *Atlas de Desenvolvimento Humano, Fundação João Pinheiro*).[7] Table 10.1 depicts the summary statistics of all variables used in this study.[8]

Spatial Weight Matrices

To conduct ESDA/CSDA it is necessary to define a spatial weight matrix *W*. This matrix imposes a neighborhood structure on the data and can be defined in a variety of ways. Because we have a large dataset (n = 5,504 observations), we faced some software-related constraints when choosing our matrices. Therefore, we opted for simple binary queen contiguity and simple binary rook contiguity. We use two matrices in our analyses to test the robustness of our results.

The simple binary queen contiguity matrix is composed of 0 and 1: if county *i* has a common boundary and/or vertex with county *j*, then they are neighbors and $w_{ij} = 1$; if county *i* does not have a common boundary and/or vertex with county *j*, then they are not neighbors and $w$ij = 0. The diagonal elements are set to 0. The rook matrix follows the same logic except that it is based on common boundary only, not including vertex. Both matrices are row standardized so that each row sums up to 1.

Spatial Autocorrelation

By using ESDA methods, we can test for spatial autocorrelation. Among statistics of global spatial autocorrelation, Moran's *I* is widely used. It provides a formal indication of the degree of linear association between the observed values and provides a formal indication of the degree of linear association between the observed values and the spatially weighted averages of neighboring values. Moran's I shows if there is clustering in the spatial distribution of a variable, and is defined as:

$$I = \frac{n}{S_0} \cdot \frac{\sum_i \sum_j w_{ij}\left(x_i - \mu\right)\left(x_j - \mu\right)}{\sum\left(x_i - \mu\right)^2} \tag{1}$$

where x_i is the observation in county i; μ is the mean of the observations across counties; n is the number of counties, and w_{ij} is one element of the spatial weight matrix W, which expresses the spatial arrangement of the data. S_0 is a scaling factor equal to the sum of all elements of W. Values of I larger than the expected value $E(I) = -1/(n-1)$ indicate positive spatial autocorrelation, whereas values of I smaller than the expected value $E(I) = -1/(n-1)$ indicate negative spatial autocorrelation. Moran's I values range from $+1$ (perfect positive spatial autocorrelation) to -1 (perfect negative spatial autocorrelation).

The global Moran's I statistics for the BF ratio, using the two spatial matrices described above, is 0.768. The spatial autocorrelation tests for BF ratio lead to the rejection of the null hypothesis of spatial randomness. The two coefficients are statistically significant at the 0.001 level, based on the permutation approach with 999 random permutations.

The BF ratio spatial distribution is characterized by a significant global positive spatial autocorrelation, which suggests that their values are spatially clustered. This means that the counties with high BF ratio values are located close to counties with high BF ratio values, and the counties with low BF ratio values are located close to districts with low BF ratio values. These results indicate that location plays an important role when examining the spatial distribution of BF ratio, when county values are compared to the country's mean. Thus, we cannot talk about spatial randomness or lack of spatial dependence when focusing on the allocation of BF in Brazil.

The Models

Because spatial autocorrelation is present in the spatial distribution of the BF ratio, we use CSDA methods as an attempt to answer our research question, taking into account each county and its geographic location relative to other counties in the country. These methods help avoid misspecification of models, inefficient coefficients, and erroneous statistical inferences that occur when spatial autocorrelation and spatial heterogeneity are not addressed (Anselin and Rey 1991).

As explained previously, the dependent variable for this model is the 2006 BF ratio. The independent variables are the Gini coefficient, infant mortality rate, and illiteracy rate, all for the year 2000. We take the following steps in specifying the model, addressing the "specific to general" model specification approach of Florax, Folmer, and Rey (2003). Step 1 is on ordinary least square (OLS)-based model estimated by:

$$BF_i = \beta_0 + \beta_1 x_{1i} + \beta_2 x_{2i} + \beta_3 x_{3i} + \varepsilon_i$$
$$i = 1, \dots, 5{,}504 \text{ and } \varepsilon \sim N(0, \sigma_\varepsilon^2 I) \quad\quad\quad (2)$$

where BF_i is the *Bolsa Família* ratio for each county i; x_{1i}, x_{2i}, and x_{3i} are the independent variables Gini coefficient, infant mortality rate, and illiteracy rate; β_0, β_1, β_2, and β_3 are the unknown parameters to be estimated; and ε is the vector of errors.

In Step 1 we carry out tests to detect the presence of spatial dependence to verify if the non–spatial OLS model is the appropriate specification. Based on the test results, we state that they are against the assumption that the same causal processes operate throughout the counties under investigation. Therefore, we apply spatial regressions, which can be in one of three forms: the spatial error model, spatial lag model, or spatial cross-regressive model. The test results reveal that the spatial lag model is the most appropriate specification. Therefore, in Step 2 the spatial lag is applied to include spatial dependence in the model specification, as an additional covariate in the model, the so-called spatial lag. According to Messner and Anselin (2004), "the spatial lag model implies that the geographic clustering of [BF ratio] is due to influence of [BF ratio] in one place on [BF ratio] in another. This [type of] model is consistent with some kind of diffusion process" (138). The spatial lag model is written as:

$$BF_i = \rho W B F + \beta_0 + \beta_1 x_{1i} + \beta_2 x_{2i} + \beta_3 x_{3i} + u_i \quad\quad i = 1, \dots, 5{,}504 \text{ and}$$
$$u \sim N(0, \sigma_\varepsilon^2 I) \quad\quad\quad (3)$$

where all the elements are defined as previously, and ρ is the spatial autoregressive parameter that indicates the extent of interaction between the observations according to the spatial pattern exogenously introduced by means of the standardized weight matrix W. The spatial lag variable WBF contains BF ratio multiplied by the weight matrix. A county i of vector BF ratio and the corresponding line of the spatial lag vector contain the spatially weighted average of BF ratio. u is the vector of errors with the usual properties.

Modeling Results

The results of the models presented in this chapter were calculated using GeoDa software (Anselin 2003). The results for all model estimations based on the queen matrix are presented in this section. Reporting the model estimates based on the rook matrix would be redundant as it leads to the same results. This fact points to the robustness of our results with regard to the choice of spatial weight matrices. Table 10.2 displays the estimation results. As one can observe, the Akaike Information Criterion

Table 10.2 Estimation results for the allocation model for Brazilian counties, 2006

	Non-spatial	Spatial
	OLS	LAG (ML)
β_0 (constant)	0.133 (0.000)	0.029 (0.03)
β_1 (Gini coefficient)	0.311 (0.000)	0.174 (0.000)
β_2 (infant mortality)	2.49 (0.000)	0.91 (0.000)
β_3 (illiteracy)	0.618 (0.000)	0.307 (0.000)
R^2-adjusted	0.66	—
Spatial lag	—	0.573 (0.000)
AIC	−7530.4	−8983.16
SC	−7503.95	−8950.1
Log Likelihood	3769.2	4496.58

Note: OBS: *p* values presented in parentheses

Source: Calculated by the author

(AIC), the Schwartz Criterion (SC), and the Log Likelihood test indicate that the spatial model performs better than the non-spatial model.

The OLS model coefficients for Gini, infant mortality, and illiteracy are all significant at the 0.1 percent level, indicating that a high *BF* ratio coincides with higher Gini, infant mortality, and illiteracy. The model's R^2-adjusted is close to 70 percent. The spatial lag model coefficients for Gini, infant mortality, and illiteracy are all significant at the 0.1 percent level, indicating that a high *BF* ratio coincides with higher Gini, infant mortality, and illiteracy. We can observe that the magnitude of the spatial lag model coefficients decreases when compared to the OLS model coefficients. The spatial lag coefficient is positive and significant, revealing that there is spatial autocorrelation between *BF* ratio in neighboring counties, which is not captured by the covariates used in the OLS-based model. Assuming that the counties do a fair job when accepting applications for *Cadastro Único*, the estimation results presented here are good news. Overall, we can affirm that *BF* funds are being allocated in counties that need them the most. There is evidence, based on the spatial lag model results, that the disadvantaged are being targeted by the 2006 *BF* allocation system.

The use of spatial econometrics methods allows us to map some results for comparison and better understanding of specific locations that may need scrutiny. Figure 10.3 displays three maps elaborated based on the results of the spatial lag model: a predicted map, a residual map, and a map that displays the dependent variable, that is, the 2006 *BF* ratio. The predicted map indicates the distribution and intensity of the three independent variables, that is, socioeconomic variables, across the Brazilian counties (Haddad and Nedović-Budić 2006). Higher predicted values (darker grey) show more intense socioeconomic variables, characterizing higher needs. We observe a strong spatial pattern in which the center-south part

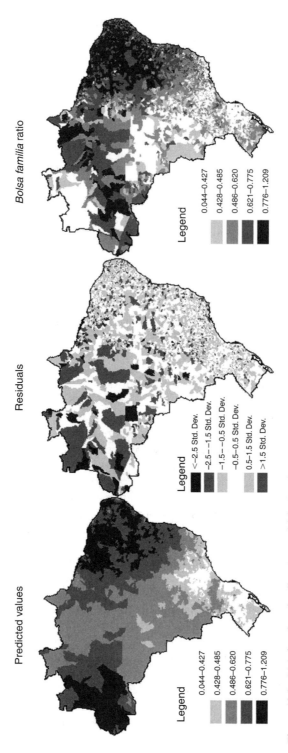

Figure 10.3 Maps based on the allocation model for Brazilian counties, 2006

Source: Calculated by the author

of the country depicts lower predicted values, and the northeast-north part of the country depicts higher predicted values. When we compare this predicted map with the *BF* ratio map, we notice a similar pattern in the spatial distribution of high and low values in both maps. This indicates that the 2006 *BF* allocation system is indeed targeting the counties characterized by higher needs.

The residual map from figure 10.3 uses standard deviation classification, in which counties are classified as underpredicted (positive values) and overpredicted (negative values) based on the spatial lag model. This map represents the difference between the predicted value of a county and the dependent variable in that same county. Table 10.3 depicts the idea of under- and overprediction in a more detailed manner. The majority of the counties—around 87 percent—do not belong to classes that present extremely high and very high values, confirming that the spatial lag model performs well. However, the counties classified as extremely high and very high are considered outliers, and suggest the existence of other variables where location and the socioeconomic variables were not sufficient to explain *BF* allocation. The outliers are the darker shades of grey and represent a greater mismatch between predicted value and the real *BF* allocation.

If policy makers are willing to improve *BF* allocation, they should direct special attention to these outliers. Let us assume that the federal government faces insufficient resources to assist this 13 percent of all counties all at once, so we can rank them. First, policy makers should concentrate on very high underpredicted counties (5.5 percent of Brazil's total) because they are characterized by high allocation, but may have low need. Second, policy makers should focus on extremely high overpredicted counties (1.4 percent of Brazil's total), since they are characterized by very low allocation, but may have very high need. Finally, policy makers should focus on very high over-predicted counties (6.2 percent of Brazil's total) since they are characterized by low allocation, but may have high need. In these two cases, counties with higher need may not be targeted by BF as they should.

Table 10.3 Percentage of Brazilian counties under- and overpredicted based on the allocation model, 2006

Interval	Scale	Percentage
< −2.5 St. Dev.	Extremely high overpredicted	1.4
−2.5– −1.5 St. Dev.	Very high overpredicted	6.2
−1.5– −0.5 St. Dev.	High overpredicted	20.6
−0.5–0.5 St. Dev.	Overpredicted and underpredicted	41.4
0.5–1.5 St. Dev.	High underpredicted	24.9
> 1.5 St. Dev.	Very high underpredicted	5.5

Source: Calculated by the author

Conclusion and Recommendations

In this chapter we examine the allocation of *Bolsa Família* from the perspective of need. We apply ESDA and CSDA methods that account for the location of the 5,504 Brazilian counties and dependency among neighboring counties. Haddad (2008) applies the same methodology described here, concluding that BF proved to be contributing to greater social equality in Brazil, when considering public-school enrollment as an input for social equity.

The empirical evidence from our models leads to a few conclusions. Counties characterized by higher need (i.e., high Gini coefficient, high infant mortality rate, and high illiteracy rate) generally are receiving more funds than counties characterized by lower need. By learning that in the northeast-north part of the country there is a higher concentration of allocation, we should be pleased, since there is also a higher concentration of the disadvantaged there (i.e., higher need).

Should President Lula continue with the same system of allocation, or should a new system of allocation be proposed? Based on the spatial analysis presented above, we believe there is no need to change the *BF* allocation system overall since it is targeting the counties with populations who need *BF* the most. There are, nevertheless, specific locations—outliers in the residual maps—that may merit some scrutiny. These locations suggest the existence of other variables where location and the independent variables are not sufficient to explain *BF* allocation. Based on our mapping procedures discussed above, policy makers are able to identify these counties and assess those that are either characterized by high allocation and low need, or vice versa. This is our methodological contribution to the literature.

Nevertheless, we have some recommendations related to children's profile, county governance, and *Cadastro Único* design. Concerning the children's profile, as Barrientos and DeJong (2006) alert, it is important to ensure that social programs that target child poverty "reach the groups of children at greater risk, such as orphans, street children, and child-headed households, which are detached from adult-headed households" (550). The figure of the mother is an essential piece within *BF*, and addressing these issues may be another challenge for President Lula's second administration.

In this study we assume that the *BF* data used in the models reflect the real people in need located in each county. However, de Janvry et al. (2005) analyze a county survey conducted in 261 Brazilian counties from four northeastern states, focusing on decentralized implementation and governance of *Bolsa Escola*. They conclude that "there is considerable heterogeneity in implementation quality and strategies by county" and "contextual factors—including governance and politics—affect implementation" (6). They state that "there was considerable variation in the process used to register potential beneficiaries, both in terms of identifying who gets registered and with regards to process used for data collection" (6). This type of behavior alerts us to the fact that the outlier counties may be associated with decentralization and governance issues. Therefore we recommend that part of the scrutiny should focus on these issues.

When assessing *Cadastro Único*, Brière and Lindert (2005) propose the use of "a detailed and disaggregated poverty map to help target the program geographically" (17) to "help provide guidelines as to which areas should adopt which type of family registry process" (18).[9] Based on the spatial analysis presented in this study, we can conclude that despite the fact that the Ministry of Social Development and Fight against Hunger was not using poverty maps in 2006, it was doing a good job in the registry process, since in 2006 *BF* was targeting the counties with greater need. Clearly, however, the use of maps helps improve allocation and assessment of the program as whole, and should be incorporated by the ministry.

Finally, to advance the type of analysis presented in this chapter, it would be advisable to change the spatial unit of analysis, since intracounty variations may be masked when working at the county level (Haddad 2003). Unfortunately, spatial disaggregated data—below the county level—is very unlikely to be available in Brazil. The ability to map estimation results should be incorporated in other studies using the smallest spatial unit available. Once this mapping process is completed, policy makers should then examine whatever locations they find intriguing and relevant.

Notes

1. The term *município* in Brazil is closer to a U.S. county than to a municipality, and "county" is used throughout this paper.
2. The existing cash transfer programs were *Bolsa Escola*, *Bolsa Alimentação*, *Auxílio Alimentação*, and *Auxílio Gás*.
3. Besides being in the per capita range of R$120.00 or lower, families who benefit from the program need to have children from 0 to 15 years old, and/or pregnant women, and/or nursing mothers as members. For families considered in extreme poverty (up to R$60.00), one member receives R$76.00, two members receive R$94.00, and three or more members receive R$112.00. For this category, even if there are no eligible members, a family receives R$58.00. For families considered to be living in poverty (between R$60.01 and R$120.00), one member receives R$18.00, two members receive R$36.00, and three or more members receive R$54.00. As announced in September 2007, the targeted population for *Bolsa Família* will be expanded starting in 2008, when 16- and 17-year-olds will also be included.
4. *Pesquisa Nacional de Amostras de Domicílios.*
5. Because we are using some data from the 2000 IBGE Census, we use a sample size of 5,504 counties (excluding islands), instead of 5,564 (which is the current number of counties in Brazil).
6. The target population for *Bolsa Família* are families with income per capita of R$60.00 or lower (considered extremely poor, or indigent), and families with income per capita of R$60.01 to R$120.00 (considered poor), with children from 0 to 15 years, and pregnant women and nursing mothers.
7. Infant mortality is measured as the number of children (out of 1,000) who died at the age of five years or younger. We divided this variable by 1,000 to scale it to the dependent variable values. The illiteracy rate is measured as the percent of people who are 25-years old or older and are illiterate. We divided this variable by 100 to scale it to the dependent variable values.

8. One can observe that there a few maxima for the *Bolsa Família* ratio that are greater than 1.00. This can be explained by the fact that, in such counties, the proxy for the target population— which comes from the 2000 IBGE Census—was not updated.

9. La Brière and Lindert (2005) propose two types of registry processes: "on-demand application process as the principle" and "survey-outreach method in very poor areas" (18).

References

Anselin, L. 2001. "Spatial Econometrics." In Badi Baltagi, ed. *A Companion to Theoretical Econometrics*. Oxford: Basil Blackwell. pp. 310–330.

———. 2003. *GeoDa 0.9 User's Guide*. Urbana-Champaign, IL: Spatial Analysis Laboratory, University of Illinois.

Anselin, L., and S. Rey. 1991. "Properties of Tests for Spatial Dependence in Linear Regression Models." *Geographical Analysis* 23(2):112–131.

Arbache, J. 2006. "Has Macroeconomic Policy Been Pro-poor in Brazil?" In Giovanni Cornia, ed. *Pro-poor Macroeconomics: Potential and Limitations*. New York: Palgrave MacMillan. pp. 326–348.

Barth, J. 2006. "Public Policy Management Councils in Brazil: How Far Does Institutionalized Participation Reach?" *Public Administration and Development* 26:253–263.

Barrientos, A., and J. DeJong. 2004. *Childhood Poverty Research and Policy Centre Report No. 4: Child Poverty and Cash Transfer*. London: Save the Children.

———. 2006. "Reducing Child Poverty with Cash Transfer: A Sure Thing?" *Development Policy Review* 24(5):537–552.

Bourguignon, F., F.H.G. Ferreira, and P.G. Leite. 2003. "Conditional Cash Transfers, Schooling, and Child Labor: Micro-simulating Brazil's Bolsa Escola Program." *The World Bank Economic Review* 17(2):229–254.

Brière, B., and K. Lindert. 2005. Reforming Brazil's Cadastro Único to Improve the Targeting of Bolsa Família Program. Social Protection Discussion Paper Series. *The World Bank*.

Cardoso, E., A.P. Souza. 2004. "The Impact of Cash Transfer on Child Labor and School Attendance." Working Paper No. 04-W07. Nashville: Vanderbilt University.

Coady, D., M. Grosh, and J. Hoddinott. 2002. "Targeting Outcomes Redux." Food Consumption and Nutrition Division Discussion Paper No. 144. International Food Policy Research Institute.

———. 2004. *Targeting of Transfers in Developing Countries: Review of Lessons and Experiences*. Washington, DC: The World Bank.

de Janvry, A., F. Finan, E. Sadoulet, D. Nelson, K. Lindert, B. Brière, and P. Lanjouw. 2005. "Evaluating Brazil's Bolsa Escola Program: Governance and Decentralization Implementation." Unpublished Report. Washington, DC: The World Bank.

Florax, R., H. Folmer, and S. Rey. 2003. "Specification Searches in Spatial Econometrics: The Relevance of Hendry's Methodology." *Regional Science and Urban Economics* 33:557–579.

Ghai, D. 2000. "Social Development and Public Policy: Some Lessons from Successful Experiences." In Dharam Ghai, ed. *Social Development and Public Policy: A Study of Some Successful Experiences*. Chimppenham, UK: UNRID. pp. 1–45.

Haddad, M. 2003. "Human Development and Regional Inequalities: Spatial Analysis across Brazilian Counties." PhD Dissertation, Department of Urban and Regional Planning, University of Illinois at Urbana-Champaign.

———. 2007. "Examining the Spatial Distribution of Urban Indicators in São Paulo, Brazil: Do Spatial Effects Matter?" In M. Joseph Sirgy, Rhonda Phillips, Don R. Rahtz, eds. *Community Quality of Life Indicators*. Blacksburg, VA: International Society for Quality of Life Studies. pp. 102–124.

———. (2008). "Bolsa Família and the Needy: Is Allocation Contributing to Equity in Brazil?" *Journal of International Development* 20:654–669.

Haddad, M., and Z. Nedović-Budić. 2006. "Using Spatial Statistics to Analyze Intra-urban Inequalities and Public Intervention in São Paulo, Brazil." *Journal of Human Development* 7(1):85–109.

Haddad, L., H. Alderman, S. Appleton, L. Song, and Y. Yisehac. 2002. "Reducing Child Nutrition: How Far Does Income Growth Take Us?" Food Consumption and Nutrition Division Discussion Paper No. 137. International Food Policy Research Institute.

Hall, A. 2006. "From Fome Zero to Bolsa Família: Social Policies and Poverty Alleviation under Lula." *Journal of Latin American Studies* 38:689–709.

Hall, A., and J. Midgley. 2004. *Social Policy for Development*. London: Sage Publications.

Lavinas, L. 2006. "From Mean-test Schemes to Basic Income in Brazil: Exceptionality and Paradox." *International Social Science Review* 59(3):103–125.

Marques, R., A. Mendes, M. Leite, and A. Hutz. 2004. *A importância do Bolsa Família nos municípios Brasileiros*. Diretoria do Departamento de Avaliação e Monitoramento, Secretaria de Avaliação e Gestão da Informação, Ministério do Desenvolvimento Social e Combate à Fome.

Messner, S., and L. Anselin. 2004. "Spatial Analyses of Homicides with Areal Data." In Michael Goodchild and D. Janelle, eds. *Spatially Integrated Social Science*. Oxford: Oxford University Press. pp. 127–143.

Mkandawire, T. 2004. "Social Policy in a Development Context: Introduction." In Thandika Mkandawire, ed. *Social Policy in a Development Context*. New York: Palgrave MacMillan. pp. 1–33.

Morley, S., and D. Coady. 2003. *From Social Assistance to Social Development: Targeted Education Subsidies in Developing Countries*. Washington, DC: Center for Global Development.

Neri, M. 2005. "Miséria em queda: Mensuração, Monitoramento e Metas." *Revista. Conjuntura Econômica* 59(12):38–40.

Oliveira, A.M.H.C., M.V. Andrade, A.N.C. Resende, C.G. Rodrigues, L.R. Souza, and R.P. Ribas. 2007. "Primeiros resultados da análise da linha de base da pesquisa de avaliação de impacto do programa Bolsa Família," (ch.1). Report Prepared for the Ministry of Social Development and Fight against Hunger, Brasília.

Schwartzman, S. 2005. "Education-oriented Social Programs in Brazil: The Impact of Bolsa Escola." Paper Prepared for the Global Conference on Education Research in Developing Countries, Prague.

Soares, F., S. Soares, M. Medeiros, and R. Osorio. 2006. "Cash Transfer Programmes in Brazil: Impacts on Inequality and Poverty." Working Paper No. 21. New York: International Poverty Centre-UNDP.

Torres, H., and G.C. Oliveira. 2001. "Primary Education and Residential Segregation in the County of São Paulo: A Study Using Geographic Information Systems." Paper Prepared for Lincoln Institute Course International Seminar on Segregation in the City. Cambridge, MA: Lincoln Institute of Land Policy.

Werna, E. 2000. *Combating Urban Inequalities: Challenges for Managing Cities in the Developing World*. Cheltenham: Edward Elgar.

CHAPTER ELEVEN

A Report Card for Lula: Progress in Education

MARY ARENDS-KUENNING[*]

Introduction

When President Lula came into office in January 2003, he inherited a government that had made progress in confronting Brazil's social inequalities. During the 1990s, the Cardoso administration together with state and local governments, focused on improving Brazil's abysmal record in education. For example, in 1990, adults over age 15 had on average only 4 years of schooling (World Bank 2007). Under Cardoso, the federal government made sweeping changes in the public education system. At the same time, mayors and governors enacted innovative conditional cash transfer programs that paid poor children to attend school. These programs evolved into the federal *Bolsa Escola* program by 2001. During Cardoso's tenure, school attendance increased, grade repetition rates fell, and teacher quality was improved. By 2002, almost all Brazilian children aged 7 to 14 were attending school. But Lula faced a difficult challenge because the relatively easy task of increasing children's school attendance had been achieved. What remained were the more difficult tasks of increasing the years of schooling completed, and raising levels of student learning.

However, Lula did not seize the opportunities to build upon the recent gains in education. During his first administration, the Lula government did not prioritize education. *Bolsa Escola*, which had focused on increasing enrollment and school attendance of poor children, was converted to a comprehensive social welfare program, the *Bolsa Família*. Therefore, the policy emphasis of social welfare programs was shifted from improving human capital to providing income transfers. Little effort was expended to develop innovative programs to improve student learning. Spending levels on education remained below standards considered to provide adequate public education.

This chapter focuses on the performance of the educational sector in Brazil during Lula's first administration in the context of the accomplishments and shortcomings of the Cardoso administration. Under Lula, access to schooling continued to increase, as enrollment rates of children aged 7 to 14 reached almost 100 percent. The high repetition rates of students continued to decline. However, Brazilian students' performance on international achievement exams continued to stagnate, and Brazil remained ranked among the lowest performing countries in Europe, Asia, and Latin America. Improving this record is the most important challenge Lula faces in his second term.

Educational Policy in the 1990s

Under President Fernando Enrique Cardoso during the 1990s, many new federal educational policies were enacted to address the high degree of educational inequality across regions and across income levels. The 1988 Brazilian Constitution required state and county governments to spend 25 percent of their revenues on public education, and county governments were required to spend 15 percent of their revenues on public education at the primary level (De Mello and Hoppe 2005). These requirements left states and counties with latitude over how to allocate spending across pre-primary, primary, secondary, and university levels of schooling, and how to allocate spending across buildings, infrastructure, and teachers' pay (Mendes 2001). Great variation existed across states and counties in per capita school spending. The legislative changes made during the Cardoso administration increased federal regulation of public schooling and redistributed educational resources from rich areas to poor areas, while providing incentives that resulted in greater decentralization of school control from the state level to the county level.

New laws were enacted to address regional inequalities in school access and school quality. The legislation focused on grades 1 to 8, defined as fundamental education. A constitutional amendment passed in 1996 mandated that 60 percent of government educational spending be spent on fundamental education (Menezes-Filho and Pazello 2004). The *Lei de Diretrizes e Bases da Educação Nacional* (LDB) (*Lei* no. 9.394) was passed in 1996. The LDB set minimum federal standards for teacher education and training and also set minimum salaries for teachers. Teachers were required to have at least 300 hours of practice teaching. Starting in 2006, all teachers were required to have training at the university level or to have in-service training. The new law required periodic licensing of teachers and provided incentives for teachers to get more training. States and counties were required to have statutes and plans governing teachers. The plans had to include entrance into teaching based on public examination, salary floors, and promotion based on degrees or increased qualifications and on evaluation of job performance. The legislation set a minimum salary that was determined by the average cost per student per year, working 20 classroom hours and providing 5 hours of activities, with an average of 25 students per teacher (Caiafa Salgado 1999).

The federal government set minimum spending levels per student for schools. States that could not generate enough revenues to meet the minimum spending levels were eligible for supplemental federal funds. The *Fundo de Manutenção e Desenvolvimento do Ensino Fundamental (Fundef)* was established in 1996 to provide resources to education and to redistribute resources from poor areas to rich areas (IPEA 2007). Resources for *Fundef* came from mandated contributions of tax revenues from counties, states, and the federal government. *Fundef* redistributed educational funding within states based on enrollment. Therefore, mayors had incentive to enroll children in county systems, and enrollment in county systems increased relative to state systems and private schools (Melo 2007, De Mello and Hoppe 2005). The *Fundef* provided funding for school projects in the Northeast and helped to equalize spending across counties within states (Gordon and Vegas 2005). Resources were transferred to poor states from the federal government. *Fundef* was successful at increasing the resources available for basic education in the poor states of the North and Northeast (Gordon and Vegas 2005).

Fundef provided another lever by which the federal government could influence the provision of education by states and counties. According to federal law, 60 percent of *Fundef* funds had to be spent on teachers' wages (De Mello and Hoppe 2005). As a result, schools spent money to hire teachers and to increase teachers' wages (Melo 2007, Menezes-Filho and Pazello 2004). The number of teachers grew by 61 percent in the Northeast and 48 percent in the North, and as a result student-teacher ratios fell (Gordon and Vegas 2005). *Fundef* was successful at reducing regional inequalities in the length of the school day and schooling levels of teachers (Mendes 2001).

The Cardoso administration put programs in place to evaluate progress in the Brazilian schooling system in order to increase accountability. The LDB mandated the federal government to carry out an evaluation process. The *Sistema de Avaliação de Educação Básica* (System for Evaluating Basic Education—SAEB) started to administer national exams in 1990. Under the 1996 law, the importance of the national exams increased. The SAEB under the Ministry of Education carried out national exams in the fourth and eighth grades and in the third year of high school (IPEA 2007). These test score results were widely disseminated by the Brazilian media and provided a portrait of progress (or, in reality, lack of progress) in student learning.

In addition to the legislative and executive activity that was occurring in educational policy at the federal level, counties and states were enacting conditional cash transfer programs. These programs provided poor families with monthly cash payments in exchange for the requirement that all children in the family aged 7 to 14 attended school regularly. Politicians associated with the *Partido dos Trabalhadores* (PT) first enacted conditional cash transfer programs in Campinas in the state of São Paulo in 1994 and in Brasília in 1995 (Melo 2007). The idea of tying welfare payments to school attendance spread across Brazil, primarily under the leadership of mayors and governors who belonged to parties opposed to Cardoso's party, the *Partido da Social Democracia Brasileira* (PSDB) (Melo 2007). Cardoso adopted the idea from the mayors and governors and made it into a national program in 2001, the *Bolsa Escola* program. This program paid poor families R$15 per month for each child who attended school, up to total of R$45 for three children.

The Cardoso administration made significant progress in improving Brazil's educational outcomes. School attendance reached almost universal levels. Student enrollment in grades five to eight increased by 19 percent between 1997 and 2002, with enrollment growing by 61 percent in the Northeast and by 32 percent in the North; 15 percent of the increase in enrollment was attributed to spending from *Fundef* (Gordon and Vegas 2005).

School quality improved. Between 1992 and 2001, the number of teachers in fifth to eighth grade almost doubled in the Northeast, compared to an increase of 41 percent in the Southeast (Arends-Kuenning et al. 2005). Educational levels of teachers improved. In 1992 in the Northeast, an astonishing 20 percent of teachers of grades one to four had not completed primary education and 30 percent had not completed secondary education. By 2001, these proportions had fallen to less than 3 percent and to 10 percent, respectively (Arends-Kuenning et al. 2005). Teachers' wages increased dramatically (De Mello and Hoppe 2005, Menezes-Filho and Pazello 2004).

However, the evidence on how the increased spending affected student academic achievement is mixed. Repetition rates for grades five to eight fell from 0.24 to 0.12 (Arends-Kuenning et al. 2005). Grade distortion, which is a measure of the extent to which students are in lower grades than they would be if they progressed through the school system on schedule, decreased for grades 1 to 4 (Gordon and Vegas 2005). According to one study, the increased spending had a positive impact on student achievement, which operated primarily through increased teachers' wages and improved school characteristics (Menezes-Filho and Pazello 2004). Gordon and Vegas (2005) found that increasing teachers' credentials slightly lowered grade distortion in grades one to four, but not in grades five to eight.

Education as a National Priority?

When Lula took office, he inherited an educational system that was improving. The Cardoso administration prioritized education. The federal government had committed resources to improve schooling in poor regions, although minimum levels of spending per pupil had been set low and remained low. In his domestic agenda, Lula decided to focus on social programs in his first term. Therefore, an opportunity to expand upon the achievements of the Cardoso administration was lost.

In the first days of his administration, president Lula announced the *Fome Zero* program, which focused on providing food to poor households. These types of programs had been discredited in the past, because they involve high overhead costs and low levels of accountability. The *Fome Zero* program was designed to address a problem that had virtually ceased to be a problem. A study issued by the Brazilian Statistical Institute based on 2003 food expenditure data showed that obesity had become a much larger problem in Brazil than hunger, with the prevalence of obesity and overweight being higher among the poor than among the rich (IBGE 2004). Lula abandoned the idea of *Fome Zero* to focus on another comprehensive social program.

The *Bolsa Família* program extended the *Bolsa Escola* programs that had started in the mid-1990s at the county level. The *Bolsa Família* program combined four previous social programs, *Bolsa Escola*, *Bolsa Alimentação*, *Cartão Alimentação*, and *Auxílio-Gás*, into one program, retaining the previous conditions that households had to meet to receive transfers such as the school attendance requirements of the old *Bolsa Escola* programs. *Bolsa Família* increased the demand for education as it encouraged children to attend school. Children's performance in school probably continued to improve, to the extent that poor performance had previously been due to absenteeism, because students had to attend school 85 percent of the days that school was in session (Soares 2006). However, *Bolsa Família* did not include incentives for children to perform well in school or for parents to become involved in governing schools.

An early positive sign for education was Lula's choice of Cristovam Buarque as his Minister of Education. Buarque was governor of the Federal District in 1994 and was one of the original advocates of the *Bolsa Escola* idea. Since 1994, the idea had spread throughout the world, with conditional cash transfer programs implemented in Bangladesh, Mexico, and Nicaragua among other countries. Buarque was an international development policy celebrity.

However, Buarque quickly became frustrated with the Lula government's priorities. Lula retained the *Bolsa Escola* program, but blunted the emphasis on schooling by combining the program with other social programs into the comprehensive *Bolsa Família* program. Buarque left the administration in 2004 and became a vocal critic of Lula, running for president against him in 2006. During the 2006 campaign, Buarque noted that he had proposed an ambitious educational program, the National Fund for Basic Education (*Fundeb*), in 2003. Lula delayed in sending the proposal to Congress for two years, and the increased spending Lula asked for was only R$1.3 billion, compared to the R$4.3 billion Buarque had originally proposed (Buarque 2006). Buarque also criticized the lack of accountability of mayors and governors for improving their school systems.

Under Lula, the proportion of GDP spent on education fell from 4.7 percent in 2000 to 4.1 percent in 2002–2004 (UNDP 2007).

Initiatives such as *Fundef* were continued, but the minimum spending levels were not adjusted upward. Funding was insufficient to make progress in school achievement. A study by Robert Evan Verhine cited in Simonneti (2005) concluded that Brazil should spend R$2,000 per student per year on infrastructure, maintaining a favorable class size, and hiring qualified teachers to assure quality education. On average, Brazil spent R$1,000 per student per year. On the other hand, the number of teachers hired in grades one to eight did continue to increase steadily under Lula (Menezes-Filho 2007).

During the election year of 2006, Lula provided new initiatives in education. The *Fundef* program was renewed in 2006. A law passed in 2006 extended fundamental education to cover six-year-old children, bringing the age of entry into school in line with the norm of other Latin American countries (IPEA 2007). School districts were given five years to implement the new law. Early in Lula's second administration, renewed attention was given to education with the introduction of *Fundeb*, which extends federal funding for schools to the preschool and high school levels. These new initiatives will be discussed in the concluding section of this chapter.

In the following sections, I examine the trends in school outcomes such as enrollment and grade-age distortion that occurred during the Lula administration at the preschool, grade one to eight, and high school levels. I consider data from national achievement tests to discover whether Brazilian children are learning in the classroom.

Early Childhood Education

Recent social science research has pointed to the importance of early childhood education for children who are from socially disadvantaged groups (for example, see the 2007 World Bank *World Development Report*). Studies by the Nobel Prize-winning economist James Heckman and colleagues have shown that early childhood programs increase the noncognitive skills of children and result in higher wages in adulthood for participants (Heckman 2006). However, until the recent passage of the *Fundeb*, very little attention had been given to early childhood education in Brazil. The educational reforms of 1996 focused on basic education and not on preschool education. As a result, counties reallocated their funding from preschool education to primary education (Menezes-Filho and Pazello 2004). In 2005, only 13 percent of children aged zero to three were enrolled in formal child care programs. From 2001 to 2005, this attendance rate increased modestly by 2.7 percentage points. The National Education Plan set a goal of having 50 percent of children aged zero to three enrolled in early childhood education programs by 2011 (Barreto et al. 2006).

Enrollment rates for children aged four to six years increased from 65.6 percent in 2001 to 72.7 percent in 2005. However, children in households with per capita income up to half a minimum salary had participation rates of 65 percent, compared to 94 percent for households with a per capita household income of three minimum salaries or more (Barreto et al. 2006). A national goal is to have 80 percent of six-year-olds attending school by 2011 (Barreto et al. 2006).

The importance of quality in formal day-care and preschool programs cannot be overemphasized. Implicit in the goals to extend public schooling to children aged zero to six is the belief that these children are better off in formal care than in a family member's care. The Ministry of Education has created a program called *Proinfantil* to offer training for preschool teachers and day-care providers who do not have adequate training. In 2005, the ministry published guidelines for providers (IPEA 2007). The IPEA report notes that the main constraint to early childhood education has been the lack of resources for this area. Only 0.3 percent of the Ministry of Education's budget was dedicated to early childhood education (IPEA 2007). However, investments in health and cognitive development made when children are aged zero to six are much more cost effective than investments made at later ages (Heckman 2006). These investments provide a foundation for achievement in primary school.

Education in Grades One to Eight

Attendance Rates

School attendance rates for children aged 7 to 14 indicate that Brazil has reached the point of universal access to schooling. In the 2004 *Pesquisa Nacional por Amostra de Domicílios* (PNAD), 97.2 percent of children aged 7 to 14 were enrolled in school. This is great progress. Figure 11.1 represents the net school enrollment rates by age. The percentages refer to the proportion of children in the age group who are enrolled in the grade level that they should be, if they enter school at age seven and progress through school at the rate of a grade a year. In 1981, only 74 percent of children aged seven to ten were enrolled in school, a percentage that increased to 86 percent in 1990, and achieved 97 percent in 1999.

This increase in enrollment rates has virtually closed the gap between rich and poor. In 2005, 91.1 percent of the children aged 7 to 14 from the poorest 20 percent of households were attending school, compared to 95.8 percent of the richest 20 percent. Gains were impressive in the rural areas, where only 66.4 percent of children aged 7 to 14 attended schools in 1992, compared to 92 percent in 2005 (Barreto et al. 2006).

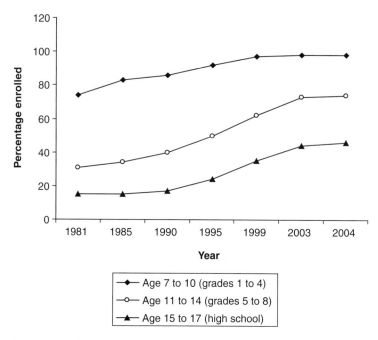

Figure 11.1   Net enrollment rates by age, Brazil 1981–2004
Source: Soares 2006

Trends in Repetition Rates and School Efficiency

Although school attendance is now universal, problems persist when examining repetition rates and the high percentage of children who are enrolled in grades that are lower than the appropriate grade for age. In 2004, for example, 29 percent of children aged 11 to 14 were enrolled in grades one to four, but according to the desired progression through the schooling system, these children should have been enrolled in grades five to eight (Soares 2006). However, the Lula administration has shown gains in these areas. By conditioning receipt of *Bolsa Família* payments on children attending schools 85 percent of the days when school is in session, the program discourages children from abandoning school in the middle of the school year or from having such low attendance that passing the grade is impossible.

Figure 11.2 shows that Brazil has made considerable progress in reducing the proportion of students enrolled in first to eighth grade who are older than the appropriate age for the grade. Students also showed progress in the 1990s, but progress is blunted by policies that encouraged social promotion. Students were advanced to the next grade regardless of their performance on exams. For example, Ferrão, Beltrão, and Santos (2002) reported that 36 percent of fourth-grade students in the state of Minas Gerais and 62 percent of the fourth-grade students in the state of São Paulo were attending schools with automatic promotion policies by 1999.

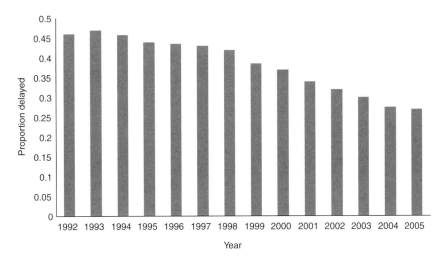

Figure 11.2   The proportion of first to eighth grade students delayed in school, 1992–2005
Source: Menezes-Filho (2007) from PNAD

Table 11.1   The proportion of children delayed in school, by grade level, 1992–2005

Grade	1st	2nd	3rd	4th	5th	6th	7th	8th
Age	up to 8	up to 9	up to 10	up to 11	up to 12	up to 13	up to 14	up to 15
1992	38.5	42.9	44.8	46.2	51.0	50.3	51.3	50.5
1993	37.7	45.0	46.4	48.5	52.3	49.0	48.2	50.3
1994	37.1	43.2	45.8	47.9	51.3	48.6	47.0	49.0
1995	36.5	41.6	45.1	47.2	50.4	48.3	46.0	47.9
1996	36.4	40.0	42.6	46.1	50.6	48.6	46.3	47.7
1997	36.1	39.4	41.6	45.1	49.6	48.0	48.0	48.0
1998	31.0	40.0	39.1	43.1	45.6	47.3	46.3	48.2
1999	26.3	34.5	39.0	40.4	45.6	43.7	43.5	47.0
2000	23.1	30.9	35.3	38.9	43.1	42.0	40.0	44.8
2001	20.9	28.3	32.8	38.3	41.4	40.7	37.8	43.3
2002	18.9	25.9	28.5	34.5	38.7	39.1	36.3	41.4
2003	17.6	22.4	27.1	31.4	36.4	36.5	35.0	39.6
2004	15.9	21.1	22.3	28.6	33.4	33.4	31.5	37.9
2005	15.5	19.9	23.4	28.0	32.7	32.5	30.6	36.1
Percentage change								
1992 to 2005	−59.7	−53.6	−47.8	−39.4	−35.9	−35.4	−40.4	−28.5

Source: Menezes-Filho (2007) from PNAD

Table 11.1 shows notable decreases in the proportion of children delayed in school for all grades. During Lula's first administration, the decreasing trend in repetition rates continued. However, note that the proportion of students who are older than the appropriate age for their grade remains high; 15.5 percent of children enrolled in first grade are older than 8, and 36.1 percent of children enrolled in eighth grade are older than 15.

High levels of repetition rates are associated with drop out as children become frustrated with the school system, give up, and drop out of school. School completion rates are still very low and vary by geographic area. For example in 2004, only 38.2 percent of children in the Northeast were expected to finish eighth grade, compared to 69.3 percent in the Southeast. Because of high repetition rates, an average Brazilian student takes 10 years of schooling to complete eighth grade (Barreto et al. 2006). This represents a great cost to the public education sector (the costs of achieving an eighth grade graduate are 25 percent greater on average than would be ideal) and to children's time.

High School Education

In 2004, 82.4 percent of adolescents aged 15 to 17 were enrolled in school. However, only 37.7 percent of the total in this age group were enrolled in high school. A high percentage (34.6 percent) was enrolled in grades five to eight, and 4.7 percent were enrolled in grades one to four (Soares 2006). Figure 11.1 shows that growth in high school attendance was concentrated in the 1990s and that since 2001, growth rates have slowed. In 2004, 46 percent of adolescents aged 15 to 17 who were enrolled in school were enrolled in secondary school.

Figure 11.3 shows that progress has been made since 2001 in lowering the proportion of high school students who are not enrolled in the appropriate grade for their age. This progress continued under Lula. All the same, Brazil has not made adequate progress in reducing the regional inequalities in high school enrollment. High school enrollment rates also vary greatly by household income, with the enrollment rates for the poorest 20 percent at 19 percent, compared to 74 percent for the richest 20 percent (Barreto et al. 2006).

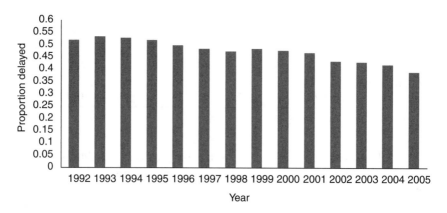

Figure 11.3 The proportion of high school students who are delayed in school
Source: Menezes-Filho (2007)

Trends in School Achievement Test Scores

Although students' progression through the educational system improved under Lula, it is not clear whether student learning is improving. Policies were enacted to support social promotion, so that the standards for passing a grade may have fallen. Achievement test scores allow for a comparison across time in student performance, and international standardized achievement tests allow for comparisons across countries.

The results of National Achievement tests show very low levels of achievement for Brazilian children. In 2003, the test results for Portuguese-language proficiency classified the performance of 60 percent of public school students in fourth grade as "critical" or "very critical." The achievement gap between students in private schools and in public schools also increased (Barreto et al. 2006).

Trends in the SAEB achievement test scores (figures 11.4 and 11.5) show a steady decline in test scores between 1995 and 2001. We would expect to see a decrease in test scores as the enrollment of students from poor backgrounds and with lower levels of preparation for school increase as a result of programs such as *Bolsa Escola*. However, we would hope to see signs of improvement over time as the students are absorbed into the schooling system and the Brazilian system changes from an emphasis on access to an emphasis on increasing school quality.

In 2003, the average achievement test score of eighth-grade Mathematics students was 248 points, considered the intermediate level according to the achievement scales devised by SAEB. By the third year of high school, the average student achievement test score of 279 points was considered to be at the critical level. From 2001 to 2005, achievement test scores continued to decline, except for fourth-grade achievement test scores in

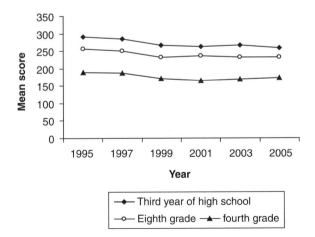

Figure 11.4   Mean Portuguese achievement test score, SAEB, 1995–2005

Source: Ministry of Education

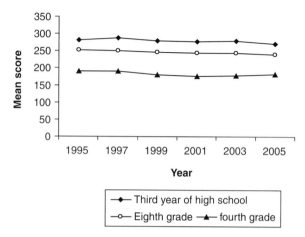

Figure 11.5 Mean mathematics achievement test scores, SAEB, 1995–2005

Source: Ministry of Education

both Portuguese and Mathematics. For high school students, the average Mathematics test score and the average Portuguese language test score decreased by about 2 percent between 2001 and 2005. For eighth-grade students, average Mathematics and Portuguese test scores declined by about 1.5 percent between 2001 and 2005. The results for the fourth grade present a glimmer of hope, because Portuguese test scores at that level improved by 4.4 percent and Mathematics test scores by 3.5 percent. These gains still place test scores for fourth graders below the test scores recorded in 1997.

How does Brazil compare internationally? Brazil participates in the OECD Programme for International Student Assessment (PISA). In the round of tests administered to 15-year-olds in 2003, Brazil ranked last out of 40 countries in Mathematics and 37th in language (ahead of Mexico, Indonesia, and Tunisia). One reason that Brazil does so poorly in this competition is high repetition rates. The test is based on students' ages and not on students' grade levels (Soares 2006).

Prospects for the Future

Early signs indicate that Lula will give more emphasis to the quality of education in his second term than he did in his first term. On April 10, 2007, the Chamber of Deputies passed the *Fundeb* legislation, which will distribute funding across preschools, grades one to eight, and high schools. The new investments would amount to R$2 billion in the first year and increase to R$4.5 billion in the third year (Folha Online 2007). Spending on the *Fundef* equaled R$450 million per year, so this represents a significant increase in spending. The government will set minimum levels of spending per student from preschool education to high school education (Folha Online 2007). In addition, the program would set a minimum salary for teachers and would provide incentives for the counties with the worst educational records to improve. However, Buarque (2007) argued that these reforms did not go far enough. He asserted that education should be a federal responsibility, with national standards for buildings, equipment, student achievement, and teacher preparation. He also called for a Law of Educational Goals, which would commit the federal government to achieving long-term aims, and a Law of Educational Responsibility that would hold politicians accountable for attaining these goals (Buarque 2007).

Increasing spending on education does not guarantee that school quality will be increased. We know much less about how to increase school quality than we know about how to increase school attendance (Arends-Kuenning, Ferro, and Levison 2006). For example, programs that provide funding for projects suggested by teachers show mixed results. Carnoy et al. (2004) did an evaluation of a program in Northeast and Central-West Brazil, the *Plano de Desenvolvimento da Escola* (PDE). This program provided funding for projects that were proposed by schools. By 2001, there were 5,600 schools participating, and the investments exceeded $1 million. Having a PDE program had no significant impact on student achievement in Math and Portuguese at the 4th, 5th or 6th grade level. However, conditional on having a program, each additional Real spent raised both Portuguese and Math scores. Spending on furniture had an especially large impact on Portuguese achievement test scores, suggesting that spending on furniture alleviates crowding problems, which benefits students. Students in PDE had higher grade passing rates and lower drop out rates than students in non–PDE schools, although the study could not determine whether teachers had lowered standards for annual advancement (Carnoy et al. 2006).

Research that examined the effects of school characteristics in Brazil on students' SAEB achievement test scores by Bezerra, Kassouf, and Arends-Kuenning (2007) found that having a computer in school was associated with higher achievement test scores for high school students. Having a television in the classroom was associated with lower school achievement test scores. The impact of the average level of teachers' schooling on children's achievement test scores was mixed, except for students in the third year of high school, whose test scores in Mathematics increased with the educational level of their teachers.

A problem with programs that rely on teachers' proposals for school spending is that the incentives faced by teachers might not match up well with the needs of students. For example, teachers might want to purchase television sets for their classrooms so that they can teach passively. A promising model is found in Mexico, where Gertler, Patrinos, and Rubio-Codina (2006) evaluated a program that provided government funding for school projects. The unique aspect of the Mexican program was that the proposals were developed by parents together with teachers. Parents were provided with training about how to manage school funds. The program had positive impacts on student learning, and the result was robust to controls for the decision to participate in such programs.

Brazil has a history of small-scale programs designed to help children who are behind the proper grade-for-age to catch up with their peers. One such program was the *Acelera Brasil* program, sponsored by the Ayrton Senna Foundation, which focused on youth who would have to repeat a grade and would be likely to drop out. Children were required to stay in school after regular classes were over, and special guidance was available for them (Arends-Kuenning, Ferro, and Levison 2006).

Currently, the *Bolsa Família* program does not condition payments on accomplishments in school. But in the future, the program could pay bonuses for grade completion. An intriguing idea is that the government might provide a substantial lump sum payment to all students who complete high school.

Achieving the goals of reducing inequality and poverty will depend in great measure on the quantity and the quality of schooling that is provided to Brazilian youth. During Lula's first administration, access to schooling continued to improve and repetition rates fell, both of which are noteworthy accomplishments. However, student achievement continued to stagnate and slight improvements in the performance of fourth graders were too modest to be acceptable. The tremendous challenge of increasing the educational attainment and cognitive skills of Brazilians remains unmet. Ultimately, the success of Lula's government in education will depend on the extent to which he can meet these challenges. Brazil is known for innovative social programs, and Lula could likewise foster innovative school programs to raise student learning. These programs should include careful evaluation, so that policy makers can learn which programs work, under what circumstances they work, and where and how they can be replicated.

Note

* The author would like to acknowledge the helpful comments of Marcia Azanha, Bruno Laranjeira, and the participants in the Lula workshop.

References

Arends-Kuenning, Mary, Andrea Ferro, and Deborah Levison. 2006. "Policy Note: Early School-leaving." Paper Prepared for the Youth at Risk in the Latin American and Caribbean Region Policy Toolkit Workshop, Washington, DC: World Bank.

Arends-Kuenning, Mary, Ana Kassouf, Ana Fava, and Alexandre de Almeida. 2005. "The Impact of School Quality and School Incentive Programs on Children's Schooling and Work in Brazil."

Paper presented at the American Agricultural Economics Association Annual Meetings, Providence, RI, July.

Barreto, Ângela, Jorge Abrahão de Castro, Martha Cassiolato, and Paulo Corbucci. 2006. "Subsídios para melhorar a educação no Brasil." In Anna Maria Peliano, ed. *Desafios e Perspectivas da Política Social*. Texto para Discussão No. 1248. Brasília, Brazil: Instituto de Pesquisa Econômica Aplicada. pp. 53–71.

Bezerra, Márcio, Ana Lúcia Kassouf, and Mary Arends-Kuenning. 2007. "The Impact of Child Labor and School Quality on Academic Achievement in Brazil." Paper Presented at the Seminar on the Quality of Education in Latin America, Universidad Iberoamericana, Mexico City, February.

Buarque, Cristovam. 2006. "Lula's Education Program for Brazil: A Grim Comedy of Errors." *Brazzil Magazine*, January30. Available at http://www.brazzil.com/articles/160-january-2006/9515.html accessed on September 2, 2008.

———. 2007. "Only a Revolution Will Take Brazil Out of the 19th Century." *Brazzil Magazine*, April 2. Available at http://www.brazzil.com/component/content/article/178-april-2007/9851. html accessed on September 2, 2008.

Caiafa Salgado, Maria Umbelina. 1999. "Training, Salaries, and Work Conditions of Teachers of the First Grades of Primary School." In Laura Randall and Joan B. Anderson, eds., *Schooling for Success: Preventing Repetition and Dropout in Latin American Primary Schools*. Armonk, NY: Columbia University Seminar Series and London: Sharpe. pp. 277–290.

Carnoy, Martin, Amber Gove, Susanna Loeb, Jeffery Marshall, and Miguel Socias. 2004. "How Schools and Students Respond to School Improvement Programs: The Case of Brazil's PDE." Forthcoming, *Economics of Education Review*.

De Mello, Luiz, and Mombert Hoppe. 2005. "Education Attainment in Brazil: The Experience of FUNDEF." OECD Economics Department Working Papers No. 424.

Ferrão, Maria Eugénia, Kaizô Iwakami Beltrão, and Denis Paulo dos Santos. 2002. "O impacto de políticas de não-repetência sobre o aprendizado dos alunos da 4ª série." *Pesquisa e Planejamento Econômico* 32(3):495–513.

Folha Online: *Folha de São Paulo*. "Câmara aprova texto base da MP que cria o Fundeb." October 4, 2007.

Gertler, Paul, Harry Patrinos, and Marta Rubio-Codina. 2006. "Empowering Parents to Improve Education: Evidence from Rural Mexico." World Bank Policy Research Working Paper No. 3935. Washington, DC: The World Bank.

Gordon, Nora, and Emiliana Vegas. 2005. "Educational Finance Equalization, Spending, Teacher Quality, and Student Outcomes." In Emiliana Vegas, ed. *Incentives to Improve Teaching: Lessons from Latin America*. Washington, DC: The World Bank. pp. 151–186.

Heckman, James. 2006. "Skill Formation and the Economics of Investing in Disadvantaged Children." *Science* 312:1900–1902.

Instituto Brasileiro de Geografia e Estatística (IBGE). 2004. "Pesquisa de orçamentos familiares— POF 2002–2003: Excesso de peso atinge 38,8 milhões de brasileiros adultos." *Comunicação Social*, December 16, 2004.

Instituto de Pesquisa Econômica Aplicada (IPEA). 2007. "Educação" Chapter in *Políticas Sociais— Acompanhamento e Análise* 13:155–192.

Melo, Marcus André. 2007. "The Politics of Service Delivery Reform: Improving Basic Education in Brazil." In Shanta Devarajan and Ingrid Widlund, eds. *The Politics of Service Delivery in Democracies: Better Access for the Poor*. Stockholm: EGDI, Ministry for Foreign Affairs. pp. 112–123.

Mendes, Marcos. 2001. "Descentralização do Ensino Fundamental: Avaliação de resultados do FUNDEF." *Planejamento e Políticas Públicas* 24:27–51.

Menezes-Filho, Naércio. 2007. "Os determinantes das matrículas no Ensino Fundamental e Médio." Presentation Prepared for the PNAD-CGEE Conference, March.

Menezes-Filho, Naércio, and Elaine Pazello. 2004. "Evaluating the Effects of FUNDEF on Wages and Test Scores in Brazil." Working Paper. University of São Paulo.

Ministério da Educação. 2007. *SAEB-2005 primeiros resultados: Médias de desempenho do SAEB 2005 em perspectiva comparada*. Brasília.

Simonneti, Eliana. 2005. "Por uma nova escola" *Desafios de Desenvolvimento* IPEA, PNUD (UNDP), 14th Ed. January.

Soares, Sergei. 2006. "Aprendizado e seleção: uma análise da evolução educacional brasileira de acordo com uma perspectiva de ciclo de vida." Texto para Discussão No. 1185. Brasília, Brazil: Instituto de Pesquisa Econômica Aplicada.

World Bank. 2007. Edstats. Available at http://devdata.worldbank.org/edstats/query/default.htm accessed on April 15, 2007.

CHAPTER TWELVE

Reforming Social Security under Lula: Continuities with Cardoso's Policies

MARIA ANTONIETA P. LEOPOLDI

During the 1990s Brazil witnessed an incremental process of mini-reforms in the social security system that, though important, cannot be considered a structural change from a public toward a private system. A sequence of changes in some procedures and rules amounts to a gradual reform within the current system, without major ruptures. These changes were inspired mostly by the government's goal of reducing the financial and actuarial disequilibria in the public pension sector. External influences also affected reforms in social pension systems. This was the case of the World Bank and the IMF recipes to privatize social security systems. Financial crises, especially during 1997–1999, made Brazil more vulnerable to the conditionalities of international agencies.

In this chapter we will discuss how these incremental changes in Brazilian social security system involved negotiations to overcome the resistance from "veto groups." The direction and the pace of the reforms depended on the government's ability to negotiate with organized groups and overcome their resistance. It also had to do with the organization of the social security institutions and their trajectories over time.

The Brazilian state had a monopoly over the pension system until the 1970s. In 1977 the military regime implemented a social security reform, creating a supplementary private pension system. Multinational and state enterprises could organize their own pension institutions for their workers and administrative personnel. Further reforms in the 1990s took the same path, enlarging the private pension system without diverging from the former model.

The Dual Face of the Social Security
System in Brazil

The present social security combines two systems with distinct purposes: the state social pension system, mandatory for all workers, and the private pension system, supplementary to the public system, for workers or other employees with high salaries. The latter system was split by the government in two categories: "open" private pension systems, operated by banks and insurers, and "closed" private pension systems, operated by pension funds, considered to be nonprofit foundations organized around the principle of solidarity instead of profit.

The 1988 Constitution initiated a debate on the reform of the Brazilian social security system. The defenders of the private system, inspired by the Chilean reform of 1979–1981, which transferred the pension system to the private sector, were linked to the financial sector (banks and insurance companies). Leftist parties, worker unions, and civil servant associations supported the public social security regime with universal coverage. During the debates at the Constitutional Assembly, pension funds, organized in the 1970s, lobbied congressmen to keep the dual pension system already in existence.

Eventually, despite all the alternatives considered by the constituents at that time, such as the private and the public-universal systems, the Constitution continued the hybrid format. Thus the pension system operating since the 1988 Constitution has two main pillars: one public and the other private.

The Public Pension Retirement System

The public pension retirement system has two branches formed by workers in the private sector and by public servants. The General Regime of Social Security (Regime Geral da Previdência Social— RGPS) has universal coverage and is mandatory for the whole labor force. It is based on a pay-as-you-go system.[1] It is operated by the National Institute of Social Security (Instituto Nacional de Seguro Social—INSS), which collects contributions and distributes benefits up to 10 minimum salaries. Urban workers and self-employed persons (*autônomos*) are the main groups under this regime. Contributions are jointly paid by employer and employee. INSS coverage presently approaches 30 million people, and its benefits correspond to nearly 8 percent of the GDP (R$165 billion or US$ 91 billion) (Giambiagi 2007: 27 and www.mpas. gov.br)

The Social Security System for Public Servants (Regime Próprio de Previdência dos Servidores Públicos—RPPS)[2] has a coverage of 4.8 million people. It works as a pay-as-you-go system but is now going through a transition to a capitalization model, which requires that all workers contribute to an individual account, regardless of whether they are employees or are self-employed.[3]

The rural social security system, created by the military regime in the 1970s, was retained in the 1988 Constitution. That document stated that rural workers have the right to a retirement benefit of one minimum salary from the age of 65, whether or not they have contributed to social security. Unlike the urban public pension system, which requires at least 15 years of contributions, the rural social security system currently transfers income to 7.7 million aged people living in rural areas. This program is not a social assistance policy, because it does not require proof of low income. The only requirement is age. The impact of this pension system on small villages in the countryside is significant, corresponding in many cases to resources greater than the budget of small counties.[4]

In 1988, disabled persons were also given the right to apply for benefits and pensions without having contributed to social security. This is a social policy aiming at transferring income—the so-called Benefícios de Prestação Continuada (Continual Benefits Installments).

Despite its objective of providing universal coverage, the current social security system does not provide coverage to all workers. As table 12.1 shows, some 52 percent of working people do not have any public or private pension. Millions of people work in the informal sector of economy and do not even have labor contracts, much less social security.

The Private Pension Complementary System

The other pillar of social security in Brazil is constituted by the private pension system. It has a supplementary character and focuses on persons earning more than 10 minimum salaries. It is based on a capitalization process through individual accounts. The prospect of accumulation for the future lies behind this system of private accounts. For a decade,

Table 12.1 Contributors to public and private pension systems: 2004 employed population

Contribution to	Number of people	Percent
Public system	37,682,382	44.5
Private complementary system	449,212	0.5
Both systems	1,972,898	2.3
Noncontributors	44,491,802	52.6
Total working population	84,596,294	100

Source: IBGE/PNAD 2004 according to IPEA, *Políticas Sociais. Acompanhamento e Analise* (12) (February 2006):40

the two systems of private pensions have coexisted: one is called the closed pension program (previdência complementar fechada) and was created in 1977. The other is the open pension program (previdência complementar aberta) formed at the time of the Real Plan (1994), which brought monetary stabilization and the possibility of private saving for the future.

Banks and insurance companies operate individual pension plans or group plans. In the individual plan only the saver contributes. It is not necessary to be a worker or a professional; access to these plans is open to all, including children. Those who opt for the individual plan enjoy income tax exemption. This program has benefited high-income recipients, who buy these plans as financial investments, diverting the program from its original purpose. Established in 1994, these open plans grew enormously after the end of inflation. Today open plans are the most profitable area in the banking and insurance sector. In 2006 there were 7.8 million individual plans and more than 100,000 group pension plans, having total assets of R$96.6 billion.[5] Forty-four companies operate in this area. Among them are three big financial groups that account for most of the operations in this sector (68 percent) as figure 12.1 illustrates:

The closed system of private pensions is formed by the pension funds and consists of contributions from employer and employee made to an individual account of the worker. As the public social security system

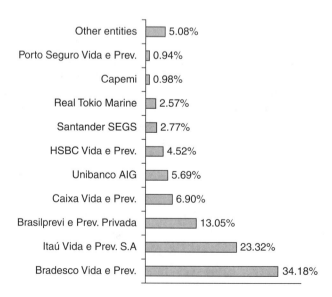

Figure 12.1 Open pension system—ranking of banks and insurers by revenue, 2006

Note: Total revenue 2006 R$22.9 billion

Source: Fenaprevi (www.fenaprevi.org.br) Dados Estatisticos December 2006

requires compulsory contributions of workers up to 10 minimum salaries, only those earning more than that amount can participate in the system. Those with such pension funds are employees of multinational firms and of large Brazilian corporations (public or private). Currently some 2,000 firms participate in the system. Such pension funds in January 2007 covered 6.3 million people. In the same year, 359 pension funds had accumulated assets equivalent to 18 percent of Brazil's GDP (R$353 billion, or US$196 billion; see table 12.2 below). Originally, pension funds operated exclusively for employees of private firms. A reform in the Social Security Law in 2001, however, extended the system to professionals and civil servants.

The Ministry of Social Security is charged with regulating the closed system pension funds. The large assets of the pension funds, especially of those of the state companies (such as Banco do Brasil/ Previ, Petrobras/ Petros) led the government to make risky investments or to invest in areas short of funds. This was the case of some privatization operations during Fernando Henrique Cardoso's administration, when pension funds were funneled into Embraer (aviation), Telemar (telecommunication) and the Companhia Siderurgica Nacional (steel). In 2005, faulty supervision by the Ministry of Social Security, along with sub rosa efforts by Lula's party, the Partido dos Trabalhadores, to win congressional support for certain bills, led opponents of the government to accuse managers of state pension funds of involvement in illegal operations such as bribing members of Congress. This resulted in the formation of two investigative committees of that body. Perhaps as a result, Lula has recently shown interest in using private pension savings to finance infrastructural projects such as roads, dams, and harbors.

Table 12.2   Assets of the 10 largest pension funds—January 2007

Pension fund	Assets (R$ billion)	Percentage on total assets of all pension funds
Previ	106.5	30
Petros	32.9	9
Funcef	23.3	7
Fundação Cesp	12.4	4
Sistel	8.8	3
Valia	8.4	2
Itaubanco	7.7	2
Banesprev	7.6	2
Centrus	7.6	2
Forluz	5.7	1
Total of ten	221.4	62
Total all pension funds	353.0	100

Source: Abrapp—Associação Brasileira de Entidades Fechadas de Previdência Complementar. Informe Estatístico January 2007

Following a period of very high inflation, the main purpose of social security reform has been to promote fiscal adjustment in the sector, reducing public expenditure on pensions, retirement plans, and other social benefits of the INSS (Instituto Nacional de Seguro Social). The Lula government has also attempted to cover wider sectors of the population, including part of the informal sector, through a new system of low dues introduced in 2007.

As far as the ratio of contributors to beneficiaries is concerned, the two systems (private and public social security) operate in very different circumstances. Currently, the contributions to the public social security nearly equal the benefits paid monthly, thus approaching the budget deficit limit. Other factors beyond the relationship contributor/ beneficiary bring actuarial disequilibrium to the public pension system: the defaulting on contributions by employers to the INSS (around R$108 billion), the lack of state contributions to the system, frauds in the system, and the aging of the national population. The government is also using social security taxes for other expenses. Therefore, there has been an increasing imbalance in public social security accounts during the last decade: the deficit of R$2.8 billion in 1997 (during Cardoso's government) rose to R$40 billion at the end of first Lula government in 2006.[6]

On the other hand, the private pension system for high-income participants has few payouts at present, because it is a relatively new system, and was able to accumulate the significant amount of R$450 billion (US$250 billion) in 2006. This sum consists of the assets of the open private system, operated by insurance companies and banks (R$96 billion or US$54 billion), and of the closed private system assets, formed by the pension funds (R$353 billion or US$196 billion). These resources of the private system are used in many areas of the Brazilian economy, such as capital markets, real estate, and industrial firms.

The regulation of the two sectors is divided between a division of the Ministry of Social Security (the Secretaria da Previdência Complementar— SPC), responsible for regulation of the closed complementary pension system, and an entity within the Ministry of Finance (the Superintendência de Seguros Privados—SUSEP), which is responsible for supervising the open pension system, formed by banks and insurers. All the attempts to concentrate this regulation into a centralized institution at the Ministry of Social Security have been frustrated.

Social Security Reform in the 1990s

The Constitution of 1988 linked the public pension system to the concept of social security. This new concept would integrate sectors until then fragmented: healthcare, pension system, and social assistance.

The health care system was established by the Constitution as a sector under state responsibility, operating through a public fund, the Universal Health Care Service (Serviço Universal de Saúde—SUS). The pension system is the second pillar of the social security system, including both public and private pension plans. Social Assistance benefits are regulated by the Social Assistance Act, and they include the compensatory benefits to poor families, disabled, and elderly people. Seen in a broad perspective, these three pillars of social welfare have yielded to a privatizing trend in the last few years. Private health care plans and private pension plans are nowadays important programs that cover millions of people. Banks as well as formal insurance companies operate in these areas.

The reform of the pension system in the 1990s followed an incrementalist trajectory. It was the first pension reform in Brazilian history that did not emerge from a decree-law issued by an authoritarian regime, as happened in the 1930s and 1960s.[7] Negotiations took place in Congress; between Congress and the presidency; and between Congress and vested interests during the period of incremental reform, spanning the years 1995–2003.

One may note several significant features of pension policies over time that may indicate path-dependence, as far as current reforms are concerned:

1. The strong presence of the state in the Brazilian pension system.
2. The fragmentation of the pension system by economic activity, separating employees in commerce, industry, banking, and railways from the 1930s to the 1960s. Today this fragmentation appears in the several pension systems of urban workers, the self-employed, rural workers, civil servants, military personnel, and complementary private pensioners.
3. The absence of a tradition of private pensions based on individual capitalization. This situation may have helped block the adoption of the Chilean privatization model in Brazil. The current Brazilian private pension system is voluntary and is complementary to the public system.
4. The political power of the civil servants in defining their pension programs. Their greatest success consists of pensions equal to full salary at the time of retirement. Bureaucrats' privileges declined, however, when Constitutional Amendment 41 of 2003 was adopted, as will be seen below.
5. The political power of urban workers' unions, defending their conquests such as the public pension system, the ceiling of 10 salaries linked to a mandatory contribution to INSS, and the linkage of benefits to the minimum salary, which is frequently raised in periods of inflation.

These characteristics explain the fact that the current pension reforms have more continuities than changes. Thus, although one can see an enlargement of the private pension system, this fact does not affect the public pension system, which is mandatory, and therefore is not losing space to the private system.

Recent changes in the pension system have affected broad sectors in Brazil. Among these groups were the unionized urban workers (Central Única dos Trabalhadores or CUT, Força Sindical[8]), bankers, insurers, industrialists, civil servants, and pension fund managers, among others. The ministers of Social Security and Finance and Presidents Cardoso and Lula set the agenda of the reform, forwarding their proposals to the Congress. In some logjams during the debates in Congress, the Federal Supreme Court (Supremo Tribunal Federal—STF) also had a voice in reform decisions by approving particular measures or declaring them invalid.

What were the main factors behind social pension reforms in the 1990s? The demographic question—the decline in the rate of population growth—posed the first problem for the system. Equally important, the population is living longer and the cost of retirement and other welfare benefits tend to increase. Such facts explain the pressure for changes in the age of retirement, in the number of years of required participation, and in the taxation of retirees. The deterioration of the number of contributors per pensioner; the default of employers in meeting their obligations to the INSS; fraud in the system; and rising costs of the administration of the complex system of more than 30 million people help explain the actuarial and financial imbalances in government accounts. A fiscal adjustment in the public social security account became necessary in the 1990s, and this crisis was the main impetus for the current reforms.

Foreign pressures also contributed to changes in the pension regime. There is a clear link between the international financial crises of 1997—1999, followed by the pressures from the IMF and the World Bank, and the first round of the reform. The Cardoso government achieved such changes in 1998, when Brazil faced financial turbulence and received an IMF loan of US$40 billion. The announcement of IMF support in September 1998, on the eve of the election that gave a second term to Fernando Henrique Cardoso, and the acceleration of the reform process in the legislature, led to the approval of the first set of reforms in December 1998 (Constitutional Amendment No. 20).

Other external pressures changing the pension system in the 1990s came from the wave of deregulation of the service sector (financial, insurance, health plans). In many countries, especially in the United States of the 1980s and 1990s, pension funds became institutional investors in the financial market. In Brazil, investments made by pension funds have focused mostly on government bonds. It is a common observation nowadays that if Brazilian pension fund managers suddenly withdraw their investments from the capital market, the São Paulo Stock Exchange (the Bolsa de Valores de São Paulo—BOVESPA), will go into default.

But the relatively minor withdrawal of the state from the retirement pension system does not mean that Brazil is going to adopt a private social security system. On the contrary, the current reform process points to a mixed model of social security that supposes these characteristics:

1. The existence of several public funds to subsidize pension and health care systems. This is the case of the INSS, RPSS (public servants fund), rural social security, and SUS (for healthcare provisions and expenses).
2. Closed complementary pension funds (fundos de pensão, previdência complementar fechada), operating through firms (Petrobras, Banco do Brasil, and others) and through occupational categories (pension funds of lawyers, teachers, civil servants—currently being organized).
3. Open complementary or voluntary private pension plans (previdência complementar aberta) operated by banks and insurers that may involve individual pension or corporate pension plans.

The Reform of Pension System of 1998: The Constitutional Amendment No. 20 of December 15, 1998—the First Round of a Gradual Reform

The pension reform of December 15, 1998 (Constitutional Amendment No. 20), clarified some points left open by the 1988 Constitution and formed a great divide in the history of social security in Brazil. The private complementary pension system now became part of the general pension system recognized in the Constitution, although its elements dated back to 1977 (the pension fund) and 1994 (the open pension plans). Therefore, Constitutional Amendment 20 ratified the hybrid system of pensions.

Changes and Continuities in the Public Social Security System

The public social security program of 1998 continues to be mandatory based on contributions and on a pay-as-you-go system. The small changes in the system aimed chiefly at achieving actuarial and financial equilibria. However, a philosophy of social protection was also present in the law, which required the social security system to provide protection for unemployment, maternity leave, illness, and disability.

The financing of public pensions henceforth was based on the following resources:

1. mandatory contributions to the INSS from workers earning up to 10 minimum salaries, plus contributions from their employers;
2. voluntary contributions of self-employed people in the INSS system;
3. taxes on the sale of rural products to finance rural workers pensions, for which no contributions were required.

For the workers linked to the INSS system, the minimum age of retirement remained the same: 60 years for men and 55 for women. As far as civil servants were concerned, the 1998 Constitutional Amendment kept several regimes in existence for government employees, despite the government effort to integrate all civil servants into a single system.

Compulsory retirement at the age of 70, voluntary retirement after 10 years of work, and "proportional" retirement, based on contributions below minimum levels, were carried over from the former pension system of civil servants. Pyramiding of two or more retirements by a single individual was prohibited, except for teachers and doctors. Workers on the verge of retirement when Amendment 20 was approved by Congress were able to follow the previous retirement regulations. Others entered a transitional regime, requiring an increase in working years prior to retirement.

Although the government intended to increase the length of career service for its employees and make pensioners pay taxes on their retirement benefits, the political power of civil servant associations prevented approval of these measures in Congress. The authors of Amendment 20 did not dare address the issue of taxing pensioners. The same "veto" worked as far as the amount of benefits by the civil servants in the RPPS pension regime. Government attempts to reduce the pensions of its retirees, establishing a difference in pay scales of working and retired people, were decisively rejected, and the salary benefits remained virtually unchanged. The parity system between working and retired officials was also extended to those in the judicial and the legislative pension systems.

The private pension system, complementary to the public system, was also affected by Constitutional Amendment 20, which determined that complementary laws would regulate issues such as the types of pension plans (plans with defined benefits or with defined contributions); mandatory and equal contributions by employer and employee in the closed system; and the portability of pension plans. The mini-reform of 2001 dealt with these issues.

The new legislation reinforced the role of regulatory agencies, responsible for the private complementary system—the SUSEP and the SPC, linked respectively to the Ministries of Finance and Social Security. Pension funds were submitted to an increased government scrutiny after 1999 because of Amendment 20. The latter mandated that by the year 2000, pension funds had to adjust to the rules of equal contributions by employee and employer; to attain actuarial equilibrium; and to implement the new age of retirement. Following this new regulation, many pension funds had to pay fines.

Pension funds had always been considered nonprofit organizations, unlike banks and insurers, and therefore were exempt from taxation. However, the government, anxious to extract revenues, reversed its position. During the Cardoso government, pension funds were required to pay taxes. When Lula was elected, however, government policies moved in another direction. Having the pension fund managers among his supporters in the 2002 elections, Lula exempted pension funds once again.

Another supervisory action from the government was focused on pension plans from the open private pension system operated by banks and insurers. Because the consumers of private open pension plans had a fiscal incentive through the exemption of pension contributions from the income tax, these plans of voluntary affiliation assumed the role of investment funds for short-term profits. Changes were made to give incentives only to plans operating over the long term, penalizing those who would make withdrawals in the short term.

The Second Round in the Reform of Social Security: Reforming the INSS and Introducing the Social Security Index (*Fator Previdenciário*)—1999

Several complementary laws emerged after the Constitutional Amendment No. 20 of 1998.[9] They gave a new configuration to the pension system of 1998. The most important measure was Law No. 9.876 of November 26, 1999, which affected the workers linked to the INSS.

Despite the veto of unions concerning the change of the age of retirement and their opposition to the extension of working time, the government created, according to this new law, an index for the actuarial reckoning of the amount of retirement benefit, combining in this index the time at work, the time of contribution to the INSS, and the age of the worker at the moment of retirement. With this measure there was more incentive to retire later, to contribute for more years, and to extend the number of years at work.

The *fator previdenciario* index was designed to keep workers actively employed longer, and this change would give them better salaries when retired. It tried to establish an equilibrium between the length of time of contribution and that of receiving the benefit, circumventing the problem of paying pensions for people living to a very old age.

Although received with suspicion by the politicians in Congress and by the worker's unions, the *fator previdenciário* put an end to the debate about the age for retirement and the time of contribution before retirement. Without the knowledge of Congress and the public at large, the executive, using the same law that created the *fator previdenciário* index (Law 9.876/1999), denied the power to set the age and conditions of retirement to the legislature, and transferred it to the Ministry of Social Security. Its officials were henceforth charged with calculating the index, tailoring it to each worker insured by the INSS.

The *fator previdenciario* index was expected to bring into balance the INSS accounts. It changed the current pay-as-you-go system for the INSS insured worker and established a new balance between the contribution and the benefit, allowing an increased control by the Social Security Ministry in the concession of benefits, now linked to life expectancy of population. Therefore, the *fator previdenciário* meant a new pact for retirement. It allows periodical changes in the limits of age for retirement without new legislation. From 1999 onward, each insured registrant at the INSS has his or her own history adjusted uniquely for the three variables: size of contribution, years at work, and age at retirement. One could say that the new index represents the end of the pay-as-you-go system for the INSS and the introduction of a capitalization calculus within the RGPS. The implementation of this index has been done gradually, within a transitional period of five years (2000–2005) and is applicable only to new pensioners.

The Third Round of Reform: 2001. Reforming the Complementary Private Pension System

The reform of the private pension system came with the Complementary Laws 108 and 109 of 2001, which made changes in Constitutional Amendment 20. Complementary Law No. 108 dealt with private pension plans, both open and closed. It extended pension funds to occupational categories and civil servants (federal level, state government level, and counties). It permitted pension funds and banks having open pension plans to operate simultaneously with many plans and enterprises (the *multipatrocinadoras*). The right of portability was enacted, giving the worker the possibility of transferring his contributions from one fund to another. Plans with final defined benefits were replaced by plans with the contribution defined, but the final benefits not defined. These measures, supported by the sponsoring enterprises of the pension funds (*patrocinadoras*), were not well received by plan subscribers, a situation creating a silent tension between the contributors to the pension fund and the *patrocinadora*.

Complementary Law No. 109 dealt exclusively with the closed pension funds of the state companies, the most important group in the ranking of the pension funds (Previ, Petros, Funcef, Valia, Centrus—in table 12.2). It established the compulsory parity of contribution, 50 percent from the insured and 50 percent from the sponsor enterprise (*patrocinadora*). It also restrained the government and state companies from replacing any losses in the pension fund finances. It furthermore spelled out criminal responsibility applicable to the fund managers, aiming at getting greater control over their actions. The main goal of this legislation was to increase regulation over the pension fund sector, and to provide more transparency for process in general.

Beginning in 2001, closed pension funds, which had previously dealt exclusively with pensions and other benefits of a single enterprise, could run the pension systems of several enterprises or professional associations. At the same time, open pension plans, tailored to individuals, began to operate with firms and professional associations. The possibility of open and closed plans operating as *fundos multipatrocinados* increased the competition among them.

The emergence of this new kind of multisponsored pension plan, in which one pension fund becomes the manager of many pension plans, was a revolution in the sector of the private pension system. From 2001 onward, instead of the growth in the number of pension fund organizations, there was growth in the number of sponsors of pension plans. The big pension funds such as Petros (originally the pension fund of Petrobrás exclusively) and Previ (Banco do Brasil) grew enormously becoming multisponsored pension funds, under the management of Previ or Petros.

The significant increase of the financial provisions[10] and the assets of the open and closed pension systems for the years 2002 and 2003, following these new rules, are shown in table 12.3. They provide evidence of the impact of the new rules on the market for pension plans.

Table 12.3 Private complementary pension plans (open and closed). Provision and assets 1994 to 2003 (thousand R$)

Year	Open private pension plan financial provisions	Pension funds (closed) assets	Assets of pension funds (closed) as % of GDP
1994	1.230	72.742	8.3
1995	1.937	74.815	8.2
1996	3.189	86.629	9.2
1997	4.616	101.033	10.3
1998	6.769	101.129	10.3
1999	9.917	125.995	12.5
2000	13.665	144.025	13.2
2001	20.782	171.152	14.4
2002	26.754	189.280	15.8
2003	34.675	240.139	18.2

Source: Fenaseg, www.fenaseg.org.br (2004) for open private pension plans; Abrapp, Consolidado Estatístico December 2003, for pension funds

In the open pension system, operated by banks and insurers, there was a great increase in individual pension plans, multisponsored pension plans (*planos multipatrocinados*), and pension plans for single companies only (*planos de patrocinadora*). In 2003 open pension plan companies had an expansion of 55 percent in the revenues coming from contributions (premiums) and an increase of 44 percent in the investment portfolio compared with the year before. This growth in one year (2002/2003) was greater than the growth of the whole period of 1977 to 1999!

Following the mini-reforms of 2001, the executive issued Provisional Measure 2222, establishing a new tax regime for the closed pension funds. In his search for more revenue, Fernando Henrique Cardoso created a new tax on pension funds, up to that point considered to be public utilities and therefore exempted from tax. There was a sound protest by the pension funds and by their sponsoring companies, especially through their association, the ABRAPP (Associação Brasileira de Empresas de Previdência Fechada). A period of tense relations now began between the pension funds and the branch of the Ministry of Social Security charged with regulating them. Eventually, pension funds had to pay taxes. At the same time that the Cardoso government forced pension funds to be more transparent in their accounts and to adopt corporate governance, the president made them pay heavy taxes for the first time in their existence. This move created sharp conflict between pension funds and the government, and the tension would last until the end of Cardoso's term in 2002.

Social Security during Lula's Government (2002–2006): The Fourth Round of Reform (2002–2006)

At the outset of his new administration, President Lula gave indications that he would continue the ongoing reform of the pension system. The complementary legislation regulating the public pension system (INSS) and the private pension plans (open and closed) had been accomplished by Fernando Henrique Cardoso's government. The missing part of the reform referred to the retirement and pension system of civil servants—the veto power that Cardoso's government had not been able to overcome. Lula made this reform his first item in the presidential agenda.

Civil servants and their associations (especially the CUT[11]) had been an important source of support of Lula in the 2002 election. But he jeopardized his backing from the CUT by forcing changes in the civil servants' pension system. His strategy however, was different from Cardoso's: At the outset of his term, in January 2003, Lula created the Council of Social and Economic Development, an organization representing various sectors of society, charged with making reform proposals.[12] Instead of forcing the Congressional agenda with Provisional Measures as Cardoso did, Lula decided to consult broader sectors of Brazilian society through its representatives in the Council. This was a significant change in the Brazilian tradition.

The Council sent to the administration a proposal to reform the civil service sector. Lula's government first discussed the project with state governors, and then forwarded it to Congress. The reform proposal arrived in Congress on April 30, 2003, as the Proposal for Constitutional amendment No. 40 (PEC 40). Congress approved it, and PEC 40 became Constitutional Amendment 41 of December 11, 2003. Consequently, despite protests from civil servants, Lula accomplished the final part of the reform of the social security system in the first year of his term.

Constitutional Amendment 41 (2003) and the Reform of the Pension System for Civil Servants

Constitutional Amendment 41 brought several changes to the federal civil servants' pension regime. It introduced a tax on retired bureaucrats, breaking a "sacred" rule by which retirees are never taxed. The parity of wages of active and retired government workers thus ended. A ceiling was also established for public servants' salaries. For the newcomers in government bureaucracy, the retirement pension now corresponds to an average of contributions paid over a certain period of time. The age of retirement remained the same: 60 years for men, and 55 for women. Financial incentives were given to officials who would stay in office beyond the retirement age. A new system of complementary pensions was created and is being implemented gradually for those who entered public service after 2003.

Although this amendment adversely affects the interests of civil servants, it did not spark broad protests, because it does not take effect immediately. Those who are near retirement will keep their former rights. Those in mid-career will have transitional rules. The amendment is only being fully enforced for the generation of civil servants entering the government after 2003.

Changes and Continuities of Lula's Reforms with Those of Cardoso

Lula followed the path of the reform established by Constitutional Amendment No. 20, 1998, which set the architecture of the new pension system. All the reforms concerning the INSS (Amendment 20 of 1998 and the *fator previdenciario* of 1999) were implemented by Lula's government. Fiscal measures designed during Cardoso's administration aiming at obtaining more resources for the social security system have been implemented during Lula's government. A rigid fiscal adjustment policy to the social security system is in process.

Beyond his commitment to Cardoso's reforms and to deepening the reform process by enacting Constitutional Amendment 41 for federal civil servant's pension plans, Lula has been trying to make his own mark on social security policy in other ways. Unions linked to the pension funds of state enterprises and managers of pension funds of big state companies connected to the Partido dos Trabalhadores made an alliance with Lula on the eve of the elections of 2002. As a result, government oversight of the pension funds continues, but less extensively than during Cardoso's government.[13]

Lula also made some concessions to workers' unions, his electoral and political base. He raised the minimum salary, and this change resulted in an increase of pensions of the INSS, which were linked to the minimum salary. The social security deficit increased, but Lula refused to consider these expenses as a mere deficit, alleging that they were social investment.

At the beginning of his second term, Lula envisaged more reforms in social security for new generations, stressing that such changes must emerge from a consensus among retirees, entrepreneurs, and current workers. To discuss the transition rules for the reforms in the public sector, Lula established the Social Security National Forum in 2007 with the charge of devising a sustainable social security system. This would include developing a program of social insurance for 28 million informal workers, and reducing inequality in the system by eliminating privileges such as highly differentiated pensions, "double-dipping" pensions, and so on. The forum has the responsibility of introducing transparency into government accounts, and addressing the issue of fiscal disequilibria. The strategy of creating consensus through new institutions within government differs from Cardoso's style of insulating reform proposals in technical groups designed to propose reforms without debate.

Immediately after his reelection, Lula declared that in his second term of office, development would have to be accompanied by income redistribution. This must be seen as a signal that although he was committed to completing reforms from the Cardoso era and overseeing monetary stability, Lula would make his mark by accelerating social inclusion. "I was reelected and I do not want to repeat what I accomplished in my first term. Now we have to innovate. And for God's sake, do not make the error of using the word development or economic growth without adding the phrase, 'redistribution of income.'"[14]

Notes

1. A pay-as-you-go system establishes that current pensions are paid out of revenues from current workers' social security contributions.
2. The armed forces have a separate pension system and are not included in the accounts of the Social Security Ministry.
3. Capitalization accounts may be linked to a bank or insurance company, or to a pension fund.

4. See Schwarzer (2000).
5. According to the Association of Open Pension Plans (ANAPP).
6. According to MB Associados Consultancy, published by *Valor*, December 7, 2006.
7. Earlier reforms during Getulio Vargas's long rule (1930–1945) were enacted by decree-law, and during the military dictatorship (1966–1977) the executive "proposed" laws that were rubber-stamped by a pliant Congress.
8. The Unified Workers' Center and Union Power.
9. The Constitution of 1998 left many questions to be regulated by complementary laws (*leis complementares*). Most reforms during the 1990's and later were made by means of this legislation, or by Constitutional Amendments.
10. Financial provisions, also known as "technical provisions," are funds determined by law and operated by insurance firms. These provisions are mandatory and act as guarantees of operations in the insurance market, as well of the pension plans. The technical provisions have to be revealed to the Ministry of Finance by the insurance companies. See www.fenaprevi.org.br
11. See above.
12. The Conselho de Desenvolvimento Econômico e Social was formed with 102 councilors: 12 from the government and 90 from different sectors of society (entrepreneurs, workers, scholars, notables, and representatives of social movements). It had the role of a consultative and advisory body. Cf. Tapia (2007).
13. Although the Secretaria de Previdência Complementar continues to seek actuarial equilibria for pension funds, in 2005 congressional investigative committees denounced the misuse of pension funds of state-owned companies. In particular, they charged that money laundering, bribery, and other forms of financial fraud had occurred.
14. *Valor*, December 7, 2006.

Bibliography

Constitutional Documents and other Official Publications

Constituição da República Federal do Brasil. 1988. Rio de Janeiro, Editora Saraiva, 11ª. Edição, 2000.

Constitutional Amendment No.20, December 15, 1998.

Constitutional Amendment No.41, December 11, 2003.

Law No. 6.435, July 15, 1977 (Complementary Social Security Law), followed by Decree No. 81.240, January 20, 1978.

Complementary Law No. 101, May 4, 2001 (Fiscal Responsibility Law. Established the General Regime of Social Security Fund, regulating article 250 of 1988 Constitution).

Complementary Law No.108, May 29, 2001.

Complementary Law No.109, May 29, 2001.

Law No.9.876, November, 26, 1999 (on the Social Security Index).

Ministério da Previdência e Assistência Social (MPAS), Secretaria da Previdência Complementar (SPC). Informações Básicas, 1998.

MPAS, Boletim Estatístico da Previdência Social. Vol 5 No. 8, agosto 2000, Brasilia, Dataprev, MPAS.

MPAS, Anuários Estatísticos (AEPS), 1995 a 1999, Brasília, Dataprev, MPAS.

MPAS, Secretaria de Previdência Social *Conjuntura Social*, Brasilia, outubro-dezembro 1994 Número Especial. Reforma da Previdência: a fase conclusiva.

IPEA, *Políticas Sociais*. Acompanhamento e Análise (12) fevereiro 2006.

Books and Articles

Abrapp (Associação Brasileira de Previdência Privada Fechada) Fundos de Pensão. Informações gerais in www.abrapp.org.br

Afonso, L.E., 1996. "Previdência Social e Fundos de Pensão." Cadernos de Seguro. Funenseg. 1(1) (July).

Barroso Leite, Celso, 1983. *Um século de previdência social.* Rio de Janeiro: Zahar.

Beltrão, K. et al. 1998. *Revolução na Previdência. Argentina, Chile, Peru, Brasil.* Rio de Janeiro: Geração Editorial.

Brant, R. 2001. "Reforma da Previdência em um ambiente democrático." MPAS, *Conjuntura Social* 12(2) (April–June):65–118 (Special Number) "A Previdência Social Reavaliada."

Chalita, Marcio, and Rui Pizarro. 2001. Interview with Solange Paiva Vieira, in *Conjuntura Econômica* FGV,RJ, 55(10) (October):56–50.

Coelho, Vera S. 1999. "A reforma da previdência e o jogo político no interior do Executivo." *Novos Estudos Cebrap* 55:121–142.

Cruz-Saco, M., and C. Mesa-Lago, Eds. 1999. *Do Options Exist? The Reform of Pension and Health Care Systems in Latin America.* Pittsburgh: Pittsburgh University Press.

Feldstein, Martin, Ed. 1998. *Privatizing Social Security,* Chicago: The University of Chicago Press.

Figueiredo, Argelina C., and Fernando Limongi. 1998. "Reforma da Previdência e Instituições Políticas." *Novos Estudos Cebrap* 51:63–90.

Giambiagi, F. 2007. *Reforma da Previdência. O Encontro Marcado.* Rio de Janeiro: Campus-Elsevier.

Giambiagi, F., and M. Moreira, Eds. 1999. *A economia brasileira nos anos 90,* Rio de Janeiro: BNDES.

Gomes, Angela C., Ed. 1992. *Trabalho e Previdência. Sessenta Anos em Debate.* Rio de Janeiro: FGV.

Leopoldi, M.A. 1999. "Democracia e Reformas Econômicas no Brasil: Desregulando o setor de seguros e previdência privada na Nova República (1985–1999)." In A. Kirshner and E. Gomes, eds. *Empresa, empresários e sociedade.* Rio de Janeiro: Sette Letras. pp. 238–256.

Malloy, James. 1986. *Política de Previdência Social no Brasil* Rio de Janeiro: Graal.

Marques, Rosa, M. Batich, and A. Mendes. 2003. "Previdência social Brasileira. Um balanço da Reforma." *São Paulo em Perspectiva* 17(1):111–121.

Melo, Marcus A. 1997. "As reformas constitucionais e a previdência social (1993–1996)." In E. Diniz and S. Azevedo, eds. *Reforma do Estado e Democracia no Brasil.* Brasilia: UnB-ENAP. pp. 295–348.

Oliveira, Francisco B. 1994. *Social Security Systems in Latin America,* Washington, DC: Inter-American Development Bank.

Oliveira, Francisco B., and K. Beltrão. 1997. *Reforma da Previdência.* Rio de Janeiro: IPEA. Texto para discussão no. 508.

Oliveira, Jaime, and Sonia F. Teixeira. 1986. *Imprevidência Social: 60 anos de História da Previdência no Brasil.* Petrópolis: Vozes.

Ornellas, Waldeck. 1999. "A Previdência Social em Fase de Transição." In João Paulo Reis Velloso, ed. *A Crise Mundial e a Nova Agenda de Crescimento.* Rio de Janeiro: José Olympio. pp. 423–453.

Pinheiro, Vinicios Carvalho, and Solange Paiva Vieira. 1999. "Reforma da Previdência no Brasil. A Nova Regra de Cálculo dos Benefícios." MPAS, Secretaria da Previdência Complementar. *Conjuntura Social* 10(4) (October–December):51–67.

Schwarzer, Helmut. 2000. *Paradigmas de Previdência Rural:um Panorama da experiência internacional.* Brasília: IPEA.

Tapia, J. 2007. "Conselho de Desenvolvimento Econômico e Social: os desafios da construção institucional." In Eli Diniz, ed. *Globalização, estado e desenvolvimento. Dilemas do Brasil no novo milênio.* Rio de Janeiro: Fundação Getulio Vargas.

Internet sites cited

www.abrapp.org.br ABRAPP Associação Brasileira de Entidades Fechadas de Previdência Complementar.

www.anapp.org.br ANAPP—Associação Nacional das Empresas de Previdência Privada Aberta.

www.dataprev.gov.br DATAPREV, MPAS.

www.fenaprevi.org.br Federação Nacional de Previdência Privada e Vida (antiga ANAPP).

www.fenaseg.org.br FENASEG Federação Nacional de Empresas de Seguro, Previdência Privada e Capitalização.

www.ipea.gov.br IPEA, Instituto de Pesquisas Econômicas Aplicadas, Ministério do Planejamento.

www.mpas.gov.br Ministério da Previdência e Assistência Social.

www.previdenciasocial.gov.br/pg_secundarias/previdencia_social_forum.asp Forum Nacional da Previdência Social.

www.spc.gov.br SPC—Secretaria de Previdência Complementar,Ministério da Previdência e Assistência Social.

www.susep.gov.br SUSEP Superintendência de Seguros Privados, Ministério da Fazenda.

PART FIVE

Regional Growth and Income Inequality

CHAPTER THIRTEEN

Social Policies, Personal and Regional Income Inequality in Brazil: An I-O Analysis

Carlos R. Azzoni, Joaquim J.M. Guilhoto,[*]
Eduardo A. Haddad, Geoffrey J.D. Hewings,
Marco Antônio Laes, and
Guilherme R.C. Moreira

Introduction

The aim of regional policy is the attainment of a more efficient and/or equitable interregional distribution of economic activity (Temple 1994). Haddad (1999) has demonstrated that in the last 20 years or so Brazil has undergone deep structural changes that have been responsible for the setback in the process of polarization reversal in the economy. After 1988, with the new constitution, the central government was hampered in advancing its regional policy agenda by a profound loss of revenues to the state and county governments. Nevertheless, the fiscal crisis reached all levels of government, decreasing their financial capability for carrying out new investment ventures. One of the major consequences has been the paucity of investment in economic infrastructure, especially transportation; this lack of investment has contributed to increasing the average cost of production. Therefore, producers' costs increased since they faced inefficient mechanisms for trade and transportation, many of which lagged technologically.

The regional deconcentration trend from the 1960s to the early 1980s was heavily influenced by active government intervention manifested in actions such as direct investments in regional development projects and tax incentives in the less developed regions of the country. However, with the fiscal crisis generalized to all levels of government, there were fewer options for new public ventures.

The agreed agenda for Brazil includes the competitive integration of the country in the global trade network, with additional domestic concerns focused on sustainable stabilization and social cohesion. This implies the attraction of foreign investments and a responsible (balanced) budget policy for all levels of government, reinforced by the promulgation of the *Lei de Responsabilidade Fiscal* (Law of Fiscal Responsibility) in 2000. The latter precludes regional policies that are based primarily on redistributional expenditures, as was the case in the 1970s. For foreign investors, the search is dominated by the search for maximum financial returns, with little concern for regional equity; location is defined on a purely economic basis.

The results presented in Haddad (1999) suggest that the interplay of market forces in the Brazilian economy favors the more developed region of the country. In other words, the trickling-down effects generated by market forces are still very unlikely to overtake the polarization effects from the Center-South. If regional equity is part of the country's development agenda, an active regional policy by the central government is still needed, in order to reduce regional economic disparities, and specifically to address the problems of the North and Northeast, traditionally backward areas reliant on low technology activities. The improvement of the economic infrastructure in those regions, as well as the establishment of enduring competitive advantages through a consistent human capital policy, are necessary to attenuate the adverse regional effects of the development strategy to be pursued by the public authorities.

Nowadays, the regional policy carried out by the central government consists of isolated subsidies and industrial incentives to growth centers, in addition to constitutional transfers to less developed regions and rural areas. In the context of the fiscal adjustment process of the 1990s, the role of the central government in stimulating directly productive activities, as well as enhancing the social overhead capital in the lagging regions, is being neglected. In the conception of the Real Plan, there was no explicit concern about the formulation of a regional development policy for the country. The Real Plan was conceived as a global stabilization plan that would include economic reforms (privatization, concessions, and deregulation) and institutional reforms (tax system, social security, and administration), without proposing any strategy for medium and long-run development. However, with the benefits from the stabilization and the reforms, a new cycle of private investments emerged. These investments tended to concentrate in the south and southeast regions, which provided a full range of nontraditional (e.g., technical skills and urban agglomeration) and traditional (e.g., friction of distance—Mercosul) locational factors to attract the incoming capital. The lack of investments by the central government, allied to the spurt in private investments, has led regional governments to engage in strong competition for private capital through fiscal mechanisms (see Baer and Hewings 2007).

Regarding the less developed regions of the North and Northeast, regional development necessarily demands direct government intervention. Their economic structure should evolve to higher levels of specialization in those activities in which the regions present dynamic competitive advantage in order to define their role in the process of interregional and international integration. In the Northeast, for instance, several studies have identified the regional competitive advantage in the productive transformation of the existing economic structure based on the restructuring and modernization of specialized industrial complexes (e.g., the petrochemical complex in Bahia, and the mining complex in Maranhão); the modernization of the agricultural sector and the agriculture-based industries; and the expansion of tourism and related activities. This strategy requires the active participation of public authorities through the adoption of regionally differentiated fiscal incentives when necessary, and more importantly, through the provision of modern economic infrastructure and the formation and development of human resources in the region, emphasizing poverty alleviation and universal primary and secondary education (see Araújo 1995, and Albuquerque and Gomes 1996). An increasing emphasis on "economic" rather than "financial" incentives throughout Brazil should give rise to a new form of regional incentive based explicitly on building up dynamic comparative advantages rather than granting fiscal handouts.[1]

Finally, the government has to identify priorities for investments in infrastructure. In this case, the government will face conflicting choices in the allocation of the scarce resources. On the one hand, it is important to create and modernize the existing economic infrastructure in the lagging regions to facilitate the operation of the forces for the centrifugal spread of economic expansion in the more developed regions, and also to consolidate their regional competitiveness through the establishment of an effective stock of social overhead capital. On the other hand, demands for economic infrastructure are also compelling in the southern part of the country, in the context of the increasing exposure to international markets. Increased trade involving the more complex economic spaces in the Center-South and foreign partners will face significant transportation costs, and unless the transportation sector can be made more efficient, Brazil will not be able to reap the full benefits of participation in a more competitive global market. In this regard, attempts to deepen the regional roots of inward productive investments should focus on the building-up of the quality of the infrastructure and the facilitation of enhanced integration with regional, extraregional, and international markets.

In this context, we can argue that nothing much has been done in the first four years of Lula's administration. In terms of what might be termed a "clearly defined" regional policy, the central government has relied only on constitutional intergovernmental transfers through regional funds[2]—FNE (Fundo Constitucional de Financiamento do Nordeste), FNO (Fundo Constitucional de Financiamento do Norte), FCO (Fundo Constitucional de Financiamento do Centro-Oeste)—and rural pensions. However, the central government has been engaged in an effort to design and implement social compensatory policies with a strong spatial

Table 13.1   Households eligible for benefits from *Bolsa Família*, 2000

Region	Number of poor households	%
North	1,574,094	0.0917
Northeast	7,140,519	0.4158
South	2,006,596	0.1169
Southeast	5,342,975	0.3111
Mid-West	1,107,909	0.0645
Total	**17,172,093**	**1.0000**

Source: Demographic Census, 2000

dimension. The pro-poor *Bolsa Família* program is one such program providing direct income transfers to the poor (with per capita income between R$60.01 and R$120), and extremely poor households (with per capita income below R$60). Given the geographical distribution of poor households in the country (see table 13.1), targeting benefits to the poor reflects an implicit concern with regional disparities in the country. Even though it cannot be considered an explicit strategy of geographic targeting to reduce poverty, it may achieve the goal of classical regional policies—namely, the reduction of regional disparities—through direct income transfers to poor households, which also happen to be concentrated in poorer regions. However, this remains to be tested.

Thus, the goal of this chapter is to assess the regional impacts of the *Bolsa Família* program from the perspective of a socially targeted regional policy. After this brief introduction, we proceed, in the next section, with an analysis of the outcomes of the 2006 presidential elections, looking at Lula's performance in the first round, by county. We estimate different models to check which economic variables were important in contributing to his victory over the other candidates. Direct income transfers through the *Bolsa Família* program can be considered one of the most robust explanatory variables for determining the better electoral performance of the Partido dos Trabalhadores (Workers' Party—PT) candidate. With this result in mind, the *Bolsa Família* program is evaluated from a regional policy perspective. The section, Economic Impacts, describes the methodology to be used in the following section, Simulation Results, where the results are presented and discussed. Final remarks follow in the concluding section, putting the results into a broader perspective of the policy initiatives to be considered in Lula's second mandate.

Voters' Evaluation: What Do the Ballots Tell Us?

In this section we evaluate the main economic determinants of votes for Lula in the first round of the 2006 presidential elections. We begin the analysis with the choropleth map of the election data. Figure 13.1 shows the data for the percentage of those voting for Lula in the first round of

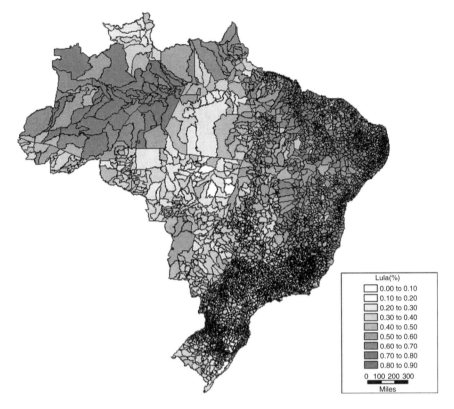

Figure 13.1 Percent of Lula votes in relation to total votes

Source: Brasil, Tribunal Superior Eleitoral (http://www.tse.gov.br/internet/eleicoes/eleicoes_2006.htm)

the presidential elections in 2006, by county. The spatial pattern of the votes is illustrated in this map; the darker the shading, the higher the proportion or votes for Lula. The suggestion of spatial clustering of similar values that follows from the visual inspection of this map needs to be confirmed by formal tests.

An exploratory spatial data analysis (ESDA) is conducted to test whether the spatial data is randomly distributed. This is accomplished using one of several global autocorrelation statistics; in this case, Moran's I was used. The underlying hypothesis is spatial randomness, that is, there is the absence of spatial dependence in the data. Intuitively, spatial randomness can be expressed as follows: values of an attribute at a location do not depend on values of an attribute at neighboring locations.

Figure 13.2 reports the global Moran's I statistics for all counties in Brazil in 2006. The statistical evidence casts doubt on the assumption of spatial randomness of the Lula performance in the elections. In fact, since the computed value of I (0.7973) exceeds its theoretical value (zero), we can reject the hypothesis of no spatial autocorrelation at the

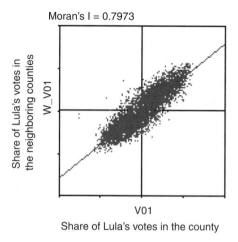

Figure 13.2 Moran scatterplot and global Moran's *I* statistic for Lula's performance in the first round of the 2006 presidential elections

Source: Authors' calculation

0.1 percent significance level.[3] These results are invariant with regards to the convention of adopting a binary neighborhood in the construction of the spatial weights (queen or rook). In addition, Moran's *I* provides clear indication that the spatial autocorrelation for Lula's performance is positive. That is, counties with a high proportion of votes for the PT candidate are also adjacent to counties with a high proportion of Lula's voters. In an analogous manner, counties with a relative low preference for Lula are adjacent to counties with a low preference as well. That is the intuitive meaning of positive spatial autocorrelation. An alternative approach to visualize spatial association is based on the concept of a Moran scatterplot, which shows the spatial lag (i.e., the average of the attribute for the neighbors) on the vertical axis and the value at each location on the horizontal axis (see figure 13.2). Note that the variables are expressed in standardized form with mean zero and standard deviation equal to one (Anselin 1999: 261).

The global indicators of spatial association are not capable of identifying local patterns of spatial association, such as clusters or spatial outliers in the data that are statistically significant. To overcome this obstacle, it is necessary to implement a spatial clustering analysis. We used the local version of Moran's *I* (LISA statistics) as the basis for testing the null hypothesis of local randomness, that is, no local spatial association. Figure 13.3 combines the information of the Moran scatterplot and the LISA statistics. It illustrates the classification into four categories of spatial association that are statistically significant in terms of the LISA concept. We find evidence of spatial grouping; overall, there are some clusters of counties where Lula obtained a better performance located in the less developed regions of the North and Northeast, as well as neighbors with high percentage of votes for Lula.

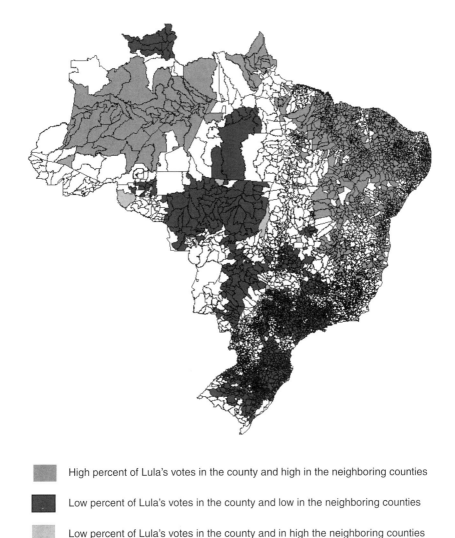

High percent of Lula's votes in the county and high in the neighboring counties

Low percent of Lula's votes in the county and low in the neighboring counties

Low percent of Lula's votes in the county and in high the neighboring counties

High percent of Lula's votes in the county and low in the neighboring counties

Figure 13.3 Moran significance map for Lula voting

Source: Authors' calculation

Likewise, there are clusters of low performance located in the center-south of the country. The question is: does Lula's performance reflect his efforts in the first mandate to fight regional inequality, or is there something else behind this seemingly paradoxical result, which shows that a government without any formal regional policy action achieved its best evaluation in the regions that were left behind?

To tackle this issue, we estimated spatial econometric models to identify the main determinants of Lula's performance in the 2006 elections. The dependent variable is the percentage of Lula's voting in the first round of the presidential elections. We considered four groups of covariates in our models: 1) Spatial structure variables—the human development index, Gini coefficient, and per capita GDP, all for year 2000; 2) Structural regional policy variables—per capita constitutional transfers and per capita rural pension payments, both in 2006; 3) Social policy variables—per capita income from *Bolsa Família*, 2006; number of households with per capita income below R$120 in 2000; 4) Economic and political variables—dummy for Mayor affiliated to PSDB, the main opposition party; share of agriculture in GDP, in 2002.

The spatial structure variables attempt to capture the spatial distribution of economic development in the country, reflecting a long-standing situation of regional dualism, and reflecting voters' perception according to different local socioeconomic profiles. The structural regional policy variables attempt to capture established regional policy, and therefore, a proper evaluation of the *extra efforts* by the central government. The set of social policy variables tries to capture not only an evaluation of the income transfer program, but also the expectation of its reinforcement in Lula's second term. Finally, the economic and policy variables reflect the economic cycle and the local political scene affecting the evaluation of the current president.

Three models were estimated. The first model was estimated using ordinary least squares (OLS) procedure. The two other models introduced space in a formal way, as suggested by the diagnostics tests. We considered 1) the estimation by means of a maximum likelihood spatial regression model that includes a spatially lagged dependent variable,[4] and 2) the estimation by means of maximum likelihood of a spatial regression model that includes a spatial autoregressive error term.[5] Results are presented in tables 13.2 and 13.3. Bold figures are statistically significant at the 1 percent level.

In terms of the spatial structural variables, HDI and per capita GDP are negatively correlated with Lula's performance in the elections, while the Gini coefficient is positively correlated. In other words, the more developed, the richer and the less unequal the county, the lower the percentage voting in Lula at that locality. Moreover, in counties that benefited from structural regional policies, Lula presented a weaker performance in the first round of the elections. In our view, this reflects the neglecting of regional policy by the current government, as these regions, traditionally reliant on government compensatory regional policies, had their expectation frustrated by the minimal efforts set in this direction.

Noteworthy is the robustness of the social policy variables. Counties with higher per capita transfers through the *Bolsa Família* program and with the potential for its consolidation in the future presented a positive evaluation of Lula's first mandate translated into greater proportion of votes. Regarding economic and political variables, the current economic situation prior to the elections, which hampered the agricultural sector (e.g., appreciation of the Real, droughts, collapse of agricultural

Table 13.2   Quantitative estimation results (dependent variable: Lula's vote as share of total)

| | Model | | |
Coefficients	OLS	Spatial lag	Spatial error
Percentage of Lula's votes in neighboring counties	–	0.74220660	–
Constant	**0.73349120**	**0.16547210**	**0.57543630**
HDI	**−0.43100760**	−0.00628164	**−0.15181800**
Gini	**0.18567520**	−0.00186970	**0.07700873**
GDP (per capita)	**−0.00051066**	**−0.00025755**	**−0.00030405**
Constitutional transfers (per capita)	**−0.00020904**	**−0.00006988**	**−0.00007210**
Bolsa Família income (per capita)	**0.00067053**	**0.00022451**	**0.00022893**
Rural pensions (per capita)	**−0.00000671**	**−0.00000540**	**−0.00000423**
Number of poor households	**0.00000153**	**0.00000027**	**0.00000001**
Mayor belongs to the party of the competitor candidate	**−0.01434254**	**−0.00659800**	−0.00399306
Share of agriculture in the economy of the county	**−0.05965714**	**−0.01389732**	−0.00703614
Lambda	–	–	0.83955020
R2	**0.5541**	**0.7870**	**0.7918**

Source: Authors' calculation

Table 13.3   Qualitative estimation results (dependent variable: Lula's vote as share of total)

| | Model | | |
Coefficients	OLS	Spatial lag	Spatial error
Percentage of Lula's votes in neighboring counties	–	(+)	–
Constant	(+)	(+)	(+)
HDI	(−)	n.s	(−)
Gini	(+)	n.s	(+)
GDP (per capita)	(−)	(−)	(−)
Constitutional transfers (per capita)	(−)	(−)	(−)
Bolsa Família income (per capita)	**(+)**	**(+)**	**(+)**
Rural pensions (per capita)	(−)	(−)	(−)
Number of poor households	(+)	(+)	(+)
Mayor belongs to the party of the competitor candidate	(−)	(−)	n.s
Share of agriculture in the economy of the county	(−)	(−)	n.s
Lambda	–	–	(+)

Note: n.s is nonsignificant; + is positive and significant; − is negative and significant
Source: Authors' calculation

insurance funds), seems to have negatively affected Lula's performance in the rural areas. Finally, from a political perspective, the role played by mayors belonging to the main opposition party, the PSDB, also negatively influenced Lula's voting in those counties.

In this context, in the next sections we take a closer look at the *Bolsa Família* program from a regional perspective. We start by describing the

Miyazawa framework, which will be used as the analytical tool for the evaluation of the program.

Economic Impacts: The Miyazawa Framework[6]

In this chapter we use a Leontief-Miyazawa model, in which the intersectoral flows in the economy can be represented by a system of simultaneous equations such as $X = AX + Y$, in which X is a $(nx1)$ vector of sectoral production values, Y is a $(nx1)$ vector of sectoral final demands, and A is a (nxn) matrix of technical production coefficients. If final demand is treated as exogenous to the system, we have $X = BY$ and $B = (1 - A)^{-1}$, with B being the (nxn) Leontief inverse matrix. If the internal consumption demand is detached from the final demand vector, the model becomes $Y = Y^r + Y^e$, in which Y^r is a $(nx1)$ vector of income related consumption demand and Y^e is the $(nx1)$ vector of exogenous demand (government expenditure, investment, exports).

The multisectoral consumption function is $Y^r = C.Q$, in which C is a (nxr) matrix of consumption coefficients, and Q is a $(rx1)$ vector of total income for each income group. The elements of matrix C are the quantity of product i consumed by the kth income group. Income distribution is introduced by $Q = V.X$, in which V is the (rnx) matrix of shares of family's income on total production, by sector and income class. This last equation connects the productive structure to income distribution.

By manipulating the above expressions, one gets $X = (1 - A - C.V)^{-1}.Y_e$. Considering that $B = (1 - A)^{-1}$, one can write $X = B(1 - CVB)^{-1}.Y_e$. The extension of the model to a multiregional setting demands the consideration of interregional flows of inputs and outputs. Let $Z_{i,j}^{Rm,Rn}$ be the monetary flow from sector i in region R_m to sector j in region R_n. Chart 13.1 presents the interregional flows.

Five macro regions of Brazil were considered, and their economic structures were split into 21 sectors. Therefore, the model uses five 21 x 21

		Sectors and regions				
		North (i ... j)	Northeast (i ... j)	Center-West (i ... j)	Southeast (i ... j)	South (i ... j)
Sectors and regions	North (i .. j)	Z_{ij} (N × N)	Z_{ij} (N × NE)	Z_{ij} (N × CO)	Z_{ij} (N × SE)	Z_{ij} (N × S)
	Northeast (i..j)	Z_{ij} (NE × N)	Z_{ij} (NE × NE)	Z_{ij} (NE × CO)	Z_{ij} (NE × SE)	Z_{ij} (NE × S)
	Center-West (i..j)	Z_{ij} (CO × N)	Z_{ij} (CO × NE)	Z_{ij} (CO × CO)	Z_{ij} (CO × SE)	Z_{ij} (CO × S)
	Southeast (i .. j)	Z_{ij} (SE × N)	Z_{ij} (SE × NE)	Z_{ij} (SE × CO)	Z_{ij} (SE × SE)	Z_{ij} (SE × S)
	South (i .. j)	Z_{ij} (S × N)	Z_{ij} (S × NE)	Z_{ij} (S × CO)	Z_{ij} (S × SE)	Z_{ij} (S × S)

Chart 13.1   Interregional flows considered in the model

Source: Authors' illustration

input-output tables, including interregional trade flows. Data referring to income distribution by sector and region comes from the 2002 National Household Survey (Pesquisa Nacional Por Amostra de Domicílios—PNAD), also produced by IBGE. Ten income brackets were considered (R$/month): from zero income to 400 (5.3 percent of total national household income); 400–600 (5.4 percent); 600–1,000 (11.5 percent); 1,000–1,200 (5.3 percent); 1,200–1,600 (8.9 percent); 1,600–2,000 (8.3 percent); 2,000–3,000 (13.7 percent); 3,000–4,000 (9.7 percent); 4,000–6,000 (11.9 percent); and 6,000 and over (19.8 percent). The household expenditure patterns for each income bracket in each region are taken into account. Consumption data comes from the 2002–2003 POF—Pesquisa de Orçamentos Familiares, implemented by IBGE.

Simulation Results

The interregional Leontief-Miyazawa model briefly described in the previous section was estimated for 2002, the last year before President Lula's first administration. The simulation strategy is to introduce a shock to that productive and distributional situation and to evaluate its impacts. The 2002 base case situation already included some influence of social programs, for they started during the previous administration. Therefore, the first step was to determine what were the amounts involved in each region. Table 13.4 presents the basic data; the columns referring to 2004, 2005, and 2006 present the effective amounts distributed by *Bolsa Família*. For 2002 and 2003, the data were not disaggregated spatially, so that some estimates had to be made. The 2003 PNAD presents a special segment on social programs, and these data could be used to make the allocation across regions. A comparison of income received by low income persons in 2005 PNAD was made with the official *Bolsa Família* data and the approximation was reasonably good. Therefore, regional shares of the 2002 PNAD data on the distribution of "interests, profits, dividends and others" to very low-income persons were considered to be the benchmark for the simulations.

As table 13.4 indicates, the average annual expenditure on the program more than doubled during the Lula administration. For the country as a whole, there was a 151 percent increase, but for the poorer northeast region, the increase was of 351 percent. For the richer southeast region, the increase was of only 92 percent. This provides an initial overview of the regional impacts of such programs. However, in order to assess their final impact, these changes in expenditure have to be introduced in the model presented in the previous section. We have shocked the earnings of the poorest income bracket in each region by the increase in government transfers to that region. We did this in two steps: initially, this extra money was introduced in the region as an absolute increase in government

Table 13.4   Government transfers to families by region—*Bolsa Família* (*)

	2002 (1)	2003 (2)	2004	2005	2006	Lula's administration
			R$1,000 of 2002			
Mid-West	130,797	219,383	226,801	300,167	376,739	1,123,090
North	119,168	242,595	482,206	618,950	805,087	2,148,839
Northeast	1,169,922	1,676,519	3,111,165	3,623,624	4,281,900	12,693,208
South	231,267	414,757	525,039	692,920	750,044	2,382,759
Southeast	756,846	891,746	1,247,910	1,720,518	1,964,509	5,824,682
Total	2,408,000	3,445,000	5,593,121	6,956,179	8,178,279	24,172,579
			Regional shares (%)			
Mid-West	5.4	6.4	4.1	4.3	4.6	4.6
North	4.9	7.0	8.6	8.9	9.8	8.9
Northeast	48.6	48.7	55.6	52.1	52.4	52.5
South	9.6	12.0	9.4	10.0	9.2	9.9
Southeast	31.4	25.9	22.3	24.7	24.0	24.1
Total	100.0	100.0	100.0	100.0	100.0	100.0

Note: (1) Based on "interests, profits, dividends, and others" received by individuals with total earnings below R$120 in the Northeast, R$130 in the North, and R$140 in the other three regions; (2) PNAD 2003, special segment on social programs; (*) Until 2003 payments to *Auxílio Gás, Bolsa Alimentação, Bolsa Escola,* and *Cartão Alimentação* were summed. These separate programs were unified in 2004 under the *Bolsa Família* program. Currency figures are expressed in R$1,000, at constant values of 2002

Sources: (1) PNAD 2002, based on "interests, profits, dividends, and others" received by individuals with total earnings below R$120 in the Northeast, R$130 in the North, and R$140 in the other three regions. (2) PNAD 2003, special segment on social programs. For 2004 on, official data from the *Bolsa Família* Program

expenditure. In the second step, we considered that this extra money had to come from reduced government current expenditures in other categories in the profile of total government expenditures. In essence, the net change in government expenditure is zero, but the allocation changes. Since the chain of interrelations in the system is different from the two forms of expenditure, it is expected that the final results on income distribution will also be different.

The size of the shock simulated is of R$ 24.172 billion, encompassing the four years of the administration. On a yearly basis, it represents 0.45 percent of national GDP, 0.82 percent of national disposable income, and 13.4 percent for the poorest income bracket. The results presented in table 13.5 indicate that this expenditure increases national GDP by 2.96 percent, averaging 0.74 percent per year. Since more money was given to poor families, the largest impacts occurred in the production of manufactured food, agriculture, rent, transportation, public utilities, textiles, chemicals and plastics, and communication. In regional terms, the northeast region is the most affected, with a GDP increase of 7.2 percent (1.8 percent per year, on average), 2.4 times the national increase. The north region is second, with 3.35 percent increase in GDP,

Table 13.5 Impacts on production by sector and region

	Impacts on production											
	Increased government expenditure (%)						Constant government expenditure (%)					
	North	Northeast	Mid–West	Southeast	South	Brazil	North	Northeast	Mid–West	Southeast	South	Brazil
Agriculture	5.31	17.1	4.21	4.40	4.65	6.26	3.21	14.1	−0.27	1.34	2.14	3.19
Mining	1.53	4.7	1.46	1.91	1.10	2.13	0.32	2.2	−1.63	0.21	0.11	0.40
Metal	1.20	2.3	1.45	1.35	1.64	1.45	0.08	1.3	−1.68	0.00	0.22	0.12
Machinery	1.54	6.0	2.46	1.52	1.20	1.56	0.40	4.1	−8.39	0.05	0.26	0.19
Vehicles	1.06	4.6	1.32	1.49	1.53	1.53	0.01	2.3	−4.59	−0.78	−0.40	−0.62
Wood & Furniture	3.97	9.0	2.90	2.27	2.48	2.75	1.36	5.4	−8.19	−0.95	0.22	−0.32
Chemicals	4.10	5.8	3.68	3.20	3.06	3.62	1.21	3.5	−5.78	0.05	0.45	0.60
Textiles	4.89	7.4	4.34	4.19	2.97	4.32	2.37	4.9	−7.35	0.45	0.87	1.10
Manufactured Food	8.22	20.9	4.25	4.63	5.34	6.62	5.20	17.3	−1.11	1.69	2.93	3.41
Other Manufacturing	1.68	8.2	2.36	2.20	2.27	2.43	−0.46	4.4	−8.52	−1.30	−0.30	−0.80
Public Utilities	5.47	9.40	2.95	3.06	3.70	4.27	2.77	6.9	−11.04	−0.52	1.16	0.16
Construction	0.20	0.4	0.17	0.20	0.24	0.23	0.06	0.2	−1.03	−0.08	0.04	−0.09
Commerce	4.31	7.6	1.89	1.95	2.65	2.92	1.29	4.9	−8.61	−0.92	0.20	−0.60
Transportation	7.46	14.4	3.00	2.60	2.97	4.66	4.72	11.5	−8.79	−0.43	0.91	1.23
Communication	5.17	6.9	2.01	2.17	2.81	3.06	2.26	4.3	−12.31	−1.11	0.33	−0.92
Financial Services	2.69	3.5	0.51	0.72	0.93	1.02	0.92	2.1	−3.68	−0.42	0.07	−0.41
Services to Families	3.34	6.8	1.34	1.69	2.38	2.65	0.97	4.1	−17.37	−1.90	−0.30	−1.80
Services to Business	3.14	6.1	2.07	1.00	2.31	1.65	−0.40	2.1	−22.74	−1.25	−0.70	−2.02
Rent	11.85	14.0	5.59	3.36	4.23	4.95	7.57	10.6	−20.32	−0.02	1.88	0.74
Public Administration	0.10	0.2	0.03	0.15	0.16	0.15	−2.94	−3.4	−21.77	−7.24	−4.24	−8.16
Non–mercantile Services	5.16	7.7	1.02	1.49	2.61	2.55	1.21	4.3	−18.29	−1.46	0.19	−1.75
All Sectors	3.35	7.2	2.15	2.13	2.77	2.96	1.15	4.6	−9.51	−0.82	0.51	−0.48

Source: Model results

and the mid-west and southeast regions are the least affected, with GDP increases of 2.1 percent.

Considering the distributive aspects, the largest disposable income increase is presented by the poorest income bracket, as expected, with a national 2.7 percent increase, but 8.6 percent in the Northeast. The national average (all income brackets) presents an increase of 2.2 percent, smaller than the increase in GDP. The national Gini moves from 0.5280 in 2002 to 0.5266 after the shocks, a decrease of 0.25 percent. This shows that the annual impact of the *Bolsa Família* program is limited, although positive (see table 13.6).

The above simulation assumes an unrealistic situation in which government increases its current expenditure to take care of the social program. The next simulation considers that government total expenditure is constant, and that the extra payment to families is subtracted from other current expenditures. For that, the previous distribution of government current expenditure was used to distribute the amount compensated among sectors and regions.

As expected, now the impact on national GDP is different, as table 13.5 shows (the five largest impacts are highlighted). As a matter of fact, it becomes negative, −0.48 percent, and average of −0.12 percent per year. This happens because the multiplier effects of the sectors negatively affected are larger than the positively affected sectors. The same sectors most affected in the previous simulation are affected now, but with lower impacts. However, some sectors are negatively affected, such as public administration, services to business, services to families, nonmercantile services, communication, other manufacturing, vehicles, commerce, financial services, wood and furniture, and even construction. The largest positive impacts accrue to manufactured food, agriculture, transportation and textiles, but rents, chemicals and plastic, mining, machinery and equipment, public utilizes, and metals also receive some positive effects.

Now the GDP in the Northeast grows only 4.6 percent, an average of 1.1 percent per year. At a lower level, the north and south regions also receive some positive effects. Negative impacts are present in the Southeast (−0.82 percent) and, mainly, in the Mid-West (−9.5 percent). This is explained by the important presence of the federal government in Brasília. As for income classes (table 13.6), only the two poorest brackets increase their values, with all other receiving less money after the shock. An average Brazilian loses 1.78 percent, a yearly average of 0.4 percent. The very poor income bracket increases its earnings by 1.72 percent (yearly average of 0.42 percent), and the second poorest by 0.33 percent. The upper income bracket presents an income decrease of 2.76 percent. This lose-gain situation is present in all regions but the Northeast, where even the richest receive income increases (1.72 percent for the four-year impact).

These changes lead to a larger change in the national Gini, which decreases 0.39 percent for the four-year impact, moving from 0.5280 in

Table 13.6 Impacts on household income by region

Income brackets (in R$ per month)	(Brazil, share 2002)	Impacts on household income											
		Increased government expenditure (%)						Constant government expenditure (%)					
		North	Northeast	Mid-West	Southeast	South	Brazil	North	Northeast	Mid-West	Southeast	South	Brazil
Up to 400 (1)	5.3	3.27	8.6	1.51	2.11	2.63	4.93	1.02	6.0	−12.77	−0.97	0.37	1.72
400–600	5.4	2.87	7.6	1.44	1.93	2.50	3.67	0.69	4.9	−13.13	−1.13	0.21	0.33
600–1,000	11.5	2.77	6.4	1.24	1.82	2.34	2.85	0.45	3.6	−14.61	−1.48	−0.07	−0.77
1,000–1,200	5.3	2.30	5.4	1.10	1.62	2.18	2.31	−0.17	2.5	−15.50	−2.05	−0.28	−1.60
1,200–1,600	8.9	2.38	5.6	0.85	1.59	2.13	2.27	−0.13	2.8	−16.52	−2.13	−0.46	−1.86
1,600–2,000	8.3	2.55	5.3	0.81	1.50	2.01	2.07	−0.01	2.4	−16.77	−2.31	−0.57	−2.13
2,000–3,000	13.7	2.29	5.4	0.73	1.42	1.97	2.00	−0.30	2.5	−17.26	−2.50	−0.73	−2.54
3,000–4,000	9.7	2.39	5.9	0.61	1.48	1.91	2.08	−0.28	3.0	−17.32	−2.43	−0.75	−2.62
4,000–6,000	11.9	2.21	5.0	0.59	1.47	2.00	1.96	−0.36	2.1	−17.17	−2.25	−0.60	−2.58
6,000 and more	19.8	2.92	4.6	0.61	1.56	2.28	2.03	0.18	1.7	−17.38	−1.90	−0.35	−2.76
All brackets		2.64	6.1	0.80	1.59	2.16	2.45	0.15	3.3	−16.55	−2.01	−0.39	−1.78

Source: Model results

Table 13.7   Impacts on income inequality

	Observed 2002	After shock			
		Increased government expenditure		Constant government expenditure	
	Gini	Gini	Change (%)	Gini	Change (%)
North	0.4659	0.4661	0.04	0.4655	−0.07
Northeast	0.4988	0.4962	−0.51	0.4961	−0.54
Mid–West	0.5353	0.5351	−0.05	0.5317	−0.67
Southeast	0.4666	0.4662	−0.08	0.4661	−0.10
South	0.4580	0.4579	−0.02	0.4576	−0.10
Brazil	0.5280	0.5266	−0.26	0.5259	−0.39

Source: Authors' calculation from the model results

2002 to 0.5259 after the shock (table 13.7). This indicates that the losing sectors present a less pro-poor profile than the sectors that benefited from the social programs. Table 13.5 allows for a comparison of the two shocks simulated here. The mid-west region presents the highest inequality 2002, probably due to the presence of the federal district, which is known for having the highest per capita income in the country. The poor northeast region comes second, with the South being the least unequal. The first shock, which assumes increase in total government expenditure in the amount of the *Bolsa Família* payments, indicates that the northeast region will present the most improvement in income inequality, a 0.51 percent decrease in its Gini indicator; the second best would be the Southeast, with -0.08 percent. Considering that the government has to compensate the extra expenditure with cuts in other programs changes the scenario, so the global improvement in income distribution is larger. The most beneficial effects are still in the northeast region, even more than in the previous case, but the highlight is the mid-west region, with the largest change in the Gini coefficient, -0.67 percent. Notwithstanding this change, the region maintains its first place in inequality levels.

As for regional concentration, the main object of this chapter, the effects are clearly favorable as table 13.8 indicates. The northeast region increases its share in national GDP from 12.9 percent to 13.56 percent and in national income from 16.9 percent to 17.78 percent; the north region moves from 4.76 percent to 4.83 percent in GDP and from 5 percent to 5.1 percent in terms of income. The southeast region loses share, from 56.11 percent to 55.92 percent in GDP, and from 54.45 percent to 54.32 percent in terms of income. The mid-west region presents the largest loss, from 7.98 to 7.26 in GDP, and from 7.24 percent to 6.16 percent in income. The south region increases its share, from 18.25 percent to 18.44 percent in GDP, and from 16.41 percent to 16.64 percent in income.

Table 13.8 Shares in production value and in income

	Base line 2002	*Without expenditure compensation*	*Holding government expenditure constant*
	Shares in GDP (%)		
North	4.76	4.77	4.83
Northeast	12.90	13.43	13.56
Mid-West	7.98	7.92	7.26
Southeast	56.11	55.66	55.92
South	18.25	18.22	18.44
	Shares in disposable income (%)		
North	5.00	5.01	5.10
Northeast	16.90	17.51	17.78
Mid-West	7.24	7.13	6.16
Southeast	54.45	53.99	54.32
South	16.41	16.36	16.64

Source: Authors' calculation from the model results

Thus, the *Bolsa Família* program exhibits a clear, favorable regional impact. Since it is targeted to poor families, and those are mainly located in poorer regions, it ends up producing a deconcentration effect. This effect is larger if government expenditures are held constant, since the regional pattern of the global effects of government expenditure is more pro-concentration than the global effects of the expenditure of poor families.

Conclusion

This chapter has shown that the *Bolsa Família* program produces positive impacts on income concentration, both at the individual level and at the regional level. Assuming that it could be continued forever, it could end up producing important improvements in income inequality in the country. However, the long-term effects of such programs, vis-à-vis other types of social intervention (education, health) should be taken into consideration. If expanded government investments in social transfers hurt other investment-related programs, it will clearly produce a setback in the future. In essence, the analysis presented here might be considered, in general equilibrium terms, a short-run analysis in which markets assume to respond only to current changes in demand rather than evaluating lon-ger-run implications that might generate a different profile—sectorally and spatially—of investment options.

Other important measures are needed to foster development in the lagging regions such as structural policies that examine both 1) the supply (human capital) and 2) the demand side (physical capital). Recent govern-ment initiatives in Brazil to promote investments in infrastructure include the Programa de Aceleração do Crescimento (Growth Acceleration Program—PAC), unveiled at the end of January 2007.[7] Investments in logistic infrastructure are estimated in US$58.3 billions in the four-year period 2007–2010, including US$33.4 billions (57.3 percent of the total) for road infrastructure alone.[8]

One important aspect of macroeconomic management in Brazil, with potential effects on the public provision of infrastructure, is the Projeto Piloto de Investimento (PPI, pilot project for investment), which permits the government to reduce the primary surplus by an equivalent amount to an increase in infrastructure expenditure. PPI will probably be increased from 0.2 percent of GDP to 0.5 percent of GDP. As the government has formally maintained the 4.25 percent of GDP primary fiscal target[9] in 2007, this will put the effective primary surplus closer to 3.75 percent of GDP.[10] In monetary terms, this may represent additional US$1.9 to 4.7 billions to be invested in infrastructure, according to FIPE estimates for the Plano Nacional de Logística e Transportes (PNLT national plan of logistics and transportation).

Concomitantly with the four-year program (PAC), the central government has also signaled its intention in reviving long-term planning in transportation in the country. The design of an ambitious PNLT has been initiated, involving different stakeholders. It aims at supporting decision makers in attaining economic objectives through policy initiatives related to both public and private infrastructure and organization of the transportation sector.[11]

Helping the poor is an important objective. In the short run, the *Bolsa Família* program has proven to produce positive results, both at the personal income level and at the regional concentration level, and has surely paid large dividends in electoral terms. Solving problems of inequality, however, might require other medium- and long-run policies that could improve the competitiveness of lagging regions.

Notes

* This author would thank FAPESP (Fundação de Amparo à Pesquisa do Estado de São Paulo) for the financial to present this paper at the *16th International Input-Output Conference.*

1. See Amann et al. (2006).
2. Almeida et al. (2006) have investigated the resources allocations of the Northeast, North and Center-West Constitutional Financing Fund loans by counties, and have established that the loans have not been directed to the poorest states or to the poorest counties.
3. Empirical pseudo-significance based on 999 random permutations.
4. Formally, this model is $y = \rho W y + X\beta + \varepsilon$, where y is a vector of observations on the dependent variable, Wy is a spatially lagged dependent variable for weights matrix W, X is a matrix of observations on the explanatory variables, ε is a vector of i.i.d. error terms, and ρ and β are parameters.
5. Formally, this model is $y = X\beta + \varepsilon$, with $\varepsilon = \lambda W\varepsilon + u$, where y is a vector of observations on the dependent variable, W is the spatial weights matrix, X is a matrix of observations on the explanatory variables, ε is a vector of spatially autocorrelated error terms, u a vector of i.i.d. errors, and β and λ are parameters.

6. The detailed model can be found in Moreira (2007).
7. The PAC will aim to raise average annual GDP growth to 5 percent per year (almost double the country's long-term average), principally through increased investment in infrastructure, which will be fostered in part through targeted tax breaks.
8. www.brasil.gov.br (Programa de Aceleração do Crescimento 2007–2010).
9. Primary nonfinancial public-sector (NFPS) balance (excluding interest payments).
10. EIU (2007).
11. www.centran.eb.br (Programa Nacional de Logística e Transportes).

References

Albuquerque, R.C., and R.M. Gomes. 1996. "Nordeste: Os Desafios de uma Dupla Inserção." In J.P.R. Velloso, ed. Fórum Nacional: *O Real, o Crescimento e as Reformas*. Rio de Janeiro: José Olympio Editora.

Almeida, M.F., A.M.A. Silva, G.M. Resende. 2006. Uma análise dos Fundos Constitucionais do Financiamento do Nordeste (FNE), Norte (FNO) e Centro-Oeste (FCO), IPEA, Textos para Discussão TD 1206.

Amann, E., E.A. Haddad, F. Perobelli, and J. Guilhoto. 2006. "Structural Change in the Brazilian Automotive Industry and Its Regional Impacts." *Latin American Business Review* 7(3–4). pp. 97–119.

Anselin, L. 1999. "Interactive Techniques and Exploratory Spatial Data Analysis." In P. A. Longley, M.F. Goodchild, D.J. Maguire, and D.W. Rhind, eds. *Geographic Information System: Principles, Techniques, Management and Applications*. New York: John Wiley, pp. 251–264.

Araújo, T.B. 1995. "Nordeste, Nordestes: Que Nordeste?" In R.B.A. Affonso and P.L.B. Silva, eds. *Federalismo no Brasil: Desigualdae Regionais e Desenvolvimento*. São Paulo: FUNDAP.

Baer, W., and G.J.D. Hewings, Eds. 2007. *Equity Distortion in Regional Resource Allocation in Brazil*. New York: Haworth Press.

Leontief, W.W. 1951. *The Structure of the American Economy*. 2nd Enlarged Ed. New York: Oxford University Press.

———. 1976. *Input-Output Analysis and the Structure of Income Distribution*. Berlin: Springer-Verlag.

Moreira, G. 2007. Políticas Sociais, Desigualdades Pessoais e Regionais da Renda no Brasil: Uma Análise de Insumo-Produto, Master Thesis, ESALQ-USP.

Temple, M. 1994. *Regional Economics*. New York: St. Martin's Press.

CHAPTER FOURTEEN

Regional Development Policies, 2003–2006

LUIZ RICARDO CAVALCANTE AND
SIMONE UDERMAN

Introduction

The high degree of regional inequality in Brazil has been widely recognized, especially since the mid-twentieth century. This feature was stressed by Williamson (1965), who concluded that the country had the highest level of regional inequalities in the world. In 1959, the Working Group for Northeast Development (GTDN) called national attention to this problem, and proposed a plan of action for the development of the northeastern region (GTDN 1959). Baer (1966: 174) and Moreira (1979: 51) claimed that economic, social, and political pressures were responsible at that time for public policies to attract and even directly transfer resources from central regions to stagnant areas. Not surprisingly, regional development policies became a recurrent subject, both in theoretical discussions and among policy makers.

The creation of federal institutions aiming at promoting the development of depressed regions stressed the role of the central government in reducing regional inequalities. As shown in the section The Instruments used during the period 2003–2006, the performances of the Bank of Northeast of Brazil (BNB), the Superintendency for the Development of the Northeast (SUDENE), the Amazonian Bank (BASA), and the Superintendency for the Development of the Amazon Region (SUDAM) were significant to support the development of the northeastern and northern regions in the 1960s and 1970s. The federal government also invested heavily in poorer regions, especially during the 1970s. The National Development Plans (PNDs) included relevant investments that reconfigured regional economic structure and supported spatial redistribution of production, as in the case of the petrochemical pole in Bahia. The regional policies conducted by the federal government, then, were based upon institutions that offered differentiated conditions to sustain the poorer regions' development, and upon the use of intensive fiscal instruments, associated with significant direct investments.

Due to the fiscal and financial crisis of the 1980s, the investment capacity of the federal government was significantly reduced and the resources formerly directed to tackle regional inequalities vanished, as macroeconomic concerns claimed most of the government's attention. During the 1990s, facing neoliberal policies and macroeconomic priorities, regional development lost importance and showed its feebleness. In 2001, with neither resources nor prestige, and apparently involved in suspicious transactions, SUDENE and SUDAM were closed and replaced by inoperative agencies, respectively the Agency for the Development of the Northeast (ADENE) and the Agency for the Development of the Amazon Region (ADA).

In this context, the convergence of GDP per capita among Brazil's states that took place between the early 1970s and the mid-1980s ceased. The absence of federal actions addressing regional inequalities stimulated fiscal competition among states, especially after the 1994 monetary stabilization plan, when a large amount of Foreign Direct Investment (FDI) flowed to Brazil. In the 2002 presidential election, the theme of regional development came up, and the re-creation of active federal regional development institutions were incorporated in the programs of the major candidates.

In the middle of 2003, president Luiz Inácio Lula da Silva announced the re-creation of SUDENE and SUDAM, and argued that the reduction of regional inequalities should be pursued through effective regional policies.[1] The guidelines for regional development policies during the first Lula administration, however, have not yet been sufficiently analyzed. We explore this subject, focusing on the regional distribution of resources over which the federal government has discretionary power. Our aim is not to evaluate the results of these policies, but to show how the federal government used the instruments available to promote regional development between 2003 and 2006.

Regional Development Policies

The Instruments used by Central Governments

Several authors in the 1950s highlighted that, following its natural trend, an economy would tend to an increasing spatial concentration. Perroux (1955), Myrdal (1957), and Hirschman (1958), proposing, respectively, the concepts of growth poles, circular and cumulative causation, and backward and forward linkages, understood the trend toward inequality as the outcome of the interplay of unfettered market forces. In tune with Rosenstein-Rodan (1943) and Nurkse (1953), these authors justified active state policies to promote development and reduce inequality through public investments (both in infrastructure and in the productive sector), as well as fiscal and financial incentives to support private investments.

In a Keynesian environment, policies of this kind flourished in several countries. According to Miyoshi (1997), "by the late 1970s, the growth pole strategies had been 'implemented, provided for, or seriously discussed' in at least 28 developed and developing countries." In the United States, for instance, the government on several occasions played an important role in sustaining redistribution processes, widely applying public policies to promote regional development (Cobb 1993, Baer and Miles 1999). This is also true for many countries in Europe, as well as, more recently, for the European Union (Dall'erba 2003). However, from the 1980s onward, the rise of neoliberal theories clearly dimmed interventionist recommendations and obscured the use of their correlated policies. This movement was also strengthened by the fiscal and financial crisis that reached many developing countries, imposing macroeconomic restrictive measures.

In the 1990s, the formal approaches proposed by the New Economic Geography School restored the regional theme, considering the trade-off between economies of scale and transportation costs (Fugita, Krugman, and Venables 1999, Fugita and Thisse 2002). The New Economic Geography put into formal models the concepts mentioned at the beginning of this section[2] and reinforced the perception that integrated markets tend to agglomerate around already developed regions. On the other hand, the idea of "social capital" (Putnam 1993) changed the focus of regional development discussions, stressing local gaps resultant from the lack of less concrete attributes, as "relational assets."[3] Difficulties involving the implementation of a state intervention agenda capable of promoting regional development, however, limited the potential of the new proposals (Uderman 2007). As a result, in spite of the new rhetoric, effective governmental intervention to promote regional development remained associated with the use of traditional instruments.

More intensively applied during the 1960s and 1970s, and less intensively used from the 1980s onward, these instruments seem to converge to a mix involving both fiscal and financial incentives, as well as capital transfers directed to the poorer regions, either as investments or as cash allowances.

Baer and Miles (1999), analyzing the role of the state in the United States regional development, associated the development of the southeastern region to local (district and state levels) policies aiming at creating a good business environment, involving low taxes and wages. In addition, federal spending directed to those localities was identified as an important lever to reduce poverty or create externalities.[4]

Describing the instruments used to promote economic development in peripheral regions of the United States, Luger (1987), focusing on policies adopted at the state level, considered eight main program areas: 1) land and building subsidies; 2) provision of debt and equity capital; 3) state tax programs; 4) postsecondary education assistance; 5) subsidized job training; 6) business regulation; 7) business recruiting or outreach; and 8) research and development (R&D) support.

Friedmann (1975: 809), in turn, suggested the following tools for implementing regional development and affecting the spatial patterns of settlement, production and welfare: 1) location (or capital) subsidies; 2) labor (or wage) subsidies; 3) other fiscal policies related to taxation and import tariffs; 4) direct controls over migration; 5) government investments in infrastructure and directly productive activities; 6) new towns; 7) land use controls; 8) licensing arrangements; 9) administrative decentralization; 10) increasing regional autonomy in matters affecting development; and 11) central planning and budgetary controls.

Cavalcante and Uderman (2006), using a more aggregated typology, proposed three kinds of incentives:[5] 1) fiscal incentives associated with tax breaks or the financing of taxes due by firms; 2) financial incentives (credit programs at lower interest rates or, more broadly, more attractive conditions); and 3) budget incentives (infrastructure provision, land and building subsidies, job training sponsored by the state, and any other incentives that directly affect the government budget).

Poverty reduction programs might be considered an indirect regional development policy as well. According to Baer and Miles (1999: 184), "since many government social programs created during and since the New Deal are aimed at reducing inequality and poverty, regions with a disproportionate amount of poor citizens get more than their share." Cash allowances are also considered an instrument that central governments may use to reduce regional inequalities. In this case, however, the impact is on the consumption levels, and not directly on the capital stock.[6]

Based on these previous studies, the typology used in this chapter assumes that governments may have four main instruments to deal with the regional distribution of economic activities:[7]

- Fiscal incentives associated with tax breaks or the financing of taxes due by firms;
- Financial incentives (long-term credit at more attractive conditions);
- Direct investments, both in infrastructure and in the productive sector; and
- Cash allowances, usually associated to poverty reduction programs and materialized in direct cash transfers to households.

Other instruments, such as job training (universities and technical schools) or R&D support provided by agencies and funds actually materialize through the previous ones. In fact, R&D support is usually provided as some sort of fiscal incentive for this kind of activity. Given the specific nature of job training and R&D support (as they focus on human capital, instead of physical capital), a more general typology could consider them as additional instruments.

As policies reflect choices available to the decision makers, the instruments are to be considered whenever the government detains discretionary power on their application. Mandatory incentives or investments (e.g., the ones established by the constitution and not submitted to government choices) should not be considered if the objective is to analyze the policies discretionarily adopted by a given administration.

Brief Review of Regional Development Policies

In Brazil, the effects of massive industrial investments in the 1950s that were concentrated in the southern part of the country amplified discussions about the relevance of federal institutions to coordinate regional economic development and integrate the national territory (Baer 1966: 162, Cano 1985: 299). The role played by government institutions and public investments in favor of some poorer regions of the country was analyzed in several studies (Barros 1970, Baer and Geiger 1978, Haddad 1978; Suzigan and Araújo 1979). The creation of the BNB in the early 1950s was an important step forward, reinforced, in 1959 by the creation of SUDENE, which provided additional financial incentives, as well as fiscal incentives, directed to the northeastern region of the country. Later on, analogous institutions (BASA and SUDAM) were created to promote the development of the northern region. The special fiscal and financial incentives aiming at stimulating new investments in peripheral areas underpinned federal actions toward regional development, stimulating a new economic dynamic in these regions.

From the 1960s onward, these instruments, as well as the influx of public investments and official credit from the Brazilian Development Bank (BNDES)[8] directed at large projects, usually associated to growth poles initiatives, supported the reduction of regional inequalities. The metallurgical investments and the petrochemical poles included in the National Development Plans (PNDs) were emblematic projects that sustained some of the results observed.

Indeed, several authors recognize that between 1970 and 1985—not by chance the period when the institutions aiming at regional development acted more intensively—regional inequalities in fact declined (Ferreira and Diniz 1995, Cano 1995). Andrade (1988: 14) also notes that the inequalities index, considering the GDP per capita, fell from 0.66 to 0.54, between 1970 and 1980. Azzoni (2001: 151) extends the convergence period up to the mid-1990s, as the inequalities indexes, calculated by this author, move from 0.2184 in 1970 to 0.1176 in 1995, after a minimum value in 1994 (0.1121). It is noteworthy, however, that from the mid-1980s onward, the convergence movements took place inside Brazil's macro regions, instead of among these regions (Cavalcante 2003).

The convergence movements observed between 1970 and 1985 seem related to the regional development policies adopted during the period. Cano (1995: 628) argues that this trend can be credited to the following factors: 1) structural changes in peripheral regions associated to the integration of the national market; 2) the capital movements toward the less developed regions that resulted from the regional development policies; 3) the incentives and investments of the Second National Development Plan (that allowed a more intensive use of the natural resources available in the peripheral regions); 4) the march to the West and the expansion of agricultural borderlines; 5) export policies and their impacts on the modernization of the agro-industrial sector in regions beyond São Paulo and the southeastern region; and 6) the 1980s crisis, whose impacts were greater in São Paulo. The first three factors mentioned were clearly associated to the development policies adopted by the federal government in favor of the less development macro regions.

By the end of the 1970s, the world economic crisis, marked by increasing oil prices and monetary instability, entailed restrictive measures that blocked the previous development programs of the federal government, and created an uncertain environment that inhibited private initiatives. During the 1980s and the early 1990s, macroeconomic disturbances became a matter of great concern. Inflation, external debts, and fiscal imbalances outweighed any other discussions, including regional development issues, from the national agenda. The prominence of liberal trends and the beginning of the privatization process also restricted governmental action in favor of peripheral regions. As a result, when the use of the regional development instruments was reduced or ceased, the convergence movements ceased as well, and growth tended to be concentrated in the center-southern part of the country. Still in the early 1990s, Diniz (1993) warned that, in the absence of effective regional policies, economic growth would be concentrated within the polygonal area limited by Belo Horizonte (MG), Uberlândia (MG), Londrina (PR), Porto Alegre (PR), and Florianópolis (SC).

In the mid-1990s, monetary stabilization and the subsequent influx of FDI caused the reappearance of regional development as a major issue, as state governments became engaged in an intense fiscal competition for investments. This fiscal war was justified by many states as an alternative to the absence of a regional development policy coordinated by the federal government. At that time, SUDENE and SUDAM were debilitated institutions, no longer capable of leading a consistent process of regional convergence. Both were extinguished in 2001, under suspicions of corruption.

This brief review of regional development policies during the second half of the twentieth century shows that convergence periods were associated with a more intensive use of some of the instruments mentioned in the section Fiscal Incentives. The reduction of regional inequalities observed in the period between 1970 and 1985, in particular, was clearly associated with an extensive use of fiscal and financial incentives, as well as direct investments in the poorer regions of the country. On the other hand, as the use of these instruments by the central government ended, the convergence among regions ceased as well.

The fact is that in the early 2000s, regional inequalities remain high in Brazil. In figure 14.1, the inequalities among Brazilian states become

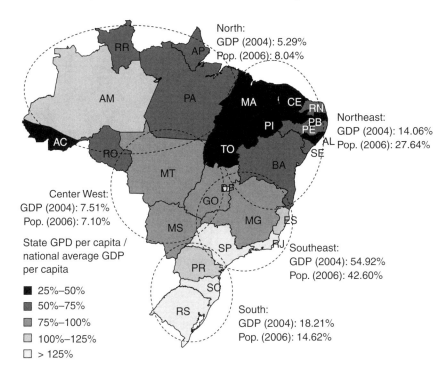

Figure 14.1   Brazilian regions: GDP, population, and GDP per capita

Source: Brazilian Institute for Geography and Statistics (http://www.ibge.gov.br). Elaborated by the authors

quite evident. In the map, states with higher levels of GDP per capita have brighter colors, while states with lower levels of GDP per capita have darker colors.

As can be seen, the higher levels of GDP per capita (i.e., above the national average) are observed in the southern states (Rio Grande do Sul [RS], Santa Catarina [SC], and Paraná [PR]), in three (São Paulo [SP], Rio de Janeiro [RJ], and Espírito Santo [ES]) out of four southeastern states, in one state of the northern region (Amazonas [AM]) and in the federal district (DF). On the other hand, the highest level of GDP per capita in the northeastern region (Sergipe [SE]) is around 70 percent of the national average, and the region is marked by the presence of very poor states (as Maranhão [MA] and Piauí [PI], whose indicators are the worst in the country).

In the 2002 presidential election, the rhetoric of the major candidates (both the pro-governmental candidate, José Serra, and the winner Luiz Inácio Lula da Silva) was against neoliberal policies and in favor of initiatives and institutions aiming at promoting regional development.[9] According to campaign promises, SUDENE and SUDAM would be re-created, and regional development policies would be put into practice. The early 2000s produced expectations that effective regional policies coordinated by the federal government would be implemented. What did really happen during the first Lula administration? Focusing on the use of the main instruments identified above, the next section examines the federal efforts made in favor of regional distribution of economic activities during the period 2003–2006.

The Instruments Used during the Period 2003–2006

We collected data on regional distribution of resources over which the federal government has discretionary power, and that are directed to promote regional development in the period between 2003 and 2006.[10] An overall comparison provides an idea about their relative relevance in monetary terms. Table 14.1 shows data on fiscal incentives granted by the federal government; credit from BNDES and regional constitutional funds; direct investments from the national budget and two important state companies; and cash allowances from the family grant program (*Bolsa Família*). This set of data provides an overview of the amount of federal resources involved in developmental actions, either supporting productive investments, infrastructure, or cash transfers. It must be noticed that job training was not considered, although the preponderant location of federal universities and technical schools in the more developed regions of the country suggests that these instruments are concentrated in the southeastern and southern regions.[11] R&D support provided by federal agencies and funds was not considered as well, as the values that could be regionalized are relatively small. At any rate, there is robust evidence that these resources are also concentrated in the more developed regions.[12] Besides, some of the actions aimed at supporting R&D activities are already included in the fiscal and financial incentives considered in the following analyses.

As one can see in table 14.1, the aggregate values for each instrument showed a very high rate of growth in the period. In fact, the resources allocated by the federal government to fiscal and financial incentives grew 77 percent and 60 percent in four years. During the same period resources directed to cash allowances more than doubled, while direct investments almost doubled. The total values allocated to each instrument, however, may be very different. Effectively, financial instruments are the most important ones, reaching almost R$60 billion in 2006. As expected, BNDES resources are by far the most significant (more than R$50 billion in 2006). Direct investments come in sequence, and Petrobras (more than R$33 billion in 2006) appears as the most relevant source, overcoming federal government budget investments (around R$15 billion also in 2006). Fiscal incentives represent around 70 percent of the financial incentives. Cash allowances, on the other hand, seem to be small when compared to the other instruments.

Table 14.1   Resources allocated by the federal government, 2003–2006, current R$ millions

	2003	*2004*	*2005*	*2006*
Fiscal incentives	**23,958**	**24,211**	**31,288**	**42,500**
Tax expenditures	23,958	24,211	31,288	42,500
Financial incentives	**36,548**	**45,536**	**53,599**	**58,337**
BNDES	33,533	39,834	46,980	51,318
BNB/FNE	1,019	3,209	4,174	4,588
BASA/FNO	1,075	1,321	976	986
BB/FCO	920	1,172	1,468	1,444
Direct investments	**26,645**	**34,469**	**39,198**	**52,156**
Federal government	5,219	9,071	10,306	15,267
Petrobrás	18,500	22,549	25,710	33,686
Eletrobrás	2,926	2,849	3,178	3,203
Cash allowances*	**3,445**	**5,593**	**6,956**	**8,178**
Family grant program	3,445	5,593	6,956	8,178

Note: *Data on cash allowances included, in 2003, Vale-Gás, *Bolsa Alimentação*, *Bolsa Escola*, and *Cartão Alimentação* unified in 2004 under the family grant program

Sources: Federal Revenue and Customs Administration, BNDES, *Ministério da Integração Nacional, Contas Abertas, Orçamento Geral da União, Petrobrás, Eletrobrás,* several years, and Azzoni et al. (2007). Elaborated by the authors

Fiscal Incentives

As was shown, governments frequently use fiscal incentives to encourage certain kinds of industries, activities, or class of persons. A useful measure of these fiscal incentives provided by governments is the concept of tax expenditures. The definition is straightforward: tax expenditures measure the difference between what is effectively collected and what would be collected in the absence of the special incentives given by the government. Over the years, the concept has been increasingly recognized as expenditure itself, and several countries and jurisdictions estimate the total amount of incentives they provide (Bordin 2003).

By law, the Brazilian Federal Revenue and Customs Administration yearly estimates tax expenditures.[13] These data are available for the macro regions of Brazil, as shown in table 14.2.

Evidently, in the period 2003 to 2006, two regions (northern and center-western) obtained shares of total tax expenditures at higher levels than their shares of total GDP. In particular, the share of the northern region (above 20 percent) seems high when compared to its share in Brazil's GDP (slightly above 5 percent). The center-western region is also noteworthy, as its average share in total tax expenditures more than doubled between the periods 1999–2002 and 2003–2006.[14] On the other hand, in spite of the allegedly high levels of fiscal incentives directed to the northeastern region, its share in the total tax expenditures is systematically smaller than its share in total GDP. These results suggest that while regional development agencies such as ADENE and ADA had their role reduced,[15] free

Table 14.2 Tax expenditures, 1998–2006, current R$ millions

	North	Northeast	Center-West	Southeast	South	Total
1998	4,586	2,376	601	7,606	2,112	17,280
1999	3,933	1,844	600	7,980	1,878	16,235
2000	3,219	2,083	783	8,772	2,106	16,963
2001	4,564	2,346	725	9,241	2,459	19,334
2002	5,286	2,285	827	11,773	3,090	23,262
2003	5,100	3,022	1,130	11,620	3,085	23,958
2004	4,853	2,480	1,264	12,472	3,141	24,211
2005	6,438	3,979	3,833	13,367	3,671	31,288
2006	8,961	4,799	4,502	19,627	4,610	42,500
Average 1999–2002 share (%)	22.4	11.4	3.9	49.8	12.5	100.0
Average 2003–2006 share (%)	20.8	11.7	8.2	47.2	12.1	100.0

Source: Federal Revenue and Customs Administration, several years. Elaborated by the authors

trade zones (such as the one located in Manaus, in the northern region of the country) keep concentrating high levels of fiscal incentives.

Financial Incentives

The role of development banks in Brazil's industrialization process has been widely recognized by several authors (Bonelli and Pinheiro 1994: 26, Além 1998: 5, Baer 2002: 293). In fact, in a financial market characterized by high levels of credit rationing and high capital costs, financial institutions that provide long-term credit at more attractive conditions can play an important role in fostering investments. The BNDES is the most important institution of this kind in Brazil. Created in the early 1950s, the bank played an important role in the developmental phase of the Brazilian economy and financed several projects in the less developed regions of the country, especially during the period between the 1960s and the early 1980s.

In the recent period, however, despite the rhetoric that the bank should contribute to reducing regional inequalities and some analysis trying to show that disbursements were directed to poorer regions (Souza 2003), the data lead to an opposite conclusion. As shown in figure 14.2, total BNDES disbursements in the period 2003–2006 (in constant 2006 R$, and segmented by state) can be compared to the share of each state in Brazilian GDP (average 2003–2004).[16] It can be easily seen that the slope of the linear adjustment $\ln(y_i) = a\ln(x_i) + b$ indicates whether the distribution of the BNDES resources effectively reflects the economic relevance of each state. Values different from the unit reflect an uneven distribution, benefiting the larger economies if $a > 1$, and the smaller economies if $a < 1$. As shown in the graph, the value obtained for a in the regression

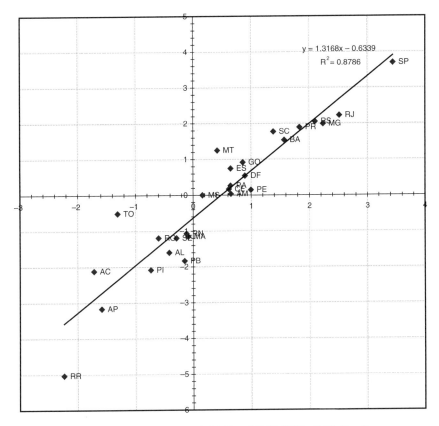

Figure 14.2   BNDES disbursements (2003–2006) and GDP (2003–2004), Brazilian states

Source: BNDES. Elaborated by the authors

Table 14.3   Regional share of BNDES disbursements, 2003–2006 (%)

	North	*Northeast*	*Center-West*	*Southeast*	*South*
2003	2.12	9.28	8.44	59.75	20.40
2004	4.91	6.87	12.96	53.47	21.80
2005	3.44	8.09	6.96	61.17	20.33
2006	3.17	9.42	7.13	61.22	19.06
Average 2003–2006 share	3.41	8.42	8.87	58.90	20.40

Source: BNDES. Elaborated by the authors

(1.3168) clearly confirms that BNDES resources are especially directed to the larger economies.[17] This technical conclusion is easily confirmed in a simpler way by table 14.3, which indicates the share of each region in BNDES disbursements in the period between 2003 and 2006.

The North and the Northeast (5.3 percent and 14.1 percent of Brazilian GDP, respectively) received, on average, only 3.4 percent and 8.4 percent of BNDES disbursements in the period. Indeed, BNDES disbursements were directed to the center-western (8.9 percent), southeastern (58.9 percent), and southern (20.4 percent) regions more than proportionally to their share in GDP (respectively 7.5 percent, 54.9 percent, and 18.2 percent). Of course, these data suggest a concentration trend, as these disbursements are clearly associated to capital formation and to higher levels of growth. This conclusion is not really different from the results obtained by Uderman (2001), who analyzed the regional distribution of BNDES resources in the second half of the 1990s, when neoliberal policies were extensively applied.

However, BNDES resources are not the only financial incentives provided by the federal government. Constitutional Regional Funds have existed for the northern (Constitutional Fund for Financing the North—FNO), northeastern (Constitutional Fund for Financing the Northeast—FNE), and center-western (Constitutional Fund for Financing the Center-West—FCO) regions since 1988, and their resources come from income taxes at the following rates: 1.8 percent to FNE, 0.6 percent to FNO, and 0.6 percent to FCO. These funds are operated by federal banks in the northern (BASA), northeastern (BNB), and center-western (Bank of Brazil—BB) regions.[18]

When the disbursements of these funds are summed to the BNDES disbursements, a reasonably good picture of the total financial incentives provided by the federal government emerges. Table 14.4 shows the distribution of these resources among the five macro regions of the country in the period between 2003 and 2006.

As shown in table 14.4, even when the constitutional funds are considered, the northeastern region receives, on average, financial incentives less than proportionally to its share in Brazil's GDP (although the values are increasing and are above the regional share in Brazilian GDP in the last two years), and the northern region just matches its share in Brazil's GPD. In line with the results obtained for fiscal incentives, financial incentives also privilege the center-western region. This macro-region, however, is not considered one of the poorest by the Ministry of National Integration in the National Regional Development Policy (Brasil. Ministério..., 2007: 11, 14).

Table 14.4   Financial incentives (BNDES, FNO, FNE, and FCO), regions, 2003–2006 (%)

	North	Northeast	Center-West	Southeast (1)	South
2003	4.89	11.19	10.26	54.93	18.72
2004	7.19	12.82	13.91	47.01	19.07
2005	4.84	14.31	8.84	54.20	17.82
2006	4.48	15.76	8.75	54.24	16.77
Average 2003–2006 share	5.35	13.52	10.44	52.60	18.09

Note: (1) FNE disbursements directed to the states for MG and ES were credited to the southeastern region

Source: BNDES. Ministério da Integração. Elaborated by the authors

Direct Investments

Direct investments include the ones by the federal government, as well as the ones by companies directly controlled by the federal government, such as Petrobrás and Eletrobrás. Data on the investments by the federal government have been obtained from the Integrated System of Financial Administration (SIAFI) through an NGO that keeps control of government expenditures (*Contas Abertas*). To capture investments by companies directly controlled by the federal government, data on Petrobrás and Eletrobrás investments (which are certainly the most representative ones) are used.[19]

Table 14.5 shows the regional distributions of investments by the federal government between 2001 and 2006. As can be seen, these resources are directed to poorer regions more than proportionally to their share in Brazilian GDP.

As some of these investments are in basic infrastructure (such as electric energy for households, water supply, and so on), it is reasonable to assume that they are more directly associated to the share of each region in the total population rather than in the total GDP. That may explain (at least partially) the larger share that relatively poorer regions exhibit in table 14.5. Interestingly, the share of the poorer regions in total direct investments by the federal government declined between the periods 2001–2002 and 2003–2006. At any rate, the average values associated to these investments, as shown in table 14.1, correspond to only one-fourth of the investments by the two companies controlled by the federal government considered in this chapter during the period 2003–2006.

Investments by Petrobrás are the largest among the ones considered in this section (table 14.1). It was not possible to access the regional distribution of these investments. Nevertheless, there is no reason to consider that these investments are not market oriented. The reports of Petrobrás, and the fact that the enterprise has commitments to its private shareholders, suggest that the spatial distribution of the investments

Table 14.5   Direct investments by the federal government, 2001–2006, current R$ millions

	North	Northeast	Center-West	Southeast	South	Total
2001	1,032	2,329	1,096	3,500	850	8,807
2002	1,389	2,861	1,476	3,802	998	10,525
2003	516	1,137	576	1,958	423	4,609
2004	853	1,849	1,053	3,653	827	8,235
2005	891	1,927	1,145	4,307	1,126	9,395
2006	1,283	2,822	5,909	3,218	945	14,176
Average 2001–2002 share (%)	12.5	26.8	13.2	37.9	9.6	100.0
Average 2003–2006 share (%)	10.4	22.2	12.2	43.5	11.7	100.0

Source: Integrated System of Financial Administration (SIAFI)/*Contas Abertas*. Elaborated by the authors

follows mainly economic and technical criteria. An exception could be the recently announced investments in Pernambuco. However, these investments do not refer to the period analyzed, and are not included in the data. The same criteria seem to apply to Eletrobrás, whose investments correspond to around 10 percent of Petrobrás'.[20]

In short, although direct investments by the federal government could have been used to promote regional development during the first Lula administration, total resources allocated are relatively small.[21] On the other hand, and despite the absence of regionalized data, the most representative share of direct investments (the ones associated to the companies controlled by the federal government) seem to have followed mainly technical and market-oriented criteria.

Cash Allowances

As indicated in section Fiscal Incentives, cash allowances (direct cash transfers to households) might be considered instruments to reduce regional inequalities. However, their impacts are not on capital formation, but rather on local levels of consumption. As a result, such programs can reduce poverty indexes in the short-run, but do not create local production capacity. In spite of these caveats, the family grant program was also considered an instrument to promote regional development during the period 2003–2006.

Since 2003, this social program gradually absorbed the *Bolsa Escola* (conditional school attendance income transfer program), the *Bolsa Alimentação* (nutrition program), the *Cartão Alimentação* (nutrition card), and *Vale Gás* (cooking fuel supplement), concentrating almost all cash allowances resources over which the federal government has discretionary power.[22] However, when compared to the previous instruments, the values associated to cash transfers remain small. Their amount, in the last year, corresponds to less than 16 percent of BNDES disbursements, and around 19 percent of the federal fiscal incentives (table 14.1).

Table 14.6 shows the regional distribution of the family grant program.

Table 14.6 Family grant program, 2003–2006, current R$ millions

	North	Northeast	Center-West	Southeast	South
2003*	243	1,677	219	892	415
2004	482	3,111	227	1,248	525
2005	619	3,624	300	1,721	693
2006	805	4,282	377	1,965	750
Average 2003–2006 share (%)	8.6	52.2	4.8	24.2	10.1

Note: *Data on cash allowances included, in 2003, *Vale Gás*, *Bolsa Alimentação*, *Bolsa Escola*, and *Cartão Alimentação* unified in 2004 under the family grant program

Source: Azzoni et al. (2007)

In the case of cash transfers to poor households, it is clear that the poorer regions should receive resources more than proportionally to their share in GDP and even in total population, as the distribution criteria are associated with the absolute number of poor people (or residences). This remark explains the high average share of the northeastern and northern region, which reach, as it can be seen, 64 percent of the total. This number, by itself, shows the importance of the program to relieve poverty and give visibility to governmental initiatives in poor areas. However, this initiative cannot define a new development path without correlated efforts. In the case of the northeastern region, for instance, the federal resources allocated to the family grant program from 2003 up to 2006 correspond to more than two times the federal investments directed to this region in the same period.

Conclusion

The aim of this chapter was to discuss regional development policies effectively adopted in Brazil during the period 2003–2006, focusing on the regional distribution of resources over which the federal government has discretionary power. It was argued that central governments have four main instruments available to deal with regional distribution of economic activities: 1) fiscal incentives; 2) financial incentives (long-term credit at more attractive conditions); 3) direct investments by the central government, both in infrastructure and in the productive sector; and 4) cash allowances, usually associated with poverty reduction programs and appearing as direct cash transfers to households. Based upon a brief literature review, it was shown that the periods of convergence among Brazilian states were associated with a more intensive use of such instruments by the federal government.

Regionalized data about these instruments collected for the period between 2003 and 2006 showed that 1) fiscal incentives are not specifically directed to the northeastern region, although the northern and the center-western regions in fact obtain these incentives more than proportionally to their shares in Brazil's GDP; 2) BNDES tends to concentrate its credits in the richer states; 3) when regional constitutional funds are considered, the average level of financial incentives provided by the federal government are, at best, neutral; 5) direct investments by the federal government benefit indeed the poorer regions; however, investments by companies directly controlled by the federal government (which handle proportionally more resources) do not seem to be used as an instrument to promote regional development; and 5) cash allowance programs are in fact directed to the poorer regions (as they have more poor people); however, the impact of these instruments on the long-term development is at least controversial, and the resources allocated are small when compared to the amounts directed to the other instruments.

In short, our main conclusion is that, even if regional funds and cash allowance programs are considered, Brazil still lacks an active regional development policy coordinated by the federal government. During the period 2003 to 2006, in spite of the atmosphere of criticism of the neoliberal policies adopted in the precedent decade, the major resources discretionarily allocated by the federal government continued to follow mainly market-oriented criteria. Hence, our conclusions extend to the period 2003–2006 the findings of Monteiro Neto (2006), who argued that during the period of "liberal inspiration" (1990–2002), the government "lost its capacity to define growth trajectories in the regional economies." Regional policies, which could play an important role in dealing with the serious distributional problems that characterized Brazil's territory, are not really being applied to mitigate structural fragilities and to support a new basis for the development of the poorer regions.

Notes

1. During the ceremony recreating SUDENE, in July 2003, the president declared: "estamos, na prática substituindo a guerra fiscal predatória e auto-destrutiva por uma verdadeira política de desenvolvimento regional [we are, in practice, replacing the predatory and self-destructive fiscal war by a real regional development policy]," *Folha de São Paulo*, July 29, 2003, translated by the authors).
2. Interestingly, Krugman (1998: 17) named them "high development theory circa 1958."
3. In Brazil, the concept of Local Productive Arrangements (APL) supports many initiatives of local development based on association and partnership (Amaral Filho, 2001; Lastres and Cassiolato, 2005).
4. The authors state that "the spending initially associated with the New Deal had social purpose." Later on, military spending became another way to promote the development of the region. In their words, "defense spending has thus been extremely important for the south" (Baer and Miles, 1999: 184).
5. Although this classification had originally been proposed for the instruments used at a state level (and not managed by the Federal Government), it seems applicable to government interventions in general.
6. Taking this into consideration, the inclusion of cash transfers among the central government instruments to promote regional development seems to be appropriate, in order to consider the poverty reduction actions taken by the Brazilian government in the recent period.
7. Although more effectively applied when central governments assumed the coordination of the process, this set of instruments can be adopted at any jurisdictional level.
8. The formerly BNDE was created in 1952.
9. During the presidential campaign, José Serra, "além da volta da Sudene,…prometeu que um eventual governo seu [teria] uma coordenação forte para as áreas de incentivos fiscais, recursos do Banco do Nordeste e investimentos [besides the recreation of the SUDENE,…promised that, if elected, his government would have a strong coordination for fiscal incentives, resources of the Bank of Northeast and investments]," *Folha de São Paulo*, April 20, 2002, translated by the authors. Also, Lula "voltou a defender a recriação da Sudene, extinta pelo governo Fernando Henrique Cardoso por acumular denúncias de irregularidades [argued in favor of the recreation of SUDENE, previously extinguished by Cardoso's government due to complaints of irregularities]," *Folha de São Paulo*, July 16, 2002, translated by the authors.
10. Constitutional obligations transfers were not considered, as they are mandatory. These transfers include rural retirement programs (which, in practice, are cash allowance programs) and the transfers to state and county governments.
11. For evidence of the concentration of federal universities in the more developed regions of Brazil, see Fagundes, Cavalcante, and Ramacciotti (2005a).

12. Total expenditures in science and technology by the Federal Government reached, in 2005, R$7.0 billion. These values take account of several kinds of expenditures, including human resources costs of the institutional structures maintained by the government in Brasília. Only a small share of these values can be regionalized, and previous works showed that these resources are highly concentrated in the richer regions of the country (Fagundes, Cavalcante, and Ramacciotti, 2005b).

13. Federal Constitution of Brazil, article 165, paragraph n. 6 (Brasil. Constituição, 1988).

14. Several hypotheses can be formulated to explain this movement. Agroindustrial expansion or growth resulting of increasing external sales (expanding the basis over which the incentives are applied) might be behind these movements.

15. Not only are resources allocated in these agencies too small, but also the requirements for accessing the funds are considerable.

16. In the graph, the logarithm of the share that each state has in the total BNDES disbursements yi is plotted against the share that each state has in the national GDP xi. In order to obtain the values of yi, all the BNDES disbursements in the period 2003–2006 were expressed in constant 2006 R$, and summed to allow the calculation of the share that each state obtained of the total amount.

17. Statistical analysis show that a can be considered higher than 1.0000 at a 99.94 percent confidence level.

18. Although mandatory, these funds are not always entirely disbursed. That explains why they were considered discretionary resources. The option for the funds instead of the disbursement of regional development banks (BNB and BASA) results from the fact that these banks are not only focused on financing long-term projects, but also on the so-called commercial operations (i.e., short term). Besides, for the long run, they use mainly constitutional funds resources, and sometimes also BNDES resources (that would be then double counted). Finally, no data on long-term credits were available for the Center-Western region, and for BASA only total credits (not segmented in long term and short term) are available.

19. According to *Contas Abertas*, the investments by the 68 state companies included in the federal budget reached, in 2005, R$28 billion. In 2006, data on the Federal Government Investment Budget indicate R$41.7 billion to the state companies. This value is practically the same obtained when the investments registered by Petrobras and Eletrobrás in their annual reports are summed. The convergence between these numbers indicates that no significant error results from the use of only these two companies.

20. Although the technical and market-oriented criteria adopted by these companies are not in question, the fact is that, in the past, some of their investment decisions took also into consideration issues related to regional development policies.

21. These investments are not only small in relation to the set of public resources considered in this paper, but also when compared to the investments made by the state companies.

22. The reason why other cash transfers such as rural retirement have not been considered in this chapter is that the government has no discretionary power on their distribution, as they are established by law.

References

Além, Ana Cláudia. 1998. "O desempenho do BNDES no período recente e as metas da Política Econômica." Texto para discussão, n. 65. Rio de Janeiro: BNDES. July.

Amaral Filho, Jair do. 2001. "A endogeneização no desenvolvimento econômico regional e local." *Planejamento e Políticas Públicas*. Brasília: IPEA, n. 23, pp. 261–286, June.

Andrade, Thompson Almeida. 1998. "As desigualdades inter-regionais de desenvolvimento econômico no Brasil." Texto para Discussão Interna, n. 156. Rio de Janeiro: IPEA. October.

Azzoni, Carlos Roberto. 2001. "Economic Growth and Regional Income Inequality in Brazil." *The Annals of Regional Science* 35:133–152.

Azzoni, C.R, J.J.M. Guilhoto, E.A. Haddad, G.J.D. Hewings, M.A. Laes, and G. Moreira. 2007. "'Neither Here nor There': Regionally Targeted Social Policy or Socially Targeted Regional Policy? The First Years of Lula's Administration." Paper Presented in the Conference Brasil: President Lula's First Administration, University of Illinois at Urbana-Champaign, April.

Baer, Werner. 2002. *A economia brasileira*. 2nd. ed. São Paulo: Nobel.

———. 1996. *A Industrialização e o desenvolvimento econômico do Brasil*. 7th. ed. Rio de Janeiro: Editora da Fundação Getúlio Vargas, 1988. Primeira edição em português: 1966.

Baer, Werner, and Pedro Pinchas Geiger. 1978. "Industrialização, urbanização e a persistência das desigualdades regionais no Brasil." In Werner Baer, Pedro Pinchas Geiger, and Paulo Roberto Haddad, eds. *Dimensões do desenvolvimento brasileiro*. Rio de Janeiro: Editora Campus. pp. 65–150.

Baer, Werner, and William R. Miles. 1999. "The Role of the State in United States Regional Development." *Revista Econômica do Nordeste* 30(2) (April–June):178–190.

Barros, José Roberto Mendonça de. [1970] 1973. "A experiência regional de planejamento." In Betty Mindlin Lafer, ed. *Planejamento no Brasil*. 2nd. ed. São Paulo: Perspectiva, pp. 111–137.

Bonelli, Régis, and Armando C. Pinheiro. 1994. "O papel de poupança compulsória no financiamento do desenvolvimento: desafios para o BNDES." *Revista do BNDES* 1(1) (June):17–36.

Bordin, Luís C.V. 2003. "ICMS: gastos tributários e receita potencial. VIII prêmio de monografia do Tesouro Nacional, 2003." Available at http://www.stn.fazenda.gov.br/Premio_TN/VIIIPremio/sistemas/MHafdpVIIIPTN/mh_pemio_tosi.pdf accessed on April 5, 2007.

Brasil. Constituição. 1988. "Constituição da República Federativa do Brasil." Available at https://www.Planalto.Gov.Br/Ccivil_03/Constituicao/Constitui%C3%A7ao.htm accessed on January 17, 2006.

Brasil. Ministério Da Integração Regional. 2007. "Política Nacional de Desenvolvimento Regional—Sumário Executivo." Brasília: Ministério da Integração Regional.

Cano, Wilson. 1985. "Desequilíbrios regionais e concentração industrial no Brasil: 1930–1970." São Paulo: Global; Campinas: UNICAMP.

———. 1995. "Auge e inflexão da desconcentração econômica regional no Brasil." In Encontro Nacional De Economia—ANPEC, 23. Salvador, Bahia. Anais. Salvador: ANPEC, 1995. 1 CD-ROM.

Cavalcante, Luiz Ricardo M.T. 2003. "Desigualdades regionais no Brasil: uma análise do período 1985–1999." *Revista Econômica do Nordeste* 4(3) (July–September):466–481.

Cavalcante, Luiz Ricardo M.T., and Simone Uderman. 2006. "The Cost of a Structural Change: A Large Automobile Plant in the State of Bahia." *Latin American Business Review* 7(3/4):11–48.

Cobb, James C. 1993. *The Selling of the South: The Southern Crusade for Industrial Development 1936–1990*. Urbana and Chicago: University of Illinois Press.

Dall'erba, Sandy. 2003. "European Regional Development Policies: History and Current Issues." Working Paper 2(4). University of Illinois EUC.

Diniz, Clélio Campolina. 1993. "Desenvolvimento Poligonal no Brasil: Nem Desconcentração, nem Contínua Polarização." *Nova Economia* 3(1):35–64.

Fagundes, Maria Emília, Luiz Ricardo Cavalcante, and Rafael Lucchesi Ramacciotti. 2005a. "Desigualdades regionais em Ciência e Tecnologia no Brasil." *Bahia Análise e Dados* 14(4):755–768.

———. 2005b. "Distribuição regional dos fluxos de recursos federais para ciência e tecnologia." *Parcerias Estratégicas* (21) (December):59–78.

Ferreira, Afonso Henriques Borges, and Clélio Campolina Diniz. 1995. "Convergência entre as rendas per capita no Brasil." *Revista de Economia Política* 15(4) (October–December):38–56.

Friedmann, John. 1975. "Regional Development Planning: The Progress of a Decade." In John Friedmann and William Alonso, eds. *Regional Policy: Reading in Theory and Applications*. Cambridge: MIT Press. pp. 791–807.

Fugita, Masahisa, Paul Krugman, and Anthony J. Venables. 1999. *The Spatial Economy: Cities, Regions, and International Trade*. Cambridge: MIT.

Fugita, Masahisa, and Jacques-François Thisse. 2002. *Economics of Agglomeration: Cities, Industrial Location, and Regional Growth*. Cambridge: Cambridge University Press.

GTDN. 1997. "Uma política de desenvolvimento para o Nordeste." *Revista Econômica do Nordeste* 28(4) (October–December):387–432. Original Publication: 1959.

Haddad, Paulo R. 1978. "As políticas de desenvolvimento regional no Brasil: notas para uma avaliação." In Werner Baer, Pedro Pinchas Geiger, and Paulo Roberto Haddad, eds. *Dimensões do desenvolvimento brasileiro*. Rio de Janeiro: Editora Campus. pp. 385–396.

Hirschman, Albert O. 1958. *The Strategy of Economic Development.* New Haven: Yale University Press.

Krugman, Paul. [1995] 1998. *Development, Geography, and Economic Theory.* 4th ed. The Ohlin Lectures; 6. Massachusetts: MIT Press.

Lastres, Helena M.M., and José E. Cassiolato. 2005. *Mobilizando conhecimentos para desenvolver arranjos e sistemas produtivos e inovativos locais de micro e pequenas empresas no Brasil.* Rio de Janeiro: UFRJ/ SEBRAE. Available at http://redesist.ie.ufrj.br/glossario.php accessed on July 28, 2006.

Luger, Michael I. 1987. "The States and Industrial Development: Program Mix and Policy Effectiveness." *Perspectives on Local Public Finance and Public Policy* 3:29–63.

Miyoshi, Takahiro. 1997. "Successes and Failures Associated with the Growth Pole Strategies." MA Dissertation, Manchester: University of Manchester.

Monteiro Neto, Aristides. 2006. "Intervenção estatal e desigualdades regionais no Brasil: contribuições ao debate contemporâneo." Texto para discussão n. 1229. Brasília: IPEA, December.

Moreira, Raimundo. 1979. *O Nordeste brasileiro: uma política regional de industrialização.* Rio de Janeiro: Paz e Terra.

Myrdal, Gunnar. [1957] 1960. *Teoria econômica e regiões subdesenvolvidas.* Rio de Janeiro: UFMG Biblioteca Universitária.

Nurkse, Ragnar. 1953. *Problems of Capital Formation in Underdeveloped Countries.* New York: Oxford University Press.

Perroux, François. [1955] 1997. "O conceito de pólo de desenvolvimento." In J. Schwartzman, ed. *Economia regional: textos escolhidos.* Belo Horizonte: CEDEPLAR.

Putnam, Robert D. 1993. "The Prosperous Community: Social Capital and Public Life." *The American Prospect* 13:35–42.

Rosenstein-Rodan, P.N. 1953. "Problems of Industrialisation of Eastern and South-Eastern Europe." *The Economic Journal* 53(210–211)(June–September):202–211.

Souza, Filipe L. 2003. "O Papel do BNDES na Distribuição Geográfica da Indústria de Transformação." *Revista do BNDES* 10(19) (June):3–20.

Suzigan, Wilson, and Aloísio Barbosa de Araújo. 1979. "Política industrial, regionalização e financiamento do desenvolvimento." In ASSOCIAÇÃO BRASILEIRA DE BANCOS DE DESENVOLVIMENTO. *Desenvolvimento e desconcentração da economia: Painéis do II Seminário de Integração Nacional.* Rio de Janeiro. pp. 7–73.

Uderman, Simone. 2001. *Estratégias de Desenvolvimento Regional: uma análise dos desembolsos do sistema BNDES para a Bahia nos anos 90.* Salvador: SEPLANTEC/SPE.

————. 2007. *Padrões de organização industrial e políticas de desenvolvimento regional: uma análise das estratégias de industrialização na Bahia.* 221 f. Tese (Doutorado em Administração)—Escola de Administração. Salvador, Universidade Federal da Bahia.

Williamson, J.G. 1965. "Regional Inequality and the Process of National Development." *Economic Development and Cultural Change* 13:3–45.

CHAPTER FIFTEEN

Northeast Brazil under the Lula Government

ALEXANDRE RANDS BARROS AND
ANDRÉ MATOS MAGALHÃES

Introduction

The Northeast is the region with the lowest per capita GDP in Brazil.[1] While average per capita GDP in 2003 was US\$4,309.24 per year, in the Northeast it only amounted to US\$2,134.34. The second poorest region in the country was the North, but its yearly per capita GDP was US\$2,731.81. This lower per capita GDP is particularly relevant when one takes into account that the Northeast is the region where 27.64 percent of Brazilian population lives. It has the second largest population in the country. It is therefore a problem that has to be tackled.

While campaigning in 2002, President Lula stressed that reducing poverty was possible and should be a priority. As poverty is not evenly distributed spatially, the regional question was one of the main issues. There was the promise that special attention to the region should be one of the government's major goals. Particularly, there was the idea that a new version of the regional development agency, SUDENE, should be created, as it has had been extinguished in the previous administration.

After four years in office, many measures were taken by President Lula's government that affected the region. SUDENE was only recently re-created, but other measures had a notable impact on the region. Thus, President Lula's reelection was most notable in the Northeast, where he got 77.13 percent of the votes. This is therefore a good point to evaluate what was done to reduce regional disparity, especially with respect to the Northeast.

It is our hypothesis that there was a crucial change in the logic of the development model adopted under Lula, one that benefited the Northeastern economy. The emphasis on growth promotion fostering efficiency and competitiveness, which started under President Collor, continued in the two terms of President Cardoso and the first term of President Lula. Nevertheless, there was a crucial change in this conception. The current Brazilian leadership endorses the proposition that most agents can be economically efficient and even internationally competitive, if they are subject to the right incentives. The previous model of the 1990s and early 2000s was rooted in the view that efficient and internationally competitive sectors would emerge only through their exposure to competition, as they already contain the intrinsic attributes needed to achieve these. The ideology of the Lula government differs in that it implicitly introduced the conception that most agents can be efficient and competitive, if there are appropriate policies to promote their necessary adjustments. Policies toward the shipbuilding and petrochemical industries, as well as those to increase the quality of education, health services, and the access to technology and credit by small farmers, are examples of this change in conception. Other examples will be mentioned below.

This change in the economic policy framework had an important impact on the Northeast, as agents working in this backward region had less ability to promptly respond to competitive incentives. The new technological developments since the 1980s have been skill-biased,[2] as education made impressive strides in the developed economies.[3] Thus, countries that had a highly educated labor force had an easier time to adjust to these new technologies. The same was the case of regions with a greater supply of more skilled labor.

When agents in the more backward regions had the opportunity to benefit from more social support to adjust, as proposed by the new development ideology, the "ability gap" to reach certain efficiency standards was reduced. Therefore, overall, Lula's government had a strong positive impact on the development of this more backward region.

A second part of the major hypothesis of this chapter is that the changes in the policy framework that benefit poorer regions also had an impact on the relative regional per capita GDP equilibrium, so that the higher growth of the Northeast is not trend-reverting. It will lead the region to reach another relative development level with lower regional inequality. It will be argued that the new logic of economic policy squeezed the sources of regional imbalances. Nevertheless, the main policies for the region still had a limited effect on some of the determinants of regional inequality. Therefore, they are still not enough to eliminate the imbalances in the long run. An even greater effort for such ends will be necessary to eliminate Brazil's regional disparities.

Some Facts on Recent Development of the Northeast

The Northeast had a per capita GDP that reached only 51 percent of the national average in 2004. It also had five among the six of the poorest states in the country (figure 15.1). Its share of Brazil's GDP increased from 10.6 percent in 1955 to 14.1 percent in 2003, but it is still quite low, given its current share of Brazilian population, which is 27.6 percent. Thus, in spite of all policies to reduce regional inequalities since the 1960s, there was very

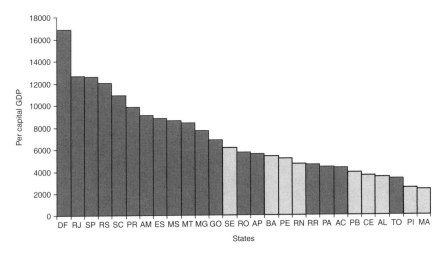

Figure 15.1   Per capita GDP in Brazilian states in 2003 (R$)

Note: States in gray are those of the Northeast

Source: IBGE—Regional Accounts

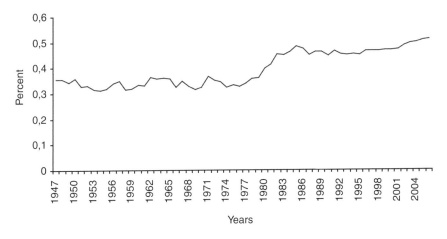

Figure 15.2   Share of Northeast per capita GDP of Brazilian per capita GDP

Source: Author's calculations based on IPEADATA

little narrowing of disparities. This indicates that there is an equilibrium inequality that tends to persist, as its causes have not been deeply affected.

Figure 15.2 shows the long-term share of Northeastern per capita GDP of that of Brazil. It can be easily observed that only in very few periods was there a substantial increase in this share. In the decade between the mid-1970s and the mid-1980s there was an important decline in the disparities. Since 2001, there also has been a gradual increase in the share. Therefore, real change in long-term regional inequality only came gradually.

Convergence theory would predict that the poorest region would grow faster than the whole country. Between 1947 and 2005, the Brazilian per capita GDP grew at an average annual rate of 2.67 percent, while the

Northeast per capita GDP grew at 3.28 percent. Nevertheless, this higher per capita growth was stronger in the decade between 1976 and 1985 and has had a new upsurge this century, especially after 2001. Therefore, the convergence observed does not seems to be an absolute one, but rather a relative one, where some disparity still would persist in equilibrium.

The Northeast also has the largest share of population living under the poverty line, as can be seen in figure 15.3. This share is almost five times the one found in the Southeast, the richest and the most populous region in the country. Poverty is so much deeper in the region because it has a higher income concentration. While the Gini coefficient in Brazil reached 0.569 in 2005, it was 0.571 in the Northeast. Thus the region not only has a very low per capita income, but also has a large share of population living under the poverty line and an extremely concentrated income distribution. These data indicate that despite almost 50 years of policy aimed at closing the gap the regional problem persists.

These inequalities spread to most areas that are relevant for economic growth. For example, the average years of schooling of the Northeast's population was only 5 years for the population of 20-years-old in 2005, while the national average was 6.5 years and in Southeast this statistic was 7.2 years.

Such a disparity can also be found in the quality of education. The last exams of SAEB and the National Exam for High School Students (Exame Nacional do Ensino Médio—ENEM) revealed such differences. The former is taken by students of fourth and eighth grades in middle school, while the latter is taken by students who finished high school. Figures 15.4 and 15.5

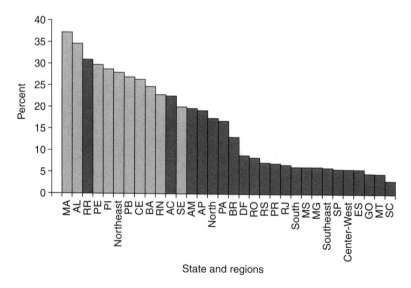

Figure 15.3 Share of population living under poverty line in Brazilian states, 2004

Note: Data for states in the North are only urban population. Poverty line is defined as half the minimum wage per capita in the household

Source: Datamétrica, calculated with data from IBGE, PNAD 2004

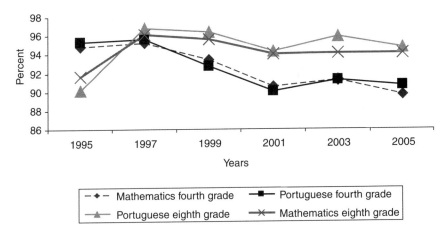

Figure 15.4 Performance of students of Northeastern urban schools as a proportion of performance of Brazilian students

Note: These are statistics from the performance of students on tests by the Sistema de Avaliação de Educação Básica (System for Evaluating Basic Education—SAEB). These tests are administered to Brazilian youth every two years. The same exams are taken by all students, and normalizations assure that results are inter-temporally comparable

Source: Original data are from the Instituto Nacional de Estudos e Pesquisas Educacionais (National Institute of Studies and Educational Research—INEP)

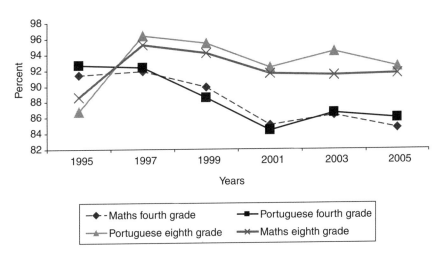

Figure 15.5 Performance of students of Northeastern urban schools as a proportion of performance of Southeastern students

Note: These are statistics from performance of students on the SAEB tests, which are taken every two years by Brazilian students. The same exams are administered to all students, and normalizations assure that results are inter-temporally comparable

Source: Original data are from INEP

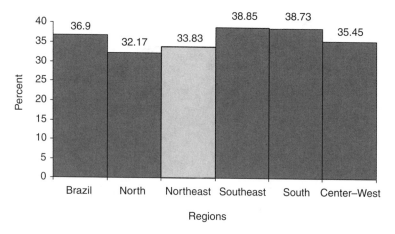

Figure 15.6 Performance of students in ENEM 2006

Note: These are statistics from performance of students on the SAEB tests, which are administered every two years to Brazilian students. The same exams are given to all youth, and normalizations assure that results are inter-temporally comparable

Source: Original data are from INEP

reveal that the performance of Northeastern students was not only worse than those of the country as a whole or those of the southeast region in the last exams, but they also have a falling relative performance since 1997. Thus, the relative educational quality has been falling in the last 10 years.

The other exam, ENEM, is made up of students who finish secondary school. Figure 15.6 shows the results of this exam for various regions in 2006. They indicate that students in Northeast performed below the national average and the ones in the most developed regions, which are the Southeast and the (Far) South. Such results also show that inequality exists even in investments in quality of education.

Recent Trends on Relative Economic Output

The relative economic performance of the Northeastern economy during the Lula government was positive. Figure 15.7 indicates that the share of regional GDP in the national one has increased during President Lula's first term. Therefore, the first obvious evidence is that the development strategy adopted in these years had a positive impact in the relative performance of the region. Nevertheless, after 1995, there was already some increase in the share of the region in the national GDP, although still small, when compared to what happened after 2002, one year before Lula's term as president began.

There are three most commonly used hypotheses to explain this phenomenon. The first and most trivial one is the convergence hypothesis, which stresses that less developed regions tend to grow faster than the others.[4] The second one states that the strong distributive policies started in Fernando

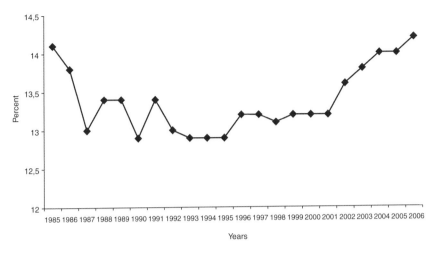

Figure 15.7   Share of Northeast GDP of Brazilian GDP

Source: IPEADATA

Henrique Cardoso's (FHC) term in office (1995–2002) benefit more agents in less developed regions and, consequently, strengthened their relative economic performance. As the Lula government continued these policies, he achieved even more. This is in line with the per capita GDP behavior since FHC era. The third hypothesis is the one stressed in this chapter that adds to the second argument an extra impulse to the performance of the region arising from the new logic of economic policies and that introduced mechanisms to help agents that are not readily efficient and competitive.

It is important to emphasize that this third hypothesis is only an extension of the second one, which incorporates the effort made by Lula's government to shift the emphasis of policies from the simple compensation for exclusion to the effort to include agents left behind the economically efficient and competitive groups. Compensatory social policies are already an instrument of protection for the less apt to succeed in a competitive environment. The idea is that in Lula's government these compensatory policies started to be seen as transitory palliatives that should be substituted as much as possible by inclusive policies, so that policies for both firms and people started to have this other inclusive logic. This could benefit the Northeast more, as it has a lower share of already efficient agents and a lower access to the human resources necessary to foster inclusion in the market.

It was already seen that the convergence hypothesis does not seem to lead to an absolute equality of per capita income, but rather to a relative one. Furthermore, the relatively faster growth in Northeast at some periods was followed by stagnation in convergence thereafter. Thus convergence alone would not explain the behavior of per capita GDP in the last four years, unless there was some change in the relative equilibrium pursued since 1985. Then this structural change in the disparity would have the same as the one presented in this chapter.

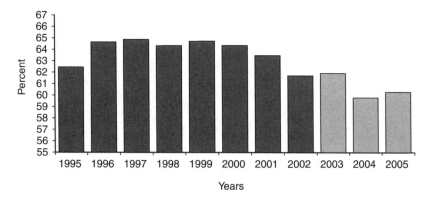

Figure 15.8   Brazil: Share of consumption of total GDP
Source: IBGE—National Accounts

It is worth noting that, although there was an expansion in transference policies for poverty alleviation in the period 2003 to 2006, private consumption declined in its share in Brazil's GDP during these years. This is shown in figure 15.8. It indicates that investment and government consumption together with exports probably had a larger role in the expansion of GDP during those years. Therefore, it is less probable that a policy that would raise private consumption becomes the leading force in explaining the relative higher performance of a region. This evidence also points to a different additional explanation for the role of fiscal transfers in the relative performance of the Northeastern economy.

Dispersion of Sectoral Expansion with Governmental Support

A main assumption of the hypothesis presented in this chapter is that there was a change in the public policy approach to agents and sectors. While in the previous model of development, most incentives were for a selected group of agents who could prosper in a more competitive environment, Lula's government moved priorities to extend incentives for those agents who could catch up if they benefit from some support. The idea is that such a framework demands less compensatory policies, so that it has an efficient cost-benefit result. If the change in approach occurred, there would be a change in the sectoral distribution of loans by BNDES, the state-owned development bank that provides credit at lower rates than the financial market and is responsible for a nontrivial share of the country's total long-term loans. It is expected that a more even distribution of these credits among sectors would arise, so that the standard deviations of the share of each sector in total credits would fall. Figure 15.9 shows the monthly standard deviations from January of 1995 to February of 2007.

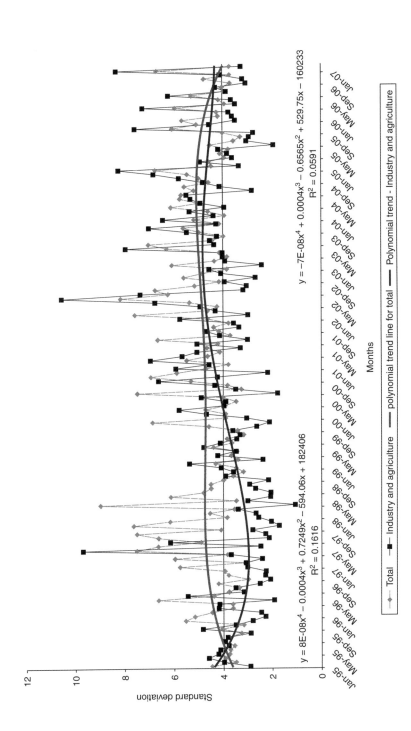

Figure 15.9 Monthly standard deviation of sectorial shares in BNDES loans

Source: Calculated from BNDES data

The time series for standard deviations shown in figure 15.9 was calculated for 41 sectors of CNAE, including economic and social infrastructure, industries, and agriculture (as one sector consolidated). It indicates that from mid-2003, it is possible to find a change in the long-term trend, so that there was a decline in standard deviations, as would happen if there was this change in the nature of economic policies as is argued in this chapter.

The Northeast According to Modern
Development Theory

To understand the impact of the changes in policies on the equilibrium of regional inequality, it is necessary to know what are the determinants of such inequality and how they can be affected. Regional disparity exists when there is a regional imbalance of per capita income among regions that is generated from market failures or different conditions from those established by the Arrow-Debreu model. It does not necessarily imply that there is a regional problem, as this one emerges when welfare of someone can improve without any loss of welfare for someone else in any of the regions involved.[5] Regional disparity can emerge mainly from seven possible sources: 1) Economies of scale in some activities with a high share of total activities;[6] 2) positive externalities arising from agglomeration of economic activities or the use of some factors of production; 3) imbalances in infrastructure, which are determined by political factors;[7] 4) the availability of natural resources;[8] 6) differences in the availability of social capital[9]; and 7) differences in the adequacy of social institutions.

There is the conviction that there is a regional problem in Brazil, so that market inefficiencies are relevant to determine regional disparities.[10] Although there is not enough rigorous empirical investigation on the relative role of these determinants of Brazil's regional problem, all the seven sources of regional imbalance are normally assumed to exist. Most are recognized by modern growth theory as also important determinants of economic growth. There is no emphasis in this literature on the existence of increasing returns to scale in particular activities or the availability of natural resources.[11] Therefore, the tackling of the regional problem in Brazil tends to coincide with a development policy, if the government focuses on the right obstacles that impede regional convergence.

Past regional policies in Brazil tended to focus on two factors determining regional disparities. The first one was the existence of scale economies in some activities. Industry was chosen as the major activity subject to such increasing return to scale. Therefore, many subsidies were allocated to investments in this sector. The second one was the imbalance in the availability in the economic infrastructure. Some investments were carried our in infrastructure in the Northeast, often more than proportionally to what the allocation of resources might have been, given the share of the region's share of national income. Nevertheless, this effort was not very successful, as political pressure from other regions was high and the results were meager. Barros and Raposo (2002) presented some estimation on the relative availability of economic infrastructure in many states in Brazil. Their conclusion was that the Northeast actually had a deficit in these infrastructures given its per capita income and population density.

There is a recent literature on the impact of institutions on economic growth.[12] The idea is that these institutions are dependent on political relations among social classes. Although Brazil is a single nation, and consequently most of the local institutional framework is the same for all regions and states, social class is also relevant to understand the relative backwardness of Northeast. The social structure of the region is peculiar and arose from particular historical circumstances. Therefore, the relationships among different social strata have local specificities. Furthermore, the working of some of its institutions also has some peculiarities. Such differences could also be an important determinant of regional disparities.

The Path for Regional Development

The goals to foster the regional development in the Northeast, given the view on development and the sources of regional disparities, are to: 1) increase the educational achievement of the local population; 2) increase infrastructure availability and their efficiency in reducing costs of production; 3) increase the availability of social capital; and 4) improve the quality of social institutions. The other sources of regional disparities that are not directly contemplated by these goals are less important in the light of modern growth theory or of economic reality.

Increasing Educational Achievements

The gap in education in the Northeast is of two sorts. One is the lower level of average schooling in this region, when compared to the most developed regions in the country, as was seen in the section Some Facts on Recent Development of Northeast. The other emerges from the lower quality of education that is provided in the region, also when compared to what is found in the most developed regions. Data in this section also indicate that there is lower quality of education in the region. Therefore, any regional policy of development has to tackle these two problems.

The availability of human capital, which has educational achievement as one of its major sources, generates externalities that are taken as crucial for development and that are not efficiently provided for incentives generated by market forces. Therefore, its accumulation is one of the major goals of promoting regional development in the region.

Increasing Infrastructure Availability

Increasing infrastructure availability can also attract more economic activities to the region. Therefore, if the Northeast had a better infrastructure availability, it would be able to attract more investments and, consequently, to grow relatively faster.

The Northeast's historical background, which is rooted in export-led growth mainly of primary commodities, assures that the local infrastructure is already biased toward long-distance trade. Therefore, not only roads, ports, and airports already point to foreign markets, but also cities are spatially dispersed and organized for this same purpose. Nevertheless, there are still vast areas that can generate exports that did not exist during the long primary commodities export era. These regions are thus poorly supplied with economic infrastructure and, consequently, their local costs of production are high. Scattered economic activities in these peripheries reduce scale economies for their local centers, weakening regional efficiency.

Increasing Social Capital Availability

There is no rigorous study that confirms that there is less social capital in the Northeast than in other regions. Nevertheless, the few indicators available, such as the rate of bad checks to the total, which is shown in figure 15.10, suggest that this is a reality. Therefore, to increase its availability of social

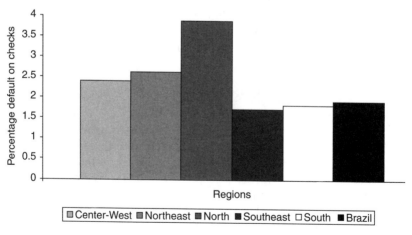

Figure 15.10   Average default on checks—September to November, 2006
Source: Telecheque

capital through policies that promote trust among agents can be a relevant way to reduce regional disparity in Brazil, making the Northeast grow relatively faster.

Improving the Quality of Social Institutions

There exist no study that indicates that social institutions in the Northeast are less apt to promote economic growth and development than in the Southeast. Nevertheless, the local institutional framework was settled under a stronger Portuguese and rural tradition, which are more bureaucratic and less efficient than other institutional cultures that had a greater influence in the southeast and south regions. It is thus reasonable to expect that the Northeastern institutional framework is relatively less efficient than the one that prevails in the most developed regions.

The National Association of Mayors created an index to measure fiscal and social responsibility. This index tries to capture a combined performance of county administrations on fiscal management and social concerns. This index was created taking into account variables that are indicators of fiscal performance, such as debts, cash flows, and salary payments, and of social performance, such as school enrollment, health expenditures, and so on. A principal component analysis was used to create the fiscal and social responsibility index. There exists such an index for most Brazilian counties. This index is to some extent an indication of institutional development, as counties with higher performance in the two areas it measures tend to have more appropriate institutions. Goods institutions tend to provide a county with better fiscal performance and social policies.

The total number of counties for which the data are available, which is 4285, was divided into five quintiles. The share of Northeastern counties in each quintile was calculated. The data appear in figure 15.11. They

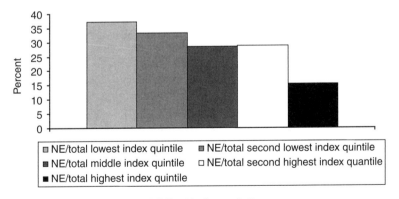

Figure 15.11 Share of Northeastern of total number of counties in each quintile of ranked fiscal and social responsibility index

Source: Elaborated by authors from index generated by Associação Brasileira de Municípios

show that the share of Northeastern counties falls when the quintiles rises. There is a higher share of Northeastern counties in those quintiles with the lowest fiscal and social responsibility index. This suggests that there is a less developed institutional environment in the Northeast than in the national average.

What Has Been Done

The Lula government does not have much of a specific policy for the Northeast. The reinauguration of SUDENE took a long time and it still does not have a final shape that can be evaluated. Nevertheless, there were several other actions that impacted the region directly. They were mainly:

- The government expanded compensatory policies with transfers to individual poor families. *Bolsa Família* and *Bolsa Escola* are the major programs in this category. These transfers were increased in Lula's government and were unevenly distributed regionally. Citizens in the Northeast benefit proportionally more, as there are more poor people in the region.
- There were important improvements in the management and control of these poverty alleviation policies in Lula's government. One was the establishment of the *Cadastro Único*, a single database for the beneficiaries of all policies. Another was the purchase of more local goods in the distribution programs for the poor, such foods in a government-calculated basic basket of goods.

All these actions benefit the Northeast not only by its share on transfers, but also because of their consequences on other determinants of the relatively lower equilibrium income in the region. The best control of *Bolsa Escola* created an incentive to increase local human capital and forced the absorption of some technologies of control, which help local agents improve their own institutions. The local purchases of goods, to be included in the bundles to be distributed to the poor, raised scale economies for local producers. As these purchases are made from cooperatives, there is one more incentive for small producers to organize in cooperatives. Consequently, this policy also promotes the creation of local social capital.

There was also a massive expansion of credit to the poor population during Lula's first term. This was for many purposes. There were productive credits from two programs, the Banco do Brasil's Fortalecimento da Agricultura Familiar (Strengthening the Family Farm—PRONAF) and the constitutionally mandated Fundo do Nordeste (FNE). These two entities helped small farmers and small Northeastern businesses, respectively. They were both offered at very low interest rates, when compared to alternatives in the market. There were also consumer credits that were raised by the linkage (*consignação*) with monthly sources of income, such as salaries and retirement disbursements. These credits were made at lower rates than those obtained in the market and could be directed to consumption. The low-income population also had more access to housing credits. All these credit opportunities raised the share of the poor population with regard to total credit availability.

Although only one of these credit lines were specific for Northeastern citizens—the FNE—the greater access of the low income population to credit and the relatively high share of Brazil's population in the Northeast assured that the region had an increased share of total credit in the country. These policies also benefited the region in two ways. First, it increased local investment and demand. These consequences tend to increase local scale economies and to improve the agglomeration effects. Both these impacts could also change the long-term relative equilibrium of local per capita GDP. Second, the rise of credit availability also reduces defaults. Consequently, local social capital tends to increase as less default tends to increase trust among agents.

There is also an audacious plan of investments in regional infrastructure projects, such as Transnordestina Railroad, diversion of portions of the São Francisco river, the widening of highway BR 101, and airport renovations. Most of these investments were announced, but are still at very preliminary stages. They will change the share of total investments predicted for the region. Table 15.1 indicates that in the construction of highways, railroads, ports, and airports and the production of energy, the predicted share of investments that benefit the region will be much higher than its share in total GDP (last row).

Table 15.1 Investments predicted by the Programa de Aceleração do Crescimento (Program of Investment Acceleration—PAC) in R$ billions for the 2007–2010 period

Regions	Logistic	Energy	Social and urban	Total	Regional share on total (%)
North	6.3	32.7	11.9	50.9	10.1
Northeast	7.4	29.3	43.7	80.4	16.0
Southeast	7.9	80.8	41.8	130.5	25.9
South	4.5	18.7	14.3	37.5	7.4
Center-West	3.8	11.6	8.7	24.1	4.8
National	28.4	101.7	50.4	180.5	35.8
Total	58.3	274.8	170.8	503.9	100.0
NE/BR identified by region benefiting (%)	24.7	16.9	36.3	24.9	NA

Source: Ministry of Finance

These infrastructure investments also tend to change the equilibrium per capita income among regions, benefiting the Northeast. As there is a relatively high proportion of such investments in the region, its equilibrium per capita GDP tends to be relatively higher in the future. Furthermore, it also will increase the local scale and agglomeration economies in the region. Thus infrastructure investment plans also will bring a structural change in the regional balances in the country.

There also has been support of the federal government for large investments in the Northeast, such as the oil refinery (Petrobrás), the textile complex, and the shipbuilding company Atlântico Sul, both in the Pernambucan port of Suape. Such projects will increase local productive capacities and will be able to attract several other investments. They will be able to increase agglomeration and economies of scale in the region, also changing the long-term equilibrium in relative per capita income in the Brazilian regions.

Lula's Government also established the FDNE, Fundo de Desenvolvimento do Nordeste, which is managed by ADENE. This fund is available to finance investment projects in the region. Although it is still in the beginning of its operational life, it tends to provide investment funds for some local projects at lower rates than those obtained from other sources in the financial market. Therefore, this fund will help foster stronger relationships among local firms and will help achieve economies of scale. Although of limited effect, this policy tends to change the long-term relative equilibrium per capita income of the region.

One of the interventions by Lula's government that assured the change in philosophy of development was the greater emphasis on clustering policies. More public policy agents extended their actions to reduce obstacles to the efficiency of less competitive agents. The Banco do Brasil, SEBRAE,[13] and the Banco do Nordeste are the major institutions relying on this policy approach. All of them have been very active in pursuing such policies in the Northeast.

These clustering policies tend to improve the quality of local institutions and to increase the social capital in the region. Most of the approaches include interactions with county and state institutions, providing them with some technical support to improve their actions or to pressure them to act according to some demands from private agents. These actions strengthen local institutions. The methods also involve the promotion of interaction of agents to achieve common interests. Consequently, they also tend to improve the level of trust among agents, increasing local social capital. It is important to stress, however, that these policies have been given priority in the whole country. There is no evidence that they have had a greater long-term impact in the Northeast than in other regions. There is thus no reason to believe they will lead to any long-term change in the equilibrium of the relative regional per capita income.

Conclusion

The government of Lula frustrated many Brazilians concerned with the regional question, as it did not have a well-defined regional policy. SUDENE is still in the process of being reestablished, four years after Lula entered office and after a first-term campaign that stressed the need for overcoming regional disparity. The focus of the development policies was completely different. There is not much spatial concern in them. The struggle against poverty was the first priority.

There were some changes in policies when compared to those of the previous administrations, which ended up having a huge positive impact in the relative performance of the Northeast. First, there was a reasonable expansion of the poverty alleviation policies, which had a proportionately greater impact in the Northeast, as should be expected, given the relatively higher share of local population in poverty in the region. Second, there was an important change in the pressure for development of competitiveness by national agents. Policy support to enhance competitiveness, in addition to introducing more competition, started to be seen as an appropriate strategy. Such changes in policies assured a relatively better economic performance of the region in the period 2003 to 2006.

These major changes in policies would have short-term impacts on relative regional equilibrium, but they are not enough to generate a long-term structural change in the relative development level of there regions. Nevertheless, they were implemented together with other development policies, often not tailored to benefit the Northeast specifically, which could affect the determinants of the long-term equilibrium of uneven regional development. Therefore, the Lula government was able not only to generate relatively higher growth for Northeast, but also to change its long-term perspective.

Brazilian regional disparity is such that it is far from any even equilibrium. Nevertheless, some steps in that direction have already been taken by the Lula's government. Although it is still too early to estimate the real impact of these policies, it is already possible to envisage that the Northeast will not be the same after the eight years of President Lula in power. Therefore, the votes he obtained in the region in the last presidential ballot are plainly justified.

Notes

1. The northeast region is defined as the contiguous states of Maranhão, Piauí, Ceará, Rio Grande do Norte, Paraíba, Pernambuco, Alagoas, Sergipe, and Bahia.
2. There is an enormous literature stressing such bias. See for example, Autor, Katz, and Kearney (2006), Autor, Levy, and Murnane (2003), and Acemoglu (1998 and 2002).
3. See Barros (1998) for a deeper discussion of this fact.
4. See Barro and Sala-i-Martin (1992) for a theoretical statement of this hypothesis.
5. For a more rigorous presentation and discussion of this concept, see Barros (1998).

6. Fujita, Krugman, and Venables (2002) present models that strongly emphasize such source. See, for example, their model in Chapter Five.
7. See, for example, Barros (2007) for a presentation of a model with such source of regional disparity.
8. See also Barros (2007).
9. Following Putnam (2000), we see social capital as anything that facilitates individual or collective action, generated by networks of relationships, reciprocity, trust, or social norms.
10. See Barros (2007) for a more exhaustive discussion of this view.
11. A recent seminar paper by Acemoglu, Johnson, and Robinson (2001 and 2005) and Acemoglu and Johnson (2005) emphasizes some social aspects that are strongly dependent on geographical conditions. Menezes et al. (2003) found some explanatory power for natural conditions to determine regional disparities in Brazil.
12. See for example Rodrik (2004).
13. Serviço Brasileiro de Apoio aos Micro e Pequenas Empresas (Brazilian Service for the Promotion of Micro and Small Enterprises).

References

Acemoglu, Daron. 1998. "Why Do New Technologies Complement Skills? Directed Technical Change and Wage Inequality." *Quarterly Journal of Economics* 113 (November):1055–1089.

———. 2002. "Directed Technical Change." *Review of Economic Studies* 69:781–810.

Acemoglu, Daron, James Robinson, and Simon Johnson. 2001. "The Colonial Origins of Comparative Development: An Empirical Investigation." *American Economic Review* 91 (December):1369–1401.

Acemoglu, Daron, and Simon Johnson. 2005. "Unbundling Institutions." *Journal of Political Economy* 113 (October):949–995.

Acemoglu, Daron, Simon Johnson, and James A. Robinson. 2005. "Institutions as the Fundamental Cause of Long Run Growth." In P. Aghion and S. Durlauf, eds. *Handbook of Economic Growth*. Vol. 1, ch.6. Elsevier. pp. 385–472.

Autor, David H., Frank Levy, and Richard J. Murnane. 2003. "The Skill Content of Recent Technological Change: An Empirical Exploration." *Quarterly Journal of Economics* 118(4):1279–1334.

Autor, David, Lawrence F. Katz, and Melissa S. Kearney. 2006. "The Polarization of the U.S. Labor Market." NBER Working Papers 11986, National Bureau of Economic Research.

Barro and Sala-i-Martin. 1992. "Convergence." *Journal of Political Economy* 100(2):223–251.

Barros, A.R.C. 1998. "Desigualdades Regionais no Brasil: Causas da Reversão da Tendência na Última Década." In *Anais do V Encontro Nacional sobre Emprego e Desenvolvimento Regional*. Lisboa (Portugal), June.

———. 2007. "Regional Inequality in Perfectly Competitive Markets When There Are Natural Resources and Economic Infrastructure." *Revista Brasileira de Estudos Sociais e Urbanas*. 1. Forthcoming.

Barros, Alexandre Rands and Isabel Raposo. 2002. "Algumas Experiências Internacionais Recentes de Políticas de Desenvolvimento Regional." *Revista Econômica do Nordeste*. Fortaleza 33(4) (October–December):774–790.

Fujita, Masahisa, Paul Krugman, and Anthony Venables. 2000. *The Spatial Economy: Cities, Regions, and International Trade*. Cambridge: MIT Press.

Instituto Brasileiro de Geografia e Estatística—IBGE. Pesquisa Nacional por Amostra de Domicílios—PNAD 2004. Available at www.ibge.gov.br accessed on March 6, 2007.

Instituto Brasileiro de Geografia e Estatística—IBGE. Contas Nacionais. Available at www.ibge.gov.br accessed on March 6, 2007.

Instituto de Pesquisa Econômica Aplicada—IPEA. Contas Nacionais. Available at www.ipeadata.gov.br/ipeaweb.dll/ipeadata?25142437 accessed on March 20, 2007.

Instituto Nacional de Estudos e Pesquisas Educacionais Anísio Teixeira - INEP (2005). Available at www.inep.gov.br accessed on March 30, 2007.

Menezes, Tatiane Almeida De, Fernando Gaiger Silveira, Luis Carlos Magalhães, and Bernardo Palhares Campolina Diniz. 2003. "Elasticidade Renda dos produtos alimentares no Brasil e Regiões Metropolitanas: uma aplicação dos micro-dados da POF 1995/96." In *XXXI Encontro Nacional da ANPEC*, Porto Seguro.

Putnam, Robert D. 2000. *Bowling Alone. The Collapse and Revival of American Community*. New York: Simon and Schuster.

Rodrik, Dani. 2004. *Growth Strategies*. Cambridge: John F. Kennedy School of Government, Harvard University.

PART SIX

The Long-run View

CHAPTER SIXTEEN

The Lula Government in Historical Perspective

JOSEPH L. LOVE

In what ways does the Lula government represent a break with the past? There are many unique features of the Lula administration, beginning with the person of the president: He is the first head of state of a Latin American nation, and one of only a handful in world history, who can claim to be genuine members of the working class. Lula moreover has had less formal education than any previous president of Brazil, and is possibly—I emphasize this is conjecture—the least Caucasian president since Nilo Peçanha (1909–1910). Could Lula be instructively compared to Getúlio Vargas (ruler of Brazil, 1930–1945, 1951–1954), who was personally honest, but allowed those around him to steal? Or, further afield, could he be compared to the current Socialist prime minister of Portugal, José Socrates, who professes socialism but pursues a "responsible" policy of fiscal orthodoxy far better than his conservative (PSD) predecessor, Pedro Santana Lopes?

Lula's party, the Partido dos Trabalhadores, at least until its rise to national power, was widely held to be unique in Brazil in having both a coherent ideological foundation and an unprecedented degree of political discipline. For example, several PT congressmen and a senator who failed to vote for the government's pension reform bill were expelled from the party.[1] Though discipline and ideology admit of degree, they seem to distinguish the Partido dos Trabalhadores from its more clientelistic and personalistic rivals. Still, one might apply the adage about the late Empire, *mutatis mutandis*: There is nothing more like a Conservative than a Liberal in power.

Lula's first term was characterized by strict fiscal orthodoxy, and some now argue that the growth model chosen may be path-driven,[2] resulting in no real option but to continue the financially orthodox and FDI-friendly policies of the first mandate. So, the president's stated objective of diminishing income inequality in Brazil may not be realized. This outcome seems to describe the situation in contemporary Chile, where, during the rapid growth of 1990–1999, income inequality remained virtually unchanged.[3] At all events, Brazil in the *World Development Report 2006* has a Gini coefficient that has remained constant over decades, despite other great transformations of the economy and society. Brazil's Gini coefficient, estimated at 0.58, ranks highest in Latin America, and third highest in the world, after two African countries.[4]

Why does this matter? The 2006 *Report* analyzes the relationship between equity and development, offering evidence that inequality of opportunity is both wasteful and inimical to sustainable development and poverty reduction. Elhanan Helpman, a leading expert on growth, also argues that income inequality and subsequent growth per capita are negatively correlated.[5] In the view of the World Bank, though equity is valuable in itself, it also matters crucially for long-term development. The *Report* shows the negative consequences for growth of the unequal opportunities resulting from imperfect markets, and the consequences of inequity for the quality of social institutions—for example, the vast qualitative differences between private and public schools that, in turn, stratify the economic opportunities of different social groups. The study makes a case for investing in human capital, broadening access to justice, land, and infrastructure, and increasing fairness in markets.[6]

Why has the problem of inequality been so intractable? Present-day students of Brazilian society are rightly concerned about the inequities of the distribution of income and wealth, and most trace the problem back to the gross inequalities of the age of slavery, an institution that lasted some 400 years in Brazil. A related problem is the extreme inequality of land tenure, historically and currently. Helpman points out that the inequality in the ownership of land has been found in some multicountry studies to be more important than that of income distribution itself in explaining low growth.[7] In Brazil the link between land tenure and political power diminished only in the twentieth century, and it remains important in many areas of the country.[8] Unlike slavery, the latifundium didn't die: it is a dynamic phenomenon, continually reproducing itself on the frontiers of the national economy.[9]

Although the studies of the distribution of income and wealth prior to 1960 are few and tentative, Zephyr Frank's recent study of wealth based on property inventories in southeastern Brazil from the 1820s to the 1860s is instructive about the extreme nature of Brazil's historical inequality. Frank has established that wealth-holding, mainly in the form of real property and slaves, shows enormous disparities among wealth holders. In the city of Rio de Janeiro, the top decile of wealth-holders held 57.4 percent of the physical wealth in the 1820s, and 59.1 percent in the 1850s.[10] Frank estimated a Gini index of 0.68 of all wealth-holders who left inventoried wills. But, he adds, if we reasonably assume that 50 percent of the population owned no wealth at all, the Gini coefficient for wealth rises to 0.85 in both the 1820s and 1850s! Therefore, although "[absolute] mean wealth-holding grew rapidly in parts of Southeastern Brazil between 1815 and 1860," the Gini index remained extremely skewed.[11]

So, perhaps the surprise is not so much the immensity of poverty and inequality, but rather that Brazil managed to grow as much as it did during most of the twentieth century, even if that growth was unequal for different social strata. According to Albert Fishlow, Brazil's per capita income from 1900 to 1979 grew on an average of almost 3 percent a year.[12] Put somewhat differently, Francisco Rigolon and Fábio Giambiagi more recently have noted that between 1900 and 1973, Brazilian per capita GDP grew at 2.5 percent annually, "a performance exceeded [on a world scale] only by Japan and Finland."[13]

But growth came to a standstill and remained so throughout the 1980s, and it has been fitful since then. If reducing income inequality is necessary for successful long-term performance, as the World Bank argues, we need to know what kind of sequencing is necessary to achieve the desired end. To attack inequality, Daron Acemoglu, Simon Johnson, and James Robinson argue for what may be called "the primacy of the political."[14] They hold that universal suffrage, effectively applied, brings the masses into the political process, and in the developed world, their power over time has forced a greater equalization of income. In the prototypical case of Britain, the state broadened the suffrage effectively to the whole adult male population between 1867 and 1884. In the same period, the British state committed itself to providing universal education; furthermore, the legalization of trade unions in this era and their steady growth increased the bargaining power of labor. In the Acemoglu interpretation, these changes slowly tilted the distribution of income toward the newly enfranchised masses. More generally, the rise of democracy in nineteenth-century Europe "shows how political institutions determine economic institutions and policies, and thus the distribution of resources."[15]

The extent of effective suffrage in Brazil only reaches "universal" levels[16] in the post–World War II period. This accomplishment required the abolition of the *régime capacitaire*—the literacy requirement—which survived until 1985. If we look at the long-term rise of suffrage from the early Republic, as measured by votes cast in presidential elections as a proportion of national population[17] we see voter participation rising from 2–3 percent between 1894 and 1926 to 6 percent in the vigorously contested race of 1930. This unprecedented political mobilization may have contributed to Getúlio Vargas's revolution, following his defeat at the polls in 1930. The rate of participation then rose to 13 percent at the outset of a new democratic regime in 1945. The rate of participation continued to rise to 18 percent in 1960, the last direct election for 29 years, owing to the military dictatorship initiated in 1964. And the presidential election of 1989 was even more of a seismic shift than that of 1945: 52 percent of the total population voted, and this percentage remained more or less stable in the next few elections. By 2006, the rate of participation had risen again—to 56 percent of the total population.[18] (By comparison, only 21 percent of the U.S. population voted in the presidential contest of 2004.[19]) In sum, there were two big quantum leaps in the growth of suffrage, in 1945 and 1989, both coming after long intervals between direct presidential elections. There was a 260 percent jump from 1930 to 1945, and a 288 percent spike between 1960 and 1989, the first presidential contest after the abolition of the literacy requirement.[20] Consequently, by this admittedly crude standard—participating voters as a share of total population—Brazil was characterized by a democratic suffrage no later than 1989.

But political structures and practices from the colonial and imperial eras died slowly. The informal institutions of familism, patronage, and mutually beneficial affective relationships (what the ancient Romans called *amicitia*[21]) lived well into the twentieth century. Slavery experienced a slow death through piecemeal legislation enacted over the years 1870–1888, but the ruling elite found other means to preserve the rigidly stratified social structure. The patron-client system may have emerged from slavery even stronger—and it cut through the formally egalitarian political and social institutions of the Republic, instituted in 1889. The operative practice was "favor," as Roberto Schwarz calls it,[22] in which the powerful dispensed privileges to obedient members of the lower orders, despite the impersonal contracts, constitutionally sanctioned political equality, and other liberal institutions that existed in theory.[23] The central force giving patronage its key role in traditional Brazil was that the protection of a powerful landlord or political boss (*coronel*) could shield the dependent against military recruitment, a practice that continued into the twentieth century.[24]

One way that patronage or favor extended its reach was by means of a broader suffrage and decentralization of government, including a greater share of revenues for the states and counties, during the Old Republic (1889–1930). This was the classic age of *coronelismo* (rural bossism). Favor receded in importance during periods of dictatorship (1930–1945, 1964–1985), and its significance in the postwar era was most notable the backward Northeast.[25]

Brazilian social and political structures in the nineteenth and early twentieth centuries may be instructively compared with their Sicilian counterparts, as revealed in Denis Mack Smith's *Modern Sicily*. In Sicily, like Brazil, peasants dreaded military recruitment and evaded it whenever possible, usually through protection of the powerful. One of the differences between the two societies is that patron-client systems were better organized in Sicily, resulting in the rise of the Mafia in the mid-nineteenth century. In Sicily, like Brazil, kinship and patronage were the central factors in politics. "Nepotism [in Sicily], far from being in any sense immoral, was recognized as a primary duty of every good family man, and almost every Sicilian belonged to a network of client-patron connections designed to defend him against other networks and even against the government."[26] Both Sicily and Brazil continually adopted and adapted liberal political institutions, usually with grotesque and tragicomic results.

One of these in Brazil was the reference in the 1823 draft constitution to the "contract" between masters and slaves.[27]

The deeply traditional, even reactionary, nature of the "real" Brazil as opposed to "formal" Brazil has been emphasized by most of the classic national character studies. I have in mind, for example, Paulo Prado, *Portrait of Brazil*; Sérgio Buarque de Holanda, *Roots of Brazil*; Gilberto Freyre, *The Masters and the Slaves*; José Honório Rodrigues, *Conciliation and Reform*; and Raymundo Faoro, *The Masters of Power*.[28]

Sérgio Buarque, in *Roots of Brazil* (1936), examines the social and political structure of traditional Brazil without the celebratory tone found in Freyre's *The Masters and the Slaves*. Buarque saw Brazilian society as evolving slowly, with a major rupture with the abolition of slavery in 1888 ("our revolution"). He felt strongly that the state, however authoritarian, could not transform civil society, but that changes in the former had to flow from the latter. Indeed, the following sentence from *Roots* seems quite Hegelian: "The external forms of society [including political movements] ought to...emerge continually from specific needs, and never from capricious choices."[29] We may infer that Buarque believed that modernization would neither come by fiat, nor even with the drafting of the 1988 Constitution.

Buarque's notion of the "cordial man" (*homem cordial*) revealed a cordiality that not only was superficial in many respects, but one limited in its application to relatives, friends, and acquaintances in the same social stratum, *or* a cordiality dispensed to the lower orders with an implicit demand for deference and obedience.[30] As the ideology of liberalism became dominant after national independence, adaptations and accommodations were made to fit the circumstances. (The cultural critic Antônio Cândido Mello e Souza uses the phrase "liberalismo ornamental.") The cordial man could neither adequately adapt to the world of the impersonal relations of the modern market and polity—moving from *Gemeinschaft* to *Gesellschaft* in Ferdinand Tönnies' famous continuum—nor to the evolving democratic practices increasingly associated with liberalism. The cordial man would probably have accepted the definition of a Spanish liberal of the 1820s, namely, that "liberalism is liberty—properly understood." In any event, the cordial man resisted Weberian rationalization and impersonalization exemplified in modern bureaucracy.[31] One may note in passing that, although *Roots* did not deal directly with the economy, today's New Institutionalists would value this essay for its implicit emphasis on the high level of "transaction costs" in a society in which impersonal trust in market relations was so lacking.

Another classic essay on the national experience emphasized the political inertia of the Brazilian state. Raymundo Faoro focused on the immobilism of the state and the self-renewing political class. He first published *The Masters of Power* in 1958; but the book had a far greater impact during the dictatorship, when it appeared in a revised and greatly expanded edition in

1975. Faoro was the first to apply and adapt Weberian analysis to Brazilian history in a systematic way. *Masters* surveys the national experience, focusing especially on the political estate (*estamento*—Max Weber's *Stand*). For Faoro, this group controlled the State, which he saw as fundamentally unaltered from its Portuguese prototype.

Regarding civil society, Faoro broke with conventional historiography, which viewed nineteenth-century Conservatives as owners of large estates. Faoro viewed them rather as controlling "mobile wealth"—slaves and credit. It was not Conservatives but Liberals, he held, who predominated among latifundists. Merchants and creditors allied with the political estate after independence in 1822. Excepting the early Empire (1831–1837) and the Old Republic (1889–1930), when relative decentralization strengthened landed elites, the political estate and its commercial allies succeeded in dominating civil society through a centralized state. The political estate has shaped the stratified character of Brazilian society; it has been impervious to the needs of the people, but also inattentive to the demands of powerful economic interests. State dominates civil society, but the ruling estate has no clear national project.

Faoro drew on Weber in his interpretation of bureaucracy, but departs from him in Faoro's ahistorical claim for the unchanging continuity of the patrimonial state. *Masters* offered an explanation of the enormous power of the Brazilian government during the military dictatorship, a regime both authoritarian and heavily engaged in parastatal enterprises.

Whether it is because of the patronage-dispensing cordial man or the dominance of the political estate, or both, formal political institutions in Brazil have counted for much less historically than they might have, had patronage and the centralized state been less powerful. The strength of these traditions surely helps account for the repeated "deinstitutionalization" of formal political parties in the last two centuries: Parties were effectively abolished or committed suicide in 1889, 1930, 1945, and 1965. Under the present constitution, parties have continued to split, merge, and reshape themselves, in part owing to proportional representation and the small parties it spawns. A fragile and fluid party system probably makes democracy in Brazil weaker than it might otherwise have been.[32]

I have described the essays by Buarque de Holanda and Faoro partly because they treat elements found in a new historical monograph by Jeffrey Needell on the origins of the conservative political tradition, which the author asserts is really at the center of the Brazilian political process in the nineteenth century, and possibly later. In *The Party of Order*,[33] Needell presents a complex and nuanced argument about the formation of the Conservative Party, and, by extension, the conservative political tradition in Brazil. He shows how the Conservatives—initially, in the form of the reactionary *saquarema* "party"—captured the State from the relatively liberal faction who ruled between the abdication of the absolutist monarch Pedro I in 1831 and the recentralization of political authority in 1837.

One of Needell's important contributions is explaining the complexity of the reception and adaptation of political liberalism in Brazil. Both *luzias* (forerunners of the Liberal Party) and *saquaremas* claimed liberal inspiration. The latter were not de Maistre-style reactionaries who wanted to repeal the French Revolution, though there were plenty of these in Spanish America. For the *saquaremas*, liberalism meant the ideology expounded by François Guizot and his *doctrinaires*, who wanted a representative government with a sharply limited suffrage. In effect, *saquaremas* and *luzias* struggled to *define* liberalism for a Brazilian political context.[34] The *saquaremas* championed representative government (as they understood it) on two fronts—against both the relatively liberal *luzias* and the potentially tyrannical and unlimited Moderating Power of the Emperor.

This is a central point for Needell, who revises the prevailing historiography by showing how the Conservatives, dominant in the middle years of the nineteenth century, faced a crisis in their struggle with the Emperor over the Rio Branco Law of 1871. This statute, the Law of Free Birth, granted conditional freedom to slaves born after that date. Needell argues that historians have failed to notice that the chief issue for the Conservative opposition to Prime Minister Rio Branco (himself a Conservative) was less the initiation of the abolition of slavery than his flagrant use of the Crown's power to get the Emperor's way against parliament. The crisis of 1871 concerned the "nature of legitimate political authority and the decline of the constitutional representative regime reconstructed by the reactionary party between 1837 and 1842."[35] This statement appears almost paradoxical, but in fact the reactionaries were the closest thing to civil society, pitted against the Emperor's "authoritarian" state.[36] The *saquaremas'* consistent adherence to constitutionality became a precedent that Conservatives tried to follow in the early twentieth century. The political process they successfully championed was designed to maintain control by a tiny elite.[37]

To enter the imperial elite, as Gilberto Freyre observed in *The Mansions and the Shantie*s, political aspirants, especially those of modest wealth, had to acquire formal higher education.[38] A university diploma became the entry ticket to politics, as early as the generation of Brazil's founding fathers, many of who had studied at Coimbra, Portugal's only university. Formal education of any kind was sharply restricted: In the census of 1872, Brazil had only 151,000 pupils in primary and secondary schools in national population of over 10 million—one pupil for every sixty-eight inhabitants—compared to one in five or six in the United States at the time. The Empire bequeathed to the Republic a literacy rate of 15 percent in 1890, a figure that had slightly decreased in the last two decades of the imperial regime.[39] Brazil's literacy rate at that time, moreover, was roughly a third that of Argentina.[40] Mass education was a process that Brazil committed to only in the middle of the twentieth century,[41] nearly a century after Britain, and as late as 1960 there were only 100,000 university students in a population of 72 million.[42]

Yet in many noneconomic dimensions of development, Brazil has advanced dramatically in the last century, especially in the last 50 years. Urbanization rose from 36.3 percent of the population in 1950 to 81.3 percent in 2000.[43] Life expectancy at birth rose from 42.1 years in 1950 to 72.0 years in 2006. Literacy more than doubled after 1950, rising from 42.6 percent in 1950 to 88.4 percent in 2006.[44] Students enrolled in all types of higher education by 2002 numbered 3.2 million[45]—32 times more than their counterparts in 1960!

Although the ethos associated with clientelism, patrimonialism, and nepotism survives, it has palpably diminished in recent decades, and we may ask: Is there a meaningful mass (as opposed to an elite-dominated) civil society today? The relatively high levels of urbanization, literacy, and university enrollments would seem to be indirect indicators of such a phenomenon, and the recent rates of high voter participation, referred to above, would be a direct indicator. Moreover, the quality of political discourse has changed significantly from that of 1945–1964, as indicated by the fact that some Brazilian historians now refer to that period of history as the Populist Republic. If *brizolismo*[46] still thrived during the 1980s and 1990s in Rio de Janeiro State, the predominance of populism at the federal level seems to have passed. Voluntary associations are thriving, and in 2007 the IBGE estimated that there were 276,000 private foundations and nonprofit organizations; these NGOs employed 1.5 million persons.[47]

The rise of the Movimento dos Sem Terra (Movement of the Landless—MST) in the mid-1980s is another indicator of increasing lower-class participation in civil society. A movement that claims a million members combines legal and extralegal tactics—for example, the mass occupation of targeted estates—to force the state to expropriate inefficient large holdings or uncultivated properties. According to one source, 350,000 families now live in MST-sponsored settlements.[48] The organization's use of extralegal tactics, however, threatens property rights. This fact may diminish investment in agriculture, and consequently it may lower overall economic growth. To date, though, there seems to be no clear evidence that the MST activity has had these effects.[49]

Such indications of lower-class political participation are important, if Acemoglu et al. are right about the primacy of politics in bringing about a redistribution of income. In his first speech after winning reelection, in the words of the *Financial Times*, President Lula stated that "whereas in the past it was said that Brazil must grow in order to distribute wealth, his view was that Brazil must first distribute wealth in order to grow."[50] For the Lula government, it would seem to be now or never.

Notes

1. Desposato (2006: 30).
2. For example, Amann and Baer (2006).
3. CEPAL (2004: 95).

4. World Bank (2006: 4).

5. Helpman adds that the mechanisms of the relationship are not yet clear. See Helpman (2004: 92–93).

6. At the international level, the report calls for dismantling trade barriers in the wealthy nations, permitting more in-migration of low-skilled persons from LDCs, and providing greater and more efficient development assistance.

7. Helpman (2004: 92).

8. See Vidal Luna and Klein (2006), ch. 8; and Amann and Baer, "The Roots of Brazil's Inequality and Lula's Attempts to Overcome Them," a companion paper in this volume.

9. For attempts to model aspects of this problem, see Alston, Libecap, and Mueller (1999), and two earlier Marxist studies: Foweraker (1980) and Velho (1976).

10. Frank (2005: 251). "Physical wealth" is net tangible property, including slaves, but excludes debts and credits, which should roughly cancel out over the whole inventoried population.

11. Ibid., 256.

12. Fishlow (1980: 107).

13. Rigolon and Giambiagi (1999: 6).

14. Acemoglu, Johnson, and Robinson (2005). Supporting Acemoglu et al., Helpman cites other studies that confirm the primacy of institutions, as compared to geography, in the long-run determination of per capita income. Helpman (2004: 132).

15. Acemoglu et al. (2005: 78).

16. Of course, Britain itself did not have universal suffrage until all adult women were enfranchised in 1928.

17. There are few historical data for age-specific populations.

18. Sources: Historical Data: João Nicolau, "A participação eleitoral no Brazil," Working Papers, Oxford, 2002, cited in Vidal Luna and Klein, p. 8; for 2006: "Election Resources on the Internet" (2006) at http://electionresources.org/br/presidente.php?election=2006; CIA, *World Factbook* (2007).

19. Data from Wikipedia.org and Wikitravel.org. Comparability is principally limited by the fact that electoral participation is required in Brazil and not in the United States; by the different age structures in the two countries; and by the fact that the minimum voting age is two years younger in Brazil than in the United States.

20. Note, however, that this interval was almost twice as long as the previous gap.

21. See Syme (1960).

22. Schwarz, "Misplaced Ideas: Literature and Society in Late-Nineteenth-Century Brazil," in Schwarz, (1992: 19–32).

23. On patronage at different levels of society in nineteenth-century politics, see Graham (1990), and Murilo de Carvalho (1988), ch. 5.

24. Beattie (2001).

25. Over time, however, coronelismo declined even there, owing to greater levels of literacy and urbanization. The phenomenon was increasingly vestigial after 1988.

26. Mack Smith (1968: 446–447). Even in the 1960s the political scientist Sidney Tarrow found that the Sicilian branch of the Italian Communist Party, which should have been ideology-oriented and highly disciplined, was honeycombed with patronage networks that sometimes trumped party discipline. Tarrow (1967).

27. Prado Júnior (1969: 52).

28. Prado, *Retrato do Brasil*; Buarque, *Raízes do Brasil*; Freyre, *Casa Grande e Senzala*; Rodrigues, *Conciliação e Reforma*; Faoro, *Os Donos do Poder*.

29. "As formas exteriores da sociedade devem…emerge[r] continuamente das suas necessidades específicas e jamais da escolhas caprichosas." *Raízes do Brasil* (1936: 161).

30. The historical tendency toward conciliation among Brazilian political actors, as José Honório Rodrigues notes in *Conciliação e Reforma*, was an intraelite phenomenon that repeatedly failed to resolve the great social problems of national society.

31. By analogy, Liliana Schwarcz has coined the term "racismo cordial" to characterize contemporary Brazilian race relations.

32. On the importance of institutionalization of parties in stable democracies, see the classic study by Huntington, *Political Order in Changing Societies* (1968).

33. Needell (2006).

34. Ibid: 209.

35. Ibid: 320.
36. Ibid: 315.
37. This adherence to constitutionalism occurred at the level of the central government, but it was those same "legalist" Conservatives who initiated a process of violence at the local level in 1848. The Conservatives "made" the elections that year, throwing their opponents out in 1849 with unprecedented violence, even forcing Liberals to flee their homes in at least one key province. This procedure, coupled with the corruption of justice, set the pattern for the rest of the Empire. Constitutionality had little application, it seems, in the provinces. For a case study in Minas Gerais, see Bieber (1999).
38. Freyre (1963), ch. 11.
39. Love (1980: 92–93); Ludwig (1985: 132).
40. Brazil's literacy rate was 15 percent in 1890, and Argentina's, 46 percent in 1895. See Ludwig (1985: 132); Vázquez-Presedo, I (1971: 27). However, the rates are not fully comparable, because the Brazilian figure is for all ages, and that of Argentina, for those aged six and older.
41. Vidal Luna and Klein (2006: 214).
42. Ludwig (1985: 126) (referring to undergraduate students).
43. Data from Oxford Latin American Economic History Data Base, online.
44. On life expectancy and literacy, see Ludwig (1985: 84, 132); and CIA (2007).
45. Vidal Luna and Klein (2006: 188).
46. The populist political style associated with Leonel Brizola, twice governor of Rio de Janeiro State in that era.
47. IBGE (2007).
48. Wright and Wolford (2003).
49. Abbey, Baer, and Filizzola (2006).
50. Wheatley (2006).

References

Abbey, Leonard A., Werner Baer, and Mavio Filizzola. 2006. "Growth, Efficiency, and Equity: The Impact of Agribusiness and Land Reform in Brazil," *Latin American Business Review* 7(2):93–115.

Acemoglu, Daron, Simon Johnson, and James A. Robinson. 2005. "Institutions as the Fundamental Cause of Long-Run Growth." In Philippe Aghion and Stephen Durlauf, eds. *Handbook of Economic Growth*. North Holland. Available at econ-www.mit.edu/faculty accessed on April 9, 2007.

Alston, Lee J., Gary D. Libecap, and Bernardo Mueller. 1999. *Titles, Conflict, and Land Use: The Development of Property Rights and Land Reform on the Brazilian Amazon Frontier.* Ann Arbor: University of Michigan Press.

Amann, Edmund, and Werner Baer. 2006. "Economic Orthodoxy versus Social Development? The Dilemmas Facing Brazil's Labour Government." *Oxford Development Studies* 14(2) (June):219–241.

———. 2008. "The Roots of Brazil's Inequality and Lula's Attempts to Overcome Them." A Companion Paper in this Volume.

Beattie, Peter. 2001. *The Tribute Of Blood : Army, Honor, Race, and Nation In Brazil, 1864–1945.* Durham: Duke University Press.

Bieber, Judy. 1999. *Power, Patronage, and Political Violence: State Building on a Brazilian Frontier, 1822–1889.* Lincoln: University of Nebraska Press.

Buarque de Holanda, Sérgio. 1936. *Raízes do Brasil.* Rio de Janeiro: José Olympio. Murilo de Carvalho, José. 1988. *Teatro de sombras: A política imperial.* Rio de Janeiro: Vértice and IUPERJ.

Central Intelligence Agency (CIA). 2007. *World Factbook.* Available at https://www.cia.gov/library/publications/the-world-factbook/index.html accessed on March 10, 2007.

Comisión Económica para América Latina y el Caribe (CEPAL). 2004. *Una década de desarrollo social en América Latina: 1990–1999.* Santiago: CEPAL.

Desposato, Scott W. 2006. "From Revolution to Rouba Mas Faz?" *Revista* David Rockefeller Center for Latin American Studies (Spring/Summer):29–32.

"Election Resources on the Internet." Available at http://electionresources.org/br/presidente. php?election=2006 accessed on April 15, 2007.

Faoro, Raymundo. 1975. *Os Donos do Poder*. 2nd enlarged ed. Porto Alegre: Globo.

Fishlow, Albert. 1980. "Brazilian Development in Long-term Perspective." *American Economic Review* 70(2) (May):102–108.

Foweraker, Joe. 1980. *The Struggle for Land: A Political Economy of the Pioneer Frontier in Brazil from 1930 to the Present Day*. Cambridge, UK: Cambridge University Press.

Frank, Zephyr. 2005. "Wealth Holding in Southeastern Brazil: 1815–60." *Hispanic American Historical Review* 85(2) (May):223–257.

Freyre, Gilberto. [1933] 2002. *Casa Grande e Senzala*. Rio de Janeiro: Record.

———. 1963. *The Mansions and the Shanties (Sobrados e Mucambos): The Making of Modern Brazil*. New York: Alfred Knopf. Original Portuguese ed.: 1936.

Graham, Richard. 1990. *Patronage and Politics in Nineteenth-Century Brazil*. Stanford, CA: Stanford University Press.

Helpman, Elhanan. 2004. *The Mystery of Economic Growth*. Cambridge, MA: Harvard University Press.

Huntington, Samuel P. 1968. *Political Order in Changing Societies*. New Haven, CT: Yale University Press.

IBGE. 2007. Instituto Brasileiro de Geografia e Estatística: Ministério do Planejamento, "As Fundações Privadas e Associações sem Fins Lucrativos no Brasil." Available at www.ibge.gov. br/home/presidencia/noticias accessed on April 18, 2007.

Love, Joseph L. 1980. *São Paulo in the Brazilian Federation, 1889–1937*. Stanford, CA: Stanford University Press.

Ludwig, Armin K. 1985. *Brazil: A Handbook of Historical Statistics*. Boston: G.K. Hall.

Mack Smith, Denis. 1968. *A History of Sicily, Vol. 3: Modern Sicily after 1715*. New York, Viking.

Needell, Jeffrey. 2006. *The Party of Order: The Conservatives, the State, and Slavery in the Brazilian Monarchy, 1831–1871*. Stanford, CA: Stanford University Press.

Nicolau, João. 2002. "A participação eleitoral no Brasil." Working Papers, Oxford, as cited in Vidal Luna and Klein (q.v.), p. 8.

Oxford Latin American Economic History Data Base. Available at http://oxlad.qeh.ox.ac.uk/ accessed on February 7, 2008.

Prado Júnior, Caio. 1969. *Evolução política do Brasil e outros ensaios*. São Paulo: Brasiliense.

Prado, Paulo. 1962. *Retrato do Brasil: Ensaio sobre a tristeza brasileira*. 6th ed. Rio de Janeiro: Jose Olympio. Original Portuguese ed.: 1928.

Rigolon, Francisco José, and Fábio Giambiagi. 1999. "The Brazilian Economy: General Overview." In BNDES, Internal Publication of Banco Nacional de Desenvolvimento Econômico e Social, June.

Rodrigues, José Honório. 1965. *Conciliação e reforma: Um desafio histórico-político*. Rio de Janeiro: Civilização Brasileira.

Schwarz, Roberto. 1992. "Misplaced Ideas: Literature and Society in Late-Nineteenth-Century Brazil." In Schwarz, ed. *Misplaced Ideas: Essays on Brazilian Culture*. London: Verso, pp. 19–32.

Syme, Ronald. 1960. *The Roman Revolution*. Oxford: Oxford University Press.

Tarrow, Sidney. 1967. *Peasant Communism in Southern Italy*. New Haven, CT: Yale University Press.

Vázquez-Presedo, Vicente. 1971. *Estadísticas Históricas Argentinas*. Vol. I. Buenos Aires: Macchi.

Velho, Otávio Guilherme. 1976. *Capitalismo autoritário e campesinato*. São Paulo: DIFEL.

Vidal Luna, Francisco, and Herbert S. Klein. 2006. *Brazil since 1980*. Cambridge: Cambridge University Press.

Wheatley, Jonathan. 2006. "Brazil Seeks Less Painful Path to Growth." *Financial Times*, October 30.

Wikipedia.org. Available at http://www.wikipedia.org/ accessed on February 8, 2008.

Wikitravel.org. Available at http://wikitravel.org/en/Main_Page accessed on February 8, 2008.

World Bank. 2005. *World Development Report, 2006*. Washington, DC: World Bank. Available at http://siteresources.worldbank.org/INTWDR2006/Resources/WDR_on_Equity_FinalOutline_July_public.pdf accessed on February 7, 2008.

Wright, Angus, and Wendy Wolford. 2003. *To Inherit the Earth: The Landless Movement and the Struggle for a New Brazil*. Oakland, CA: Food First Books.

INDEX

Note: Please note that page numbers in *italics* indicate end notes.

Acemoglu, Daron, 4, *300*, 307, 312
ADENE. *see* Agência de
    Desenvolvimento do Nordeste
Agência de Desenvolvimento do
    Nordeste (ADENE), 264, 271, 298
Agência Nacional de Energia Elétrica
    (ANEEL), 96
Agência Nacional de Telecomunicações
    (ANATEL), *64*, 95, 103–105, 108, *113*
agriculture
    agrarian policy and, 140–142
    in colonial times, 27–28
    economy and, 38–39, 250, 254, 256,
        292, 312
    environmental policy network and, 146
    foreign policy and, 175
    modernization of, 245
    policy under Lula, 136–140, 142–143
    postcolonial, 28–29
    PRONAF and, 296
ALCA. *see* Free Trade Area of the
    Americas
Almeida, Paulo Roberto de, 3, 167–182
Amann, Edmund, 2, 27–41
ANATEL. *see* Agência Nacional de
    Telecomunicações
ANEEL. *see* Agência Nacional de Energia
    Elétrica
Arbache, J., 191
Área de Livre Comércio das Américas. *see*
    Free Trade Area of the Americas
Arends-Kuenning, Mary, 217
Asian crisis, 123–124
Azzoni, Carlos R., 4, 243–260

Baer, Werner, 1–4, 27–41

Bahia, 18, 21, 245, 263
Banco Central
    Fraga, Armínio and, 124
    Franco, Gustavo and, 122, *132*
    inflation-targeting policies, 35
    Meirelles, Henrique and, 94, 128
    public policy and, 61
    tax exemptions and, 57–58
Banco do Brasil, 138, 225, 229, 233, 296,
    298
Banco Nacional de Desenvolvimento
    Econômico (BNDE), *278*
Banco Nacional de Desenvolvimento
    Econômico e Social (BNDES), 171,
    267, 270–274, 276, 277,
    279, 290
Bank of Brazil. *see* Banco do Brasil
bankruptcy reform, 68, 78, 81
Barelli, Walter, 153
Barrientos, A., 191, 200
Barros, Alexandre Rands, 4, 283–299
Bezerra, Jocildo, 2, 67–86
Bezerra, Márcio, 217
BNDE. *see* Banco Nacional de
    Desenvolvimento Econômico
BNDES. *see* Banco Nacional de
    Desenvolvimento Econômico e Social
Bolsa de Valores de São Paulo
    (BOVESPA), 229
Bolsa Escola (School Fund)
    Bolsa Família and, 208–209
    cash allowances and, 276
    creation of, 190–191, 205
    governance of, 200
    Lula da Silva and, 296
    school achievement test scores, 215

Bolsa Família (Family Fund)
  accountability and, *62*
  analysis of, 187–201
  education and, 205, 209, 212, 218
  eligibility for, 246
  inequality and, 27, 35–39, 41, *42*
  Northeast Brazil and, 296
  regional development policy and,
    250–251, 253, 256, 258–260, 270
  studies of, 3, 4
Bourguignon, F., 191
BOVESPA. *see* Bolsa de Valores de São
  Paulo
Brazilian Agency of Agro-Pastoral
  Research. *see* Empresa Brasileira de
  Pesquisa Agropecuária
Brazilian Institute for the Environment.
  see Instituto Brasileiro do Meio
  Ambiente
Brazilian Institute of Geography and
  Statistics. *see* Instituto Brasileiro de
  Geografia e Estastística
Brazilian Social Democratic Party.
  see Partido da Social Democracia
  Brasileira
Brazilian Telecommunications. *see*
  Telecomunicações Brasileiras
BRIC countries (Brazil, Russia, India,
  China), 72–73, 174, 180, 197
Buarque de Holanda, Sérgio, 309, 310

capital. *see also* human capital
  domestic, 132
  foreign, 3, 51, *86*, 132, 179
Cardoso, Fernando Henrique
  agrarian policy and, 141
  Bolsa Família and, 190–191
  education and, 205–206, 207–208
  environmental policy and, 148
  exchange rate policy and, 115–117, 119,
    122, 125–129, 131
  foreign policy and, 168, 170, 177
  growth and, 74–76, 85, *87*
  inequality and, 34–35
  labor policy and, 152–157, *162*
  Northeast Brazil and, 283, 289
  regulation and, 95, 97, 100–101, 104
  social security and, 221–236
  studies of, 1, 2–4
  SUDENE and, *278*

cash allowances, 265–266, 270–271,
  276–277
cash transfer programs, 35, *42*, 190–193,
  201, 205, 207, 209, 266, 270,
  276–277, *278*, *279*. see also *Bolsa
  Escola*; *Bolsa Família*
Cavalcanti, Luiz Ricardo, 4, 263–278
Cavalcanti, Tiago V. de V., 2, 67–86
Ceará, 18, 36
Center-South, 3, 244, 245
Central Bank. *see* Banco Central
Central Única dos Trabalhadores (CUT),
  153–154, 156, 160–161, *163*, 228,
  234
Chamber of Deputies, 10–11, 15, 19, 21,
  156, 161, 216
Chávez, Hugo, 178–179
Cheibub, José Antonio, 2, 9–22
clientelism, 11, 17, *23*, 37–38, 312
Coes, Donald V., 3, 115–132
coffee, 28–29, 137–138, 179
Collor, Fernando, 152, *162*, 168–170, 283
colonos, 29
Comissão Técnica Nacional de
  Biossegurança (CTNBio), 144–146,
  149
competitiveness, 17–22, 117–120, 131,
  158, 245, 260, 283, 299
complementary laws, 230–232, *237*
Confirmatory Spatial Data Analysis
  (CSDA), 188, 194, 195, 200
Conselho de Desenvolvimento
  Econômico e Social, *237*
Consolidação das Leis do Trabalho
  (CLT), 151, 155–157, 160–161
Consolidation of Labor Laws. *see*
  Consolidação das Leis do Trabalho
Constitution, 9, 12, 17, 146, 154–158,
  160, 310–311
  1988, 97–98, 143, 152, 206, 222–223,
    226, 309
  Amendment 8, 95
  Amendment 20, 228, 229–231, 232
  Amendment 32, *62*, *63*
  Amendment 40, 235
  Amendment 41, 227, 235–236
Constitutional Assembly, 48–49, 222
Contribuição Provisória sobre a
  Movimentação ou Transmissão de
  Valores e de Créditos e Direitos

de Natureza Financeira (CPMF),
55–57, 79, 156
coronelismo (rural bossism), 308, *313*
corruption, 2, 9, 13, 16, 20–21, 170, 268,
314
cotton, 28, 137
Council of Economic and Social
Development. *see* Conselho de
Desenvolvimento Econômico e
Social
CPMF. *see* Contribuição Provisória sobre
a Movimentação ou Transmissão de
Valores e de Créditos e Direitos de
Natureza Financeira
"crawling peg" policy, 116–119
Crusius, Yeda, 156
CTNBio. *see* Comissão Técnica Nacional
de Biossegurança
CUT. *see* Central Única dos
Trabalhadores

Dean, Warren, 28–29
debt, moratorium on, 115, 130

economic development, 27–41
agriculture and, 135–140
Bolsa Família and, 36–38, 187–192
CNDES and, 54
economic infrastructure and, 243–246
exchange rate policy and, 115–132
foreign policy and, 167–174, 177–182
growth constraints and, 76–85
hydroelectric projects and, 147
income concentration and, 38–39
income distribution during 1980s and
1990s, 31–32
income distribution during ISI period,
29–31
labor and, 153–154, 157, 159–160, 161
Lula government and, 34–35, 153–154,
157, 159–160, 161
neoliberal policy and, 32–34
poverty and distribution under Lula,
35–36
primary goods export economy, 28–29
property and income concentrationin
colonial times, 27–28
reform and, 67–68
regional development and, 263–272,
277, 292–293, 295

regulation and, 97, 101–102,
106, 111
service sector and, 39–40
social security and, 234, 236
education. see also *Bolsa Escola*; school
attendance
attendance rates, 211
Bolsa Família and, 37, *42*
conditional transfer-for-education
(CTE), 190
early childhood education, 210–211
economic growth and, 77, 180–181,
188, 245, 265, 284, 286, 288
grades one to eight, 211–214
high school, 214
history in Brazil, 307, 311–312
human capital and, 82–84
industrial policy and, 84–85
Lula da Silva and, 3–4, 205–218
as national priority, 208–210
policy in 1990s, 206–208
prospects for future, 216–218
regional development and, 293–294
repetition rates and school efficiency,
212–214
school achievement test scores,
215–216
service sector and, 39–40, 41, *42*
elections
federalism and, 12–13
legislative, 11, 17–22
PNAD and, 127
presidential, 58, 162, 246–250,
307–308
PSDB and, 59
PT and, 127, 236
reducing competitiveness and
preserving representativeness,
17–22
reform and, 14, 16
electricity, *41*, 95, 96–97, 99, 102, 112,
147–148, *149*, 275
EMBRAPA. *see* Empresa Brasileira de
Pesquisa Agropecuária
employment, 3, 36, 58, 78, 81, 152–154,
160, 229. *see also* labor unions;
service sector
Empresa Brasileira de Pesquisa
Agropecuária (EMBRAPA),
137–139

environmental policy, 143–148, 175
ESCELSA. *see* Espírito Santo Centrais
  Elétricas S.A.
ESDA. *see* Exploratory Spatial Data
  Analysis
Espírito Santo Centrais Elétricas S.A.
  (ESCELSA), 96
Espirito Santo Energy Distributing
  Company. *see* Espírito Santo
  Centrais Elétricas S.A.
Estado Novo, 3
ethanol, 178, 180
Evaluation System for Elementary
  Education. *see* Sistema de Avaliação
  da Educação Básica
exchange rate, 3, 94, 103, 115–132,
  141, 168
  external pressures and end of anchor,
    122–125
  future of policy, 129–132
  Plano Real and the first Cardoso term,
    117–122
  policy inheritance of Lula government,
    125–129
  pre-*Plano Real* policies, 116–117
Exploratory Spatial Data Analysis
  (ESDA), 188, 194, 200, 247

Family Fund. see *Bolsa Família*
Faoro, Raymundo, 309–310
Federação das Indústrias do Estado de São
  Paulo (FIESP), 52, 58, 60
federalism, 12–13, 15, 17
Ferreira, Aloysio Nunes, *162*
Ferreira, F.H., 191
Ferreira, P.C., *86*
FIESP. *see* Federação das Indústrias do
  Estado de São Paulo
financial incentives. *see also* subsidies
  Northeast Brazil and, 4
  policy networks and, 137–139
  regional policy and, 243–245,
    264–268, 270, 272–274, 277
  regulation and, 93
  social security and, 231, 235
  tax incentives, 53
  Zona Franca and, 55
fiscal anchor, 124–125
fiscal incentives, 55, 231, 245, 266–268,
  270, 271–272, 274

Fome Zero (Zero Hunger Program),
  42, 62, 209
Força Sindical (FS), 153, 228
foreign direct investment (FDI), 32–33,
  35, 102, 244–245, 264
foreign policy, Lula da Silva and, 167–182
  Brazil and world order, 167–168
  international order and, 179–182
  main priorities of, 173–175
  strategies and main focus, 175–179
Fortalecimento da Agricultura Familiar,
  296
Fórum Nacional do Trabalho (FNT),
  157–158, 160
Fraga, Armínio, 124
Franco, Gustavo, 122
Franco, Itamar, 117, 152, 155, 168, 170
Frank, Zephyr, 306
Free Trade Area of the Americas (FTAA),
  3, 168, 170, 175, 177–179
FS. *see* Força Sindical
FTAA. *see* Free Trade Area of the
  Americas
Fund for the Maintenance and
  Development of Elementary
  Education. see *Fundo de Manutenção
  e Desenvolvimento do Ensino
  Fundamental*
Fundef. see *Fundo de Manutenção
  e Desenvolvimento do Ensino
  Fundamental*
*Fundo de Manutenção e Desenvolvimento do
  Ensino Fundamental (Fundef)*,
  207–208, 210, 216

GDP (Gross Domestic Product)
  Bolsa Família and, 37, 189, 191
  economic policy and, 35
  education and, 209
  exchange rate policy and, 126–127, 129
  foreign policy and, 177, 180
  GNI compared to, *42*
  growth and, 67, 69–76, 79–81, 85, *86*,
    307
  income concentration and, 38–39
  income distribution and, 29–32
  infrastructure and, 100, 102
  MP 252 and, 53
  Northeast Brazil and, 283–286,
    288–290, 297–298

policy networks and, 4
PPP and, 59–60
regional development policy and, 264,
    267, 269, 271–275, 277, *279*
regional income inequality and, 250,
    254, 256, 258–260
social security and, 222, 225
Giambiagi, Fábio, 307
Gini coefficient, 3–4, 30, 35–37, 39, 126,
    181, 192, 194–197, 200, 250–251,
    256, 258, 286
Gini index, 4, 306
Gross Domestic Product. *see* GDP
growth
    bankruptcy reform and, 81
    Brazil's lack of, 67–86
    constraints on, 76–85
    demographic, 29, 31, 228, 244, 260,
        267–268, 270
    economic, 2–3, 31–32, 35, 41, 53,
        59–60, 67–86, 99–102, 120,
        126–128, 131–132, 147–148, 153,
        169, 180–181, 189, 192, 286, 289,
        292–294
    government and tax reform, 79–81
    human capital accumulation, 82–84
    industrial policy and, 84–85
    international comparisons, 69
    labor market rigidity, 81–82
    worldwide slowdown, 72–76
growth poles, 264–265, 267
growth theory, 292–294
Grupo de Trabalho para o
    Desenvolvimento do Nordeste
    (GTDN), 263
Guilhoto, Joaquim J.M., 4, 243–260
Guizot, François, 311

Haddad, Eduardo A., 4, 243–260
Haddad, Mônica A., 3, 187–201
Hall, Michael M., 3, 151–162
health care, 80, 187, 189–190, 227, 229
Helpman, Elhanan, 306, *313*
Hewings, Geoffrey J.D., 4, 243–260
Hirschman, Albert O., 264
Holanda, Marcos, 1
human capital. *see also* service sector
    accumulation of, 82–84
    Bolsa Família and, 187
    economy and, 2, 39, 41, 85

education and, 205, 296
GDP and, 39
Northeast Brazil and, 294
regional development policy and, 266
social policy and, 244, 259, 306
hyperinflation, 31, 32, 37, 68, 120. *see
    also* inflation

IBAMA. *see* Instituto Brasileiro do Meio
    Ambiente
IBGE. *see* Instituto Brasileiro de
    Geografia e Estastística
Import-Substitution Industrialization
    (ISI), 29–31, 68, *86, 87*
income concentration, 27–28, 30, 38–39,
    259, 286
income distribution, 2, 4, 29–31, 35–37,
    39, 41, 82, 126–128, 181, 252–254,
    258, 286, 306
industrial policy, 84–85, *87*
industry. *see also* Import-Substitution
    Industrialization (ISI)
    exchange rate policy and, 125
    foreign policy and, 170–171, 175, 177–180
    growth and, 4, 68–69, 71–72, 80, 82,
        84–85
    income distribution and, 29–31
    inequality and, 2
    labor policy and, 153, 158
    Lula da Silva and, 38–41, 52–53, 56–61
    Northeast Brazil and, 284, 292
    regional development policy and,
        267–268, 271–272
    regulation and, 93, 95
    social security and, 227–228, 244–245
inflation, 268. *see also* hyperinflation
infrastructure
    economic, 189, 191, 243–245, 293–294
    education and, 206, 210
    environment and, 146–148, *149*
    foreign investment and, 102
    growth and, 77, 81
    increasing availability, 294
    investment in, 35, 38, *64*, 84, 144, 225,
        259–260, 264, 266, 270, 275, 277,
        297–298, 306
    Lula da Silva and, 175, 177–178, 181
    regulation and, 93–102
INSS. *see* Instituto Nacional do Seguro
    Social

Institute of Applied Economic Research. *see* Instituto de Pesquisa Econômica Aplicada

Instituto Brasileiro de Geografia e Estastística (IBGE), 113, 190, 253, 312

Instituto Brasileiro do Meio Ambiente (IBAMA), 143–144

Instituto de Pesquisa Econômica Aplicada (IPEA), 37, 68, 211

Instituto Nacional de Seguro Social (INSS), 222, 226–230, 231–232, 234, 235–236

International Monetary Fund (IMF), 31–32, 35, 123, 168, 170, 221, 228

IPEA. *see* Instituto de Pesquisa Econômica Aplicada

judiciary
bankruptcy reform and, 81
growth and, 77, 81, 85
labor policy and, 160
Lula da Silva and, 47, 50
policy networks and, 145
political reform and, 22
regulation and, 93, 109–110
social security and, 230

Kassouf, Ana Lúcia, 217
Keynes, John Maynard, 265

Labor Ministry. *see* Ministério do Trabalho
labor unions, 3, 31, 104, 108, 151–161, 222, 228, 231–232, 236
Laes, Marco Antônio, 4, 243–260
Land. *see also* Movimento dos Sem Terra
agriculture and, 27–28, *41*, 137–142
distribution of, 3
land reform, 137–142, 265–266
land tenure, 2, 28, 306
ownership, 28–29, 31, 37–38, 39, 40
Langoni, Carlos, 31
latifundium, 306
Law of Fiscal Responsibility. *see* Lei de Responsibilidade Fiscal
Law of Free Birth, 311
Law on the Directives and Bases of Education. *see* Lei de Diretrizes e Bases da Educação

LDB. *see* Lei de Diretrizes e Bases da Educação
legislative elections, 11
lei complementar. see complementary laws
Lei de Diretrizes e Bases da Educação (LDB), 206–207
Lei de Responsibilidade Fiscal, 125, 244
Leopoldi, Maria Antonieta P., 4, 221–236
Love, Joseph L., 1–4, 305–312
Lula da Silva, Luiz Inácio
agrarian policy and, 140–143
agricultural policy formation, 136–140, 142–143
Bolsa Família and, 187–193, 200
education and, 205–218
environmental policy and, 143–148
exchange rate policy and, 115–132
foreign policy and, 167–182
growth and, 74–76, 85–86
historical perspective of government, 305–312
labor policy and, 151–162
macroeconomic policy and, 27–41
Northeast Brazil and, 283–299
overview, 1–4
policy making, 47–62
political reform and, 9
regional development policy and, 264, 269–270, 276
regulation and, 93–112
social policy and, 246–254
social security and, 221–236

Maddison, Angus, 74
MAE. *see* Mercado Atacadista de Energia
Magalhães, André Matos, 4, 283–299
Mantega, Guido, 127
Marchezan, Nelson, 156
market concentration, 34, 123
market rigidity, 81–82
Mata, Maria Eugénia, 1
Matland, Richard E., 19
Medidas Provisórias (MPs), 47, 49–57, 59, *62, 63, 64,* 162
Meirelles, Henrique, 94, 128
Mercadante, Aloísio, 127
Mercado Atacadista de Energia (MAE), 96
Mercosul, 3, 244
Mercosur. *see* Mercosul

Minas Gerais, 21, *64*, 212, *314*
minimum wage. see *salário mínimo*
Ministério do Meio Ambiente (MMA),
    143–144, 148, *149*
Ministério do Trabalho, 151–154, 161,
    162
Ministry of the Environment. *see*
    Ministério do Meio Ambiente
Miyazawa framework, 252–253
MMA. *see* Ministério do Meio Ambiente
mobilization, political, 4, 52, 156, 161,
    175–176, 307
Monteiro Neto, Aristedes, 278
Moreira, Guilherme R.C., 4, 243–260
Movement of the Landless. *see*
    Movimento dos Sem Terra
Movimento dos Sem Terra (MST),
    141–142, 312
MST. *see* Movimento dos Sem Terra
Mueller, Bernardo, 2, 93–112
Mueller, Charles C., 3, 135–148
multipartyism, 10–11, 14
Myrdal, Gunnar, 264

National Agency of Electrical Energy.
    see Agência Nacional de Energia
    Elétrica
National Bank of Economic and Social
    Development. *see* Banco Nacional
    de Desenvolvimento Econômico e
    Social (BNDES)
National Bank of Economic
    Development. *see* Banco Nacional
    de Desenvolvimento Econômico
    (BNDE)
National Household Survey. *see* Pesquisa
    Nacional por Amostragem em
    Domicílio
National Institute of Social Security. *see*
    Instituto Nacional do Seguro Social
National Labor Forum. *see* Fórum
    Nacional do Trabalho
National Sanitation Plan. *see* Planasa
National Technical Commission on
    Biosecurity. *see* Comissão Técnica
    Nacional de Biossegurança
National Telecommunications
    Agency. *see* Agência Nacional de
    Telecomunicações
Needell, Jeffrey, 310–311

neoliberalism
    impact of policies, 32–34
    labor policy and, 152–153, 157, 160
    regional development policy and,
        264–265, 269, 274, 278
nepotism, 308, 312
Neves, Aécio, 156
Northeast Brazil
    Bolsa Família and, 3, 36, 38
    colonial era and, 27
    dispersion of sectoral expansion,
        290–292
    education and, 207, 208, 214, 217,
        293–294
    history of policy in, 296–298
    infrastructure, 294
    modern development theory and,
        292–293
    overview, 283–284
    path for regional development,
        293–296
    quality of social institutions, 295–296
    recent development of, 284–292
    regional development policy and,
        263–264, 273–274
    social capital availability, 294–295
    social policy and, 244–245, 248, 256
    trends in relative economic output,
        288–290
Nuclear Non-Proliferation Treaty
    (NPT), 170, 176
Nurkse, Ragnar, 264

OECD. *see* Organization for Economic
    Co-operation and Development
Oliveira, André Rossi de, 2, 93–112
Organization for Economic Co-operation
    and Development (OECD), 39,
    72–73, 170, 176, 178, 180, 182, 216

Pack, H., 84
Paes de Barros, Ricardo, 37, 42
Paiva, Claudio, 1
Partido da Social Democracia Brasileira
    (PSDB), 48, 59, 156, 208, 250–251
Partido dos Trabalhadores (PT)
    education and, 207
    exchange rate policy and, 125,
        127–129, 131, *132*
    foreign policy and, 171–172, 175, *183*

Partido dos Trabalhadores—*continued*
   Lula da Silva and, 61, *62*, 305
   policy networks and, 140, 148
   regulation and, 104
   social policy and, 246, 248
patrimonialism, 29, 310, 312
pension system, 4, 53, 60, 221–236, 245,
   250, 305
Perroux, François, 264
Pesquisa Nacional por Amostra em
   Domicílios (PNAD), 36, 126–127,
   211, 253–254
Pessôa, S., 84
Planasa, 97–98
Plano Cruzado, 117, 118, 122
Plano Real, 32, *62*, 116–120, 122,
   124–127, 129, 141, 168
Planos Color, 117
PNAD. *see* Pesquisa Nacional por
   Amostra em Domicílios
policy networks, 135–148
   agrarian policy, 140–142
   agricultural policy, 136–140
   environmental policy, 143–148
   tradeoffs in policymaking, 142–143
   truncated dialectical policymaking,
     136
political mobilization, 4, 156, 161,
   175–176, 306
PPPs. *see* public-private partnerships
Prado, Caio Jr., 27–28
Prado, Paulo, 309
presidentialism, 10, 11, 12–16, 59
privatization
   growth and, 68
   Lula da Silva and, 60
   neoliberal policy and, 32–35
   Real Plan and, 244
   regional development policy and, 268
   regulation and, 93, 95–97, 100, 107
   social security and, 221, 225, 227
PRONAF. *see* Fortalecimento da
   Agricultura Familiar
property concentration, 27, 30–31, 34, 39
property rights, 1, 2, 76, 85, 312
proportional representation, 11–13, 310
protection, economic, 32, 68, 82, 138
Provisional Laws. *see* Medidas Provisórias
PSDB. *see* Partido da Social Democracia
   Brasileira

Public Servants' Social Security Fund.
   see Regimes Próprios de Previdência
   Social
public-private partnerships (PPPs),
   58–60, *63, 64*

reform. see also *Bolsa Família*
   agrarian policy and, 140–142
   bankruptcy reform, 81
   CTNBio and, 146
   economic, 68, 76–77, 79–82, 84–86,
     170, 172, 181–182, 244
   education and, 210–217
   electricity and, 96–97
   environmental policy and, 148
   federalism, 12–13
   inadequacy of existing proposals,
     13–17
   labor policy and, 152, 154–161
   legislative elections, 11
   Lula da Silva and, 48–49, 54–58, 108,
     128
   pension system, 305
   policy networks and, 138
   preserving representativeness,
     17–22
   presidentialism, 10
   reducing competitiveness, 17–22
   sanitation and, 97–98
   social security and, 221–236
   tax reform, 79–81
   telecommunications and, 95–96
Regimes Próprios de Previdência Social
   (RPPS), 222, 229–230
regional development, 263–278
   cash allowances, 276–277
   creation of, 4
   direct investments, 275–276
   financial incentives, 272–274
   fiscal incentives, 271–272
   foreign policy and, 178
   instruments used (2003–2006),
     270–277
   instruments used by central
     governments, 264–267
   Northeast Brazil and, 283, 293–296,
     299
   overview, 263–264
   review of policies, 267–270
   social policy and, 243–244

regulation
  Cardoso, Fernando Henrique and, 168
  constraints on, 98–99
  economy and, 78, 80, 82, 99–102, 244
  education and, 206
  effect on investments and growth,
    99–102
  elections and, 13, _23_
  electric energy sector and, 96–97
  governmental attempts to change,
    103–106
  infrastructure sectors and, 95–102
  institutional constraints and safeguards,
    106–112
  labor and, 3, 85, 161
  Lula da Silva and, 2, 3, 93–112, 181
  MPs and, 47
  policy networks and, 144, 145
  sanitation sector and, 97–98
  social security and, 225, 227–228,
    230–234
  telecommunications sector and, 95–96
Rigolon, Francisco, 307
Rio Branco Law (1781), 311
Rio de Janeiro, 18, 21, 269, 306, 312
risco Brasil, 123, 125, 128, 131
Rodrik, Dani, 76–77, 85
Roett, Riordan, 1
Rosenstein-Rodan, P.N., 264
Rossi, J.L., _86_
RPPS. _see_ Regimes Próprios de
    Previdência Social
rural bossism. see _coronelismo_
Russian crises, 123–124, _132_, 170

SAEB. _see_ Sistema de Avaliação da
    Educação Básica
Saggi, K., 84
salário mínimo, 125
São Paulo
  Bolsa Família and, 188
  education and, 207, 212
  foreign policy and, _183_
  labor policy and, 153, 156
  land tenure and, _41_
  Lula da Silva and, 52, 53
  policy networks and, 147
  political reform and, 21, 26
  regional development policy and,
    268–269

  wages and, _42_
São Paulo Federation of Industries. _see_
    Federação das Indústrias do Estado
    de São Paulo
São Paulo Stock Exchange. _see_ Bolsa de
    Valores de São Paulo
saquaremas, 310–311
Sarney, José, 117, 122, 152, 169
school attendance, _42_, 187, 191, 205,
    207–209, 210–214, 217, 276. _see also_
    education
School Fund. see _Bolsa Escola_
Senate, 12, 59, 104, 111, 144, 146,
    156–157, 161
Serra, José, 127, 128, 269, _278_
service sector, 39–40, 153, 228. _see also_
    human capital
Silva, Marina, 144, 148, _149_
Sistema de Avaliação da Educação Básica
    (SAEB), 207, 215–217, 286
slavery, 2, 27–29, 306, 308–311, _313_
Strengthening the Family Farm. _see_
    Fortalecimento da Agricultura
    Familiar
subsidies, 3, _42_, 68, _87_, 137–139, 247,
    265–266, 292
SUDAM. _see_ Superintendência de
    Desenvolvimento da Amazônia
SUDENE. _see_ Superintendência do
    Desenvolvimento do Nordeste
sugar production, 27–28, _41_, 137–138,
    178–180
Summers, Larry, 76
Superintendancy for the Development of
    Amazonia. _see_ Superintendência de
    Desenvolvimento da Amazônia
Superintendancy for the Development of
    the Northeast. _see_ Superintendência
    do Desenvolvimento do Nordeste
Superintendência de Desenvolvimento da
    Amazônia (SUDAM), 263–264, 267,
    268–269
Superintendência de Seguros Privados
    (SUSEP), 226, 230
Superintendência do Desenvolvimento
    do Nordeste (SUDENE), 263–264,
    267–269, _278_, 283, 296, 299
Superintendency of Private Insurance.
    see Superintendência de Seguros
    Privados

supply-side reform, 80–81
SUSEP. *see* Superintendência de Seguros Privados

tax burden, 51–52, 55, 57–58, 79–80, *86*, 180, 191
tax on capital transfers. *see* Contribuição Provisória sobre a Movimentação ou Transmissão de Valores e de Créditos e Direitos de Natureza Financeira
tax reform, 79–81
TELEBRÁS. *see* Telecomunicações Brasileiras
telecommunications, 95–96, 102, 103–104, 108, 225
Telecomunicações Brasileiras (TELEBRÁS), 95
Tosta, Luciano, 1
trade, foreign, 56, 61, 68
Trade Union Power. *see* Força Sindical
trade unions, 175, 307
Trade Unions' Organization. *see* Central Única dos Trabalhadores

Uderman, Simone, 4, 263–278

Velasco, A., 73, 77
Verhine, Robert Evan, 210
Vianna Monteiro, Jorge, 1, 2, 47–62
voting
    ballots and, 246–252
    Bolsa Família and, 190
    exchange rate policy and, 125, 127–128
    growth and, 82
    labor policy and, 152, 156–157
    Lula da Silva and, 4, 38, 283, 305, 307–308, 312
    Northeast Brazil and, 299
    policymaking and, 49, 52, 58, 61–62
    political reform and, 10–22
    scandal and, 111

wages
    education and, 207–208, 210
    exchange rate policy and, 127
    income distribution and, 29–31
    labor policy and, 155–157
    minimum wage, 37, *42*
    post-slavery, 29, *41*
    privatization and, 34
    regional development policy and, 265–266
    social security and, 235
water, 95, 97–98, 112. *see also* Planasa
Welch, John, 1
Workers' Party. *see* Partido dos Trabalhadores
Working Group for the Development of the Northeast. *see* Grupo de Trabalho para o Desenvolvimento do Nordeste
World Bank, 4, 71, 75, 80–81, *86*, 205, 210, 221, 228, 306–307
World Trade Organization (WTO), 174
WTO. *see* World Trade Organization

Zero Hunger Program. see *Fome Zero*